T0383112

Frontiers in the Economics of Gender

Gender is now recognized as a fundamental organizing principle of economic as well as social life, and related research has grown at an unprecedented pace in recent decades across branches of economics. This book takes stock of the research, proposes novel analytical frameworks and outlines further directions. The book has grown out of the Summer School of International Research in Pontignano, University of Siena, which traditionally brings together the most prominent scholars in the field.

The thirteen essays included in this book cover recent advances in gender related issues across disciplinary branches, from economic history and the history of economic thought to macroeconomics, household economics, the economics of care work, labour economics, and institutional and experimental economics.

The book is primarily addressed to graduate students in economics and is an essential companion for researchers in the area of gender economics. For intrinsic reasons, however, research on gender tends to transcend disciplinary boundaries. The author's effort to use non technical language whenever feasible makes most texts accessible to a wider audience, including students and specialists in sociology, demography and history.

Francesca Bettio is Professor of Labour Economics at the University of Siena, Italy.

Alina Verashchagina is a PhD candidate in Economics at the University of Siena, Italy.

Routledge Siena studies in political economy

The Siena Summer School hosts lectures by distinguished scholars on topics characterized by a lively research activity. The lectures collected in this series offer a clear account of the alternative research paths that characterize a certain field. Different publishers printed former workshops of the school. They include:

Macroeconomics: A Survey of Research Strategies
Edited by Alessandro Vercelli and Nicola Dimitri
Oxford University Press, 1992

International Problems of Economic Interdependence
Edited by Massimo Di Matteo, Mario Baldassarri and Robert Mundell
Macmillan, 1994

Ethics, Rationality, and Economic Behaviour
Edited by Francesco Farina, Frank Hahn and Steffano Vannucci
Clarendon Press

Available from Routledge:

The Politics and Economics of Power
Edited by Samuel Bowles, Maurizio Franzini and Ugo Pagano

The Evolution of Economic Diversity
Edited by Antonio Nicita and Ugo Pagano

Cycles, Growth and Structural Change
Edited by Lionello Punzo

General Equilibrium: Problems and Prospects
Edited by Fabio Petri and Frank Hahn

Cognitive Processes and Economic Behaviour
Edited by Nicola Dimitri, Marcello Basili and Itzhak Gilboa

Environment, Inequality and Collective Action
Edited by Marcello Basili, Maurizio Franzini and Alessandro Vercelli

Inequality and Economic Integration
Edited by Francesco Farina and Ernesto Savaglio

Legal Orderings and Economic Institutions
Edited by Fabrizio Cafaggi, Antonio Nicita and Ugo Pagano

Frontiers in the Economics of Gender
Edited by Francesca Bettio and Alina Verashchagina

Frontiers in the Economics of Gender

Edited by
Francesca Bettio and
Alina Verashchagina

LONDON AND NEW YORK

First published 2008
by Routledge
2 Park Square, Milton Park, Abingdon, Oxon OX14 4RN

Simultaneously published in the USA and Canada
by Routledge
270 Madison Ave, New York, NY 10016

Routledge is an imprint of the Taylor & Francis Group,
an informa business

© 2008 Editorial matter and selection, Francesca Bettio and
Alina Verashchagina; individual chapters, the contributors

Typeset in Times New Roman by Keyword Group Ltd
Printed and bound in Great Britain by TJI Digital, Padstow, Cornwall

British Library Cataloguing in Publication Data
A catalogue record for this book is available
from the British Library

Library of Congress Cataloging in Publication Data
A catalog record for this book has been requested

ISBN 10: 0-415-44572-8 (hbk)
ISBN 10: 0-203-92769-9 (ebk)

ISBN 13: 978-0-415-44572-6 (hbk)
ISBN 13: 978-0-203-92769-4 (ebk)

Contents

Tables

Figures

Contributors

A. Haroon Akram-Lodhi is Professor of International Development Studies at Trent University, Peterborough, Canada.

Alessandro Cigno is Professor of Economics in the Faculty of Political Science of the University of Florence.

Alessandro Innocenti is Associate Professor of Economics at the University of Siena.

Ali Skalli is a Maitre de Conference at the Universite of Paris II, Pantheon-Assas.

Alina Verashchagina is PhD Candidate in Economics, University of Siena.

Ann Mari May is currently working as a Visiting Associate Professor of economics at Middlebury College.

Annalisa Rosselli is Professor of Economics and History of Economic Thought at the University of Rome Tor Vergata.

Catherine Eckel is Professor of Economics and Director of the Center for Behavioral and Experimental Economic Science (CBEES) at the University of Texas at Dallas.

Francesca Bettio is Professor of Labour Economics at the University of Siena.

Graciela Chichilnisky is UNESCO Professor of Mathematics and Economics at Columbia University.

Lucia C. Hanmer is Senior Economic Advisor in the South Asia Division of the United Kingdom's Department for International Development.

Maria Cristina Marcuzzo is Professor of Economics at the University of Rome, 'La Sapienza'.

Maria Grazia Pazienza is Assistant Professor of Public Economics at the University of Florence.

Marina Malysheva is Senior Research Associate at the Institute of Socio-Economic Studies of Population within the Russian Academy of Sciences.

Nancy Folbre is Professor of Economics at the University of Massachusetts, Amherst.

Oscar Marcenaro-Guttierez is Lecturer at the University of Malaga.

Pat Hudson is Professor of History at Cardiff University.

Peter Dolton is a Professor of Economics at Royal Holloway College, University of London and Senior Research Fellow at the London School of Economics.

Shelly Lundberg is Castor Professor of Economics and Director of the Center for Studies in Demography and Ecology at the University of Washington.

Foreword

Gender is now recognized as a fundamental organizing principle of economic as well as social life; and the related research has grown at an unprecedented pace in recent decades across branches of economics. The book takes stock of this research, proposes novel analytical frameworks and outlines further research directions. It has grown out of the Summer School of International Research in Pontignano, University of Siena, which traditionally brings together the most representative scholars in the field.

The way in which the term 'gender' is used within economics and other social sciences often gives rise to ambiguity. Sometimes the 'economics of gender' is a catch-all expression used for any economic analysis that explicitly distinguishes men and women. In social and economic policy circles, 'gender approach' is often the new fangled name for the older 'equal opportunities for women' approach. In academic circles 'gender economics' may refer to an area that largely overlaps with the economics of female labour; or it may be understood as feminist research in a 'softer' guise. When the American historian Joan Wallach Scott first advocated the use of 'gender' in lieu of 'sex' to denote socially as opposed to biologically constructed differences between men and women, she could not have foreseen that, because of its very success, the term 'gender' would in its turn become a source of ambiguity.

We like to think that the spirit inspiring this collection of essays adheres to Scott's proposed meaning of the term in at least two important respects. Because gender is a social, and hence intellectual and historical, construct, its precise features vary across time and space. Likewise, the economics of gender cannot be identified with one or another specific ideology that inevitably influences the analysis, but should cross ideological boundaries. Because, moreover, gender is an all-pervasive social construct, within economics it cannot be confined to the study of such phenomena as fertility, labour market participation or the wage gap that, for historical and biological reasons, are more closely associated with women.

The book makes a special effort, in fact, to present gender research not only in labour or population economics but also in the history of economic thought, economic history, macroeconomics, institutional economics, experimental and behavioural economics. Of course, since labour and population economics were the first disciplinary fields to be renovated by recognition that gender divisions matter, some imbalance in their favour are still visible in this collection of essays. To our knowledge, however, this volume is the first systematic attempt to explore how a gender perspective has opened up, and continues to do so, research horizons across disciplinary fields within economics.

Section one assesses the visibility and the conceptual impact of the category of gender within both the history of economic thought and economic history. It combines exploration of new research topics with a fascinating review of research on women and by women in both disciplines. The second section presents novel theoretical perspectives. Two of these perspectives adopt, respectively, a microeconomic and biology oriented approach and a general equilibrium welfare oriented analysis to re-examine the root causes of gender disparities at work, while the third one challenges conventional macroeconomics by introducing unpaid labour at home into macroeconomic modelling. Section three looks at gender from within the household and in light of two partially complementary approaches: intra-household bargaining and the economics of care work. Both approaches are now well established and are compellingly reviewed in this section, but it is apparent from such reviews that they still offer considerable potential for further development. Section four examines gender from within the labour market and inevitably focuses on the two disparities that have received the widest research attention to date, namely segregation and the wage gap. The question implicit in the three essays making up this section is what type of research is still needed and how it should be carried out, and the analysis divides between thorough investigation of methodology and comparative evidence. Section five offers fresh experimental evidence on differences in behaviour between men and women in the laboratory, reviews past evidence and provides a fascinating exploration of how differences in the labs may be sustaining actual disparities in the market. In contrast to labour market analysis, differences between men and women have never been a primary object of interest in experimental economics, but they are nevertheless becoming one of its most interesting research 'spillovers'. Section six fittingly draws the volume to a close by addressing the changing position of women in higher education from the standpoint of institutional economics.

Due to chance more than choice, some important gaps remain, despite the wide variety of issues and disciplinary areas covered by the six sections. Neglect of the well-developed gender research in development economics is perhaps the most glaring omission. However, a perfectly balanced representation of gender research in economics across fields and countries was never the main priority in assembling this book. Following the tradition of the International Summer School in Siena, from which the book originates, participating scholars were asked to prioritize, on the one hand, evaluation and assessment of consolidated methodologies and, on the other, to bring to the fore advances in research methodologies and ideas.

In view of the strong focus on methodology and ideas, the book is primarily addressed to graduate students in economics, and it is an essential companion for researchers in the area of gender economics. For intrinsic reasons, however, research on gender tends to transcend disciplinary boundaries not only within economics but also externally to it. Whenever feasible, we have thus requested the authors to use non-technical language so that the texts are accessible to a wider audience, including students and specialists in sociology, demography and history. At the same time, we have also asked the authors to buttress each chapter with clear references to key technical contributions and with a comprehensive and up-to-date reference list.

Francesca Bettio and Alina Verashchagina

Part 1

Historical perspectives

1 The history of economic thought through gender lenses

Maria Cristina Marcuzzo and Annalisa Rosselli

Introduction

The History of Economic Thought (HET) studies the making of economic ideas and their evolution through time, or, borrowing the definition from the most famous book in HET of the twentieth century, written by Joseph Schumpeter and published in 1954: HET is ' the history of the intellectual efforts that *men* have made in order to *understand* economic phenomena' (Schumpeter 1994 [1954]: 3; the first emphasis is ours[1]).

Several arguments can be used to support the importance of HET for economists. Here we will consider two of them. First, only the most naïve among us can believe that the market for ideas is so efficient that the best ideas prevail and are fully contained in the theory taught today, while the forgotten ideas were totally worthless and deserved oblivion. Many factors influence the path that a science follows and not just 'the search for truth'. The second argument – which is more relevant here – is that economic ideas are not invented by machines, but by human beings under the influence of the social, ideological and cultural context of their times. By studying the role that these influences have played in the past we enhance our awareness that economics is not 'neutral' with respect to nationality, political ideology or, for that matter, gender.

This chapter tries to summarize some of the findings of the recent feminist approach to HET which can throw some light on the points mentioned above. One word of warning: inquiry into HET through gender lenses is still in its early stages. There are not many people involved in this research yet, and they are almost exclusively in the Anglo-Saxon countries, mainly North America and Australia, although the annual conference of the European Society for the History of Economic Thought often has a session devoted to it. We were unable to find more than 10 articles on HET in the 12 volumes of *Feminist Economics,* and no more than 20 articles have been published on the subject in the most important HET journals.

It is too early, therefore, for a full assessment of the results. The most important of those achieved so far seem to lie largely in identification of the questions we should be asking, while in many cases the answers are still very tentative.

The main points that have been raised are:

a)   What has been the contribution of women to the development of economic ideas?
b)   Why have these contributions been neglected for so long? Were they deemed worthless, or were the women who provided them actively discriminated against?
c)   What is the difference – if any – in men and women's approaches to economics, in terms of subjects and style of research? In other words, if there were more women in the profession, above the 'critical mass', would the profession be different?
d)   What has economics had to say about the role played by women in the market and non-market economy?
e)   How has gender bias shaped economic theory?

If these are the questions that lie behind the research carried out so far, it is interesting to note that HET has, albeit unintentionally, followed the same route traced by studies on women in science. In a survey article on the ample literature which has been addressing the issue of the place of women in science since the 1970s, Londa Schiebinger identified four approaches (Schiebinger 1987: 307). The first aims to 'brush off the dust of obscurity' from women who have been ignored by all mainstream history of sciences. The second, which complements the first, focuses on the institutions of science and on the limited access women have to them. The third looks at how sciences – such as the biological and medical science – have defined the nature of women. The fourth approach 'seeks to unveil distortions in the very norms and method of science that have resulted from the historic absence of women from any significant role in the making of modern science' (ibid.). It is the same route that we will follow here.

Who were the women economists?

Those like the authors of this chapter who began studying economics in the 1970s were convinced that they belonged to the first generation of women setting out to pursue an academic career in economics. Of course there were exceptions, notably Joan Robinson, who was doubtless a theorist (and of whom we will have more to say below), and a few other women scholars in economic history. But most of our teachers, in Italy and in London (where we did our post-graduate work), were men, and together with our women colleagues we felt that we were entering an entirely male-dominated profession for the first time in history. Our impression was shared by the majority of the profession: as late as 1985, William Baumol, in an article for the centenary of the American Economic Association, observed that 'before World War I, as today, a (distressingly) few women *were* contributing to the literature' (Baumol 1985: 11). He added that his research assistant had found only seven articles by four women.

When Baumol delivered his speech, the only book which had tried to rescue a few eminent women economists from oblivion had been the pioneering work by Dorothy L. Thompson, *Adam Smith's Daughters*, a book that the author had published with difficulty and that had received scant attention when it first came out in 1975.[2] After that came important contributions by the late Michèle Pujol (1992), and a few other works: for example Groenewegen (1994); Dimand *et al.* (1995); Dimand and Nyland (2003).

However, we are still in the preliminary stage, since some of the basic tools for research are yet to become available. The questions like 'Who were the women economists?', 'What did they write?', 'Where are their papers preserved, if still extant?' have been answered only partially, especially as far as the non-Anglo-Saxon countries are concerned. *A Biographical Dictionary of Women Economists* (Dimand *et al.* 2000) was published not long ago, and it is very incomplete, by admission of the editors themselves. A bibliography of works by women economists has recently come out (Madden *et al.* 2005); it took several years to complete since the widespread use of initials makes the task of identifying the sex of the authors of articles in journals particularly tiresome.

Although incomplete, the above mentioned biographical dictionary of women economists contains – to the surprise of many – 120 entries covering a period of 200 years. The dictionary excludes women who were still active in the year 2000 and includes only women 'who were important, either because they made a substantive contribution to the field or, in a few cases, because they were historically important, such as being the first woman (of whom we were aware) in a particular country to contribute to the discipline' (Dimand *et al.* 2000: xvi). Table 1.1 shows the breakdown in the entries of the dictionary by nationality. The largest group is from the US, but this does not entitle us to infer that US women economists were more numerous. They were just better researched.

In general, the attention that a woman economist has drawn is not necessarily proportional to her merits, because it also depends on the motivations behind this

Table 1.1 Women economists by nationality in *A Biographical Dictionary of Women Economists*

Country	Number of female economists	Country	Number of female economists
USA	58	Italy	2
UK	24	Russia	2
Germany	6	Brazil	1
France	5	Hungary	1
Austria	4	India	1
Canada	4	The Netherlands	1
Greece	3	Poland	1
Japan	3	Spain	1
Denmark	2	Sweden	1

Source: Marcuzzo 2002a.

first stage of the search for our predecessors. We believe that, over and above curiosity and genuine interest, some of the recent studies in feminist HET were animated by the (unconscious?) desire to redress a possible injustice. Notorious examples in other sciences have revealed how little fairness there is in the scientific world when it comes to acknowledging the merits of women. Therefore we can suspect a secret hope of finding unknown geniuses whose gifts were sacrificed to the greater glory of the male. In other words, the Rosalind Franklin[3] or the Lise Meitner[4] of economics.

For this reason perhaps, women partners of famous male economists were the first to be investigated, with the strong suspicion that their talent was hidden in the works of their husbands/partners. More than one essay is devoted to Harriet Taylor, the friend of John Stuart Mill and, after the death of her first husband, his wife for the short time before her death (Pujol 1995, 2000; Forget 2003). Mill expresses his admiration for her talent not only in his posthumous *Autobiography*, but in many of his works, *Principles of Political Economy* included, where, in a limited number of copies, given small circulation out of respect for her husband who was still alive at the time, he says that many of his ideas 'were first learned from herself' (Hayek 1951: 122). Mill's long and enthusiastic expressions of admiration and gratitude elicited sceptical comments of disbelief from their very first appearance. However, if we read the detailed account of her contribution to the *Principles* that Mill provides in his autobiography, we find that Mill's words may have been unusual, but not so hard to believe:

> The first of my books in which her share was conspicuous was '*The Principles of Political Economy*'. The 'system of logic' owed little to her except in the minutes matters of composition [...] The chapter of Political Economy which has had a greater influence on opinion than all the rest, that on 'the Probable Future of the Labouring Class' is entirely due to her: in the first draft of the book that chapter did not exist [...] She was the cause of my writing it and the more general parts of that chapter, the statement and discussion of the two opposite theories respecting the proper condition of the labouring class, was wholly an exposition of her thoughts, often in words taken from her lips.
>
> (quoted in Hayek 1951: 117)

Hayek, too, was puzzled by this confession, but he refused to consider it the mere effect of love and delusion in a man with an 'eminently sober, balanced and disciplined mind' (Hayek 1951: 15). Therefore, unlike other historians who denied any influence of Harriet Taylor over Mill without attempting further inquiry, he investigated the matter and published the correspondence between Mill and Taylor that was available to him. The editing is, as usual with Hayek, extremely accurate. Hayek himself refrains from commenting on the new material he had found apart from a short conclusion attributing to Harriet Taylor's influence 'the rationalist element in Mill's thought' (ibid.: 17). Hayek, of course, had expected her to have stressed his sentimental side.

Pujol (1995) and Seiz and Pujol (2000) represent rehabilitation of Harriet Taylor as an original thinker[5]. Her originality lies precisely in the absence of gender prejudice. Unlike Mill, she did not oppose the participation of married women in the labour market. In an age when the virtues of the free market were extolled, Harriet Taylor saw the contradiction between the liberal standpoint which favoured competition in all sectors and the limited access of women to the better paid jobs and professions. She called the male control over the labour market a 'monopoly' and argued in her book *Enfranchisement of Women* (1851): 'so long as competition is the general law of human life, it is tyranny to shut-out one half of the competitors.' (quoted in Pujol 1995: 88). Taylor also recognized the ability of women to perform a multitude of tasks, required but not adequately rewarded by the market: 'the varied though petty details which compose the occupation of most women, call forth probably as much of mental ability, as the uniform routine of the pursuits which are the habitual occupation of a large majority of men.' (quoted in Pujol 1995: 90).

Various other partners of famous male economists have been investigated, for example, Sophie De Grouchy, the wife of Nicolas Condorcet. She was a friend of Thomas Paine and an advocate for the extension of political rights to all races, and to women. She translated Adam Smith's *Theory of Moral Sentiments* into French in 1798, during the Terror, when the issue of what can keep society together was of utmost importance, and added eight 'letters' on this subject, where, with the excuse of clarifying Smith, she expresses her own ideas (Forget 2003). Or, to move to more recent times, Mary Paley Marshall, Alfred Marshall's wife, taught economics for over 40 years to the women of Newnham College in Cambridge. Before her marriage she wrote a book with her future husband, *The Economics of Industry,* praised by Keynes who found it 'an extremely good book; nothing more serviceable for its purpose was produced for many years, if ever' (Keynes 1972 [1933]: 239). Marshall let it go out of print when there was still great demand for it, and decided to replace it with one bearing his name alone, probably when he 'came increasingly to the conclusion that there was nothing useful to be made of women's intellect' (*ibidem*: 241; see also McWilliams Tullberg 1992).

In the recent wave of feminist studies in HET attention has also been given to the popularizers of economics, with the aim of showing – successfully, in a number of cases – that they were original thinkers in their own right. We have essays on Jane Haldimand Marcet (1769–1858), who has been considered a popularizer of David Ricardo's *Principles*, although she published her most famous book *Conversations in Political Economy*, a dialogue between a Mrs. B and her pupil, in 1816, whereas the first edition of Ricardo's *Principles* appeared in 1817. It seems that her book launched the fashion of governesses acquainted with Political Economy. The book was praised by all the major Classical Economists, including Ricardo, Malthus and Say, and was the only book on Political Economy which became a successful bestseller, reaching the 14th edition. Her readership was large, and by no means confined to young people and women. She also wrote a short book for the working class, in the belief that knowledge could improve its lot; the landowners and employers who appreciated her optimistic attitude and denial of class conflict were to buy it and distribute it among the poor, but the venture was not as successful as expected (Polkinghorn 1995: 75).

In the same line Harriet Martineau (1802–1876) published tales to illustrate the principles of Political Economy by means of examples taken from everyday life. She, too, was extremely successful. The first volume sold over 10,000 copies, compared with Dickens's novels which rarely reached 3,000 copies. She was single, became economically independent and pursued a career as a scientific popularizer in many fields for the rest of her life. Marx despised her, like all other 'vulgar' economists who accepted the wage fund theory, but he adds sexism to his insults by choosing to call her an 'old maid' (Marx 1954: 594). In her case too, attempts at rehabilitation have been made (Levy 2003), but whether or not Jane Marcet and Harriet Martineau were original thinkers is beyond the scope of this chapter. What matters here is the importance they both attached to the diffusion of science and their belief that it contributed to the betterment of humanity. They grasped the political implications of the prevailing theories (which they accepted by and large) and did not hesitate to use simple language and easy examples to make themselves understood. How are we to account for the fact that it was two women – but none of the men involved in it – who carried out the task of explaining the results that the new science of Political Economy had reached? And they were not alone. Millicent Fawcett was another great popularizer. Joan Robinson, too, apart from being a theorist in her own right, was also to some extent a popularizer. Can we detect in these women a particular need for 'moral responsibility and social relevance' that we do not find in their male contemporaries, as has been argued (Polkinghorn 1998: x; Kerr 2006)?

Strategies of survival

It would be very unfair, however, to depict the first feminist studies in HET as if they were concerned only with the question whether a woman was 'better' than her husband/partner, according to a measure of excellence which is the male norm. Indeed, as soon as systematic exploration of the history of economics was applied to the search for women pioneers in the discipline, the question changed from 'why so few?', as Baumol had asked in 1985, into 'how so many?', as Peter Groenewegen and Susan King could only wonder, after finding 222 articles (5.3% of the total) written by 112 women between 1900 and 1939 in the five most important journals in the English language of those years: the *American Economic Review, Economic Journal, Economica, Journal of Political Economy* and the *Quarterly Journal of Economics* (Dimand, R. 1995: 17). Thus attention shifted to the individual and collective strategies followed by women to survive in a hostile environment. It is noteworthy that the period covered by Groenewegen and King is that of the professionalization of the discipline, when political economy broke away from the moral sciences and turned from a subject investigated by philosophers and political scientists into an autonomous discipline, with its own academic curricula (the Tripos in economics was established in Cambridge in 1903), its scientific societies such as the American Economic Association (founded in 1885) and the Royal Economic Society (founded in 1902), and its journals. This professionalization implied that the barriers women had to face rose even higher: not just prejudice, but limited access to academic positions, research funds and all that makes research possible even today.

The collective strategies pursued by women included the construction of networks and the mentoring of women by women. Perusing the biographies of women economists we find that behind every successful woman there is often another gifted woman (teacher, relative or friend) who provided encouragement and advice (see Thorne 1995). An attempt to reconstruct the networks of women economists before 1940 was ventured upon by Mary Ann Dimand (1995), but much more work is required. In particular, the role played by academic institutions for women has not been thoroughly investigated (here we have in mind historical institutions such as Bedford College in London, Girton College and Newnham College in Cambridge, or the famous 'seven sisters' in the US – Vassar, Barnard, Wellesley etc., to name but the most famous).

Individual strategies have been examined in an interesting essay by Evelyn Forget, who analysed the PhD dissertations in economics in all the PhD-granting universities in the US in the period 1912–1940, as listed in the *American Economic Review*. She notes that the percentage of PhD dissertations by women out of the total of dissertations in economics grew steadily to peak at 19 per cent in the early 1920s. The period after World War I was a golden age for women's education, since the war had taken its toll of lives of many young men and there were vacancies to be filled in the institutions of higher education. After that short period the percentage of PhD dissertations by women began to decline, 10 years before the downward trends in other fields, and was down to just over 5 per cent by the beginning of World War II (see Figure 1.1). It was only in the 1970s that it showed signs of picking up again. Why economics began to exclude women before other disciplines is still an unsolved mystery.

Moreover, Forget argues that at PhD stage women did not show a particular interest in 'women's issues' broadly defined, such as 'Women in the labour market' or 'Social Policy'. The slight difference between men and women in the choice

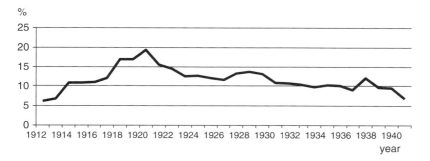

Figure 1.1 Percentage of PhD in economics by women in the US, 1912–1940
Source: Forget 1995.

of subjects to be seen at the beginning of the century had completely disappeared by 1935. Yet, in the same years, the publications by women in academic journals were disproportionately focused on areas of 'women's issues', which, by the way, remained popular among women well into the 1970s, when the whole discipline had turned its attention to other fields.

Forget explains this difference between the subjects of the PhD dissertations and those of the articles as a survival strategy pursued by women, and identifies different kinds of such strategies. The first strategy is subordination, i.e. accepting marginalization in second-rate jobs and/or institutions. For example, women's colleges provided a supportive environment and good work opportunities, although they could not offer research facilities of the same excellence as the leading research institutions.

The second strategy is separatism. Women chose to write articles in particular areas where they had a comparative advantage. By becoming the majority in a field, they had less male competition to face. These two tactics can be called 'realistic': they accept the prevailing stereotypes and division of roles between the sexes but try to exploit them with the aim of carving out a niche for women in the discipline. The third strategy is innovation, i.e. some sort of reaction to the constraints imposed upon women and to the traditional standards of success. (It must be noted that the distinction between separatism and innovation is subtle, since they are both based upon the revaluation of fields neglected by the majority of the discipline). It has been defined as an 'idealistic' strategy, (Rossiter 1982: xvii), sometimes openly confrontational. Identifying cases when it was practised in the history of economics is not easy, but it would certainly be worth investigating. As Forget observes: 'A slightly different perspective encourages us to ask whether women ever challenged the constraints directly and whether they had a measurable impact on the nature of the discipline itself' (Forget 1995: 36).

We have deliberately omitted a fourth strategy: super performance, i.e. outperforming the male colleagues. This is an effective way to gain success and recognition, but unfortunately it is open only to a few women with extraordinary talents. Joan Robinson is the most striking example in the history of economics. It is worth devoting particular attention to her case not only on account of her academic performance, but also in the light of her personal and intellectual life.

A case study: Joan Robinson (1903–1983)

Joan Robinson, née Maurice, offers an interesting case study. She was the wife of an economist, Austin, but also the greatest female economist of all times, with over 400 items in her bibliography (Marcuzzo 2002b). She enjoyed a worldwide reputation, which led Kaldor to remark in her (anonymous) obituary 'that after Keynes, Joan Robinson would be widely regarded as the most prominent name associated with the Cambridge School of Economics' (King's College Annual Report 1984: 34). In fact, she was the first woman to be made Honorary Fellow of King's College, in the year (1979) when women became eligible for fellowships, although she was not a College member.

In the years prior to the First World War, in Cambridge, women were taught in separate courses, tutorials being given in the presence of a chaperone. Their presence in the classroom was experienced with discomfort even by someone like Keynes, who later staunchly supported Joan Robinson, but who in his first year of teaching in 1909, wrote:

> I think I shall have to give up teaching females after this year. The nervous irritation caused by two hours' contact with them is <u>intense</u>. I seem to hate every movement of their minds. The minds of the men, even when they are stupid and ugly, never appear to me so repellent.
>
> (J.M. Keynes to D. Grant, 16 February 1909,
> quoted in Moggridge 1992: 183–4)

The situation improved slightly in the 1920s when Joan Robinson was an undergraduate; however, still no more than 500 women could enter the university, and their exams were taken in separate rooms. It was only in 1948 that women could become full members of Cambridge University.

Soon after marrying Austin in 1926, Joan Robinson followed her husband to India, where he had been appointed tutor of the Maharajah of Gwalior, and stayed there as a young *mem-sahib* for three years, getting involved in a dispute between the local and the central government of India on a matter of taxation. Her background in economics, even with a modest 2.1 in the Cambridge Tripos of 1925, gave her leverage on the issues involved.

The role of economist's wife was short-lived for Joan Robinson. It lasted just a few months after her return to England (ahead of her husband), when she was looking for a place for them to stay in Cambridge and she busied herself making sure that Austin would be appointed to a lectureship. It surfaces in a few instances, as when she stepped down to allow him to give a seminar originally scheduled for her at the Keynes's Political Economy Club.[6]

On the other hand, people in Cambridge grew particularly conscious that she was Austin's wife whenever they felt that she might embarrass him with her outward behaviour and assertive views. Such was the case when, early in her career, she came under fire from her colleagues, because they felt she was too fervently advancing her own ideas when teaching, or in general because she was seen as excessively opinionated and stubborn in discussion (see for instance the opinions expressed by her male colleagues in the Faculty of Economics, C.R. Fay[7], A.C. Pigou[8] and J.R. Hicks[9]). Keynes stepped in to prevent a great injustice being made and she was allowed to teach the course of her liking (J.M. Keynes to C.R. Fay, 5 March 1935, in Kahn's papers RFK/14/99/209–14).

By the mid 1930s she had established herself academically with the publication of her first book (Robinson 1969 [1933]), and several articles which, at least in one case, aroused admiration and surprise that they were written by a woman.[10] By the 1970s it was being rumoured that she might be a candidate for the Nobel Prize, which of course she was never awarded, in part at least because of her radical political views.

Was her case an example of that individual strategy that Evelyn Forget describes as 'out-performing male colleagues'? For Joan Robinson it was a very tough game, John Maynard Keynes and Piero Sraffa – two of the greatest economists of all times – being the economists with whom she had constant contact, and occasional contrast. However, she also enjoyed the close collaboration of another great economist, Richard Kahn, warm ties of affection playing an important part.

These three economists were associated with her in the three major revolutions occurring in Cambridge between the late 1920s and 1960s (imperfect competition, effective demand and capital theory); some idea of what it may have meant to her to be a woman economist may, perhaps, be gained by looking more closely into her relations with them.

There has been much speculation on the nature of the collaboration between Kahn and Joan Robinson on *The Economics of Imperfect Competition* (EIC). In the opening paragraphs of her Preface she acknowledged Kahn's contribution:

> […] I have had the constant assistance of Mr. R.F. Kahn. The whole technical apparatus was built up with his aid, and many of the major problems […] were solved as much by him as by me. He has also contributed a number of mathematical proofs which I should have been incapable of finding for myself.
>
> (Robinson 1969 [1933]: xiii)

Kahn reacted strongly to the suggestion that he co-authored her book. He wrote to her:

> You are attributing to me very much more than I am responsible for. What I did was to read what you had written. Most of my attempts to do constructive work (e.g. in regard to Discrimination and Exploitation) ended in failure and it was almost invariably you who found the clue.
>
> (R. F. Kahn to J. V. Robinson, 30 March 1933,
> quoted in Rosselli 2005a: 262)

Having made a thorough investigation of their correspondence we are in a better position to assess the matter. As one of us wrote:

> [Kahn's] contribution in the initial phase of drafting, when efforts concentrated on a rigorous result, was indeed enormous […] However, once the result was demonstrated, the exposition and the capacity to raise new questions lay entirely in the domain of J. Robinson, who acquired growing confidence *vis-à-vis* Kahn as the *EIC* was drafted.
>
> (Rosselli 2005a: 262)

The relationship between Joan Robinson and Kahn lasted throughout their lives, as witnessed by the amount of letters passed between them which number in to the thousands over the years. They spent much time together, shared common intellectual and personal pursuits, and together built Cambridge economics as it stood until the 1960s. This relationship appeared as a case of *her* outperforming *him*, but it was he who – as a caring and protective partner – provided her with strength and confidence.

The relationship with Keynes was of course entirely different. Joan Robinson's acquaintance with him began slowly and was facilitated by her association with Kahn, who was Keynes's favourite pupil. She was a member of the 'Circus', the discussion group that led Keynes from the *Treatise* to the *General Theory*, the proofs of which she was asked by Keynes to read, along with Harrod, Hawtrey and Kahn. Again on the basis of the correspondence we have a good understanding of their relationship:

> Keynes trusted Robinson's judgment, was appreciative of her work and took account of her opinion. For her part, J. Robinson, always respectful of Keynes's authority, was rarely intimidated by him and often held her own position without giving ground... At times she would try to lead him to a line other than the one he had chosen, and on several occasions attempted to get Keynes to change his mind on specific issues.
>
> (Marcuzzo and Sardoni 2005: 189)

Joan Robinson is rightly considered as the torch-bearer of the Keynesian revolution – perhaps the economist (together with Kahn) most identified with it. Interestingly, however, although she was perceived as single-minded and sectarian by outsiders, within Keynes's closer circle she stood up as a critical and independent mind.

The most interesting and intriguing of her relationships with male colleagues was that with Sraffa. She and Kahn attended his lectures in the academic year 1928–29, and Sraffa's 1926 article was a major source of inspiration for her first book. While writing *The Economics of Imperfect Competition* she was apprehensive of Sraffa's criticisms, and indeed she never persuaded him of it.

In the following years their relationship became much closer, but only after the war did Sraffa's work again have a major impact on her, in the critique of neo-classical theory and the ensuing capital controversy. A letter from Joan Robinson to Sraffa following upon publication of his *Production of Commodities by Means of Commodities* (Sraffa 1960) reveals the characteristics of this relationship as it had evolved over the years:

> Dear Piero: all the work that I have been doing the last 10 years has been very much influenced by you - both our conversations in the old days and by your Preface [to Ricardo's Principles]... Since, quite apart from worldly success, I have had a lot of fun I have a deep feeling of gratitude to you. The fact that you reject it does not affect the case at all.
>
> (J.V. Robinson to P. Sraffa, 18 June 1960,
> quoted in Marcuzzo 2005: 447)

Once again Joan Robinson occupies a special position, being the only economist of the Cambridge group who attempted to integrate Keynes's approach with Sraffa's. Although the attempt has had very mixed results, it is noteworthy of the role she played in that group. A revealing clue is given by her own assessment of her work. In the midst of her third nervous breakdown,[11] in November 1952, she wrote to Kahn:

> I have realized more than ever after this do how much one's whole personality is involved in one's 'purely intellectual' work. I think the reason I have done so much more with a much weaker brain than any of us is because of my extremely simple minded attitude.
> (letter of 3 November 1952 in RFK Papers, 13/90/5/352–5, quoted in Marcuzzo 2003: 558)

In conclusion, it seems to us that the closest we can get to characterizing Joan Robinson as a woman[12] is her role as mediator and facilitator in conveying different views and modes of thought, without however reneging her individual standing. She is reported as saying 'It's much easier being a woman. You can be so creative having a child'(Narasimhan 1983: 218). But the urge to be intellectually 'creative' – in a milieu of such outstanding male achievers – never abandoned her.

Is there a way of 'doing economics' that is specific to women?

After considering the contributions of so many female economists, one may naturally wonder whether the history of economics shows that there is a way of 'doing economics' that is specific to women. However, it is a question that would probably lead us to a fruitless search. All female economists have faced barriers so high, their freedom of expression have come up against so many limitations, that it is too hard to distinguish what was done out of necessity and what out of choice. Not to mention the risk of identifying as 'truly feminine' what is only the product of the present process of construction of a gender identity. One thing most women economists seem to have in common, however, is they have proved less likely to be blinded by prejudice where 'women's issues' were concerned, unlike the majority (though not all) of their fellow male economists, who have often shown no hesitation in contradicting the principles of their discipline in order to reassert the privileges of their gender.

Let us take a couple of examples of the latter phenomenon. The first goes back to the years of the French Revolution. Throughout the eighteenth century a 'scientific' explanation of the universal subordination of women was developed which took the place of the justifications grounded on religion and passages from the Bible. The Enlightenment proclaimed that the life of people is shaped not only by Nature but also by cultural habits, economic organization and political institutions. But if the transformation into servitude of women's alleged innate inferiority was a human action, how could one get away from the logical conclusion that a change was possible? Two women above all saw this contradiction and advocated for their sex the same freedom available to men, including sexual freedom. They were Mary Wollstonecraft, the wife of Godwin, and the above mentioned Sophie Condorcet. As Chris Nyland argues (2003: 123–125), it is surely significant that Malthus wrote the first edition of his famous *Essay on Population* to criticize the views of Condorcet and Godwin. Being a gentleman, he could not attack women, and addressed their husbands instead. But he did attack their claims, providing a useful argument to deny women the same freedom as men. Population explosion is inevitable – says Malthus – if women are not constrained by social control and have the means to support their children. Single mothers must be banished from society; women must be dependent on men for their survival. The double standard of morality for men and women is a necessary evil to avoid an even greater evil, a rate of population growth naturally exceeding the rate of growth of the means to feed it. As we know, Malthus's view became prevalent among the Classical economists.

The second example is reconstructed by Pujol (1984, 1992). The question of women's lower wages was at the centre of the economic debate between the end of the nineteenth century and World War I. The explanations provided by the profession were grounded on the lesser needs of women, who always had a husband or a family to support them, on their lower productivity, the lower price of the goods they produced or their alleged absenteeism. However, in 1857 Barbara Bodichon had already provided a perfect explanation. She wrote:

> There are fewer paths open to women, and these are choke full. We are sick at heart at the cries that have been raised about distressed needlewomen, and decayed gentlewomen, and broken down governesses... There is no way of aiding governesses or needlewomen but by opening more ways of gaining livelihoods for women. It is the most efficacious way of preventing prostitution. At present the language practically held by modern society to destitute women may be resolved into Marry – Stitch – Die – or do worse.
>
> (quoted in Sockwell 1995: 110)

Her call for the end of male monopoly in the labour market went unheeded. No better fortune attended later attempts, by Millicent Fawcett and Ada Heather Briggs, to explain the lower wages of women with the segregation existing in the labour market (Millicent Fawcett and Ada Heather Briggs). The prevailing theories remained strongly influenced by the dominant ideology which saw the proper place for women in the home. Edgeworth, Marshall and Pigou, as Pujol shows, gave these theories the force of their authority, neglecting contradicting evidence. Marshall, who was usually very cautious when it came to identifying a causal relationship, firmly maintained that working mothers increase infant mortality and the 'degradation' of the working class.

The history of economics offers many examples of how prejudice creeps into even the greatest minds, and it reminds us that gender prejudice is one of the strongest.

Conclusion

The above examples confirm what feminist research has been showing over the last 20 years: economic science, which claims to be value-neutral, is instead permeated by androcentric values in its method, language and cultural assumptions. It has been argued (Harding 1986; Nelson 1986) that economics, like other sciences, has been constructed to conform to an ideal of masculinity based on rigour, rationality and objectivity, progressively excluding all that cannot be subjected to quantitative measurement and mathematical formulation, and ultimately neglecting important aspects of social life.

HET can be an important tool in this work of unmasking an impossible neutrality and pervasive gender-blindness. A gender-sensitive reading of past works and theories opens our eyes to the gradual shifts in meaning of the terms, the slow movement of the boundaries of the discipline, the progressive exclusion from it of whole areas of economic activity (housework for example) and of concepts which, though meaningful, lack a quantitative dimension. Not much work has yet been done in this direction, but the initial results show that this may prove one of the most promising fields of research in HET. For example, Brennan (2006) reconstructs the evolution of the dichotomy productive/unproductive labour from Adam Smith to the present-day feminist efforts to define the boundaries of 'production' so as to include women's contribution to human welfare. Nelson (1986) analyses the statutory statements of the goals of two important scientific associations – the American Economic Association and the Econometric Society – and their changes over time. She uses this as an illuminating illustration of how economic science was conquered by an ideal of detachment of the researcher from their object, and of separation between research and its applications. In a profession made almost exclusively of men, this ideal of detachment and domination might reflect masculine hopes and fears and the prevailing dichotomy between what is masculine/positive and what is feminine/negative.

Julie Nelson also provides an interesting agenda for 'a history of gender influences in economic thought' (Nelson 1986: 56–59). She suggests investigating the relationship between changes in social beliefs about gender and about science, or how gender has influenced the language of economics itself. Or how and when issues like marriage, fertility, crime and sex were excluded from economics until recently? Or how, since they have been back in the reckoning, economics still represents male power and privilege as 'efficient', 'functional' or the outcome of women's own choices? Other interesting questions (and wise warnings of the pitfalls that feminist research in HET faces) are raised by Janet Seiz (1993). Margaret Lewis (1999), in an excellent review of the gender-sensitive HET literature, adds to the agenda investigations into the methods adopted to assess the worthiness of a contribution to economics.

There is no shortage of subjects and it is not an agenda only for women, whose participation in the economics profession, and in the field of HET, is still despairingly low. Gender awareness, instead of gender neutrality, is in the interest of all who care for the quality and the relevance of economic research.

Notes

1 Although Schumpeter follows the tradition of his times of using 'men' to mean both men and women, this use is likely to reflect his own convictions. To the best of our knowledge, only four women are included in his monumental history of economics.
2 A second edition, with two new chapters and a fair amount of revision, was published by B. Polkinghorn 25 years later (Polkinghorn and Thomson 1998).
3 Rosalind Franklin's research data and X-ray photographs contributed to the discovery of the double helix by Crick and Watson, who had got hold of them without her consent. Her contribution was totally denied by Watson in the book where he reconstructs the discovery that brought him, together with Crick and Wilkins, the Nobel Prize in 1962 (see Maddox 2002).
4 Lisa Meitner contributed crucially to the discovery of nuclear fission, for which the Nobel Prize was awarded to Otto Hahn. Being a Jew, she was obliged to leave Berlin where she had been working with Hahn and her name could not appear in the German publication that reported the discovery. Her contribution was acknowledged only after the disclosure of the correspondence between her and Hahn, who continued to call her 'my assistant' (see Lewin 1996).
5 The complete works of Harriet Taylor Mill, together with her correspondence, have recently been edited by Ellen Jacobs and Paula Harms Payne (1998).
6 'I find that Austin would like to read his paper on size of firms to the Club. Could I resign in his favour?' letter of J.V.Robinson to R.F. Kahn, 25 December 1933, in Kahn Papers, King's College Modern Archives, Cambridge, (henceafter RFK) 13/90/1/270–3.
7 'I agree about Mrs R[obinson]'s high talents and so does Oxford and London. But it is an awful pity she is so bloody rude. Her conduct to the other ladies on the day of the Taussig luncheon […] made me first blush for the fair name of Cambridge and her great friend at Oxford tells me she glories in it' (C.R. Fay to J.M. Keynes, 6 March 1935, in Kahn Papers, King's College Modern Archives, Cambridge, RFK/14/99).
8 'The parrot-like treatment of your stuff is due to the lectures and supervision of the beautiful Mrs. R.[obinson] – a magpie breeding innumerable parrots! I gather that she puts in the Truth, with an enormous T, with such Prussian efficiency that the wretched men become identical sausages without any minds of their own! Obviously there's nothing we can do about this at present, but, I think, if peace ever comes, we ought to introduce some counter-irritant in their territory. Even the muddle into which they all got when Denis [Robertson] and the beautiful lady were lecturing against one another seems better than this drill sergeant business' (A.C. Pigou to J. M. Keynes, 12 June 1940, in Keynes Papers, PP/45/254/44–5).
9 'the truth was that the idea of a female economist at once suggests Joan Robinson to him [Pigou]. He is really very attached to Austin, and very sorry for him! I assured him that my future wife has a wider range of conversational subjects' (John Hicks to his fiancée Ursula Webb, 14 October 1935 quoted in Marcuzzo et al. 2006: 26).
10 'Who is Joan Robinson' – Haberler asked Kahn – 'The Christian name sounds like a woman's, but the article seems to me much too clever for a woman' (Joan Robinson's Papers, King's College Modern Archive, Cambridge, JVR/7/181).
11 Joan Robinson suffered from a serious breakdown in 1937–38, when she spent almost six months in a clinic. In a very short period (1934–37) she had given birth to two daughters and published three books. Overwork, complex relations with Sraffa and Kahn and the spectre of war made a devastating mixture (see Rosselli and Besomi 2005). Other, but milder, crises occurred in 1932 and 1953.

12 Others have singled out her style as the characteristic revealing her gender. See Pasinetti
    (2007: 102): 'in spite of her bold attacks and her satirical mood, her literary style is
    surprisingly feminine'.

References

Baumol, W. (1985) 'On Method in U.S. Economics a Century Earlier', *American Economic Review*, 75 (6): 1–12.

Brennan, D. (2006) 'Defending the Indefensible. Culture's Role in the Productive/Unproductive Dichotomy', *Feminist Economics*, 12 (3): 403–25.

Dimand, M.A. (1995) 'Networks of women economists', in M.A. Dimand, R. Dimand and E. Forget (eds) *Women of value*, Aldershot, UK and Brookfield, USA: Edward Elgar. pp. 39–59.

Dimand, M.A., Dimand, R. and Forget, E. (eds) (1995) *Women of value*, Aldershot, UK and Brookfield, USA: Edward Elgar.

Dimand, M.A., Dimand, R. and Forget, E. (eds) (2000) *A Biographical Dictionary of Women Economists*. Cheltenham, UK and Northampton, MA, USA: Edward Elgar.

Dimand, R. (1995) 'The neglect of women's contribution to economics', in M.A. Dimand, R. Dimand and E. Forget (eds) *Women of value*. Aldershot, UK and Brookfield, USA: Edward Elgar. pp. 1–22.

Dimand, R. and Nyland, C. (eds) (2003) *The Status of Women in Classical Economic Thought*. Cheltenham, UK and Northampton, MA, USA: Edward Elgar.

Forget, E. (1995) 'American women economists, 1900–1940: doctoral dissertations and research specialization', in M.A. Dimand, R. Dimand and E. Forget (eds) *Women of value*. Aldershot, UK and Brookfield, USA: Edward Elgar. pp. 25–38.

Forget, E. (2003) 'Cultivating Sympathy: Sophie Condorcet's Letters on Sympathy', in R. Dimand and C. Nyland (eds) *The Status of Women in Classical Economic Thought*. Cheltenham, UK and Northampton, MA, USA: Edward Elgar. pp. 142–61.

Groenewegen, P. (ed.) (1994) *Feminism and Political Economy in Victorian England*. Aldershot: Edward Elgar.

Harding, S. (1986) *The Science Question in Feminism*. Ithaca and London: Cornell University Press.

Hayek, F. (1951) *John Stuart Mill and Harriet Taylor. Their friendship and subsequent marriage*. Chicago: University of Chicago Press.

Jacobs, J.E., Payne, P.H. (eds) (1998) *The complete works of Harriet Taylor Mill*. Bloomington, IN: Indiana University Press.

Kerr, P. (2006) 'Knowledge without pain', in B. Gibson (ed.) *Joan Robinson's Economics*. Cheltenham, UK and Northampton, MA, USA: Edward Elgar.

Keynes, J.M. (1972) [1933] *Essays in Biography*. Vol. X of *The Collected Writings*. D. Moggridge (ed.), London: Macmillan.

King's College Annual Report (1984), Cambridge.

Levy, D. (2003) 'Taking Harriet Martineau seriously', in R. Dimand and C. Nyland (eds) *The Status of Women in Classical Economic Thought*. Cheltenham, UK and Northampton, MA, USA: Edward Elgar. pp. 262–84.

Lewin, S.L. (1996) *Lise Meitner. A life in Physics*. Berkeley: University of California Press.

Lewis, M. (1999) 'History of economic thought', in J. Peterson and M. Lewis (eds) *The Elgar Companion to Feminist Economics*. Cheltenham: Edward Elgar.

McWilliams Tullberg, R. (1992) 'Alfred Marshall's attitude to The Economics of Industry'. *Journal of the History of Economic Thought*, 14 (2): 257–70.

Madden, K., Pujol, M. and Seiz, J. (eds) (2005) *A Bibliography of Female Economic Thought up to 1940*. London: Routledge.

Maddox, B. (2002) *Rosalind Franklin. The dark lady of DNA*. London: HarperCollins publishers.

Marcuzzo, M.C. (2002a) Review of A Biographical Dictionary of Women Economists, edited by Dimand Robert, Dimand Mary Ann and Forget Evelyn, *Economic Record*, 78: 497–99.

Marcuzzo, M.C. (2002b) The Writings of Joan Robinson, in the Palgrave Archive edition of *Joan Robinson, Writings on Economics*. Vol. 1, London: Macmillan. pp. xxxii–lxxiii.

Marcuzzo, M.C. (2003) Joan Robinson and the Three Cambridge Revolutions, *Review of Political Economy*, 15 (4): 545–60.

Marcuzzo, M.C. (2005) Piero Sraffa at the University of Cambridge, *European Journal of the History of Economic Thought,* 12 (3): 425–52.

Marcuzzo, M.C. and Sardoni, C. (2005) 'Fighting for the Keynesian Revolution', in M.C. Marcuzzo and A. Rosselli (eds) *Economists in Cambridge. A study through their correspondence, 1907–1946*. pp. 174–95.

Marcuzzo, M.C., Hirai T., Nishizawa T. and Sanfilippo E. (eds) (2006) *The Letters between John Hicks and Ursula Webb. September–December, 1935*, Kobe: Working Paper, n. 207, Institute for Economic and Business Administration Research, University of Hyogo.

Marcuzzo, M.C. and Rosselli, A. (eds) (2005) *Economists in Cambridge. A study through their correspondence, 1907–1946*. London: Routledge.

Marx, K. (1954) *Capital*. Vol. 1, London: Lawrence and Wishet.

Moggridge, D. (1992) *Maynard Keynes. An Economist's Biography*. London: Routledge.

Narasimhan, S. (1983) 'Joan Robinson: in the radical vein. A Laywoman's Homage', *Cambridge Journal of Economics,* 7: 213–19.

Nelson, J. (1986) *Feminism, objectivity & economics*. London: Routledge.

Nyland, C. (2003) 'Women's Progress and "the end of History"', in R. Dimand and C. Nyland (eds) *The Status of Women in Classical Economic Thought*. Cheltenham, UK and Northampton, MA, USA: Edward Elgar. pp. 108–26.

Pasinetti, L. (2007) *Keynes and the Cambridge Keynesians*. Cambridge: Cambridge University Press.

Polkinghorn, B. (1995) 'Jane Marcet and Harriet Martineau: motive, market experience and reception of their works popularizing classical political economy', in M.A. Dimand, R. Dimand and E. Forget (eds) *Women of value*. Aldershot, UK and Brookfield, USA: Edward Elgar. pp. 71–81.

Polkinghorn, B. and Thomson, D.L. (1998) 'Introduction', in Polkinghorn Bette and Lampen Thomson Dorothy (eds) *Adam Smith's daughters*. Cheltenham, UK and Northampton, MA, USA: Edward Elgar.

Polkinghorn, B. and Lampen, T.D. (1998) *Adam Smith's daughters*. Cheltenham, UK and Northampton, MA, USA: Edward Elgar.

Pujol, M. (1984) 'Gender and class in Marshall's "Principles of Economics"', *Cambridge Journal of Economics*, 8 (3): 217–34.

Pujol, M. (1992) *Feminism and Anti-Feminism in Early Economic Thought*. Aldershot, UK and Brookfield, USA: Edward Elgar.

Pujol, M. (1995) 'The feminist economic thought of Harriet Taylor (1807–1858)', in M.A. Dimand, R. Dimand and E. Forget (eds) *Women of value*. Aldershot, UK and Brookfield, USA: Edward Elgar. pp. 82–102.

Pujol, M. (2000) 'Harriet Hardy Taylor Mill', in M.A. Dimand, R. Dimand and E. Forget (eds) *A Biographical Dictionary of Women Economists*, Cheltenham, UK and Northampton, MA: Edward Elgar. pp. 307–11.

Robinson, J. (1969) [1933] *The Economics of Imperfect Competition*. London: Macmillan.

Rossiter, M. (1982) *Women Scientists in America*. Baltimore and London: Johns Hopkins University Press.

Rosselli, A. (2005) 'An enduring partnership. The correspondence between Kahn and J. Robinson', in M.C. Marcuzzo and A. Rosselli (eds) *Economists in Cambridge. A study through their correspondence, 1907–1946*. London: Routledge. pp. 259–91.

Rosselli, A. and Besomi, D. (2005) 'The unlooked for proselytiser. Joan Robinson and the correspondence with Sraffa, Harrod and Kaldor', in M.C. Marcuzzo and A. Rosselli (eds) *Economists in Cambridge. A study through their correspondence, 1907–1946*. London: Routledge. pp. 309–29.

Schiebinger, L. (1987) 'The History and Philosophy of women in science: a review essay', *Signs: Journal of Women in Culture and Society*, 12 (Winter): 305–32.

Schumpeter, J. (1994) [1954] *History of Economic Analysis*. New York: Oxford University Press.

Seiz, J. (1993) 'Feminism and the History of Economic Thought', *History of Political Economy* 25 (1): 185–201.

Seiz, J. and Pujol, M. (2000) 'Harriet Taylor Mill', *American Economic Review Papers and Proceedings,* 90 (2): 476–9.

Sockwell, W. (1995) 'Barbara Bodichon and the Women of Langham Place', in M.A. Dimand, R. Dimand and E. Forget (eds) *Women of value*. Aldershot, UK and Brookfield, USA: Edward Elgar. pp. 103–23.

Sraffa, P. (1960) *Production of Commodities by Means of Commodites*. Cambridge: Cambridge University Press.

Thorne, A. (1995) 'Women mentoring women in economics in the 1930s', in M.A. Dimand, R. Dimand and E. Forget (eds) *Women of value*. Aldershot, UK and Brookfield, USA: Edward Elgar. pp. 60–70.

2 The historical construction of gender

Reflections on gender and economic history

Pat Hudson

Introduction

Gender is the social construction of sexual difference. It concerns the features that different societies ascribe to individuals, and to objects, processes and behaviours, based upon perceptions of differences between the sexes. Gender is a social rather than a biological construction, and it has a history. Most, though not all, historical work has a diachronic emphasis while much social science, including economic analysis, is present-centred and/or synchronic. It is thus the case that historical work raises issues about gender that may be much less obvious to economists, and other social scientists, than to historians.

This chapter considers the impact of gender theory and gender research on the writing of economic history. Some examples of the impact of gender-oriented research in altering perspectives in economic, demographic and social history are given. Ways in which a gender perspective is challenging our understanding of economic motivations and behaviour and our conceptions of the scope of economic analysis are emphasised.

The impact of a gender approach upon history

Recognition of the importance of gender has begun to radically influence research and writing in history, including economic history, in several different ways. First, it alerts historians to the gender bias in recording and writing about the past. Because men have held more political, economic, social and cultural power than women in all past societies of record, men have been the subject of most historical writing. Until the second half of the twentieth century women barely figured as historical subjects. This is not only because of male domination of the historical profession but also because of the privileging, in professional history, of formal documentary evidence (evidence mostly written by men and about men) over less formal sources, and because of dominant ideas about the legitimate scope of history. These elevate political history over most social and cultural history, the public world of politics, business and diplomacy over the private world of everyday social reproduction. Thus the first way in which recognition of the importance of gender affects the writing of history is in encouraging more research on women and on the ordinary, everyday, business of life that has been hidden from the public gaze and omitted from public record.

The growth of women's history since the 1960s has done much to further this project but gender history differs markedly from women's history in recognising the need to do more than write parallel histories of women's lives to match those that we have of men. It recognises two additional things: first that the history of women's lives often fits badly into the sub-disciplinary divisions and agendas that dominate conventional history and second that chronological phases and turning points that have arisen from male-oriented history are often inappropriate when the remaining half of the population is included in the account. Thus gender history often challenges established agendas and chronologies suggesting that we should not just try to fit women back into the conventional historiography as if they had somehow slipped out. Instead we should recognise that adding women to history may necessitate a fundamental rethink about the boundaries, and even the existence, of conventional research priorities and specialisms, and to question the validity of long-accepted narratives of the timing of development and change.

Gender history also differs from women's history because it involves the study of men and male identity as much as it involves the study of women and female identity. Gender is constructed in culture and constructed through difference: women are defined as what men are not, and vice-versa, hence the need to consider constantly the production and reproduction of both men and women. In Natalie Zemon Davies's words:

> It seems that we should be interested in the history of both women and men, that we should not be working only on the subjected sex any more than a historian of class can focus entirely on peasants. Our goal is to understand the significance of the sexes, of gender groups in the historical past...to find out what meaning they had and how they functioned to maintain the social order or to promote change.
>
> (Davies 1975a)

The concern of gender history is thus in recognising the social construction of sexual difference, how this social construction with respect to the two sexes works, how this came to be and how it is sustained or changed over time. This involves analysing the binary opposition male: female in historical context and questioning the hierarchy involved in the construction (male = superior, dominant; female = inferior, subordinate).

Gender also affects research and writing in history by altering the way in which sources are perceived and evaluated. This has two aspects: the first concerns the identification of legitimate sources, the second concerns their interpretation. Gender history suggests that some of the older popular sources and practices of history need to be rehabilitated, often those that predominated before the professionalisation of history in the late nineteenth century: oral traditions and oral testimony, collective memory, folk tales and stories. More importantly it insists that we require a different and more questioning use of all evidence, including documentary sources: more reading against the grain. This involves more inference and more listening to the silences and unwitting testimony of documents. It also involves more recognition of the influence of past gender relations upon the generation, construction, survival and the language of evidence.

Gender theory and language

The development of gender theory has found expression as part of the more general post-modern and specifically post-structural approach that advocates (after Derrida) the deconstruction of all linguistic expression of 'facts' and 'knowledge', paying particular attention to the role of ideology and political agendas in forming vocabulary and expression in speech and writing: the power of normative discourse and of unspoken assumptions (Scott 1986; 1988). The key point endorsed by recognition of the importance of gender, and by a post-structural approach is that knowledge is not a value-free neutral thing but a form of power. The most interesting developments in history arising from the so-called 'linguistic turn' have occurred in deconstructing the language contained in documents from the past, and in the historical literature itself, and seeing the words and terms used as themselves embodying a gender-specific view of the world and of the past.

Most key words important for understanding sources and writing history have been coined by a male dominated culture with a view to understanding male experience. They have become accepted as value-free or part of common sense understanding when they should really be questioned. Words such as 'class', 'politics', 'work', 'the economy', 'family', 'skill', 'knowledge', 'employment', 'unemployment', 'choice', 'rationality' all take on different meanings when women are the focus of study.

From this perspective it is the case that one can never aspire to historical research that is free from gender bias without a full investigation of language (used by both historical actors and by historians): its gendered structure and composition. Language constructs meaning and there is no meaning without language.

From current gender theory we thus have the following propositions:

i) that gender is the primary way of indicating and conveying inequalities of power (of all kinds) in society
ii) that gender differences and gender perceptions are therefore important for understanding all spheres of history (not just women's history, men's history or the history of the family, but also for understanding political history, economic history, the history of institutions, science, technology, religion and all other spheres)
iii) that gender was and is the product of discourse
iv) that opposing notions of male and female must be seen in relation to one another and are constantly changing over time and space

v) that deconstruction of language is vital for understanding the gendered nature of texts and sources and in uncovering the importance of gender in all types of academic (and other) writing

Until these propositions were incorporated into gender history from the late 1980s gender had been largely used only in a descriptive sense to refer to relationships between the sexes and to social identities in history. Hence it was confined mainly to women's history and the history of the family, generally to endorse a functionalist view and one rooted ultimately in biology. 'Although gender in this usage asserts that relationships between the sexes are social it says nothing about why these relationships are constructed as they are, how they work, or how they change' (Scott 1988: 32–33). It also tells us nothing about (because it is not concerned with) how gender permeates all aspects of society and polity. What was needed in Joan Scott's view, writing in 1986, was a way of using gender as a category of analysis so that it could be focused upon aspects of history not normally associated with it, such as the realm of political and ideological change, war, diplomacy, science and religion. One could also add: the economy, business history, micro-economic decisions, macro-economic policy making. Scott asks 'How does gender give meaning to the organisation and perception of historical knowledge?' (Scott 1988: 31). She cites as one example of the legitimising function of gender, Pierre Bourdieu's study of how agricultural production in the past was often organised according to concepts of time and season that invoked the opposition between masculine and feminine. She also cites Natalie Davis's study of the way in which concepts of masculine and feminine underpinned the rules of social order in early modern France and Caroline Bynum's study of medieval spirituality, showing the relationship between religious behaviour and the defining characteristics of gender inequality (Bourdieu 1980; Davis 1975; Bynum 1982, 1987).

The history of imperialism provides further illustration of the operation of gender in relation to history. Ann Laura Stoler, for example, asks in what ways were gender inequalities essential to the structure of imperial authority and racism. Why were colonial writers and agents so mysogynist? Was it merely a practical response to the conditions of conquest? Stoler focuses on French Indo China and the Dutch East Indies arguing that the assertion of European supremacy in terms of patriotic manhood and racial virility was not just an *expression* of imperial domination but also a defining feature of it. She shows that imperial authority and racial distinctions were fundamentally structured through perceptions of gender: '…the categories of colonizer and colonized were secured through notions of racial difference constructed in gender terms'. Sexuality served as a loaded metaphor for domination (Stoler 1996: 209–266).

Gender, then, provides a way to decode meaning and to understand the connections between various forms of human interaction. Concepts of gender structure our perception of the concrete and the symbolic aspects of all social life. To the extent that this establishes differential control over, or access to, material and symbolic resources, gender becomes implicated in the conception and construction of power itself.

Gender and social science

This brings us to consideration of the methodological implications of a gender approach to social science history and to economic history in particular. The growing importance of gender in the practice of historical research and writing, particularly since the closer identification between gender history and post-structural theory, has done much to undermine the role of conventional social science ideas and methodology. These have come to be seen as too positivistic, essentialist and deterministic. Marxist-influenced views of gender are also viewed as problematic because patriarchy is seen to develop and change as a function of the relations of production rather than having an enduring, independent dynamic. Even in more sophisticated versions of Marxism that admit considerable autonomy of the psychic structuring of gender identity, gender in the last instance is reduced to its materialist determination and has little or no analytical status of its own. In historical work the methodological shift of emphasis, inspired by a gender perspective, has involved a general rejection of the mechanical models and analogies that underpin both Marxian and non-Marxian social-scientific investigation (and that imply a detachment of subject and object, with the goal of objectivity), in favour of a hermeneutic approach to knowledge. A hermeneutic approach is one that involves the conscious interaction between subject and object, between researcher and sources, analogous to the interaction between reader and text. In relation to science and specifically to economic theory, the feminist challenge has involved recognition of the ways in which the Cartesian approach is masculinist (Poovey 1998; 1988). 'In the Cartesian view, the abstract, general, detached, emotionless, 'masculine' approach taken to represent scientific thinking is radically removed from, and clearly viewed as superior to, the concrete, particular, embodied, passionate, 'feminine' reality of material life' (Ferber and Nelson 1993: 25). Overall, methodologically, the growing importance of gender in historical research and writing has favoured, and been favoured by, the current privileging of a post-structurally oriented cultural history over positivistic forms of social and economic historical research, of qualitative over quantitative work and of inductive over deductive enquiry. In turn this has been an important ingredient (though not the only one) in the declining popularity of economic history, in Western Europe at least, in recent decades.

It is certainly the case that the entire basis and procedures of academic study and discourse in history and in other disciplines have been challenged by the development of gendered approaches in recent years. So much so that it is fair to suggest that as gender becomes more central, history might become an entirely different subject generating a very different account of all aspects of the past and using different research methodologies. While cultural and social history are progressing and changing in this direction, in economic history the radical challenge that gender might pose remains muted. The challenge of gender has coincided with a decline in the popularity of economic history (encouraged by the declining influence of social science and Marxian models) rather than by any marked attempt to reform it from within.

We now turn to some illustrations of research in economic history where, in different ways, gender is making a difference and also where it might develop much further in the near future. The illustrations mainly concentrate upon research in British economic history between the eighteenth and twentieth centuries, although similar trends are characteristic in research on other periods, geographical areas and fields. I have elsewhere analysed ways in which a gender perspective was quick to begin to alter our view of the structural shift in the British economy away from the primary sector to the secondary and tertiary sectors, during industrialisation; our understanding of productivity growth and technological change; and the development of social class and of crime and punishment in the period of Britain's industrial revolution (Hudson 1995). In the case of crime, for example, it has been shown that the 'crime wave' traditionally seen to have accompanied industrialisation and urbanisation was absent in the case of women, but that gender ideology and social attitudes to both female crime and to the punishment of female offenders lies at the heart of understanding this phenomenon. The causes, chronologies and types of crime varied markedly between men and women, as did the policing of female crime and punishment. The older research agendas and priorities of historians of crime are considerably undermined when one disaggregates the criminal experience by sex and when one examines the gender attitudes and stereotypes that governed policing and the law. Here we concentrate upon population growth during industrialisation, the demographic transition, business networks and information, work, and consumption. This is followed by some analysis of the way in which gender influences our understanding of all aspects of everyday behaviour and what this may mean for conceptualising 'the economic sphere' and for analysing economic behaviour, past and present.

Demographic history: the population boom of the industrial revolution period

The demographic history of England was revolutionised in the 1970s and 1980s by the publication of research from the Cambridge Group for the History of Population and Social Structure. First, Laslett produced evidence from early household listings that the nuclear rather than the extended family dominated in the early modern period and did not arise, as was thought, as a result of industrialisation (Laslett 1965; 1969). Second, Wrigley and Schofield made a study of population change in England over more than two centuries by using vital event totals from over 400 parish registers, and allowing for under registrations by using back projection from the later census figures (Wrigley and Schofield 1981). This demonstrated that increases in fertility were two and a half times more important than mortality improvements in accounting for the unprecedented, sustained, acceleration of population growth in the eighteenth century. The fertility side of the equation was altered partly through rising illegitimacy, together with some increase in fertility rates within marriage, but the real key lay in nuptiality, in changes in the age and rate of marriage (Wrigley and Schofield 1981; Wrigley 2004). Laslett had shown that household size remained roughly stable and that the nuclear family was the norm, Wrigley and Schofield proposed that nuptiality ages and rates depended upon the ability of young people to form a new household. Real wage changes were the key, they argued, and they backed this up with a, subsequently much criticised, correlation analysis between the Phelps, Brown and Hopkins real wage index (an index formed primarily from adult male wages in the building trades of London) and national nuptiality rates. The correlation analysis indicated a positive relationship both before and during the population rise of the eighteenth century but only if a lag of 20 years or so was introduced into the real wage series. In the population acceleration of the later eighteenth century the age of marriage, rather than the rate of marriage, was shown to be the key variable. The demographic regime was therefore characterised by Wrigley and Schofield as one of a natural balance between population and resources, operating through a Malthusian-style prudential, preventive check, creating a 'dileatory homeostasis' (Wrigley 2004).

A gender perspective provides a challenge to this analysis and to these conclusions in several important respects. First Laslett's conclusion was tempered by research emphasising that households are not families and that the boundaries of households are sufficiently fluid to question the assumption that young people achieved economic independence at marriage. The material supports of the extended family, both vertically and horizontally, could be maintained in an environment where extended families lived in households close to one another rather than in the same household. Research on neighbourhood networks of kinship and reciprocity have highlighted the role of gender in these networks: informal social and economic roles, particularly those expected of women (in their capacity as mothers, grandmothers, daughters and sisters) often took in several households and involved significant inter-household and intergenerational transfers and reciprocities concerning material resources (Chaytor 1980; Hill 1989; Janssens 1993; Sabean 1990, 1998; O'Hara 2000). It is perhaps no accident that female historians have predominantly undertaken such studies. Using a variety of qualitative evidence and analysis, this research has highlighted some of the drawbacks of an excessively quantitative approach that takes too little account of relationships that refuse to be captured in the neat categories of recorded data, amenable to statistical manipulation. Such qualitative research is generally seen as outside the legitimate sphere of interest of demographers but it often has the capacity to significantly undermine their analysis and conclusions (Frederici *et al.* 1993).

A major plank of criticism of the Wrigley and Schofield analysis has been their instrumental treatment of marriage decisions: that marriage in the period from the sixteenth to the nineteenth century was largely determined by wage levels, rising wages enabling more marriages. This involves the assumption that men and women react in the same way to the same economic circumstances, that young men and women have the same desires and aspirations with respect to marriage, and that couples make their courtship and marriage decisions in harmony with one another's needs and desires rather than in conflict. However, gender-oriented research has shown that courtship and marriage decisions were often complex and contradictory, subject to contingencies of all kinds and often vitally dependent upon inheritance, parental support and the passing on of economic niches or access to jobs rather than real wage levels (Hill 1989; King 1999; O'Hara 2000; Duhamelle and Schlumbohm 2003; Agren and Eriksson 2005). Research on the Yorkshire textile region has, for example, suggested the importance of the expansion of employment opportunities together with pre-mortem inheritance and aid from both parents and from poor relief in framing marriage decisions for young people in the eighteenth century. An increasing preference for marital endogamy, and chance and contingency also played a role (Hudson and King 2000; King 1999).

More damaging for ostensibly scientific and value-neutral demographic research on marriage has been the finding that women's decisions about when and whether to marry or remarry were often based on factors entirely distinct from those that may have influenced men. This is a crucial finding because, demographically speaking, it is the lowering of the female marriage age (enabling more childbearing years within marriage) that is seen as the key variable driving population growth. Rising wages and employment for young women have in many localities and regions been shown to have led to pressure to stay longer in the parental home in order to contribute to family income. And in periods of low or unstable wages for women research has shown a tendency for young women to leave home and to marry earlier because of the need for families to shed unproductive members (Hill 1989; Wall 1978; Sharpe 2002; O'Hara 2000). In these circumstances it was often desperation and the desire to avoid pauperism that drove women into marriage and indeed remarriage. Thus the marriage age of women may have been analysed in an entirely misleading manner by demographers who have assumed that men and women would react to economic stimuli in the same rather than in a polar opposite manner. The assumptions of modern economic analysis make it difficult to analyse decision making that is fraught with relationships of patriarchal or intergenerational dependence, obligation and power (Ferber and Nelson 1993). This is particularly so regarding decision making about marriage and fertility (Folbre 1983).

Demographic history: the fertility transition

Gender perspectives have had a similar impact upon research concerning the fertility transition of the late-nineteenth and early-twentieth century. The earliest analyses of this transition relied upon a modernisation paradigm in which a play off between additional children and greater wealth in material goods was envisaged, a play off that started in the middle classes and eventually spread to the entire population. The model recognised the impact of lower levels of infant and child mortality and the greater emphasis placed upon the education of children, but the key idea was one that saw couples making harmonious decisions based largely upon material considerations that eventually influenced the whole population in a similar way. Gender perspectives challenged this view by pointing to a number of variables that better accounted for occupational, regional and local differences than did models based on class or upon the idea of unitary responses to material circumstances. Some of these factors are neatly summarised in MacKinnon's challenging article: 'Were women present at the demographic transition?' which rightly criticised the blindness to gender that characterised most of the demographic literature on this topic (MacKinnon 1995).

First there appeared to be large variations between areas where stable paid work was available for women, including married women, and where it was not. It has been argued not only that the opportunity cost of multiple pregnancies in such areas would influence procreative decisions but that the culture of communities such as those dominated by factory textile production would give more power to the role of women in family decision making. Women involved in the wage labour market in large numbers had more self-confidence and had access to more knowledge concerning contraception (Gittins 1982). Szreter has identified regional and local variations with respect to contraception, based partly on occupational structures and the availability of women's work but also upon wider cultural variables (Szreter 1996). Oral history from the early twentieth century, carried out by Gittens in particular, has indicated that the responsibility for contraception varied, partly associated with occupational and local cultures and that this was often reflected in different forms of fertility restriction from abstention and coitus interruptus (where male compliance was required) to abortion and infanticide (the latter two being more desperate measures associated almost entirely with women's agency) (Gittens 1982). The demographic evidence itself shows variation in birth spacing and timing that helps to identify regional, local and occupational variation in fertility restriction caused predominantly by greater spacing or by earlier stopping of births, again indicating a variety of responses, motivations and conditioning variables for what, at first sight, might appear to be a general phenomenon (Garrett *et al.* 2001). It has been gender-oriented qualitative research that has done most to unsettle the analysis and conclusions derived from conventional demographic analysis.

In conventional demographic history as a whole the dominant theory has been the cultural diffusionist model of change. In this model occupational and spatial differences are seen in terms of consensual rational choice decisions about marriage and fertility being taken largely in response to material circumstances and with backward regions and classes eventually catching up with the leaders on the road to modernity and progress. However, a gender perspective suggests the need for a more sensitive and nuanced analysis of the ways in which relationships of power and knowledge (public and private) act to form a specific response to material stimuli within a variety of regional and local contexts where gender and material life interact in different ways (Seccombe 1992a, 1992b; Garrett *et al.* 2001). The lessons learned in the historiographical development of demographic history might well be instructive for economists with the current vogue to interpret marriage and divorce decisions largely via general maximisation models (see the debate later in this volume). Only time and further research will tell whether such gender-inspired qualitative approaches to the history of marriage and fertility decisions will provide a fundamental challenge to what has become mainstream economic theorising.

Information and social capital

A gender perspective has also radically altered the historiography concerning the accumulation of capital and its roots in social and cultural networks based on families and co-fraternities.

The story of capital accumulation during the period of Britain's industrialisation, for example, used to be analysed in entirely economic terms emphasising savings and investment ratios and the rise of various formal instruments and institutions such as mortgages, bills of exchange, trusteeships, banks and discount houses that gradually assisted in the more efficient mobilisation of funds in the service of business and commerce. The legal position of women made it difficult for them to function as entrepreneurs in a formal way and the documentary evidence for their role in business and investment has always been limited. However it has long been recognised that widows and spinsters were the holders of significant savings balances. New research has shown that the gender specific risk aversion associated with the social, economic and cultural position of women and their preference for an annuity income made wealthy widows and spinsters very significant investors in government stocks and bonds (Green and Owens 2003). Their role in riskier business as trustees and investors in manufacturing and commerce is also becoming more recognised. Some secondary and tertiary activities, such as millinery, running lodging houses, inns and schools, were particularly marked by female entrepreneurship (Kay 2004; Barker 2006). The widespread phenomenon of widows taking over family businesses has also been researched (Berg 1993; Owens 2002). The bulk of gender-oriented research on entrepreneurship and capital formation has concerned women as a 'hidden investment' in enterprise through their role, not just behind the scenes in a variety of practical capacities in businesses large and small, but also through their work in cementing commercial networks of trust and knowledge based on extended families, religious co-fraternities and civic and philanthropic circles (Davidoff and Hall 1987; Morris 2005). In the high-risk, high-uncertainty climate of the early decades of industrialisation the gender specific roles of different family members in creating and endorsing commercial networks was vital. This depended partly upon social, religious and civic reputation and respectability in which family life, entertaining and consumption all played an important part, and in which the activities of wives and daughters was as important as that of men. Female sociability, kinship and friendship networks complemented the contacts made in the male world of the counting house, the coffee house or the gentleman's club (Sabean 1998; Rose 2000).

Information is also important in this context, although insufficient historical research on information and gender has been done to explore it in detail. The efficiency of markets in the past, as in the present, depended upon the extent and accuracy of commercial information, which was not only conveyed via formal business connections and business correspondence, but also in the informal socialising, networking and letter writing of women (Hudson 2004; Morris 2005; Sabean 1998). Gender played an important role in all conduits of information but particularly in informal networks of friends and families. Kahneman and Tversky's work has demonstrated that the way in which information is presented, communicated, perceived and processed is subject to bias and that gender can be important in this bias (Kahneman and Tversky 1979). It may therefore be the case that research will now start to uncover the cognitive as well as the psychological and social influence of gender in this area of historical research and in interpreting the importance and variability of social capital past and present.

Work, provisioning and consuming

Gender perspectives have been important for altering our understanding of shifts in patterns of work, payment structures and divisions of labour during the industrialisation period, and beyond, for some time. The impact of such perspectives on the rise of a consumer oriented society is much more recent but equally important.

The idea that both long-enduring and newly emerging divisions of labour were a product of sex-specific physical strengths or mental proclivities has long been abandoned in favour of an acknowledgement that ideology rather than biology has been the major determinant of the nature and distribution of work for men and women, past and present. Gendered ideas of what is fit work for women and for men and a shifting ideology of idealised social roles for women and men have played the key roles. The congruence of home and work in pre-industrial times, both in agriculture and in manufacturing, allowed for some flexibility of roles within the household as a unit of production, particularly at harvest time when maximal effort was demanded in a short period. The seventeenth to nineteenth centuries in Europe were marked by the expansion of rural and semi-rural domestic manufacturing for distant markets which usually incorporated the labour of all family members. This 'proto-industrialisation' was sometimes accompanied by a blurring of gender roles but more often there appears to have been a clear cut division of labour with men taking the skilled and supervisory roles, working with female and child assistants in tasks clearly delineated along gender lines (Cerman and Ogilvie 1996).

The separation of home and work that gradually occurred with the coming of industrial society can be seen to mark a turning point in solidifying pre-existing tendencies to a separation of spheres with men engaging in the public world of politics, commerce and waged work whilst women were increasingly confined to the domestic sphere of home making and childrearing. Although women at all levels of society were impelled to find ways of crossing these boundaries, the ideology of a domestic sphere reserved largely for women (even though this was far from the reality), and the rise of the male breadwinner wage norm, did much to endorse male/female distinctions based on notions of male physical and mental superiority and upon the necessary subordination of the 'weaker sex'. Notions of appropriate forms of motherhood and fatherhood, and of the socialisation of girls and boys were radically affected. Once the male breadwinner norm was accepted by employers and trade unionists as well as by the state, it became even more difficult for women to command a wage on equal terms with men, male control of their wives' financial assets and of the assets of the marriage was endorsed, and the female wage labour market continued to be dominated by jobs that were unskilled, casual and low paid (Creighton 1996; Seccombe 1993). Women came to be concentrated in low productivity, manual, low-tech and casual occupations in the nineteenth and early-twentieth centuries and were paid accordingly, their wage being seen as supplementary 'pin' money for a household. Even in the textile industries where women were employed in large numbers in mechanised factories on relatively high rates of pay by the 1840s and 1850s, a period of restructuring quickly followed so that the more capital intensive, supervisory and higher paid jobs within factories were confined to men, and women lost the skill traditions necessary to reassert their position, on equal terms, thereafter (Valverde 1988).

The above story is well known but when we link the demand to the supply side of the economy during the process of industrialisation a gender perspective is beginning to reveal that male and female roles were changed in different ways. The shift from part-time by-employments in domestic manufacturing to the emergence of a full-time manufacturing workforce, largely outside the home, has been argued to have been driven by an industrious revolution where women were at the forefront of change. This involved a massive transfer of labour out of self-provisioning and household subsistence in favour of wage earning and entering the market for everyday necessities as well as luxuries (de Vries 1993; 1994). Further research on consumption and consumerism in the industrial revolution has hinted at the ways in which gender (and appeals to gender ideals via advertising and retailing schemes) profoundly influenced patterns of spending and consumption. Dominance of the male breadwinner wage norm gave women a high profile and public role in consumption and provisioning via the market (Weatherill 1988; Vickery 1998; Breward 1999; Berg 2005; de Grazia and Furlong 1996). Women appear to have been at the forefront of a radical shift in the culture of appearances. This was felt in a marked change in attitudes to the consumption of clothes and home wares that signalled much about rapidly changing society and social relations (Roche 1990; 1994). Male oriented fashion histories and models of male 'rational' choice, based on stable tastes, are not therefore the most appropriate for analysing demand in industrial societies past or present (Nelson 1993).

Everyday life

Among the most fundamental challenges to conventional economics and economic history posed by a gender perspective is the importance that one might attach to everyday life. We have so far glimpsed this in relation to the historiographies of self-provisioning and procreation and to the communication of information via familial and social networks and gossip. It is now time to say a little more about the concept of everyday life, embodied in locality, work, home and family and how this may help to emphasise the potential impact of gender upon economic analysis.

Everyday life essentially encompasses the daily tasks of reproduction. It covers a pragmatic world of habit, routine and regularity, neither questioned nor consciously valued but assimilated as common sense. It is taken for granted as a sort of second nature in which people orientate themselves with little deliberate reflection. It dominates existence even in sophisticated commercialised societies but perhaps more so in societies close to subsistence where a large amount of time is devoted to physiological necessities such as resting, eating and drinking – that usually occur in a limited number of locations. It includes habits of waking and sleeping, the routines and rhythms of the day, the year, the life cycle; responding to light and dark, the weather, the state of the soil; preparing food and eating, cleaning, washing and provisioning, nurturing, work routines, familial and social reciprocities, day to day sociability, the list is long. As Eagleton has suggested, the territory includes

> the whole of our sensate life: the business of affections and aversions, of how the world strikes the body on its sensory surfaces, of what takes root in the gaze and in the guts and all that arises from our most banal biological insertion into the world.
>
> (Eagleton 1996:2)

Everyday life crosses the boundaries of public and private. It is not just a women's thing, although it could be argued that women's lives, so wrapped up in day-to-day provisioning and nurturing, are embedded particularly deeply in it. Certainly a gender approach to economic history brings to the forefront time and again the importance of habit and routine – the everyday – in framing choice and action.

Everyday life in this sense – habitual and unreflective – has not traditionally been the province of either history or social science. And although it influenced the cultural approach of Schmoller and others of the biologically rooted historical school, it is particularly absent from economics (and hence from theoretically informed economic history) which rests upon theories of deliberately considered rational action and choice. One might argue that the growing literature on fertility and other household-based decisions has drawn economic analysis closer to the sphere of everyday material reproduction, but the essential distinction between this literature and the approach being discussed here is the prominence of conscious calculative decision making in the former and its absence in the latter.

Everyday life always takes place in, and relates to, the immediate environment of a person. It is thus most directly experienced in relation to home and to face-to-face communities and localities involving all of the population – men and women, young and old. All of the writers working in this tradition stress the importance of home and of locality and community, emphasising a sphere which, if not gender neutral, is at least gender inclusive (Heller 1979, 1984; De Certeau 1984; Wright 1985; Highmore 2002). The everyday involves all private as well as public actions and behaviour that impact upon material life. To acknowledge the importance of the everyday not only involves acknowledging the material roles of women and children, past and present, but it also enlarges our conception of where the economic sphere, and economic behaviour, begin and end. It can lead to a gender-neutral conceptualisation of the economy and of economic activity.

Home is at the centre of everyday life, the hub around which most other experiences turn. In the home,

> Particularistic interests are harmonised …with the customs, values and norms of external authority, options are assessed in the light of conscience, experiences are remembered and reinterpreted in the light of age, feelings are framed and arranged …in a way that fits them to the …tasks and demands of the external world.
>
> (Wright 1985:11)

Home also concerns the recognition and use of skills and potentials that have little opportunity for realisation in wider society. These are practised or exploited behind closed doors but have a wider importance in generating notions of self and in influencing motivations and behaviour. Such features of the home environment act to encourage or to discourage shifts from self-provisioning to waged work and spending, for example. They influence how economic choices are perceived and the nature of responses to them.

Home is also a major site of stories, myths and gossip that play a prominent part in interpreting and making sense of the wider world. The household selects or rejects information and narratives from outside. It discusses and rehashes. Bauman stresses the role of stories in connecting what he calls historical memory with the everyday process of 'making sense'. But 'The historical memory of a group is institutionally carried and it does not always surface to the level of verbal communication'. It finds its expression in the group's proclivities to some rather than other behavioural responses. For Bauman historical memory and the behaviour that it encourages or supports, is reinforced daily by micro-social individual experience: the actions and reactions of men and women, largely in the private sphere (Bauman 1982: 2, 27).

Face to face localities and communities, complement home in providing the locus of actions that constitute everyday life. Each locality has its own distinctive sense of place, collective memory, discursive and practice-based knowledge, common-sense understandings and behavioural dispositions. Like the home, localities generate a sense of belonging and being, but the importance of this is not so much identification with a collectivity but the modification of behaviour and action which this entails (Calhoun 1980). Such groupings do not leave their members free to go their own way and explore every possible avenue of action. They operate with a set of implicit rules or standards that define appropriate behaviour in an array of circumstances. The rules operate to reduce conflict by defining what it is that people can expect from certain of their fellows (Calhoun 1980: 20). Shared understandings and a common value system define and sanction acceptable and unacceptable forms of behaviour. Such understandings and values reduce chaos and uncertainty and provide the trust and security within which economic choices can be made and everyday material life can carry on and reproduce itself.

> Community is a matter of long term co-operation and many of the results of this co-operation are assimilated as common sense and are not conscious goals in the minds of participants.
>
> (Calhoun 1980:126)

According to Heller, the four most important and binding norms without which everyday life would be impossible are: keeping a promise, telling the truth, gratitude and loyalty. She emphasises the role of often localised and particularistic customs in strengthening such norms (Heller 1984: 8–27, 152–57). It is worth noting here that it would be difficult to incorporate gratitude and loyalty into the assumptions of a neo-classical economic model of any kind. And recent game theoretic developments in economics accept no such restrictions on the range of human responses as keeping a promise or telling the truth. In fact one could say that accepting the force of gender-inclusive everyday norms and habits flies in the face of both rational choice and game theory in economics.

Everyday common sense and economic analysis

What does this discussion of everyday life imply for the study of economic history? Micro-economic analysis, whether contemporary or historical, is dominated by 'constrained maximisation models peopled by rational, calculating, self interested individuals' (Humphries 1995: xiv). Despite the rise of new neo-classical and institutionalist approaches that pay more attention than previously to interest groups and social norms, constraints upon knowledge and bounded rationality, the foundation of the subject remains the privileging of the individual over the social in explanations of economic behaviour.

Formal modelling is not good for helping to understand the social realm which is governed by social rules – rights, obligations prerogatives, possibilities and limits. Yet the everyday experience of subsistence and relationships within home, neighbourhood and workplace create 'natural attitudes' and common sense understandings which are likely to govern patterns of consumption and production, savings and investment, pricing, work practices, expectations, time preferences and a host of other important economic phenomena which are rarely analysed in other than neoclassical individualist terms.

Study of the economics of everyday life involves a broader conceptualisation of the economic than is conventional and a hermeneutic rather than an exclusively formal or mechanical approach to the subject. It also involves a more thoughtful approach to gender. Feminist economists have advocated a methodological shift that emphasises a broader and more inclusive definition of 'the economic' for some time now. This can open up to careful scrutiny of those gender-specific habits, routines, behaviours and understandings to which economics has largely been blind and to which economic history is only partly open.

In my research on industrialising townships in West Yorkshire such insights have helped to explain many phenomena. For example, when, as happens frequently, an apparently profitable opportunity is not exploited an economist would normally avoid explanations that involve non-maximising behaviour, content with wealth already acquired, the force of routines and traditions or shifts in preferences. Rather he would postulate the existence of costs (monetary or psychic) of taking advantage of these opportunities and thus eliminating their profitability. But if research fails to find these costs empirically, some of the much avoided possibilities must be faced such as entrenched altruism, goals of sufficiency or stability, a weight of habit and gender specific norms routed in vernacular cultures. Such arguments might be brought to bear to explain the preference of weavers, especially male weavers for harvest labour even in years where it must have resulted in a marked loss of income; the greater localised geographical mobility of young women than young men despite similar or less advantageous push and pull factors; persistence with the production of certain sorts of cloth long after other patterns and types had proved more profitable. But what we might term force of habit was not always conservative. It might involve resistance to externally imposed values and culture, but it can also provide networks and institutions that support economic and social change, often moulding that change to suit the environment. In the textile producing regions of the north of England in the eighteenth century, for example, the social networks and interdependence involved in belonging to village and parish social life were probably the most important conduits through which new designs and technologies were conveyed and improved. The tacit knowledge involved in collective innovation and invention, rooted in localities and families, in vernacular speech and in day-to-day socialising, underpinned economic transformation (Hudson 2004).

Geographers and economic sociologists have been more ready than historians or economists to stress the importance of local cultures and institutions, involving the everyday, home and locality (hence women as well as men), in the successful development of dynamic specialised regions serving global markets. They have stressed the relationship between firms and their environments, the embeddedness of the economic within social and cultural interaction: the importance of social and economic networks, the processes of institution building amongst employers, workers and families; the existence of common forms of understanding, routines and myths (Polanyi 1944; Grabher 1993; Todtling 1994; Amin and Thrift 1994; Amin and Cohendet 2004). In all of these areas gender perspectives have opened up new lines of enquiry and understanding: the importance of women in skills transmission and budgeting in domestic manufacturing before the factory, the role of wives and daughters in entrepreneurship, in credit networks and in the spread of information about markets and fashions; the material importance of female gossip in creating and sustaining the unwritten rules and regulations of locale. These aspects of cultural interaction are seen to lie behind the dynamism of industrial regions. The current literature on industrial agglomerations has thus turned from emphasis upon economic reasons for their existence and persistence such as product specialisation, vertical or horizontal integration, to social and cultural reasons such as extensive institutional support and structures encouraging innovation, social consensus, common purpose, high levels of inter-family and inter-firm collaboration, local skill traditions, the circulation of ideas, the advantages of local trust and reciprocities and the presence of a common discourse (Storper 1993; Scott 1996; Hirst and Zeitlin 1989; Hudson 2004). This also neatly describes the foundation of success for many industrialising localities in the past. By adopting a gender-aware approach the economic sphere is enlarged and the boundaries between the economic, the social and the cultural rightly become blurred.

Conclusion

I have chosen to consider a limited number of areas of recent research and writing in economic history where gender is having an impact and in doing so I have also tried to flag topics where a gender perspective is likely to bear further fruit in the near future. In concluding it is a good idea to refer to the opening discussion about the very different ways in which recognising the importance of gender might have an impact upon research in economic history. In some areas of research the most important influence has been in identifying the shortcomings of the sources and the neglect of women's motivations, behaviours and roles. It is clear that these were often very different to those of men and need different tools of analysis. Of more weight in transforming broader approaches to history, however, is the role of gender in identifying how conventional chronologies, disciplinary boundaries, research agendas and methodologies arose and have been perpetuated. In this respect the gender critique of language and of research methodologies, particularly of formal (supposedly gender neutral) rational choice theory in material decision making, would seem to be a vital areas for debate and discussion.

References

Agren, M. and Erickson, A. L. (eds) (2005) *The marital economy in Scandinavia and Britain, 1400–1900*. Aldershot: Ashgate.

Amin, A. and Cohendet, P. (2004) *Architectures of Knowledge: firms, capabilities and communities*. Oxford: Oxford University Press.

Amin, A. and Thrift, N. (eds) (1994) *Globalisation, institutions and regional development in Europe*. Oxford: Oxford University Press.

Barker, H. (2006) *The business of women: female experience and urban development in northern England, 1760–1830*. Oxford: Oxford University Press.

Bauman, Z. (1982) *Memories of class: the pre-history and afterlife of class*. London: Routledge and Kegan Paul.

Berg, M. (1993) 'Women's property and the industrial revolution', *Journal of Inter-disciplinary History*, 24 (2): 233–50.

Berg, M. (2005) *Luxury and pleasure in eighteenth century Britain*. Oxford: Oxford University Press.

Bourdeiu, P. (1980) *Le Sens Practique*. Paris: Les Editions Minuit.

Brewer, J. and Porter, R. (eds) (1993) *Consumption and the world of goods*. London: Routledge.

Breward, C. (1999) *The hidden consumer: masculinities, fashion and city life, 1860–1914*. Manchester: Manchester University Press.

Bynum, C. W. (1982) *Jesus as mother: Studies in the spirituality of the high middle ages*. Berkeley: University of California Press.

Bynum, C. W. (1987) *Gender and Religion: on the complexity of symbols*. Boston: Beacon Press.

Calhoun, C. (1980) 'Community: toward a variable conceptualization for comparative research', *Social History*, 5 (1): 105–109.

Cerman, M. and Ogilvie S. (eds) (1996) *European protoindustrialisation*. Cambridge: Cambridge University Press.

Chaytor, M. (1980) 'Household and kinship: Ryton in the late sixteenth and early seventeenth centuries', *History Workshop Journal*, 10 (Autumn): 25–60.

Creighton, C. (1996) 'The rise of the male breadwinner family: a reappraisal', *Sociological Review*, 44 (1): 204–224.

Davidoff, L. and Hall, C. (1987) *Family fortunes: men and women of the English Middle class, 1780–1850*. London: Routledge.

Davis, N. Z. (1975a) 'Women's history in transition: the European case', *Feminist Studies*, 6 (3): 90.

Davis, N. Z. (1975b) 'Women on top', in N.Z. Davis, *Society and culture in early modern France*. Stanford: Polity Press. pp. 124–151.

De Certeau, M. (1984) *The practice of everyday life*. Berkeley: University of California Press.

De Grazia, V. and Furlong E. (eds) (1996) *The sex of things: understanding consumption in historical perspective*. Berkeley: University of California Press.

De Vries, J. (1993) 'Between purchasing power and the world of goods: Understanding the household economy in early modern Europe', in J. Brewer and R. Porter (eds), *Consumption and the world of goods*. London: Routledge. pp. 85–132.

De Vries, J. (1994) 'The industrial revolution and the industrious revolution', *Journal of Economic History*, 54 (1): 249–270.

Downs, L. L. (2003) 'From women's history to feminist history', in S. Berger, H. Feldner and K. Passmore (eds) *Writing History: theory and practice*. London: Arnold. pp. 261–281.

Duhamelle, C. and Schlumbohm, J. (eds) (2003) *Ehesschliessungen im Europa des 18 und 19 Jahrhunderts: Muster und Strategien*. Göttingen: Vandenhoek & Ruprecht.

Eagleton, T. (1996) *Literary theory: an introduction*. Oxford: Oxford University Press.

Ferber, M. A. and Nelson J. A. (1993) *Beyond Economic Man: feminist theory and economics*. Chicago: University of Chicago Press.

Friedland, R. and Robertson, A. F. (eds) (1990) *Beyond the marketplace: rethinking economy and society*. New York: De Gruyter.

Floud, R. and Johnson, P. (eds) (2004) *The Cambridge Economic History of Modern Britain*, vol. 1. Cambridge: Cambridge University Press.

Folbre, N. (1983) 'Of patriarchy born: the political economy of fertility decisions', *Feminist Studies*, 9 (2): 261–284.

Frederici, N., Oppenheim, M. K. and Sogner, S. (eds) (1993) *Women's position and demographic change*. Oxford: Clarendon Press.

Garrett, E., Reid, A., Schurer, K. and Szreter, S. (2001) *Changing family size in England and Wales, Place, class and demography, 1891–1911*. Cambridge: Cambridge University Press.

Gittins, D. (1982) *Fair Sex: family size and structure, 1900–1930.* London: Hutchinson.

Grabher, G. (ed.) (1993) *The embedded firm: On the socio-economics of industrial networks.* London: Routledge.

Green, D. R. and Owens, A. (2003) 'Gentlewomanly capitalism? Spinsters, widows and wealth holding in England and Wales, c.1800–1860', *Economic History Review,* 56 (3): 510–536.

Heller, A. (1984) *Everyday Life.* London: Routledge and Kegan Paul.

Heller, A. (1979) *A Theory of feelings.* Assen: Van Gorcum.

Highmore, B. (2002) *Everyday Life and cultural theory.* London: Routledge.

Hill, B. (1989) 'The marriage age of women and the demographers', *History Workshop Journal,* 28: 129–147.

Hirst, P. and Zeitlin, J. (1989) *Reversing industrial decline? Industrial structure and policies in Britain and her competitors.* Oxford: Oxford University Press.

Hudson, P. (1995) 'Women and industrialization', in J. Purvis (ed.) *Women's History: Britain, 1850–1945.* London: University College, London Press. pp. 23–49.

Hudson, P. (2004) 'Industrial organization and structure', in R. Floud and P. Johnson (eds) *The Cambridge Economic History of Modern Britain,* vol. 1 Industrialisation, 1700–1860. Cambridge: Cambridge University Press. pp. 28–56.

Hudson P. and King S. (2000) 'Two textile townships c.1680–1820: a comparative demographic analysis', *Economic History Review,* 53 (4): 706–741.

Humphries, J. (2004) 'Household economy', in R. Floud and P. Johnson (eds), *The Cambridge Economic History of Modern Britain, vol. 1, Industrialisation, 1700–1860.* Cambridge: Cambridge University Press. pp. 238–267.

Humphries, J. (ed.) (1995) *Gender and Economics* Introduction. Aldershot: Elgar.

Janssens, A. (1993) *Family and social change. The household as a process in an industrializing community.* Cambridge: Cambridge University Press.

Kahneman, D. and Tversky, A. (1979) 'Prospect theory: an analysis of decision under risk', *Econometrica,* 47 (2): 263–292.

Kay, A. (2004) 'Small business, self employment and women's work-life choices in nineteenth century London', in D. Mitch, J. Brown and M.H.D. van Leeuwen (eds), *Origins of the modern career.* Aldershot: Ashgate.

King, S. A. (1999) 'Chance encounters? Paths to household formation in early modern England', *International Review of Social History,* 44 (1): 23–46.

Lash, S. and Urry, J. (1992) *Economies of signs and space: after organised capitalism.* London: Sage.

Laslett, P. (1965) *The World we have lost.* New York: Methuen.

Laslett, P. (1969) 'Size and structure of the household in England over three centuries', *Population Studies,* 23 (1): 199–223.

MacKinnon, A. (1995) 'Were women present at the demographic transition? Questions from a feminist historian to historical demographers', *Gender and History,* 7 (2): 222–240.

Mitch, D., Brown, J. and van Leeuwen, M.H.D. (eds) (2004) *Origins of the modern career.* Aldershot: Ashgate.

Morris, R. J. (2005) *Men, women and property in England, 1780–1870: a social and economic history of family strategies amongst the Leeds middle classes.* Cambridge: Cambridge University Press.

Nelson, J. A. (1993) 'The study of choice or the study of provisioning? Gender and the definition of economics', in M. Ferber and J.A. Nelson *Beyond economic man.* Chicago: University of Chicago Press. pp. 23–36.

O'Hara, D. (2000) *Courtship and constraint: rethinking the making of marriage in Tudor England.* Manchester: Manchester University Press.

Ohmae, K. (1990) *The borderless world.* New York: Collins.

Owens, A. (2002) 'Inheritance and the life cycle of family firms in the early industrial revolution', *Business History*, 44 (1): 21–46.

Polanyi, K. (1944) *The Great Transformation.* Boston: Beacon Press.

Poovey, M. (1988) *The ideological work of gender in mid Victorian England.* Chicago: University of Chicago Press.

Poovey, M. (1998) *A history of the modern fact.* Chicago: University of Chicago Press.

Roche, D. (1994) *The culture of clothing: dress and fashion in the ancien regime.* Cambridge: Cambridge University Press.

Roche, D. (2000) *A history of everyday things; the birth of consumption in France.* Cambridge: Cambridge University Press.

Rose, M. (2000) *Firms, networks and business values: the British and American cotton industries since 1750.* Cambridge: Cambridge University Press.

Sabean, D. W. (1990) *Property, production and family in Neckarhausen, 1700–1870.* Cambridge: Cambridge University Press.

Sabean, D. W. (1998) *Kinship in Neckarhousen, 1700–1870.* Cambridge: Cambridge University Press.

Scott, A. (1996) 'Regional motors of the global economy', *Futures*, 28 (5): 391–411.

Scott, J. W. (1986) 'Gender: a useful category of historical analysis', *American Historical Review*, 91 (5), reprinted in J.W. Scott, *Gender and the politics of history*: 28–50.

Scott, J. W. (1988) *Gender and the politics of history.* New York: Columbia University Press.

Scott, J. W. (ed.) (1996) *Feminism and History.* Oxford: Oxford University Press.

Seccombe, W. (1992a) *A millenium of family change: Feudalism to capitalism in north west Europe.* London: Verso.

Seccombe, W. (1992b) 'Men's "marital rights" and women's "wifely duties": Changing conjugal relations in the fertility decline', in J. R. Gillis, L. A. Tilly and D. Levine (eds), *The European experience of declining fertility, 1850–1970: the quiet revolution.* Oxford: Oxford University Press.

Seccombe, W. (1993) *Weathering the Storm: working class families from the industrial revolution to the fertility decline.* London: Verso.

Sharpe, P. (2002) *Population and society in an East Devon parish: reproducing Colyton, 1540–1840.* Exeter: Exeter University Press.

Storper, M. (1993) 'Regional worlds of production: learning and innovation in the technology districts of France, Italy and the United States', *Regional Studies*, 27 (5): 433–455.

Stoler, A. L. (1996) 'Carnal Knowledge and imperial power: gender, race and morality in colonial Asia', in J. W. Scott (ed.), *Feminism and History.* Oxford: Oxford University Press. pp. 209–266.

Szreter, S. (1996) *Fertility, class and gender in Britain, 1860–1940.* New York: Cambridge University Press.

Todtling, F. (1994) 'The uneven landscape of innovation poles: local embeddedness and global networks', in A. Amin and N. Thrift (eds) *Globalisation, institutions and regional development in Europe.* Oxford: Oxford University Press. pp. 68–90.

Valverde, M. (1988) '"Giving the female a domestic turn": the social, legal and moral regulation of womens' work in British cotton mills, 1820–1850', *Journal of Social History*, 21 (4): 619–634.

Vickery, A. (1998) *The Gentleman's Daughter: Women's lives in Georgian England.* New Haven: Yale.

Weatherill, L. (1988) *Consumer behaviour and material culture.* London: Routledge.

Wall, R. (1978) 'The age of leaving home', *Journal of Family History*, 3 (2): 181–202.

Wright P. (1985) *On living in an old country. The national past in contemporary Britain.* London: Verso.

Wrigley, E. A. (2004) 'British population during the 'long' eighteenth century, 1680–1840', in R. Floud and P. Johnson (eds) *The Cambridge Economic History of Modern Britain, vol. 1 Industrialisation, 1700–1860.* Cambridge: Cambridge University Press. pp. 57–95.

Wrigley, E. A. and Schofield, R. S. (1989) [1981] *The population history of England, 1541–1871: a reconstruction.* Cambridge: Cambridge University Press.

Part 2
Theoretical developments

3   A gender-neutral approach to gender issues

Alessandro Cigno

Introduction

In this chapter, I attempt to explain a number of facts, adverse to women, without assuming that the latter are discriminated against in the labour market, that mothers love children more than fathers do, or that parents treat sons better than daughters. Nor do I assume that individual behaviour is subject to any sort of social conditioning – in particular, that women feel compelled to stay at home and look after their children just because they are women. I do this not because I believe it to be necessarily true in all circumstances, but in order to show that none of those assumptions is necessary to explain why, for example, girls might receive less education than boys, and women might participate in the labour market less than men or get less than their fair share of household consumption. I also provide a rationale for the institution of the dowry, and point out a possible link between compulsory education and equal-sharing arrangements.

For analytical convenience, as well as because of its intuitive appeal, I shall assume that parents are altruistic towards their children in the sense that they derive direct utility from the latter's well-being. But similar results can be achieved if we assume that parents are ultimately self-interested, and that any apparent generosity is actually a rational response to the existence of a self-enforcing family constitution (Cigno, 2006). By contrast, I do not assume that spouses are altruistic to each other. That, too, is only an analytically convenient simplification, but much the same results are obtained if we allow for mutual altruism so long as people care for their own consumption at least a little more than they do for their partner's.

The approach I follow is in the tradition of Manser and Brown (1980), McElroy and Horney (1981) and Lundberg and Pollak (1996). In those seminal contributions, the allocation of family resources, and the distribution of consumption between husband and wife, are modelled as a Nash-bargaining game with exogenous threat point. Two more recent contributions, Lundberg and Pollak (2003), and Basu (2006), endogenize the threat point by making the reserve utility of the spouses depend on their actions. The actions modelled in these two papers have (or, rather, are modelled as if they had) no lasting consequences. If the action in question stopped, the game could be played all over again with the same initial conditions.

In what follows, I model family interactions as a game (not necessarily co-operative) with endogenous reserve utilities as in the last two papers, but take the consequences of certain individual actions to be *irreversible*. The actions in point are the birth of a child (which I assume to be an inevitable consequence of marriage, but in a more general formulation would be the outcome of a further decision), and the allocation of the couple's time between labour and child care. Assuming that human capital accumulates not only with formal education, but also with work experience, the consequences of withdrawing from the labour market to look after a child include not only an immediate loss of earnings, but also a permanent loss of earning potential.

In order to explain why women might supply less labour and get less consumption than their husbands without assuming either sex discrimination, or different preferences and endowments, I focus on the case where the only ex-ante difference between husband and wife is of sex. Sex differentiation is modelled by stipulating that a child requires at least a certain amount of specifically maternal time. Above that minimum, the father and mother's time are perfect substitutes in the production of child care. That is sufficient to explain also why parents might give a daughter less education than a son, without assuming that they like boys better than girls. Children are modelled as a local public good. The analysis builds on Cigno (1991), and Cigno and Rosati (2005).

The basic model

Take a woman, f, and a man, m. If they marry, they have one child. I assume that f and m have exactly the same preferences and endowments. I further assume that a child needs t_0 units of maternal time. That is the only asymmetry between the sexes I shall allow. Above t_0, the father's time is perfectly substitutable for the mother's in caring for the child.

Suppose that f and m get married. Let a_i denote i's consumption ($i = f, m$). Let c be the amount of money, and t the total amount of time over and above t_0, that the couple spends on the child. The utility of partner i over what is left of his or her life is given by

$$U_i(a_i, c, t) = u(a_i) + \beta U^*(c, t), 0 < \beta \leq 1. \tag{3.1}$$

The term $U^*(c, t)$ may be interpreted as the maximum lifetime utility that the child can achieve given c and t. The constant β is a measure of parental altruism. The functions $u(.)$ and $U^*(.)$ are increasing and concave. Since $\beta U^*(c, t)$ is the same for both partners, the child's well-being has the nature of a local public good.

At marriage, i is endowed with a stock of human capital, h_i. After marriage, the stock accumulates at the rate αh_i (where α is a positive constant, the same for f and m) per unit of work experience. If h_i is produced entirely by education, this formulation of the on-the-job learning technology implies that well educated workers learn from experience more quickly than less well educated ones. After marriage, i's wage rate is given by

$$w_i = (1 + \alpha L_i) h_i \omega, \tag{3.2}$$

where ω is the market rate of return to human capital, and L_i the amount of time worked by i. By using the same value of ω for both partners, I am effectively saying that there is no sex discrimination in the labour market.

Since neither f nor m derives utility from leisure, the time not spent in the care of the child is inelastically supplied to the labour market. Normalizing the time endowment of each partner to unity, the woman's labour supply is then

$$L_f = 1 - t_0 - t_f, \tag{3.3}$$

where t_f is the amount of time, in addition to t_0, that she spends caring for the child. The man's labour supply is

$$L_m = 1 - t_m, \tag{3.4}$$

where t_m is the amount of time that he spends caring for the child.

For the assumption that t_f and t_m are perfect substitutes,

$$t_f + t_m = t. \tag{3.5}$$

I shall assume that t will never be so large that the woman could not look after her child single-handed,

$$t_0 + t \le 1. \tag{3.6}$$

Efficiency

An efficient allocation of domestic resources maximizes some weighted average of the utilities of the two partners,

$$\Lambda = \lambda U_f + (1 - \lambda) U_m, 0 \le \lambda \le 1, \tag{3.7}$$

subject to (3.5), and to the couple's joint budget constraint. Using (3.2)–(3.4), we can write the latter as

$$a_f + a_m + c = ((1 - t_0 - t_f)[1 + \alpha(1 - t_0 - t_f)]h_f$$
$$+ (1 - t_m)[1 + \alpha(1 - t_m)]h_m)\omega. \tag{3.8}$$

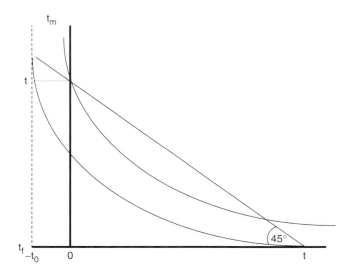

Figure 3.1 Efficient division of labour.

Since U_i is not a function of t_i, we can characterize first the efficient allocation of any given t between f and m by finding the (t_f, t_m) that minimizes the opportunity-cost of caring for the child,

$$p(t_0+t) \equiv \big((t_0+t_f)\big[1+\alpha(1-t_0-t_f)\big]h_f + (1-t_m)[1+\alpha(1-t_m)]h_m\big)\omega,$$
(3.9)

subject to (3.5), and then look for the efficient levels of all the other variables.

The solution to the cost-minimization problem is illustrated in Figure 3.1. The straight line with absolute slope equal to unity is an isoquant, satisfying (3.5). The convex-to-the-origin curves, with absolute slope,

$$-\frac{dt_f}{dt_m} = \frac{1+2\alpha(1-t_0-t_f)}{1+2\alpha(1-t_m)} \frac{h_f}{h_m},$$
(3.10)

diminishing as t_m is substituted for t_f, are isocosts satisfying

$$p(t_0+t) = \text{const.}$$

For any (h_f, h_m) satisfying

$$\frac{h_f}{h_m} \le \frac{1+2\alpha}{1+2\alpha(1-t_0-t)},$$
(3.11)

$p(t_0+t)$ is minimized if the mother looks after the child single-handed $(t_f = t,\ t_m = 0)$. For the opportunity-cost to be minimized at the opposite corner

$(t_f = 0, t_m = t)$, f's human capital endowment would have to be strictly larger than m's. For f and m matched at random, the chances of that are obviously less than 50/50.

The picture in Figure 3.1 is drawn under the assumption that

$$h_f = h_m = h. \tag{3.12}$$

That is the assumption I shall make through the rest of this section. In this case, it is efficient for the mother to take complete responsibility for the care of the child, and for the father to specialize completely in market work. Given this domestic division of labour, the woman will end up with less human capital than her husband despite starting out with the same endowment.

Given (3.12), an efficient (a_f, a_m, c, t) maximizes (3.7) subject to

$$a_f + a_m + c = ((1 - t_0 - t)[1 + \alpha(1 - t_0 - t)] + 1 + \alpha)h\omega. \tag{3.13}$$

It will thus satisfy the first-order conditions

$$\lambda u'(a_f) = \beta U_c^* = (1 - \lambda)u'(a_m) \tag{3.14}$$

and

$$\frac{U_t^*}{U_c^*} = 1 + 2\alpha(1 - t_0 - t)h\omega, \tag{3.15}$$

where U_k^* is the partial derivative of U^* with respect to $k = c, t$.

It is clear from (3.14) that the weight attributed to each spouse affects only the distribution of parental consumption. In view of (3.10), the efficient allocation of time depends only on human capital endowments. In view of (3.15), the efficient allocation of household income between parental consumption and expenditure for the child equates the child's Marginal Rate of Substitution (MRS) of money for child-care time to the marginal opportunity-cost of the latter. In other words, it is efficient to substitute money for parental time in the care of the child only to the point where the child's marginal valuation of parental attention equals the opportunity-cost of the latter, minimized by division of labour.

Bargaining

Suppose that λ, and thus the distribution of the private consumption good between the partners, is the outcome of a Nash-bargaining game. Suppose, also, that this game is played *before* the wedding. This implies that the parties can credibly commit (e.g. by signing a legally binding contract) to a division of the benefits before the marriage takes place. Let R_i denote i's ex-ante reserve utility. Assuming, for simplicity, that the best alternative to the prospective wedding is being single (in which case, i's time would be spent entirely for working in the market), this utility is the same for both partners.

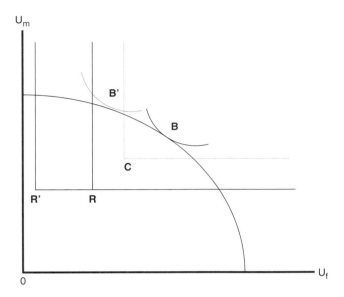

Figure 3.2 Ex-ante bargaining, ex-post bargaining and non-cooperative equilibrium.

Bargaining will maximize

$$\Pi = (U_f - R)(U_m - R),\tag{3.16}$$

subject to (3.1)–(3.8). The solution is illustrated in Figure 3.2.

Let a superscript B identify the value taken by a variable in the solution to this constrained maximization problem. The point **R**, with co-ordinates (R, R), is the threat point of the game. The concave-to-the-origin curve is the utility-possibility frontier implied by (3.1), (3.5) and (3.8). Since **R** lies on the 45° line, the continuous, convex-to-the-origin curve is a contour of (3.17). Π is maximized at the point **B**, with co-ordinates (U^B, U^B). Since **B** lies on the utility-possibility frontier, the equilibrium is efficient. In this bargaining equilibrium, the spouses have the same utility level. Since the public good is valued equally by both partners, their consumption of the private good must be the same too.

What if a binding pre-marital commitment to $\left(a_f^B, a_m^B, c^B, t^B, t_m^B\right)$ is either impossible, or too costly? If the woman accepts to take complete responsibility for the care of the child, she will then expose herself to the risk of opportunistic bargaining on her husband's part. Once the child-care season is over, and the woman's human capital potential irretrievably curtailed, f's reserve utility will in fact fall to

$$R_f' = u((1 - t_0 - t)[1 + \alpha(1 - t_0 - t)]h\omega) < R,$$

while m's will remain the same,

$$R'_m = u((1+\alpha)h\omega) = R.$$

Her bargaining power will consequently fall.

In Figure 3.2, the ex-post threat point is **R'**, with co-ordinates $\left(R'_f, R'_m\right)$. Given this new threat point, the contours of Π will now look like the dotted, convex-to-the-origin curve shown. As **R'** lies to the left of **R**, the ex-post bargaining equilibrium is at point **B'**, with co-ordinates $\left(U_f^{B'}, U_m^{B'}\right)$. As **B'** lies on the utility-possibilities frontier, North-West of **B**, it is clear that the allocation is still efficient, but less favourable to the woman than the ex-ante bargaining equilibrium.

Non-cooperation

As an alternative to engaging in ex-post bargaining, f might prefer to retain control over her own earnings (e.g. by having a separate bank account), and contribute money and time to the care of the child in a non-cooperative fashion. As m would then do the same, the outcome would be a Cournot-Nash equilibrium. Bergstrom (1996) describes a non-cooperative marriage as a kind of war of attrition ('harsh words and burnt toast'). But the hallmark of a Cournot-Nash equilibrium is lack of communication, not attrition. It thus seems more appropriate to characterize a non-cooperative marriage as one where the spouses lead effectively separate lives, foregoing the efficiency gain that would come from division of labour just to prevent conflict. A third possibility is that f and m decide to stay single. Since this case is not very interesting,[1] however, I shall assume that marriage is always better than no marriage for both parties.

In a non-cooperative marriage, the joint budget constraint (3.8) is replaced by two individual budget constraints – one for each partner. Using (3.5), and denoting i's contribution to c by c_i, we can write f's budget constraint as

$$a_f + c - c_m = (1 - t_0 - t + t_m)[1 + \alpha(1 - t_0 - t + t_m)]h\omega, \tag{3.17}$$

and m's as

$$a_m + c_m = (1 - t_m)[1 + \alpha(1 - t_m)]h\omega. \tag{3.18}$$

The woman now chooses (c, t) to maximize her own utility, subject to (3.18), taking (c_m, t_m) as parameters. Her choice will satisfy the first-order conditions

$$u'(a_f) = \beta U_c^*(c, t) \tag{3.19}$$

and

$$\frac{U_t^*(c, t)}{U_c^*(c, t)} = [1 + 2\alpha(1 - t_0 - t + t_m)]h\omega. \tag{3.20}$$

The man chooses (c_m, t_m) to maximize his own utility, subject to (3.19), taking (c, t) as parameters. His choice will satisfy

$$u'(a_m) = \beta U_c^*(c, t) \tag{3.21}$$

and

$$\frac{U_t^*(c, t)}{U_c^*(c, t)} = [1 + 2\alpha(1 - t_m)]h\omega. \tag{3.22}$$

Equations (3.20)–(3.23) imply that, in equilibrium, f and m consume the same amount of the private good,

$$a_f = a_m, \tag{3.23}$$

and thus enjoy the same utility level,

$$U_f = U_m. \tag{3.24}$$

They also supply the same amount of care time,

$$t_0 + t_f = t_m. \tag{3.25}$$

and thus of labour. It is thus clear that the domestic allocation of time is inefficient, and that the opportunity-cost of parental care time is too high. Since, in view of (3.21) and (3.23), each parent's opportunity-cost of child-care time is equated to the child's MRS of c for t, and given that this MRS is decreasing in t, it then follows that non-cooperative parents spend relatively too little time with (and too much money for) their child. There are thus two reasons why a non-cooperative marriage is inefficient. One is that the spouses do not exploit their comparative advantages in the allocation of time. The other is that they give their children the wrong mix of money and personal attention.

Let a superscript C identify the value of a variable in the Cournot-Nash equilibrium, and a superscript B' that of a variable in the ex-post bargaining equilibrium. The marriage will be cooperative if and only if

$$U_i^{B'} \geq U_i^C, i = f, m. \tag{3.26}$$

In both Figure 3.2 and Figure 3.3, the non-cooperative equilibrium is represented by point **C**, with coordinates (U^C, U^C). As the equilibrium is inefficient, **C** lies inside the utility-possibility frontier. The difference between the two figures lies in the position of **B'** relative to **C**. In Figure 3.2, **B'** lies outside the segment of the utility-possibility frontier that satisfies (3.27). The couple will then play the Cournot-Nash game, and end up at **C**. In Figure 3.3, by contrast, **R'** lies close enough to **R** for **B'** to fall inside the segment that satisfies (3.27). The couple will

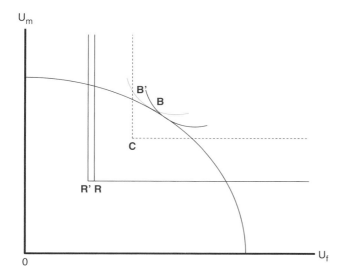

Figure 3.3 Ex-ante bargaining, ex-post bargaining and non-cooperative equilibrium with money and human capital endowments.

then play the Nash-bargaining game, and the equilibrium will be at **B'**. In general, therefore, a woman *may* be better-off submitting to her husband's opportunistic bargaining, than refusing to cooperate.

Lundberg and Pollak (1996) assume post-marital bargaining, and take the non-cooperative equilibrium to be the threat point. In the present context, however, the non-cooperative equilibrium ceases to be available the moment *f* and *m* marry, because her human capital potential is then irreversibly curtailed. The comparison between **B'** and **C** serves only to determine which kind of game will be played after the marriage.

The model with money endowments

Does it make any difference if individual endowments include money or other conventional assets instead of, or as well as, human capital? In many legal systems, spouses can opt for either a joint or a separate property regime, but this applies only to assets acquired after marriage. Assets acquired before marriage are individually owned anyway. Additionally, the disposal of any assets that the woman might have received from her own parents at the time of marriage ('dowry') are typically subject to legal restrictions that put them beyond the reach of rapacious (or imprudent) husbands. I shall thus assume that property rights are vested in the individual, rather than in the couple. To maintain symmetry, I shall also assume that the spouses start out with the same endowment of money, as well as of human capital.

Let b denote the common value of f's and m's initial money endowment. Ex-ante, f and m have again the same reserve utility,

$$R_i = u(b + (1+\alpha)h\omega) \equiv R.$$

Their pre-marital bargaining power is thus unaffected by the presence of money endowments.

Ex-post, however, f's reserve utility is now given by

$$R'_f = u(b + (1 - t_0 - t)[1 + \alpha(1 - t_0 - t)]h\omega),$$

and m's by

$$R'_m = u(b + (1+\alpha)h\omega).$$

For any positive h, it thus remains true that R'_f is smaller than R'_m, and that the cooperative equilibrium with post-marital bargaining is more favourable to m than to f. But it is clear that, the larger is b relative to h, the smaller will be the difference between R'_f and R, and thus between R'_f and R'_m. If h were equal to zero, R'_f would be actually equal to R'_m.[2] If human capital at marriage were entirely the result of education, and f and m were totally uneducated ($h=0$), point **B'** would coincide with point **B**, and the woman would then have nothing to fear from ex-post bargaining.

Let us now look at non-cooperative marriages. With money and human capital endowments, the woman's budget constraint is

$$a_f + c - c_m = b + (1 - t_0 - t + t_m)[1 + \alpha(1 - t_0 - t + t_m)]h\omega, \qquad (3.27)$$

but the first-order conditions on her choice of (c, t) are still (3.20)–(3.21). The man's budget constraint is

$$a_m + c_m = b + (1 - t_m)[1 + \alpha(1 - t_m)]h\omega, \qquad (3.28)$$

and the first-order conditions on his choice of (c_m, t_m) are again (3.22)–(3.23).

In the non-cooperative equilibrium, it is then again true that the spouses consume the same amount of the private consumption good, supply the same amount of child care time, and give their child the wrong mix of money and care time. As in the basic model, the equilibrium is thus inefficient.

Continuing to assume that pre-marital contracts are unenforceable, which of the two available alternatives will prevail? Once again, it all depends on the position of the post-marital bargaining equilibrium – **B'** – relative to the non-cooperative one – **C**. Now, however, the probability of a post-marital bargaining equilibrium is an increasing function of the relative weight of conventional assets. This provides a rationale for the institution of the dowry and for the special protection that legislations afford to dotal goods.

Discussion

We have seen that the traditional domestic division of labour, where men go out to work, and women stay at home to look after children, can emerge even if husband and wife have exactly the same preferences and endowments. That is sufficient to explain a bias against women in the division of the benefits of marriage, and in the amount of education that they receive from their family of origin. It also provides a rationale for giving a daughter more money and less education than a son.

All that is needed to produce these results is some recognition that

(i) the mother cannot be entirely replaced by the father in the care of a child;
(ii) work experience has a permanent effect on earning ability; and
(iii) a man and a woman cannot credibly commit to any particular division of consumption after marriage.

In relation to (i), I postulate that a child requires at least a certain amount of specifically maternal time. Beyond that, the father and mother's time are perfectly substitutable for each other in the care of the child. In relation to (ii), I postulate that human capital accumulates with work experience, and that the accumulation rate increases with education. Taken together with (i), this implies that it is efficient for the father to specialize completely in market work, and for the mother to take complete responsibility for the care of the child. In view of (iii), if the woman accepts to withdraw from the labour market to look after a child single-handed, she exposes herself to the risk of opportunistic bargaining on her husband's part once the child care season is over, and her human capital potential compromised.

A woman can avoid being exploited by her husband by refusing to specialize in child care, and retaining control over her own earnings (e.g. by keeping a separate bank account). This may not be socially acceptable in certain contexts. If it is, however, it will have efficiency costs. One arises from the fact that the domestic division of labour will not exploit comparative advantages. The other arises from the local public good nature of the child's well-being. Non-cooperative parents spend too little time with their children. The analysis assumes that spouses, while altruistic towards their children, are not altruistic to each other. Allowing for reciprocal altruism would moderate the extent to which a spouse will exploit a domestic bargaining advantage. So long as each spouse cares a little more about his or her own consumption than about the spouse's, however, the results will remain qualitatively the same.

The rationale for giving a daughter less education than a son comes from the fact that, while the marginal benefit of education depends on how much the educated person will work in subsequent life, and thus on the domestic division of labour, the marginal benefit of money and other conventional assets is independent of it. This explains why girls traditionally got less education than equally gifted boys. The reason was not necessarily that parents liked sons better than daughters. It may have been that a girl's interest was better served by giving her money, rather than an education she would not be able to use to the full. By limiting parental freedom to choose the mix of money and education to give a child, compulsory education makes it less likely that a girl will have a cooperative marriage, and more likely that it will be characterized by equal sharing of child care and market work. All of this assumes that education gives utility only indirectly, by raising the recipient's earning capacity. If education gives also direct utility, or has a direct effect on a person's domestic bargaining power, the argument for giving a daughter money rather than education becomes weaker.

Notes

1 Each of them would then consume $(1+\alpha)$ $h\omega$ of the private good, and zero of the public one. Utility would be $u((1+\alpha)$ $h\omega)$ for both of them.
2 In that limiting case, however, there would be nothing to gain from domestic division of labour.

References

Basu, K. (2006) 'Gender and Say: A Model of Household Behaviour with Endogenously Determined Balance of Power', *Economic Journal,* 116: 558–580.

Bergstrom, T. C. (1996) 'Economics in a Family Way', *Journal of Economic Literature,* 24: 1903–1934.

Cigno, A. (1991) *Economics of the Family*, Oxford and New York: Clarendon Press and Oxford University Press.

Cigno, A. (2006) 'A Constitutional Theory of the Family', *Journal of Population Economics,* 19 (Special Issue on Political Economy and Population Economics): 259–283.

Cigno, A. and Rosati, F. C. (2005) *The Economics of Child Labour*, Oxford and New York: Oxford University Press.

Lundberg, S. and Pollak, R. A. (1996) 'Bargaining and Distribution in Marriage', *Journal of Economic Perspectives,* 10: 139–158.

Lundberg, S. and Pollak, R. A. (2003) 'Efficiency in Marriage', *Review of Economics of the Household*, 1: 153–167.

McElroy, M. B. and Horney, M. J. (1981) 'Nash-Bargained Household Decisions', *International Economic Review*, 22: 333–349.

Manser, M. and Brown, M. (1980) 'Marriage and Household Decision Making: a Bargaining Analysis', *International Economic Review*, 21: 31–44.

4   The gender gap

Graciela Chichilnisky[1]

Introduction

The gender gap, like the minority achievement gap, has lately become a hot topic. Women are underpaid, undervalued, and overworked across the board. But in our rational economy, what could explain the persistence of this phenomenon? A preferential demand for lower paid women should drive their salaries up until they reach the level of men's. The logic seems impeccable, but it is not borne out by the facts.[2] This article provides an explanation based on the coupling of two institutions: the family and the market. Families are about sharing and using common property resources. Firms, instead, use private property to produce private goods, and maximize profits. As far as institutions go, the family and the market could not be further apart, yet they are undeniably intertwined. The way that each responds to the other is critical in understanding and resolving the unequal situation of women in our society.

I hope to explain the seemingly illogical actions of the family-market system by introducing a game between the two components. This game helps to explain the gender gap in salaries, and why men and women allocate time differently between work and home. I show that inequality at work leads to inequality at home, and vice versa. This vicious circle creates a persistent gender gap. The government may regulate the workplace, but it cannot regulate the family. Since one inequality cannot be solved without the other, this may explain why the gender gap has been so difficult to overcome.

The current situation has evolved over time. Women had lower salaries historically, and therefore performed most housework because men could make a higher income working in the marketplace. Under the conditions, the traditional division of labour is a rational way to maximize family income. However, the burden of excessive housework decreases the time and the energy that women can bring to the marketplace. Therefore the family produces externalities on the firm.[3] My point is that under these conditions a firm will perceive women as being more risky than men because they are not available in case of emergencies and ill health, since, for example they are the main providers of the medical needs of the family, or are less productive than men, since they have demanding second jobs at home that men do not have.[4] If workers are assets, then women are riskier assets even when they are equally productive. This riskiness is in turn used to justify women's lower wages, closing the vicious circle. From this game between the family and the marketplace, the gender gap emerges as a rational but undesirable situation that is similar to the classical prisoner's dilemma.

The perception that women are more risky workers is felt most acutely in the most demanding and highest paid jobs where constant availability is required. This means that at the highest levels, there should be a larger gap in female participation and salaries. This could be an explanation for the glass ceiling, the somewhat perverse phenomenon that leads the more productive women to face higher differentials between their compensations and men's (Meyersson Milgrom *et al.* 2001; Meyersson Milgrom and Petersen 2003).

The empirical and experimental evidence appears to confirm the above observations. Bonke *et al.* (2005) found that larger differences between men and women's work at home are associated with larger differences in market salaries, and recent experiments by Gneezy *et al.* (2003) show that women perform worse than men in competitive environments. Both make sense. Due to their lower salaries, women spend more time working at home where the most important skills involve sharing and cooperation. One can therefore expect women to adapt to the cooperative family 'mores', while men adapt instead to the competitive 'mores' of the marketplace. After all, success in the marketplace requires competitive skills – while success at home requires instead cooperative skills.[5] Recent work validates the empirical conclusions reached in this chapter (Chichilnisky and Shachmurove 2007).

This article formalizes a toy game where women and men share their time between the family and a Walrasian market economy. They learn by doing, in the sense that the more they work, the more productive they are. This follows Becker's classic article (Becker 1985), which provides the standard argument for specialization of women and men, at home or in the marketplace respectively.[6] In contrast with Becker's assumption, however, I follow Arrow's 1962 seminal article where he introduced learning by doing. In Arrow's formulation there are decreasing returns after a certain number of hours per day (Arrow 1962). I show that Arrow's model reverses Becker's findings in the sense that specialization is no longer necessary for efficiency at higher levels of productivity. There is now another, rational, solution in which women and men are paid the same and share the work equally in both institutions. This fair outcome emerges at higher levels of output, when the economy is richer and more productive. Once production exceeds a minimum level we enter Arrow's regime where the learning curve is concave rather than convex as in Becker's work. I show that a new equilibrium emerges that leads to more welfare at home, more family services, and simultaneously to higher productivity and profits in the marketplace. Inequality is no longer the only solution. Now fairness is Pareto efficient.

If such equitable solutions exist, one may ask, why aren't they observed more often? The answer is that under current economic and social conditions, the equitable solution seems riskier, as is the optimal solution in the prisoner's dilemma. It can be seen that there are missing contracts between the players. Equal treatment in the family depends on equal treatment in the marketplace, and vice versa – but neither institution can safely depend on the other, and they do not have contracts to implement the optimal solution. In the conclusions I suggest how certain incentives or firm informational structures can help overcome the problem, and even the introduction of new contractual arrangements that can help overcome the lack of contracts between the parties and help reach efficient and equitable social solutions.

The firm

The economy has several identical competitive firms producing a good x. A representative firm uses two types of workers, men and women. Their labour is denoted L_1 and L_2 respectively with possibly different wages w_1 and w_2. The firm's production technology is described by a function f

$$x = f(L_1) + f(L_2)$$

The firm's goal is to maximize profits π, namely the difference between the firm's revenues and its costs:

$$Max_{L_1 L_2}(\pi) = Max_{L_1 L_2}\left[p_x(f(L_1) + f(L_2)) - (w_1 L_1 + w_2 L_2)\right] \qquad (4.1)$$

Since firms are competitive they take the price of goods x, p_x and wages w_1 and w_2, as parametrically given. Maximizing profits implies the standard condition that wages must equal the marginal product of labour:

$$w_1 = \frac{\partial f}{\partial L_1} \text{ and } w_2 = \frac{\partial f}{\partial L_2} \qquad (4.2)$$

In the following I assume that there are two parameters γ_1 and γ_2 which vary with the person's work at home and influence their productivity in the marketplace. The firm takes these parameters as given; they represent an externality[7]:

$$x = f(L_1, \gamma_1) + f(L_2, \gamma_2)$$

so for each given γ_1, γ_2 profit maximization implies

$$w_1 = \frac{\partial f}{\partial L_1}(\gamma_1) \text{ and } w_2 = \frac{\partial f}{\partial L_2}(\gamma_2)$$

The family

There are several identical families. Neglecting distributional issues we refer to a 'representative' family whose welfare derives from family services h, and from the consumption of goods x. The family goal is to optimize welfare:

$$Max(U(x, h)) \qquad (4.3)$$

Family services are produced according to a technology g

$$h = g(l_1) + g(l_2) \tag{4.4}$$

where l_1 and l_2 are the two types of labour in the household, men's and women's respectively. Let K be the total amount of hours that a person can feasibly work in a given period of time, at home and in the market. As an example, in a given day, this could be $K = 15$. When all labour is utilized

$$L_1 = K - l_1 \text{ and } L_2 = K - l_2 \tag{4.5}$$

The family's income equals the wages that its members, a man and a woman, earn in the marketplace plus the firms' profits, since families own the firms. The value of what the family buys $p_x x$ must equal its income:

$$p_x x = w_1 L_1 + w_2 L_2 + \pi \tag{4.6}$$

where as before profits π are the firm's revenues minus its costs:

$$\pi = p_x(f(L_1, \gamma) + f(L_2, \gamma)) - (w_1 L_1 + w_2 L_2) \tag{4.7}$$

We normalize by assuming that the price of x is one, $p_x = 1$, so that the family's 'budget' equation is

$$x = f(L_1, \gamma) + f(L_2, \gamma) \tag{4.8}$$

The family's trade-off

The family faces a trade-off in deciding whether to use labour at home or in the marketplace. The more labour is used at home, the more family services are produced, but the lower is the family's income and therefore the fewer market goods it consumes. The family has to reach an optimal use of labour at home and in the marketplace to optimize its welfare.

When women and men are paid differently, $w_1 \neq w_2$, the family's decision problem by (4.5), (4.4), and (4.8) is to choose l_1, l_2 to

$$Max_{l_1, l_2} U(f(K - l_1, \gamma) + f(K - l_2, \gamma), g(l_1) + g(l_2)) \tag{4.9}$$

The family considers the productivity parameters γ_1 and γ_2 as given. [8] From (4.2) this implies

$$\frac{\partial U}{\partial x}(-w_1) + \frac{\partial U}{\partial h}\frac{\partial g}{\partial l_1} = 0 \tag{4.10}$$

and

$$\frac{\partial U}{\partial x}(-w_2) + \frac{\partial U}{\partial h}\frac{\partial g}{\partial l_2} = 0$$

Therefore wages determine the productivity of each type of labour at home, and the amount of time each works at home

$$\frac{\partial g}{\partial l_1} = \frac{\frac{\partial U}{\partial x}}{\frac{\partial U}{\partial h}}w_1 \text{ or } w_1 = \frac{\partial g}{\partial l_1}\frac{\frac{\partial U}{\partial h}}{\frac{\partial U}{\partial x}} \tag{4.11}$$

$$\frac{\partial g}{\partial l_2} = \frac{\frac{\partial U}{\partial x}}{\frac{\partial U}{\partial h}}w_2 \text{ or } w_2 = \frac{\partial g}{\partial l_2}\frac{\frac{\partial U}{\partial h}}{\frac{\partial U}{\partial x}} \tag{4.12}$$

Equivalently, we obtain the standard result that the marginal rate of substitution between home services and market goods equals their marginal rates of transformation, which in turn equal the ratio of wages:

$$\frac{\frac{\partial U}{\partial h}}{\frac{\partial U}{\partial x}} = \frac{\frac{\partial g}{\partial l_1}}{\frac{\partial g}{\partial l_2}} = \frac{\frac{\partial f}{\partial L_1}}{\frac{\partial f}{\partial L_2}} = \frac{w_1}{w_2} \tag{4.13}$$

Public goods and common property resources

We may consider a family that acts as a single unit, making choices about how to allocate women and men's labour, namely l_1 and l_2. This means that the family's labour is treated as common property. Furthermore, since there is a single welfare level for the entire family, this means that family services are shared as a 'public good' within the family (see also Apps and Rees 1997; Aronsson *et al.* 2001).

This is summarized by saying that the family produces a public good using common property resources. Family services are better described as a 'local' public good within the family, because they are not shared with other families.

Learning by doing

Becker pointed out that the more time we spend in a given activity the better we become at doing it (Becker 1985). This is called *learning by doing*. It means that marginal productivity $\dot{g}$ increases with time. Under these conditions, each person in the family (man or woman) should specialize – one should specialize in working at home, and the other in the marketplace. Both are more productive, at home and in the marketplace, thus increasing family welfare. As a direct consequence of Becker's assumption, when women's salaries are lower than men, women should do all the housework. Men should only work in the marketplace.

Since in fact women's salaries are lower than men's in most economies, both historically and currently, Becker's assumption leads directly to a division of labour where women stay at home and men work in the marketplace. Under Becker's assumptions the current situation where most household work is done by women seems a rational and efficient solution.

There is indeed learning by doing in our society and therefore Becker's assumption is reasonable, but only up to a point. Human beings need rest after a number of working hours, and this implies a decrease in productivity beyond a certain number of hours of work.

Accordingly, we assume here that the time derivative of the home production function $\dot{g}$ is initially positive, but after a maximum is reached $\dot{g}$ starts to decrease since humans cannot work productively without rest.

If $g(t)$ is the amount of h produced with t hours worked, then we may assume that increases in productivity follow a modified quadratic form, increasing initially and then decreasing as was just postulated,

$$\dot{g}_t = H(g_t) = \beta g - \gamma g^2 \text{ with } \beta, \gamma > 0$$

This equation integrates to yield the classic logistic curve that is used often to describe the evolution of biological populations over time:

$$g(t) = \frac{\beta g_0}{\gamma z_0 + (\beta - \gamma z_0)\exp(-\beta t)}$$

The logistic function $g(t)$ has an inflection point: e.g. when $g_0 = 1$, the inflection point is at $g = \frac{\beta}{\gamma}$. Assuming that $g_0 = 1$, the evolution over time of labour productivity increases with the number of hours worked, until it reaches a maximum increase at $g = \frac{\beta}{\gamma}$ and declines afterwards. The second derivative is positive until the inflection point and negative afterwards. The graph of the function is therefore convex until the value $\frac{\beta}{\gamma}$ and it is concave thereafter.

The convex part is similar to Becker's assumption and yields similar results. On the other hand the concave part, which occurs after the inflection point is reached yields very different results as shown further. The inflection point determines a change from one regime to the other; it appears in the diagram as the maximum of the quadratic curve, which is the derivative of g (Figure 4.1).

Assumption 1.   In the following we assume that production has reached the inflection point at home and at the marketplace, an assumption that seems to make sense in highly productive economies. We describe this as having achieved higher levels of output.

Equity at home improves welfare

Proposition 1.   At higher levels of output, equity benefits the family. In other words, distributing home labour equally between men and women produces more

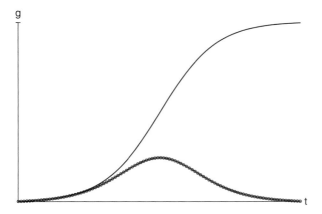

Figure 4.1 Logistic function g(t).

household services for the same total labour. Formally, if

$$\frac{l_1 + l_2}{2} > \frac{\beta}{\gamma}$$

where β/γ is the inflection point of the logistic, then

$$l_1 \neq l_2 \Rightarrow g(l_1) + g(l_2) < 2g\left(\frac{l_1 + l_2}{2}\right)$$

Proof:

$$2g\left(\frac{l_1 + l_2}{2}\right) > g(l_1) + g(l_2) \Leftrightarrow g\left(\frac{l_1 + l_2}{2}\right) > \frac{g(l_1)}{2} + \frac{g(l_2)}{2},$$

which is implied by the definition of concavity. Recall that above its inflection point the logistic curve g is concave, since its second derivative is negative. This proves the inequality. In words: equity is a more efficient use of resources at home whenever

$$\frac{l_1 + l_2}{2} > \frac{\beta}{\gamma},$$

as we wished to prove.

Inequality at work leads to inequality at home

There is historic difference in the average pay of men and women, about 25 or 30 per cent in the US. What is the optimal response by the family to this inequality, in terms of allocating labour at home? The following proposition provides a response:

Proposition 2.   Inequality at work leads to inequality at home when women are paid less than men in the marketplace, $w_1 > w_2$, the family's optimal response is that women should work longer hours at home than men. When the difference in wages is large enough, $\frac{w_1}{w_2} > M = \frac{\sup \frac{\partial g}{\partial l_1}}{\inf \frac{\partial g}{\partial l_2}}$, it is optimal for the family that women should do all the housework, and men should work only in the marketplace.

Proof :   Proof: From (4.3) and (4.9) the family's goal is

$$Max_{l_1, l_2} U(f(K - l_1) + f(K - l_2), g(l_1) + g(l_2))$$

From (4.13)

$$\frac{\frac{\partial g}{\partial l_1}}{\frac{\partial g}{\partial l_2}} = \frac{w_1}{w_2}$$

so that at an optimum

$$w_1 > w_2 \text{ implies } \frac{\partial g}{\partial l_1} > \frac{\partial g}{\partial l_2}.$$

Therefore women (over)work at home, in the sense that they work up to the point where their marginal productivity is lower than men's.[9] As we saw in the section learning by doing, when $g(t) > \frac{\beta}{\gamma}$, the marginal productivity of labour $\frac{\partial g}{\partial l_2}$ is a decreasing function of the time allocated, so that lower productivity means longer hours for women at home.

When the ratio of salaries exceeds M, the ratio of the supremum and the infimum productivity of g, namely when

$$\frac{w_1}{w_2} > M = \frac{\sup \frac{\partial g}{\partial l_1}}{\inf \frac{\partial g}{\partial l_2}} \tag{4.14}$$

it is optimal that women should completely specialize in housework. This completes the proof.

Proposition 2 implies that it is always optimal for the family to use more female labour at home when they have lower salaries than men. If women's housework hours are less than the maximum feasible, K, then it would be rational that women should also work in the marketplace in addition to their work at home – at their reduced salaries. Furthermore, when salary differentials are large enough, it is optimal for the family that women do all the housework and that they work also in the marketplace receiving lower salaries than men, while men, on the other hand, work only in the marketplace and receive higher salaries.

The logic of the situation and (4.13) imply that when $w_1 > w_2$, then women's marginal productivity is lower than men's at home and also in the marketplace. When production functions f and g are concave, this implies in turn that women work more hours than men at home and also in the marketplace, because marginal productivity decreases with the time worked, so that:

$$L_1 > L_2 \text{ and } l_1 > l_2 \tag{4.15}$$

However on the other hand,

$$L_1 = K - l_1 \text{ and } L_2 = K - l_2$$

so that

$$L_1 > L_2 \Rightarrow l_2 > l_1 \tag{4.16}$$

How should we reconcile the apparent contradiction between (4.15) and (4.16)? In the next section we show that the externality that the home produces on the firm, namely the parameter γ, reconcile these two apparently contradictory inequalities.

Externalities: inequality at home reduces women's productivity in the market

As already pointed out, the amount of work that a person performs at home has an impact on their productivity in the marketplace. The first hour that a woman works at the firm may be the sixth hour of work that day, since she may have already worked five hours at home.

Yet in a competitive market, the number of hours that a person works at home before going to work at the firm is private information and not known to the firm, nor can the firm control them. This is an externality that the family causes the firm. Formally, l_1 and l_2 are treated as parameters by the firm even though they have an impact on the firm through worker's productivity. These observations may be formalized as follows:

Assumption 2. There exists a parameter $\gamma > 0$ representing an 'externality' on the firm so that

$$\text{for } i = 1, 2 \qquad \frac{\partial f}{\partial L_i} = \frac{\partial f}{\partial L_i}(\gamma) \text{ where } \frac{\partial^2 f}{\partial \gamma \partial L_i} < 0.$$

A simple example of this phenomenon would be

$$f(L_i) = \gamma(l_i) L_i^{\alpha}$$

where

$$\gamma = \gamma(l_i) \text{ and } \partial\gamma/\partial l_i < 0.$$

Under assumption 2.

Proposition 3.   Inequality at home leads to lower productivity of women at work, and to lower salaries for women. This is an immediate consequence of assumption 2 and (4.13).

The interpretation of the result is simple: as we already discussed, the productivity of women in the marketplace depends on the amount of time they work at home. This breaks the symmetry between productivity at work and hours worked, because even if the production function f is concave, those who spend more time working at home have a lower productivity in the marketplace while working fewer hours than the rest. Recall that the production function f depends not only on L but also on l, and at higher levels of l the graph of $f(L)$ shifts downwards due to the externality, i.e.

$$f(L) = f(L, \gamma) \text{ with } \partial f/\partial\gamma < 0.$$

The externality thus resolves the apparent contradiction between (4.15) and (4.16).

Inequality lowers family welfare

We saw that inequality at work leads to inequality at home and that inequality at home reduce productivity at work for those working longer hours at home. If women are subject to this inequality, then obviously they are worse off under these conditions. Is it possible however that the entire family is better off as a whole? The following proposition provides a response.

Proposition 4.   At higher levels of output, inequality lowers family welfare, decreasing both family services h and the family's consumption of market goods x.

Proof: We have already shown that, under the conditions, the family produces more home services h with the same total amount of labour if the work load is distributed equally between the two genders. Namely when $\frac{l_1+l_2}{2} > \frac{\beta}{\gamma}$

$$l_1 \neq l_2 \Rightarrow 2g\left(\frac{l_1+l_2}{2}\right) > g(l_1) + g(l_2)$$

Therefore inequality leads to less family services h.

Yet it is still possible that inequality at home could increase family income sufficiently to compensate for the loss in family services. We show that this is not possible under the conditions. By definition, inequality at home means $l_1 < l_2$ which implies

$$L_1 = K - l_1 > L_2 = K - l_2$$

This under the conditions implies that women's marginal productivity at work is lower than men's, see (4.13). Since the firm has a logistic production function f then for the same total amount of labour $L_1 + L_2$ an equal workload among women and men increases total output:

$$2f\left(\frac{L_1 + L_2}{2}\right) > f(L_1) + f(L_2) \text{ when } L_1 \neq L_2$$

as shown in proposition 1. Therefore the total production of market goods x is lower than when men and women share work equally. Since all production is consumed by families, the family consumes less market goods x as well as fewer family services. Therefore inequality at home lowers the family's welfare as we wished to prove.

Inequality leads to lower output and lower profit

Proposition 5.   At higher output levels, inequality reduces the firm's output and lowers its profits.

Proof: We saw in proposition 4 that under the conditions, inequities decrease the market's output of x. For the same total amount of work the production of the firms is higher when men and women divide equally the work load:

$$2f\left(\frac{L_1 + L_2}{2}\right) > f(L_1) + f(L_2) \text{ when } L_1 \neq L_2,$$

This proves the first part of the proposition. It remains to consider the impact of inequality on profits, namely on the function

$$\pi(L_1, L_2) = f(L_1) + f(L_2) - w_1 L_1 - w_2 L_2$$

We wish to compare

$$\pi(L_1) + \pi(L_2) \text{ with } 2\pi\left(\frac{L_1 + L_2}{2}\right)$$

By concavity (since we are above the inflection point of f) profits increase with the level of output, namely

$$\frac{\partial \pi}{\partial x} > 0$$

Since equity increases output, and profit is an increasing function of output, it follows that equity increases profits as well. Equivalently, inequality decreases output and profits as we wished to prove.

A mixed economy and a Nash-Walrasian solution

This section describes the functioning of the economy as a whole. The economy consists of a Walrasian market where firms maximize profits, and of families that produce public goods using common property resources, maximizing welfare. There are three traded goods in the economy: the market goods x, women's labour, and men's labour.[10]

This economy is partly Walrasian, and partly based on a common property resource that is used to produce a public good. There are no benchmarks for studying such a mixed economy. Indeed, the family is not Walrasian; its services h are shared among the members, which make them similar to (local) public goods. Furthermore, the resources such as labour l_1 and l_2 that are used to produce h are allocated by common decision within the family so as to maximize the family's welfare. Therefore the family treats resources as common property. Additionally the family produces an externality on the firm γ which depends on the hours that men and women work at home, $\gamma = \gamma(l_i), i = 1, 2$. Since there are no benchmark models to analyze the functioning of such a mixed economy, we will propose a natural solution that is partly a Nash equilibrium and partly a Walrasian equilibrium, interacting with each other. For this we need some definitions.

- If $w_1 \neq w_2$ we say that *the market is unfair*. If $w_1 = w_2$ we say that *the market is fair*.
- If $l_1 \neq l_2$ we say that *the family is unfair* and if $l_1 = l_2$ we say that *the family is fair*.

Proposition 6.   Finding a solution for the mixed economy. Given wages for the two types of labour w_1 and w_2 from the family's welfare optimization behaviour (4.3) it is possible to determine the amount of family services it produces, the employment of men and women's labour at home, l_1 and l_2, the offer of labour of the two types to the marketplace, $K - l_1$ and $K - l_2$, the family's demand for market goods, the family's income, its welfare level, and the value of the externality parameters $\gamma_1(l_1)$ and $\gamma_2(l_2)$ which modify the firm's production function. On the other hand, the firm has expected values for the parameters γ_1^e and γ_2^e and from the firm's profit maximization behaviour (4.1) it is possible to determine the amount of labour the firm wishes to employ (men and women), how much it produces, what are its profits, and the productivity of its labour. The rest is a standard microeconomic exercise.

In proposition 6 the family and the firm may have contradictory goals in terms of the productivity parameters γ_1^e and γ_2^e, the market goods produced and consumed, and people employed. A *solution* for this economy arises when firms and families behave consistently:

Definition. A *solution* for this mixed economy consists of wages for men and for women w_1^*, w_2^* and expected values of the parameters γ_1^e, γ_2^e leading to consistent behaviour by the family and the firm. The levels of employment and consumption that derive from profit optimization by the firm and from welfare optimization by the family clear all three markets. Furthermore, the value of the externality produced by the family on the firm equals the values expected by the firm.

In particular:

(1) Expectations are confirmed;

$$\gamma(l_1) = \gamma_1^e \text{ and } \gamma(l_2) = \gamma_2^e$$

(2) Supply of men's labour equals demand for men's labour by the firm;

$$L_1^D(w_1, w_2) = N.\arg\max \pi(w_1, w_2) = L_1^S(w_1, w_2) = K - l_1(w_1, w_2)$$
$$(4.17)$$

(3) Supply of female labour equals demand of women's labour by the firm;

$$L_2^D(w_1, w_2) = N.\arg\max \pi(w_1, w_2) = L_2^S(w_1, w_2) = K - l_2(w_1, w_2)$$
$$(4.18)$$

and

(4) Supply by the firm of x equals the family's demand for x,

$$x^S(w_1, w_2) = f(L_1^D(w_1, w_2), L_2^D(w_1, w_2)) = x^D(w_1, w_2)$$
$$= w_1 L_1 + w_2 L_2 + \pi \qquad (4.19)$$

The existence of a solution shows that the model as postulated is internally consistent.

Proposition 7. There exists a *solution* for this mixed economy as defined above. See Appendix for the proof.

A particular example: the market – family game

This section illustrates the mixed economy with a game with two players, the market and the family. The *market's objective* is to maximize profits as defined in (4.1). The *family's objective* is to maximize welfare as defined in (4.3). The players choose their strategies to achieve their goals. The *market's strategy* is to set wages for men and for women, w_1 and w_2, and expectations about their productivity γ_1^e and γ_2^e, while the *family's strategy* is to allocate labour at home among men and women, l_1 and l_2.

Definition.   A Nash equilibrium for this game is a set of strategies for the market and for the family $(w_1^*, w_2^*, \gamma_1^e, \gamma_2^e, l_1^*, l_2^*)$ leading to a solution for the economy in which each player reacts optimally to the other's strategy, and so neither has an incentive to deviate.

Proposition 8.   At high levels of output:

1   Nash equilibrium where women have lower salaries. The family reacts by allocating more house work to women. Conversely, at a Nash equilibrium where the family allocates more housework to women, women productivity is lower in the marketplace and they receive lower salaries than men. This Nash equilibrium is called unfair-unfair.
2   Nash equilibrium where women have the same salaries as men. Women have the same productivity. The family reacts by sharing equally housework between men and women. Conversely, at a Nash equilibrium where women and men share housework equally, their wages in the marketplace are the same as men's. This is a fair-fair Nash equilibrium.

Theorem.   The unfair-unfair Nash equilibrium is Pareto inferior. The fair-fair Nash equilibrium is Pareto efficient, but it is perceived as riskier.

Proof :   We use the results proven in the former section. When women have the same salaries as men, both bring to the family the same income for the same hours in the marketplace. By (4.13) their productivity is the same at an optimum, and given the assumptions, it is more productive for both men and women to work the same hours in the marketplace. At the same time, by proposition 1 women work at home the same number of hours as men, since under the conditions, sharing work equally at home provides more family services for the same total amount of labour.

Reciprocally, when women and men share work equally at home, then from (4.13) it is optimal for the firm to pay both equally. The fair-fair pair of strategies just described is a Nash equilibrium of the market-family game because when following such a pair of strategies, each player is responding optimally to the others' move.

At a Nash equilibrium where women's salaries are inferior to men's, it is optimal for the family to choose an unfair distribution of household work by proposition 2. Women work more at home, and their productivity at home is lower as shown in proposition 2 and in the section entitled *Inequality lowers family welfare*, and so is their productivity at work by (4.13). This is an unfair-unfair Nash equilibrium, with both players responding optimally to each other. Nevertheless, it is a Pareto inferior solution.

The first fair-fair equilibrium is Pareto optimal. The following section illustrates why the fair-fair equilibrium is riskier under the conditions.

Illustration: a matrix game

The matrix below illustrates a game where the horizontal strategies represent the market's and the vertical represent the family's. The payoffs for the market are sub-indexed 1 and those for the family are sub-indexed 2.

$$\begin{pmatrix} & w_1 \neq w_2 & w_1 = w_2 \\ l_1 \neq l_2 & (A_1, A_2) & (C_1, D_2) \\ l_1 = l_2 & (D_1, C_2) & (B_1, B_2) \end{pmatrix}$$

In this matrix game, proposition 8 can be summarized by the inequalities

$$C_1 < A_1 < B_1 < D_1$$

and

$$C_2 < A_2 < B_2 < D_2$$

when (A_1, A_2) is the outcome of the unfair-unfair Nash equilibrium, (B_1, B_2) is the outcome of the fair-fair Nash equilibrium. The fair-fair Nash equilibrium is Pareto efficient because $A_1 < B_1$ and $A_2 < B_2$.

The Pareto efficient Nash equilibrium is more risky, because $C_1 < A_1$ so if the market plays fair but the family plays unfair the market will be worse off, this is proposition 3. Conversely, $C_2 < A_2$ implies that the family will be worse off if it plays fair while the market plays unfair, by proposition 2.

The family-market game is similar to prisoner's dilemma

The matrix presented above is similar to that of the 'prisoner's dilemma game' when in addition to the inequalities:

$$C_1 < A_1 < B_1 < D_1$$

and

$$C_2 < A_2 < B_2 < D_2$$

the two players are symmetrically situated, so that

$$A_1 = A_2, B_1 = B_2, C_1 = C_2, D_1 = D_2$$

A numerical example of the prisoner's dilemma is

$$\begin{pmatrix} 5,5 & 3,10 \\ 10,3 & 9,9 \end{pmatrix}$$

while a numerical example of our situation need not be symmetrical – for example

$$\begin{pmatrix} 5,6 & 3,10 \\ 9,4 & 8,9 \end{pmatrix}$$

where

$$
\begin{aligned}
A_1 &= 5 & A_2 &= 6 \\
B_1 &= 8 & B_2 &= 9 \\
C_1 &= 3 & C_2 &= 4 \\
D_1 &= 9 & D_2 &= 10
\end{aligned}
$$

Conclusion

We show that the coupling of two distinct institutions – the market and the family – can lead to asymmetric allocations of effort and of rewards to two identical groups of people, men and women. In principle the asymmetries could be in favour of either group. However, given initial conditions, historically given differences in wages that favour men, the coupling leads to a rational but inferior solution that involves a disproportionate allocation of home responsibilities to women, and simultaneously to lower women's wages in the marketplace. However, as we showed, there is a cooperative solution that is better for all, involving equity at home and in the workplace. This latter solution is Pareto superior – but it seems riskier. The risks derive from missing contracts between the family and the marketplace. The family loses if it plays fair when the market doesn't, and vice versa (Edin and Richardson 2002; Elul *et al.* 2002; Engineer and Welling 1999).

What social institutions can help resolve this problem? Waldfogel (1998) and others have considered similar issues.

A prenuptial agreement that specifies women and men's roles in the family could be a start. It should have penalty, for example through 'bonds' that are posted in advance, if the parties default from what was promised initially. Using such a legal agreement women can present themselves at work as fully able to deliver so a fair employer is not misled about the nature of the labour it hires.

Similarly, strengthening equal pay provisions in the marketplace should support the execution of these prenuptial agreements. This requires enforcing the *Equal Pay Act* – and perhaps making this enforcement contingent on the availability of the prenuptial agreement just discussed. This way the firms would not risk being penalized for playing fair.

Other solutions to the prisoner's dilemma have been proposed over the years, most of them encourage cooperation among the players. Often this requires repeated games among the players, which is not realistic in the case of marriage over small single digits (Lagerlöf 2003). In any case, any solution that encourages a cooperative outcome between the family and the market will benefit both. The moral of this article is that equity may appear to be riskier – and indeed, it may be – but it is after all the Pareto efficient allocation.

Another approach, suggested by O. Hart (in private communication), is to consider what informational structures within the firm are more likely to produce incentives that lead to equal pay to equal labour. It has been argued that piece-rates, when women are 'residual claimants', could do the job. An example would be women who own so-called 'franchises', where after paying a fixed rate for the name and the fixed costs, women act as self-employed and pay themselves the marginal product of labour. If this works, we should observe no gender gap in firms of this nature. This becomes an empirical question to be determined in future work.

In any case, the results of this article suggest that the gender gap is more problematic in firms where performance is difficult to observe, and that women who have more obligations at home – for example those who take care of children – face a larger gender gap. The existing empirical evidence for this seems reasonably good. Similarly, executive jobs that demand constant dedication would be most affected by the externality produced by the family that is mentioned in this article, and therefore in such jobs one would expect a glass ceiling to emerge: the higher a woman's level of accomplishment, the larger the gap between her salary and those of men. This glass ceiling is a direct implication of the results of this chapter and is extensively documented in the empirical literature. The empirical results discussed are validated by recent empirical work in Chichilnisky and Shachmurove (2007) based on data from the American Time Use Survey (ATUS).

Appendix

Proof of the existence of solution in proposition 7.

We show existence of a solution in a simple case; the most general case requires the use of a fixed point argument. The simplest (non trivial) case is when $\frac{w_1}{w_2} > M$ as defined in (M). Under the conditions, as we saw in proposition 2, women will do all the housework and men will only work in the marketplace. From (4.11) we obtain the total amount of hours that women work at home, denoted l_2, which as already discussed, produces an externality on the productivity of women at the firm. There is no externality in the case of men, since men do not work at home. Therefore the total amount of hours that men work at the firm is L_1 and is determined from (4.11) and so is the marginal productivity $\frac{\partial f}{\partial L_2}$. Since we know the ratio of wages $\frac{w_1}{w_2}$ from (4.11) we may now derive the number of hours L_2 that women work at the firm together with the value of the externality γ – the two values L_2 and γ_2 must satisfy the following two equations

$$\frac{w_1}{w_2} = \frac{\frac{\partial f}{\partial L_1}(\gamma).}{\frac{\partial f}{\partial L_2}(\gamma).} \tag{4.20}$$

74   *Graciela Chichilnisky*

and

$$K - L_2 = l_2.$$ (4.21)

To solve the model we need to find the values of the two variables, γ^* and L_2^*, that satisfy the two equations (4.1) and (4.2). One shifts the production function using the externality parameter γ until the two equations are satisfied. At a solution, the productivity of women at the firm will be lower than men's, since women work most of their time at home. The vector $(w_1^*, w_2^*, \gamma^*, l_1^*, l_2^*)$ is a solution for this economy.

Notes

1 Graciela Chichilnisky is the UNESCO Professsor of Mathematics and Economics at Columbia University and a Professor of Statistics at Columbia, and the Director of Columbia Consortium for Risk Management. This paper was presented at the economic theory Workshop of Columbia University in 2004, and at the June 2005 International School for Economic Research (ISER) on 'Gender and Economics' at the University of Siena, http://www.wcon-pol.unisi.it/iser.html. It appeared first in the book 'Gender and Economics' edited by Professor F. Bettio and G. Forconi (Chichilnisky 2005), and has been validated empirically in Chichilnisky and Shachmurove (2007). The author thanks the participants of the 2005 ISER for valuable comments and suggestions, and Oliver Hart for valuable insights on incentives and contracts in this model of gender discrimination.
2 The problem persists across all occupations and income levels, and is typically worse at the top. See Blau and Kahn (2004), Ginther (2004), Rosholm and Smith (1996), NCES (2004), Meyersson Milgrom *et al.* (2001), Meyersson Milgrom and Petersen (2003), Bureau of Labor Statistics (2003), Gupta *et al.* (2003).
3 In economic terms, there are *externalities* between the market and the family because the more persons work at home, the less reliable or productive they can be in the marketplace. In legal terms, there are missing *property rights* and missing *contracts* between the two institutions. Both of these issues impede the work of the market; they tie down the invisible hand.
4 Health service is an important sector, representing about 16% of the US GDP.
5 To clarify this issue their experiments (Gneezy *et al.* 2003) should be augmented to ask the women and the men who participate the amount of time they spend in each of the two institutions. In the case of students, the question may be better posed in terms of the amount of time they expect to spend on each of the two institutions - or the amount of time that their 'gender role models' - such as parents of teachers - themselves spend at home and in the marketplace.
6 Holmstrom and Milgrom (1991) examine people who share their time among different activities and predict specialization as does Becker. Their production functions have increasing productivity, and as a result each task is the responsibility of a single person thus predicting hierarchies. Under our conditions, instead, we show that at higher levels of employment equal sharing at home and at the marketplace emerges as the more productive strategy. This increases family welfare, and is more productive in the workplace.
7 In the following without loss we assume that the parameter is the same for the genders, $\gamma_1 = \gamma_2$.
8 Without loss of generality, we have assumed $\gamma_1 = \gamma_2$.
9 The consideration of leisure in the utility function would reinforce the results obtained in this chapter.
10 Recall that we normalized the price of x so that $p_x = 1$.

References

Apps, P. F. and Rees, R. (1997) Collective Labor Supply and Household Production, *Journal of Political Economy*, 105 (1): 178–190.

Aronsson, T., Daunfeldt, S.-O. and Wikström, M. (2001) Estimating Intrahousehold Allocation in a Collective Model with Household Production, *Journal of Population Economics*, 14(Part 4): 569–584.

Arrow, Kenneth (1962) Economic Implications of Learning by Doing, *Review of Economist and Statistics* 29: 155–173.

Becker, G. S. (1985) Human Capital, Effort, and the Sexual Division of Labor, *Journal of Labor Economics*, 3 (1): 33–58.

Blau, F. D. and Kahn, L. M. (2004) *The US Gender Pay Gap in the 1990's: Slowing Convergence*, NBER Working Paper Series, Working Paper 10853.

Bonke, J., Gupta, N. D. and Smith, N. (2005) Timing and Flexibility of Housework and Men and Women's Wages, IZA Discussion Paper no. 860, published in D. S. Hamermesh and G. A. Pfann (eds) *The Economics of Time use in Contributions to Economic Analysis*, Amsterdam: Elsevier, 2005.

Bureau of Labor Statistics (2003) *Highlights of Women's Earnings in 2002*, Report 972, U.S. Department of Labor.

Chichilnisky, G. (2005) The Gender Gap, Presented at the 2004–2005 Economic Theory Seminar of Columbia University and the CSWEP Session on Gender Discrimination at the 2005 American Economic Association Annual Meetings, Philadelphia, Pennsylvania, circulated in 2005 and 2006 as Working Paper of the Department of Economics, Columbia University, and published in F. Bettio and G. Forconi (eds.) *Gender and Economics, Proceedings of the 2005 ISER Conference*, University of Siena, June 2005. Available: http://www.econ-pol.unisi.it/iser.html/ (Accessed 27 February 2007).

Chichilnisky, G. and Shachmurove, Y. (2007) *Household Work and the Gender Gap: an Empirical Analysis of Gender Discrimination*, Working Paper, Columbia University, Graduate Center CUNY and University of Pennsylvania, February 2007.

Edin, P.-A. and Richardson, K. (2002) Swimming with the Tide: Solidary Wage Policy and the Gender Earnings Gap, *Scandinavian Journal of Economics*, 104 (1): 49–67.

Elul, R., Silva-Reus, J. and Volij, O. (2002) Will you marry me? A Perspective on the Gender Gap, *Journal of Economic Behaviour and Organization*, 49: 549–572.

Engineer, M. and Welling L. (1999) Human Capital, True Love, and Gender Roles: is sex destiny? *Journal of Economic Behaviour and Organization*, vol. 40: 155–178.

Ginther, D. K. (2004) Why Women Earn Less: Economic Explanations for the Gender Salary Gap in Science, *Awis Magazine*, 33 (1): 6–10.

Gneezy, U., Niederle, M. and Rustichini, M. (2003) Performance in Competitive Environments: Gender Differences, *The Quarterly Journal of Economics*, August 2003: 1049–1074.

Gupta, N. D., Oaxaca, R.L. and Smith, N. (2003) *Swimming Upstream, Floating Downstream: Comparing Women's Relative Wage Positions in the US and Denmark*, International and labour relations review, 59(2): 243–266.

Holmstrom, B. and Milgrom, P. (1991) Multitask Principal – Agent Analyses: Incentive Contracts, Asset Ownership and Job Design, *Journal of Law and Economic Organization*, 7 (Spring): 24–53.

Lagerlöf, N.-P. (2003) Gender Equality and Long-Run Growth, *Journal of Economic Growth,* 8: 403–426.

Meyersson Milgrom, E.-M., Petersen, T. and Snarland, V. (2001) Equal Pay for Equal Work? Evidence from Sweden and a Comparision with Norway and the US, *Scandinavian Journal of Economics* 103 (4): 559–583.

Meyersson Milgrom, E.-M. and Petersen, T. (2006) Is There a Glass Ceiling for Women in Sweden, 1970–1990? Life Cycle and/or Cohort Effects. In *The Declining Significance of Gender?* edited by F. Blau, M. Brinton, and D. Grusky. New York: Russel Sage Foundation.

NCES (2004) *Trends in Educational Equity of Girls & Women: 2004*, U.S. Department of Education, Institiute of Education of Education Sciences, NCES 2005-016.

Rosholm, M. and Smith, N. (1996) The Danish Gender Wage Gap in the 1980s: A Panel Data Study, *Oxford Economic Papers*, 48 (2): 254–279.

Waldfogel, J. (1998) The Family Gap for Young Women in the United States and Britan: Can Maternity Leave Make a Difference? *Journal of Labor Economics*, 16 (3): 505–545.

5   Ghosts in the machine

A post Keynesian analysis of gender
relations, households and
macroeconomics

A. Haroon Akram-Lodhi and Lucia C. Hanmer

Introduction

Gender relations are a set of social norms, values, conventions and rules
that informally or formally regulate the parameters of the practical day-to-day
relationships between men and women within a society (Akram-Lodhi 1996).
There is however one parameter of gender relations that apparently seems
to transcend the myriad and multifaceted complex of gender-based cultural
differences that can be found across societies and, as such, can claim the
status of a 'stylized fact' of gender analysis. That parameter is that there are
systemic asymmetries of social power between men and women, to the benefit
of men. These systemic asymmetries are constructed on the basis of dominant
gender ideologies that emphasize those aspects of life experience that differ
between men and women. The power of gender ideology lies most fundamentally
in its capacity to conflate the biological with the social and thus render as
'natural' the allocation of tasks by gender. Biological sex is a powerful, available
metaphor for organizing society, generating a system of symbols which can
interact with social institutions to asymmetrically structure relationships between
men and women. Biological difference is thus used in the construction of a
subjectivity that invests shared experience with different meanings, and in so
doing becomes transformed into gender ideologies that shape cultural and social
norms and, in turn, affect and effect material practices (Akram-Lodhi 1992a).
The most notable material impact of gender ideologies is in the division of
labour within the household, where women have a distinct role in performing
the caring, maintenance and service activities that can be said to comprise
'household production'. At its most minimal, these activities can consist of the
biologically-necessary tasks of food preparation, child care, sanitation and family
reproduction.

   The arena within which gender relations are played out, in the first instance, is
thus the household. The household is

> a social institution that embodies a particular pattern of relationships among
> individuals as biological and social beings...(and) an ideological concept
> through which people express their ideals about how biological and social

reproduction ought to be coordinated…Both as an institution and as a conception,…(it) mediates between people's definitions of themselves as individuals and as members of society.

(Coontz 1988: 12–13)

In households three material elements affect the pattern of gendered social relations: production, consumption and reproduction. It is worth noting that three types of reproduction simultaneously occur: biological reproduction, labour force reproduction and social reproduction (Edholm *et al.* 1977). The specific way in which these three material elements are constructed forms the basis of the differential engagement in work activities by gendered economic agents. The household is thus the locus of a complex web of material and ideological forms (Akram-Lodhi 1992b).

A standard dictionary defines macroeconomics as 'a branch of economics that focuses on the general features and processes that make up a national economy and the ways in which different segments of the economy are connected' (Encarta 2001). In so doing, macroeconomics places particular stress on aggregate output levels, price levels and employment, focusing on either short run fluctuations around a trend or the factors that contribute to the long-term expansion of productive capacity and economic activity. Macroeconomic theory is concerned with understanding the relationship between a set of key variables that determine national output and income, including consumption, investment, savings, government expenditure and trade, while macroeconomic policy seeks to alter the relationship between these key variables so as to alter the overall level of economic activity, with the usual objective of increasing the rate of growth of aggregate output and income.

For many – possibly most – macroeconomists, the focus of their attention on aggregate variables appears to preclude an analysis that integrates the set of gender relations that operate within and between households. The purpose of this chapter is to demonstrate the fallacy of this presumption. The chapter begins by discussing why there is a need to introduce gender into macroeconomics. Having established the point, the chapter explores a specific way by which households, as a locus of gender relations, could be incorporated into macroeconomic analysis by presenting a post Keynesian two-sector macroeconomic model that explores the dynamic relationship between household production and commodity production. The model generates results that are not only interesting but which are also quite sensible, resulting in the conclusion that a well-rounded understanding of macroeconomic growth and accumulation requires a full analysis of the relationship between gender-mediated household production and gender-mediated commodity production.

Why macroeconomics is not gender-neutral

Theoretically, it is difficult to precisely trace the impact of macroeconomics on gendered individuals. Households mediate the relationship between macroeconomic variables and outcomes, and understanding the basis by which the mediation is undertaken is essential if the identification of the gendered individual effects of macroeconomic variables is to be made (Akram-Lodhi 2002). For this reason, the analysis of the economic role of the household has been dominated by a branch of neo-classical microeconomics termed the 'new household economics' (NHE) (Becker 1981). In NHE analysis agents, operating in a more or less competitive market environment, face exogenous constraints when seeking to marginally optimize their production and consumption decisions. The NHE approach thus makes two claims (Braunstein and Folbre 2001). The first claim is that the household acts for the benefit of all its gendered members: the household is an altruistic unit. The second claim is that the gender division of labour within the household is, in economic terms, efficient. In making both claims, the NHE approach is being consistently neo-classical in banishing contestation, conflict and collective action, and this remains the key weakness of the approach. In that they cannot deal with the empirically well-documented presence of conflict within the household, microeconomic models of the household operating within the NHE framework continue to face major theoretical and empirical difficulties, particularly with regard to assumptions concerning labour substitutability, resource pooling, joint utility maximization and the presence of a household production function (Akram-Lodhi 1997). As a consequence, recent research in the microeconomics of the household has sought to move beyond the 'unitary' approach used by many of those that operate within an NHE approach (Folbre 2004; World Bank 2001; Haddad *et al.* 1997).

By way of contrast, the macroeconomic analysis of the household and the gender relations that operate within it remains, despite a great deal of work (Çağatay *et al.* 1995; Grown *et al.* 2000) in its infancy. The analytical variables that are considered relevant to macroeconomics are, as aggregates, deemed by most macroeconomists to be not relevant in understanding the social identities that reflect and affect gender relations in households. Thus, the tools of macroeconomic theory and policy are seen as being gender-neutral. This perception of gender-neutrality is incorrect, for two interrelated reasons. The first reason is that the perception of gender-neutrality, in large part, reflects an orthodox neo-classical conceptualization of the domain of macroeconomic analysis as one that assumes that the distribution of aggregate output is given, and is thus analytically exogenous. This assumption, which is not shared by heterodox macroeconomics of a structuralist or post Keynesian persuasion, is fundamentally challenged by feminist economists (Çağatay and Erturk 2004) because it is, at best, misleading and, at worst, wrong. The error of the assumption lies in the fact that the distribution of aggregate output is a function of a series of distributive options that are not given but which are, rather, the outcome of a series of explicit and implicit social choices (Evers 2003). Gender relations are an extremely important determinant of the structure of these choices, and hence the distribution of aggregate output, most particularly with regard to those choices that are implicit. This has two implications. The first is that factors effecting the distribution of aggregate output must be investigated. The second is that gender relations are a key factor in structuring the distribution of aggregate output. Gender, as a power relationship, affects the division of labour in the performance of household maintenance and service activities and, as a consequence, the division of labour between paid work in the commodity-producing economy and the caring labour engaged in household production. As a result, the labour market is segmented on the basis of gender. This gender-based distortion can, in turn, be transmitted into other economic processes that can, as a consequence, be segmented on the basis of gender. For example, constraints on female labour supply as a result of the gender division of labour have implications for the output gap between potential and actual production. Therefore, factor market segmentation affects production, productivity and incomes, and thus both the distribution of aggregate output and macroeconomic growth processes. Thus, the distribution of time, the distribution of income and the distribution of wealth, in that they are often gender-differentiated within and between households, can affect consumption and investment choices, productivity, and, again, the distribution of aggregate output and macroeconomic growth processes. Gender inequalities can, as a result, generate 'hidden' inefficiencies that affect aggregate investment, aggregate production, distribution and economic growth, leading to sub-optimal outcomes (Hanmer *et al.* 1999). For example, it is well established that gender inequality in early childhood education for females reduces long run growth (King and Hill 1995). The response of a government to such gender-based inefficiencies can affect its budgetary position. Moreover, the efficiency and equity of public spending can be subject to gender-based distortions, in that the two reasons that are cited to justify the economic case for public intervention – market failure and redistribution – can both be the outcome of the structure of gender inequalities (Akram-Lodhi 2002). Thus, gender relations can act as a structural constraint on the macro economy (Folbre 1994).

The second reason that the perception of macroeconomic gender-neutrality is incorrect is related to the first. The behaviour of economic agents reflects their social identity as gendered individuals (Çağatay and Erturk 2004, Akerlof and Kranton 2000). This microeconomic phenomenon has macroeconomic implications, suggesting that patterns of consumption (Dwyer and Bruce 1989), investment (Arndt and Tarp 2000; Warner and Campbell 2000) and savings (Seguino and Floro 2002) at an aggregate level may be gender-differentiated. Once again, it appears that gender relations can act as a structure of constraint on the macro economy. This suggests, in turn, that macroeconomic variables should not necessarily be treated as homogenous, but should rather be partitioned into heterogeneous subsets of the aggregate variable. Once more, this perspective is consistent with structuralist and post Keynesian macroeconomics, but not with orthodox neo-classical macroeconomics.

In light of these points, it appears that in order to properly integrate gender structures into macroeconomic analysis it is necessary to introduce three key propositions that differ from those in orthodox macroeconomics but which are essential to an engendered macroeconomic analysis (Grown *et al.* 2000). The first proposition is that economic institutions – states, markets and households – bear and transmit gender bias. The second is that the macro economy must be defined so as to include the unpaid caring work that goes into household production and whose supply is by and large inelastic with respect to non-caring work. The third is that gender relations affect the division of labour, the distribution of productive inputs, the distribution of employment, the distribution of income, the distribution of output and the distribution of wealth. In so doing, gender relations affect aggregate production, aggregate savings, aggregate investment, and aggregate net exports, and thus macroeconomic processes.

Efforts at seeking to understand the structural role of gender relations on macroeconomic processes by integrating these three propositions into macroeconomic analysis can take one of four approaches (Çağatay *et al.* 1995; Grown *et al.* 2000). The first approach is to use conventional macroeconomic analysis but to disaggregate the variables contained within such an analysis on the basis of gender (Collier 1994) or to include social reproduction as a set of analytical variables (Fontana and Wood 2000). A subset of this approach is that variant which seeks to formalize the microfoundations of macroeconomics through the use of computable general equilibrium models. In the latter the macro economy is taken to be the sum of the rational and self-interested individual activities of economic agents and, as the terrain of analysis is the individual agent, there is, in theory, space for gender-differentiated agents to be introduced. However, in practice, such is not the case. Computable general equilibrium models predicated on the 'microfoundations of macroeconomics' approach require the introduction of 'representative agents': that is to say, individuals that can be aggregated and, in so doing, represent, in a microeconomic sense, the behaviour of the sum total of economic agents in the macro economy. Needless to say, this approach obscures the very issue that feminist economists find objectionable: namely, that asymmetrical power relations between men and women mean that the very notion of a gender-neutral 'representative agent' is a fiction that cannot be substantiated because no single representative agent can encapsulate the different material positions of men and women in the micro economy (Evers 2003; Kirman 1992). Thus, the gendering of economic agents, while an important contribution to the domain of microeconomic analysis, does not deal with the reality of gender that, as a social institution, fosters a structural macroeconomic constraint, which in turn effects labour flows between household production and commodity production. Moreover, from an empirical point of view data on unpaid household production remains far too scarce, meaning that the formal modeling of this approach tends to neglect the dynamics of household production.

The second approach is to introduce gendered variables into macroeconomic models (Elson 1995). However, this approach often fails to question the underlying logic of the macroeconomic analysis itself: in common with the first approach, gender relations and households are 'added on' to conventional macroeconomics and as such fail to recognize the extent to which gender relations permeate macroeconomic structures and variables and, as a consequence, require a fundamental rethinking of macroeconomic processes from first principles.

The third approach is to treat household production as a separate sphere of economic activity and then to examine the ways in which the two spheres impact upon each other (Taylor 1995; Walters 1995). This approach, however, fails to interrogate the dynamic interaction between household and commodity production. The fourth approach combines two or more of the three previously-mentioned approaches (Elson *et al.* 1997).

So far, efforts at seeking to integrate gender relations and household production into macroeconomics remain less than satisfactory because of an unwillingness to rethink fundamental macroeconomic propositions. Gender relations and households remain 'ghosts' – they 'haunt' the margins of macroeconomic analysis without assuming form and substance because the assumption of form and substance would require a reconsideration of macroeconomics at its very foundations. Yet surely, given the universal nature of gender relations and household production, a reconsideration of macroeconomics from its very foundations is precisely what is required. A possible basis by which reconsideration might be attempted is offered in the following section.

Modelling the macroeconomics of gender relations

A starting point by which to offer a preliminary formalization of some of the propositions contained in the previous section is the gender critique of the circular flow of income and product (Elson 1999). As is well understood by all students of macroeconomics, in order to grasp the complexities of the fairly abstract sets of social interactions between people that takes place at the level of the economy as a whole the macro economy is modelled by macroeconomists. The model of the circular flow of income and product is presented, in a simple form, in Figure 5.1.

In the circular flow, households provide inputs – primarily labour – to firms for wages. Firms use those inputs to produce goods and services which can be sold to households for cash. Firms also receive investment funds from financial markets to buy plant and equipment to increase their capacity to produce goods and services in the future. The household gets the money from the sale of labour to make the payment for goods and services produced by the firm that they in turn consume. Alternatively, households can save, or they may be forced to save by making tax payments to the government. Governments use these taxes to buy

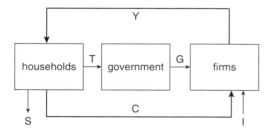

Figure 5.1 The circular flow.

goods and services from firms. There are thus: flows of income (Y), which are payments for labour which are in turn used for payments for goods and services; flows of production (C), in that the flow of labour resources from households are turned into goods and services that are consumed by the household; leakages, in the form of savings (S) flows into financial markets and forced savings (T) that flow to the government; and injections, in the form of investment (I) financed from financial markets and government spending (G).

This simplified conventional account is gender-blind. It assumes that households collectively act in a unified way, but there is little basis, either theoretically or empirically, for this assumption. It also assumes that households do not produce, but this is clearly incorrect, in that consumer goods and services often have to have work performed on them prior to their final consumption, which suggests in turn that the purchase of goods and services should not be equated with the final consumption of goods and services in either the micro or the macro economy. Most fundamentally, however, the orthodox circular flow ignores the care economy, which is the household production and community service that is not paid, that maintains health, that develops skills, and which builds 'social assets': the relational rules, norms, and values of civic responsibility and social community. Moreover, as has been suggested, the care economy does not just spend what is produced: without the care economy and the household production that takes place within it the production and sale of goods and services in the commodity economy could not take place.

Orthodox macroeconomists have long recognized some of the inherent limitations of this approach to modelling the macro economy. They have thus, for example, recognized the need to construct 'satellite accounts' that seek to monetarily capture the value of uncosted environmental and household production activities, in order to better quantify the size of the macro economy (Beneria 2003; Smith and Ingham 2005). However, feminist economists have argued that it is not enough to simply 'add on' gender variables to the macroeconomic analysis that is undertaken. Rather, it is necessary to fundamentally reconceptualize the production of national income and output as the interaction of the private sector, commodity production economy of firms and markets, the public service economy of government and the household and community care economy. This means, in turn, that the circular flow of income and product should be engendered (Unifem 2000). A widely-adopted gender-aware circular flow is therefore presented in Figure 5.2.

In the gender-aware circular flow the private sector commodity economy of firms and, as a regulatory actor, markets, supplies consumption and investment goods and services to the government public service economy and to the household and community care economy. The informal private commodity sub-sector is by and large undercounted in developed market, developing and transition economies, which may have gender implications. The government public service economy provides social and physical infrastructural investment used for consumption and investment in both the private commodity economy and the household and community economy. As a result, the public service economy affects the

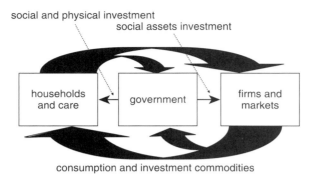

Figure 5.2 A gender-aware circular flow.

overall flow of income and product. Like the private sector commodity economy the public service economy is market-regulated, but less so than the private commodity economy. The employment pattern in the public service economy may have gender implications. Household production and the care economy produce goods and services for use by individuals, households and communities. This supports the private commodity and public service economies by supplying human capital and social assets. Work in household production and the care economy is not formally paid, although some aspects may be supported by transfer payments. Work patterns are regulated by social norms and conventions, and are gendered.

The gender-aware circular flow offers a very different macroeconomic model to that offered by conventional macroeconomics. Its recognition of household production and the care economy, and the role of these sectors in sustaining the private and public spheres, emphasizes both the necessary role of the care economy in the performance of the macro economy as well as the dynamic flow relationships between economic sectors. At the same time, however, gender relations *per se* do not directly enter into the model; rather, they are seen to operate across the macro economy, although special emphasis is paid to the way in which gender relations in household production and the care economy structure an engendered engagement in the activities of other economic sectors.

A previous joint article sought to offer a series of preliminary propositions designed to shed light on the dynamic interaction between household production and commodity production that is demonstrated in the gender-aware circular flow of income and product (Hanmer and Akram-Lodhi 1998). In so doing, the article attempted to reconsider the fundamental position of household production, as the central arena within which gender relations are constructed, within macroeconomic analysis. Next section seeks to formalize the preliminary propositions contained in this earlier article. Before doing that, however, a justification is elaborated that substantiates the relevance of structuralism and post Keynesianism for an engendered macroeconomics.

Structuralism, post Keynesianism and macro dynamics

The domain of imperfect markets

It has already been noted that the attractiveness of structuralist and post Keynesian approaches to feminist macroeconomics is that key macroeconomic variables can be partitioned into heterogeneous sub-variables, as well as the fact that the distribution of output is within the terrain of analysis. These are far from the only reasons why structuralist and post Keynesian analysis offers a favourable analytical framework for feminist macroeconomics. Structuralist and post Keynesian economic analysis is rooted in an exploration of the dynamic interrelationship between two economic domains: the market and the state. However, unlike neo-classical economics, which explores resource allocation decisions reflecting efforts at utility maximization in these spheres, structuralist and post Keynesian economics is concerned with issues of economic growth. Accumulation drives the analysis, which is a function of distributional relationships between, on the one hand, workers motivated to consume and capitalists motivated to earn profit and, on the other hand, the various sectors into which the macro economy can be partitioned, and in particular sectors within and between agriculture and industry.

The starting point of a structuralist and post Keynesian analysis stresses the relevance of social institutions in economic activity (Arestis 1992). As Kalecki (1970: 311) put it, 'the institutional framework of a social system is a basic element of its economic dynamics'. However, social institutions operate in a very different manner in structuralist and post Keynesian analysis when compared to neo-classical theory. In Kaleckian-inspired post Keynesianism in particular, the setting from which microfoundations are derived is one in which the capitalist market economy is dominated by oligopolistic firms that control large shares of the markets in which they operate. Control over markets by oligopolistic firms confers economic power to capitalists in both the production and the distribution of the goods and services which they produce. Control over markets has two major implications for the way in which markets, and hence, at one remove, the macro economy, operates.

The first implication is that markets are highly imperfect. Control over markets permits capitalists to price private goods and services based upon a mark-up over costs. The extent of the mark-up will itself reflect the degree of control of the capitalist in the product markets in which they operate: what Kalecki termed the degree of monopoly. Thus, the more control exercised by the capitalist in the product market the higher the mark-up. This is because control in the product market will permit capacity under-utilization to be deliberately maintained by the capitalist so that when the business cycle moves into a new period the capitalist can capture the benefit of economies of scale. Capacity under-utilization in turn permits the maintenance of a reserve army of labour, which sustains real wage discipline. The presence of a reserve army of labour produces a segmented labour market which, by limiting the number of skilled primary sector jobs and by rendering the less-skilled secondary sector more competitive, generates antagonism within the labour market which reinforces the control of the capitalist. Moreover, there is at best only very limited cyclical mobility between the segments because of the human capital investment requirements of the primary sector. Labour markets are therefore also imperfect.

The second implication of capitalist control of markets is that market failures extend beyond mark-up pricing and segmented labour markets. Markets in a range of goods and services may be interlocking: demand in one market is conditional upon supply in another market, or vice versa. Moreover, markets may be incomplete in their capacity to provide a range of goods and services: public goods, for example. Indeed, markets may be missing and, because of the nature of the good or service required, may be incapable of being created under the conditions of a capitalist market economy.

Macro dynamics: effective demand, investment and expectations

The capacity of the capitalist to control the product market and utilize mark-up pricing has an impact upon the distribution of income within an economy, and thus macro dynamics. In effect, wage and profit shares are determined as a consequence of the market control of the capitalist. The oligopolistic structure of the product market thus determines wage shares and, in conjunction with productivity, the real wages which accrue to households. It should be noted, though, that the segmentation of the labour market means that in the secondary sector real wages may be flexible.

Given their control in product markets, it might appear that a profit-oriented capitalist would simply continually mark-up in order to accumulate. In practice, it is not as simple as that. The capitalist faces two interrelated problems. On the one hand capitalists face the problem of 'realization': they must be able to sell what they produce in order to realise a profit. They therefore require effective demand for the goods and services that they produce. The effective demand for goods and services produced by capitalists comes from workers, whose motivation is that of consumption. In a structuralist and post Keynesian world workers do not by and large save; they spend what they earn, and thus act as a source of effective demand for the goods and services produced by capitalists. However, workers must have goods and services on which to spend what they earn. This is then the second problem which capitalists face. Capitalists must continue to provide the goods and services which workers can buy. This means that capitalists must invest, in order to continue to meet the effective demand of workers. As a consequence, the spending decisions of capitalists, particularly on investment, determine the level of economic activity and hence of capitalist profitability. In a sense, in structuralist and post Keynesian economics capitalists earn what they spend.

However, to invest capitalists must be reasonably certain that effective demand will be forthcoming for the goods and the services which they produce. This implies that capitalists must be reasonably confident that workers will express a preference for the goods and services that they produce. Therefore, investment by capitalists is primarily a function of their expectations. Indeed, if production and effective demand are central economic issues then in structuralist and post Keynesian economics expectations play a major role in the oscillations of production and effective demand.

Expectations have been an important area of debate in post Keynesian economics in particular. In Keynes' own work it is assumed that while in the short run expectations are generally met in the long run expectations are capable of violent and unforeseen change: the 'animal spirits' which cannot be deduced. Some have argued that as a consequence Keynes has no understanding of long run behaviour. Lawson (1985) disputes this. Following conventional thinking, Lawson argues that in Keynes there is an emphasis that existing circumstances form a disproportionate influence on long term expectations. This is because while individuals are uncertain of the future they are knowledgeable about the present. However, rather than using this to dismiss long run expectations Lawson uses it to explore the basis of short run expectations. According to Lawson's exposition of Keynes, in the short run existing conventions shape much understanding. Keynes saw convention in part being formed by demonstration effects. As he put it, 'knowing that our own individual judgement is worthless, we endeavour to fall back on the judgement of the rest of the world which is perhaps better informed. That is, we endeavour to conform with the behavior of the average' (Keynes 1937: 214). However, knowledge of what exactly are the conventions of the present is obtained through the direct acquaintance of the individual in social practice – experience, perception and understanding. Indeed, as Lawson emphasizes, it would appear that for Keynes it is by taking part in social practices that individuals become knowledgeable about social practices (Lawson 1985: 916–917). Thus, individual rational behaviour is guided by the context and setting within which knowledge is obtained. Expectations thus reflect the knowledge that the capitalist has of the society within which they operate which in turn is a consequence of being a member of that society.

In post Keynesian analysis then the expectations of capitalists will be consequence of the degree of monopoly that they have in the product markets in which they operate. The state of the distributional struggle will affect the level of effective demand. Specific factors which result in a reduction in effective demand through a cut in real wages will be self-reinforcing because of their impact upon expectations. The alteration in the expectations of capitalists arising from a fall in effective demand will lead to a cut in investment which in turn reduces both the level and the profitability of economic activity. Unlike orthodox economics, then, in situations where labour is not a constraint on production an under-employment equilibrium is both possible and probable. This will in turn effect the expectations of workers and capitalists in a self-reinforcing manner.

The domain of the state – and the household?

It is at this point that the second domain of economic analysis addressed by structuralists and post Keynesians can be introduced: the state. In their analysis, the state is an arena of conflict and struggle between capitalists and workers. However, the state is not a class instrument. Rather, the role of the state is to prevent an under-employment equilibrium by stabilizing the economy through intervention designed to counter-cyclically boost effective demand in the short run and thus contribute to an alteration of expectations. In the longer term the role of the state is to regulate the development of human capital in a manner consistent with social convention. These objectives are achieved through the provision of economic services and through the establishment of legislative parameters.

In this framework, there is clearly much that has implications for the household. The determination of real wages in oligopolistic product markets has implications for the level of incomes obtained by households, and in turn, for the allocation of household members to particular activities. That labour is obtained by oligopolistic firms through segmented labour markets has further implications for the levels of income received by households and for the types of labour market participation undertaken by members of households. Combined, both will effect the allocation of household resources within and between households and the capacity of households to make a contribution to effective demand. Effective demand will also be affected by the way in which household consumption requirements combined with expectations shape preferences, in which the role of demonstration effects noted by Lawson (1985) will be extremely important. Moreover, the types of choices made by households will be constrained by missing markets and by expectations. Finally, the state has a role to play in intervening in the household in order to shape the process of social reproduction. It should therefore be possible to take these structuralist and post Keynesian methodological points and apply them to a third, missing, domain: the household. This task is carried out formally in the next section.

A two-sector model

Gender relations, household production and post Keynesianism

In the analysis contained within the previous joint article, a theory of household choice was introduced which sought to recognize the role of co-operation and conflict between household members in the formation of household preferences, consistent with Lawson's exposition of Keynes noted earlier (Hanmer and Akram-Lodhi 1998). It then attempted to examine how the allocation of resources within households in light of preferences was constrained by social relations, technical progress, the labour market and the state, in light of the post Keynesian framework previously discussed. The article thus tried, in a novel way, to uncover the macrostructural determinants of household decisions. In so doing, the article wanted to better understand the ways in which households provide the primary institutional mechanism through which non-price adjustments to labour market demand take place. In this section a formal presentation of some of these propositions will be made, using a structuralist and post Keynesian understanding of the macro economy derived from the work of Kalecki (1976) as developed by FitzGerald (1983, 1989, 1990, 1993).

Consistent with both the post Keynesian methodology already noted as well as with the gender-aware circular flow presented earlier, in this section the macro economy is partitioned into a set of sectors and the flow relationships between the sectors are examined in order to understand the dynamics of growth and accumulation. Historically, this sectoral partition of the macro economy has focused on distinctions between capital goods and wage goods and between industry and agriculture. For feminist economists the most common way of sectorally partitioning an economy has been to define sectors as being female- or male-dominated (Darity 1995). Here, a fresh way of sectorally partitioning the macro economy is proposed: the household sector and the commodity sector.

Households and commodities

The household sector produces a range of goods and services. Some of these goods and services fall, in principle, within the boundaries of national income accounts. Others do not. Examples of the former include: the production of cooked meals; home repairs and maintenance; housework; and child care (Smith and Ingham 2005). All of these products have an opportunity cost: the scarcity value so central to standard economic theory. Examples of the latter include: nurturing; love and care; wisdom; and the various components of 'social assets' (Folbre 2001). Note that the concept of 'social assets' used here differs from the concept of social capital, which is conventionally presented in the literature. In the literature, social capital is typically a stock variable which can be accumulated and allocated in a manner consistent with conventional neo-classical economic theory. The conception here is different: social assets are fundamentally relational in character, and the accumulation of social assets is thus an outcome of their relational characteristics. It is important to stress that typically these latter products cannot be marketed and are valued outside the domain of economics, by the deontological or spiritual values that are attributed to them. At this point in the development of the model, the community service economy, despite its clear importance, is not explicitly part of the model, and so can be considered, at this time, as being part of the household sector.

The second sector in the model is the commodity sector, which produces all the goods and services that are typically manufactured in the formal economy. Thus, the commodity sector comprises the production of wage goods and investment goods. Production of wage and investment goods is performed by enterprises and by other economic institutions, including the state. Thus, the government sector is, in this model, encapsulated within the commodity sector.

The model[1]

To begin, focus attention on the household sector (S_1), as opposed to the commodity sector (S_2). The total value (V) of the output of the household sector is:

$$V = Y + Y' = Q_1 P \tag{5.1}$$

where Y is the revenue generated by the household sector, Y' is the 'conditional revenue' generated by the household sector which is discussed below, Q_1 is the physical quantity of goods and services produced by household sector, and P_1 is the price vector of the goods and services produced by the household sector.

Now examine the components of equation (5.1) in more detail. The revenue (Y) generated by the household sector is:

$$Y = \phi Q_1 P_1 \tag{5.2}$$

where $0 < \phi < 1$. The parameter ϕ thus shows how much of the total product of the household sector is actually marketed. In that the total product of the household sector includes goods and services, it includes socially reproduced labour that is marketed. The parameter ϕ is the subject of household choice and as such will be influenced by the bargaining process within households and the consequent gender division of labour, which was discussed earlier. These aspects of the post Keynesian household will be formalized in future research.

The remaining portion of household product generates what is here called 'conditional revenue' (Y'):

$$Y' = (1 - \phi) Q_1 P_1 \tag{5.3}$$

Some components of this output could, in principle, be marketed, but are not. Examples would include child care, housework and socially reproduced labour that is not marketed. However, other components of this output are unmarketable. Examples here include love, nurturing and wisdom. This output cannot generate revenue that can be realized in economic values. Thus, this output can have no price. However, its production is a precondition of the marketing of household sector goods and services, including socially reproduced labour, and it is in this sense that this revenue is 'conditional'.

In that some of the components of Y' cannot have a price the vector of prices that makes up P_1 is incomplete: some prices will always be missing from it. The use of incomplete vectors is well established in the physical sciences, and it can be suggested that using an incomplete price vector offers an important new way of conceptualizing the macroeconomics of household production. Furthermore, it should be noted that the focus on produced output departs from the neo-classical model of the household. In the neo-classical model the focus is on the allocation of inputs, the cost of which can be assessed by the opportunity cost of time. In such an approach, it must be assumed that all labour time is used productively in the creation of 'goods'. The approach used here does not require this assumption: whether labour time is used productively to create 'goods' or is used unproductively to create 'bads' is not an issue which affects the model's outcomes.

Empirically, in developed market economies the revenue obtained from the marketing of goods and services produced in the household sector will, of course, be dominated by socially reproduced labour. The revenue obtained from marketing goods and services produced in the household sector is equal to the cash income (wL) available to the household sector. Therefore:

$$\phi Q_1 P_1 = wL \tag{5.4}$$

Thus, while cash income is equal to the marketed total product of the household sector, this is argued to be an outcome of bargaining processes within the household. It is assumed that households save via institutions, through pension schemes and social insurance contributions. As such, these savings are retained in the commodity sector (S_2). Thus, the income portrayed in equation (5.4) is the total disposable income accruing to the household sector.

Socially reproduced labour in the household sector is employed in the commodity sector. Employment (L) therefore depends upon the total output (Q_2) of the commodity sector and is given by the labour coefficient (γ) of that output. Thus:

$$L = Q_2 \gamma \tag{5.5}$$

Prices (p_2) in the commodity sector are given by a fixed mark-up (g) over labour costs, which, in the tradition of Kalecki, is a reflection of the degree of monopoly:

$$p_2 = (1+g)w\gamma \tag{5.6}$$

The formal model thus contains five endogenous variables (Y, Y', P_1, p_2, L) and two exogenous variables (Q_1, Q_2), which are considered predetermined in the short run. Output of both sectors is fixed in the short run by the state of technology, and by social relations and norms governing custom, ideology and tradition.

The implications of phi

Before solving the model it is worth briefly discussing the implications of the parameter ϕ within the fully specified model. Recall equation (5.4):

$$\phi Q_1 P_1 = wL$$

Rearranging (5.4):

$$Q_1 P_1 = (w/\phi)L = V \tag{5.7}$$

Equation (5.7) demonstrates that the value of the household sector's output depends on the relative magnitudes of w and ϕ. The lower the value of ϕ in relation to the wage rate the higher the value of the household sector's output. Thus, it would be expected that high value household sectors would be located in those economies where the wage rate was high, but only a small proportion of total household product was traded with the commodity sector. Conversely, a low value household sector would characterize economies where wage rates were low and where social organization and the economic system combined to result in a large amount of the household sector's output being traded with the commodity sector.

It is thus the case that there need not be a high correlation between the value of the output produced in the commodity sector and the value of the output produced in the household sector. This is because the high value of the household sector's output may stem from the fact that $(1-\phi)$, rather than the wage rate, is high. Some developing countries may be characterized by such circumstances. Granted, there will be a minimum amount of wage income needed by the household sector. The demand for labour from the commodity sector at the given wage rate must be able to secure this minimum amount of income. Nonetheless, the overall value of the output of the commodity sector may be fairly low even as the overall value of the household sector's output is high.

By way of contrast, the macro economy could develop in such a way that a high wage rate is only secured when the value of ϕ is also high. In such cases, the value of the household sector's output will be low. The type of economic development which has extended working hours at the expense of time spent in the family and community captures this sort of dynamics. A recent example would be the ongoing retrenchment of social provision in many developed market economies. In such a case the value of the commodity sector's output will be fairly high, but the amount of output that the household sector can produce will be small. Hence, the value of the household sector's output will be low.

It can be suggested that the relative magnitude attached to w and ϕ is an important way of exploring a 'care regime' (Bettio and Plantenga 2004). A care regime can be defined as the basis on which care responsibilities are allocated, with particular reference to the specific balance between the household, the market and the state as the providers of care. In recent comparative research on Europe 'the relative reliance on informal care and formal care, and the different modalities of formal care provisioning, like leave arrangements, financial provisions and social services' (Bettio and Plantenga 2004: 108) were identified as important markers of the pattern of care provision. Links from the care regime to labour markets, poverty and macroeconomic dynamics have also been identified in this research. It might be thought, in this light, that a high value of ϕ would suggest the possibility of a relatively more formal care regime, while a low value of ϕ would suggest a more informal care regime. However, this need not be the case; the character of the care regime can only be identified by examining the magnitude of ϕ in relation to w.

Solving the model

Formal solutions for a two-sector model of the type developed earlier have been established by FitzGerald (1989, 1990, 1993). The real value of household revenue $(\overline{Y})$ is:

$$\overline{Y} = \phi Q_1 P_1 / p_2 \tag{5.8}$$

$$= Q_2 / (1 + g) \tag{5.9}$$

Defining the profit function (R) in the normal way gives:

$$R = gwL \tag{5.10}$$

and so the real value of profits $(\overline{R})$ is:

$$\overline{R} = gwL/p_2 \tag{5.11}$$

$$= Q_2/(1+g) \tag{5.12}$$

Defining savings from the commodity sector (s_2), the market clearing mechanism for the commodity sector is established as:

$$p_2 Q_2 = (wL + (1 - s_2)R) + (\lambda I + I_c) \tag{5.13}$$

Consider equation (5.13). Inside the first bracket on the right hand side are the commodities produced by the commodity sector which are consumed by either the household sector or by the institutions that comprise the commodity sector. The second bracket on the right hand side consists of the investment goods produced by the commodity sector. Total investment goods are divided in two, as in standard structuralist macroeconomics. The investment goods produced by the commodity sector and used by the household sector consist of (λI). The investment goods produced by the commodity sector and used by the commodity sector consist of (I_c).

In the economy as a whole total investment (I) is:

$$I = I_1 + I_2 \tag{5.14}$$

Investment in I_2 is simply made up of the investment goods produced by the commodity sector for the commodity sector, and is thus:

$$I_2 = I_c \tag{5.15}$$

By way of contrast, investment in the household sector (I_1) has two components:

$$I_1 = \lambda I + \delta I \tag{5.16}$$

The first term, (λI), has already been introduced and is easily interpreted as the social investment used by the household sector that is produced in the commodity sector. Examples of such investment would include health services and education. The second term, (δI), is more complex. It can be formally defined as:

$$\delta I_t = \lambda I_{t-n} + \delta I_{t-n} \tag{5.17}$$

Thus, equation (5.17) states that part of the current investment within the household sector is an outcome of past investment in the household sector. Part of that investment (λI_{t-n}) is previous social investment. However, a second part of that investment (δI_{t-n}) can be interpreted as the knowledge, wisdom, capabilities, social networks and social assets upon which the household can draw. Such 'investment', which is not recognized in orthodox economics, is a product of history and culture as well as previous allocations of social investment. It is, in the context of this model, and as will be explained below, an important variable in understanding macro dynamics.

The implications of the model

In order to explore the implications of the post Keynesian two-sector model attention is focused on the physical goods and services (Q_1) produced by the household sector. As already stated, in the short run the physical volume of goods and services produced in the household sector is considered fixed. However, in the long run:

$$Q_1 = f(I_1) \tag{5.18}$$

Equation (5.18) is a standard formulation which simply states that growth and accumulation in the household sector is a function of the investment in it. The empirical evidence that supports this proposition is now reasonably well-established (King and Hill 1995). Investment in the household sector can be used in the production of goods and services that are consumed within the sector as well as being traded with the commodity sector. As shown in equation (5.16), part of this investment (λI) is produced in the commodity sector. Therefore, the allocation of resources between the three components of the commodity sector's output – wage goods, investment goods for the commodity sector and investment goods for the household sector – will determine, in part, the amount produced by the household sector. The key determinants of this allocational choice, which is realized in the commodity sector amongst its key actors, will be public action designed to construct intersectoral principal-agent relationships between households acting as principals and the state acting as the regulating agent.

   The second implication of the two-sector model is that the household's standard of living, in both its income and its non-income dimensions, is determined by the balance between the real value of the revenue generated by households ($\overline{Y}$) and the real value of the conditional revenue ($(1-\phi)Q_1 P_1$) generated by households. As is emphasized in conventional macroeconomics, the level of economic activity in the commodity sector is of great importance: it determines the amount of labour demanded and, through the wage-price ratio which prevails in the commodity sector, the real value of disposable income accruing to households. However, the level of economic activity in the commodity sector is not the end of the story. The goods and services that comprise conditional revenue also determine the standard of living of the household. The goods and services that comprise conditional revenue have some components that are in principal marketable. However, they also have some components that are unmarketable and unvalued in economic terms. This has an intriguing implication: economic policies which foster increased amounts of this unmarketable and unvalued output may *increase* the standard of living. This in turn suggests the need to invest in the full range of activities which take place in the household sector. Granted, there may well be a trade off: the organization of production in the commodity sector could mean that accrued prior investment in the household sector (δI) depreciates more rapidly than it can be replaced. At the same time, the share of social investment accruing to the household sector (λI) has to compete with the need for investment in the commodity sector. Nonetheless, it is clear that a key determinant of the standard of living is the relative allocation of resources between investment in the household sector and investment in the commodity sector (Unifem 2000). In other words, the characteristics of the care regime have important implications for the standard of living, the quality of life and human well-being.

Conclusion

In light of the clear need to engender macroeconomics, and in light of dissatisfaction with existing attempts to integrate gender relations and household production into macroeconomic analysis, this chapter has developed a post Keynesian two-sector model of the macro economy in order to examine the dynamic flow relationship between household production and the commodity sector. Two primary conclusions have emerged. The first is that there need not be any correlation between the value of household production and the value of the output of the commodity sector. High-value household production can be associated with both low-value and high-value production within the commodity sector. The second is that investment in household production, including critical unmarketed outputs, is a functional requirement of improvements in the standard of living. Caring and nurturing, activities which many – possibly most – economists deem to be outside the realm of economic analysis, can have an important bearing upon accumulation and living standards within an economy. However, for them to perform that role requires investment: an investment which many policymakers appear to be quite unwilling to make. It can be suggested that the failure of policymakers to confront the 'ghosts' inhabiting the macro economy is an important possible explanation for the failures of macroeconomic policy in developed market, developing and transition economies.

Acknowledgements

The preliminary ideas for this chapter were presented to the Out of the Margins 2/International Association for Feminist Economics Conference in Amsterdam, the Netherlands on 4 June 1998. In further developing this work, the advice of E.V.K. FitzGerald, Ardeshir Sepehri, Alex Izurieta, Irene van Staveren and Nicky Pouw are gratefully acknowledged. The usual disclaimers apply.

Notes

1 Readers interested in the full formal solution to the model, which is methodologically quite orthodox by Kaleckian and post Keynesian standards, are advised to consult the important work of E.V.K. FitzGerald (1989, 1990, 1993), where the analytical dynamics are explored in full.

References

Akerlof, G.E. and Kranton, R.E. (2000) 'Economics and identity', *Quarterly Journal of Economics*, 115 (3): 715–753.

Akram-Lodhi, A.H. (1992a) 'Peasants and hegemony in the work of James C. Scott', *Peasant Studies*, 19 (3 & 4): 179–202.

Akram-Lodhi, A.H. (1992b) 'Women's work and peasant class differentiation: a methodological and empirical study in political economy with reference to Pakistan', unpublished PhD dissertation, The University of Manitoba, Winnipeg: Canada.

Akram-Lodhi, A.H. (1996) ' "You are not excused from cooking": peasants and the gender division of labor in Pakistan', *Feminist Economics*, 2 (2): 87–106.

Akram-Lodhi, A.H. (1997) 'The unitary model of the peasant household: an obituary?', *Economic Issues*, 2 (1): 27–42.

Akram-Lodhi, A.H. (2002) ' "All decisions are top-down": engendering public expenditure in Vietnam', *Feminist Economics*, 8 (3): 1–20.

Arestis, P. (1992) *The Post-Keynesian Approach to Economics: An Alternative Analysis of Economic Theory and Policy*, Aldershot, UK: Edward Elgar.

Arndt, C. and Tarp, F. (2000) 'Agricultural technology, risk and gender: a CGE analysis of Mozambique', *World Development*, 28 (7): 1307–1326.

Becker, G. (1981) *A Treatise on the Family*, Cambridge, MA: Harvard University Press.

Beneria, L. (2003) *Gender, Development And Globalization: Economics As If People Mattered*, London: Routledge.

Bettio, F. and Platenga, J. (2004) 'Comparing care regimes in Europe', *Feminist Economics*, 10 (1): 85–113.

Braunstein, E. and Folbre, N. (2001) 'To honor and obey: efficiency, inequality and patriarchial property rights', *Feminist Economics*, 7 (1): 25–44.

Çağatay, N., Elson, D. and Grown, C. (1995) 'Introduction', *World Development*, 23 (11): 1827–1836.

Çağatay, N. and Erturk, K. (2004) 'Gender and globalization: a macroeconomic perspective', International Labour Organization World Commission on the Social Dimensions of Globalization *Working Paper*, no. 19.

Collier, P. (1994) 'Gender aspects of labour allocation during structural adjustment: a theoretical framework and the Africa experience', in S. Horton, R. Kanbur and D. Mazumdar (eds) *Labour Markets in an Era of Adjustment Volume 1*, Washington: The World Bank.

Coontz, S. (1988) *The Social Origins of Private Life: A History of American Families 1600–1900*, London: Verso.

Darity, Jr., W. (1995) 'The formal structure of a gender-segregated low-income economy', *World Development*, 23 (11): 1963–1968.

Dwyer, D. and Bruce, J. (eds) (1989) *A Home Divided: Women and Income in The Third World*, Palo Alto, CA: Stanford University Press.

Edholm, F., Harris, O. and Young, K. (1977) 'Conceptualizing women', *Critique of Anthropology*, 3 (9 & 10): 101–130.

Elson, D. (1995) 'Gender awareness in modeling structural adjustment', *World Development*, 23 (11): 1851–1868.

Elson, D. (1999) 'Gender-neutral, gender-blind or gender-sensitive budgets? Changing the conceptual framework to include women's empowerment and the economy of care', in *Gender Budget Initiative: Background Papers*, London: Commonwealth Secretariat.

Elson, D., Evers, B. and Gideon, J. (1997) 'Concepts and sources', University of Manchester Genecon Unit *Working Paper*, Number 1.

Encarta (2001), Seattle: Microsoft Ltd.

Evers, B. (2003) 'Broadening the foundations of macro-economic models through a gender approach: new developments', in M. Gutierrez (ed.) *Macro-economics: Making Gender Matter*, London: Zed Press.

FitzGerald, E.V.K. (1983) 'The problem of balance in the peripheral socialist economy: a conceptual note', *World Development*, 13 (1): 5–13.

FitzGerald, E.V.K. (1989) 'The analytics of stabilization in the small semi-industrialized economy', in E.V.K FitzGerald and R. Vos (eds) *Financing Economic Development*, Aldershot, UK: Gower.

FitzGerald, E.V.K. (1990) 'Kalecki on financing development: an approach to the macroeconomics of the semi-industrialised economy', *Cambridge Journal of Economics*, 14 (2): 183–203.

FitzGerald, E.V.K. (1993) *The Macroeconomics of Development Finance*, London: St Martin's Press.

Folbre, N. (1994) *Who Pays For The Kids? Gender and The Structures of Constraint*, London: Routledge.

Folbre, N. (2001) *The Visible Heart*, New York: The New Press.

Folbre, N. (2004) 'A theory of the misallocation of time', in N. Folbre and M. Bittman (eds) *Family Time: The Social Organization of Care*, London: Routledge.

Fontana, M. and Wood, A. (2000) 'Modeling the effects of trade on women, at work and at home', *World Development*, 28 (7): 1173–1190.

Grown, C., Elson, D. and Çağatay, N. (2000) 'Introduction', *World Development*, 28 (7): 1145–1156.

Haddad, L., Hoddinott, J. and Alderman, H. (eds) (1997) *Intrahousehold Resource Allocation in Developing Countries: Models, Methods and Policy*, London: The Johns Hopkins University Press.

Hanmer, L.C. and Akram-Lodhi, A.H. (1998) 'In "the house of the spirits": towards a Post Keynesian theory of the household?', *Journal of Post Keynesian Economics*, 20 (3): 415–433.

Hanmer, L.C., Pyatt, G. and White, H. (1999) 'What do the World Bank's Poverty Assessments teach us about poverty in Sub-Saharan Africa?', *Development And Change*, 30 (4): 795–823.

Kalecki, M. (1970) 'Theories of growth in different social systems', *Scientia*, 40 (5–6): 1–6.

Kalecki, M. (1976) 'The problem of financing economic development', in *Essays on Developing Economies*, Hassocks, Sussex, UK: Harvester.

Keynes, J.M. (1937) 'The general theory of employment', *Quarterly Journal of Economics* 51 (2): 209–223.

King, E. and Hill, A. (1995) 'Women's education and economic well-being', *Feminist Economics*, 1 (2): 1–26.

Kirman, A. (1992) 'Who or what does the representative individual represent?', *Journal of Economic Perspectives*, 6 (2): 117–136.

Lawson, T. (1985) 'Uncertainty and economic analysis', *Economic Journal*, 95 (380): 909–927.

Seguino, S. and Floro, M. (2002) 'Does gender have any effect on aggregate saving? An empirical analysis', *International Review of Applied Economics*, 17 (2): 148–166.

Smith, J.P. and Ingham, L.H. (2005) 'Mother's milk and measure of economic output', *Feminist Economics*, 11 (1): 41–62.

Taylor, L. (1995) 'Environmental and gender feedbacks in macroeconomics', *World Development*, 23 (11): 1953–1962.

Unifem (2000) *Progress of the World's Women 2000*, New York: United Nations Development Fund for Women.

Walters, B. (1995) 'Engendering macroeconomics: a reconsideration of growth theory', *World Development*, 23 (11): 1869–1881.

Warner, J. and Campbell, D.A. (2000) 'Supply response in an agrarian economy with non-symmetric gender relations', *World Development*, 28 (7): 1327–1340.

World Bank (2001) *Engendering Development: Through Gender Equality in Rights, Resources and Voice*, Oxford: Oxford University Press.

Part 3

A fresh look at households

6 Conceptualizing care

Nancy Folbre

Introduction

Most people care about other people, to varying degrees. In more economistic terms, people often value the welfare of others, even when this might lower their own consumption. Large transfers of money and time that take place within the family, the community, and the state are particularly important for the welfare of dependents – children, the elderly, the sick, and the disabled. The quantity and quality of these transfers is shaped, in part, by individual and cultural negotiation.

What, exactly, is being negotiated? In everyday discussions the word 'care' is used in a variety of ways. Recent feminist research on care work offers many alternative definitions. But when care is used to describe direct provision of a service, it typically conveys a sense of emotional engagement and personal connection. This chapter emphasizes the need to distinguish motivations for care from consideration of who benefits from it and where it takes place. It also explains why the provision of care services differs from other forms of work.

Definitions

The meaning of care is often mediated by prepositions. To care for someone is different than to care about; 'to care' is distinct from 'take care' which is less specific than to 'take care of.' Two different verbs are often used in conjunction with care: giving and taking. The synonymity between care taking and care giving implies a two-way relationship, though we think of the former more often in conjunction with houses or gardens and the latter more often in conjunction with children or other dependents. Sometimes we exhort loved ones to 'take care of yourself' or just 'take care' as though it were there for the taking.

The word care generally carries both positive and negative valence, as defined in the *American Heritage Dictionary*. As a verb, it seems cheerful and engaged: '1. To be concerned or interested. 2. To provide needed assistance or watchful supervision'. As a noun, it seems gloomy: '1. A burdened state of mind, as that arising from heavy responsibilities; worry. 2. Mental suffering; grief'. The contrast emphasizes the larger argument many feminist scholars have made: the act of care itself can create a burden. To be carefree is, in a sense, to be liberated. To be careless, on the other hand, is to shirk responsibility. It seems hard to find the right balance between the two.

Motivations

Non-pecuniary motivations almost always play a role in the provision of care (Van Staveren 2001; Jochimsen 2003). Kari Waerness emphasizes the extent to which care departs from traditional definitions of work as an activity performed only for pay (Waerness 1987; Leira 1994). Emily Abel and Margaret Nelson write 'Caregiving is an activity encompassing both instrumental tasks and affective relations. Despite the classic Parsonian distinction between these two modes of behavior, caregivers are expected to provide love as well as labor, "caring for" while "caring about" ' (Abel and Nelson 1990).

Some care theorists go even further, suggesting that family care is so intensely personal and emotional that it should not be termed work. Even paid care often retains its personal quality, resisting 'complete commodification' (Gardiner 1997; Himmelweit 1999). For that reason, some argue, care should not even be considered labour (Jochimsen 2003). Care is often framed in ethical rather than economic terms, as a morally transcendent activity that women are more likely to embrace than men (Gilligan 1982; Noddings 1984). Care can be situated within a larger political analysis of rights and justice (Tronto 1987; Kittay 1999). The economics of care, however, remains underdeveloped.

All seemingly non-economic motivations for providing care services can be subsumed under the rubric of utility maximization. Individuals can derive utility either directly from the well-being of others or indirectly from 'doing the right thing'. Economists sometimes argue that women have more caring preferences than men. In the event of divorce, mothers often fight harder for child custody than fathers do, despite the economic burden it imposes (Fuchs 1988). Similarly, women may choose to specialize in care work, despite the lower wages it offers, because they derive non-pecuniary satisfaction from it (Filer 1981).

From this perspective, virtue always has its own reward. But this statement is true only by definition. There is no way to empirically test the claim that individuals maximize their utility if one presumes that whatever they do must represent maximization and whatever they maximize must be their utility. The number and variety of possible compensating differentials is infinite. One person may accept lower pay in a job because they enjoy risk, while another may accept lower pay because they dislike risk. Most people have particular preferences that affect their choice of jobs, but the salaries that are offered for a job are based on the overall supply of workers, not individual preferences.

Differences in the types of preferences that can motivate provision of care services have potentially important consequences. Care providers may care only about the happiness of a care recipient and not at all about their own happiness – what we could call perfectly sacrificial or selfless preferences. They may place a higher weight on others' happiness than their own, which we could call unselfish preferences. They may place a weight on other's happiness that is equal to or less than their own well-being. It is worth noting that the Christian bible's New Testament injunction to 'love thy neighbour as thyself' seems to ask only for equality of weights.

Altruistic preferences can take different forms as well as different weights. Care providers may place a higher priority on the well-being of recipients than their happiness, as in 'take your medicine' or 'it's for your own good' (Pollak 2003). Care providers may also value the process of providing care – they not only want to improve a care recipient's well-being but also receive a warm glow for being the ones who improve it (Andreoni 1989). Interdependent preferences complicate the story. The effort to make someone happy if they also want to make you happy can lead to coordination problems (Folbre and Goodin 2004).

People who provide care for others don't necessarily have altruistic preferences. They may act out of a sense of moral obligation, or simply to seek approval. They may simply derive pleasure from the care activity itself. Alternatively, they may provide care only in the hope of receiving a reward, either in the form of future reciprocity or actual payback. They may even be forced to provide services on pain of punishment.

We can list these different motivations from what might be termed the 'most intrinsic' to the most 'extrinsic' (or the least likely to be combined with intrinsic motivation) (Folbre and Weisskopf 1998).

- Coercion or threat of punishment;
- Expectation of pecuniary reward;
- Hope for reciprocity;
- Desire for social approval;
- Sense of obligation to or responsibility for care recipient;
- Concern for happiness or well-being of care recipient.

Many different types of motivation may coexist or interact with one another, and motivation is, of course, difficult to directly observe. But caring for others requires more than merely acting on a preference; it entails acting in such a way as to strengthen or reinforce a preference. It often involves commitment.

Beneficiaries of care

Care work often benefits others. Its third-party effects are often celebrated as the 'work of looking after the physical, psychological, emotional, and developmental needs of one or more other people' (Daly 2002). For this reason, care work is often assigned to the realm of reproduction rather than production. Maren Jochimsen writes that caring activities aim at 'the long-term maintenance, sustenance, and repair of these physical and social relationships which are indispensable for continuing human existence in a social context' (Jochimsen 2003: 11). But most forms of production ultimately contribute to reproduction. Is there any work that does not involve looking after others in some indirect, if not direct way?

Care work can and often is narrowed down to the care of dependents. Diemut Bubeck defines care as 'meeting a need that those in need could not possibly meet themselves' (Bubeck 1995). She aims to exclude provision of personal services to able-bodied adults, such as waiting hand-and-foot on men. But the substantive definition of dependency is hard to operationalize. Infants are dependent on others for survival, but children begin taking care of themselves (and their younger siblings) long before they attain formal autonomy. Likewise, many elderly individuals care for themselves and others part of the time.

Care work often goes beyond fulfillment of basic needs to develop the capabilities of its recipients – health, abilities, skills useful to themselves and others. The work of nurturing children at home or teaching them in school, for instance, contributes to their human capital (England and Folbre 1999; England *et al.* 2002). But while it is easy to conceptualize caring for children as a form of investment, the same may be said of care for adults – an activity that maintains existing human capital and also slows its inevitable (at least with current medical technology) depreciation.

Although children and other dependents are the most vulnerable recipients of care, it seems misleading to define care services by reference to them. The very term 'dependent' is misleading, insofar as it presumes its opposite, 'independent'. Most adults fit neither category; they are interdependent, providing and receiving care from friends and family. While the exchange of care services among adults may be less pressing than other types of care, it clearly affects daily routines and quality of life. The process of finding a partner and trying to develop a stable and satisfying relationship requires considerable effort, and many market services, ranging from speed-dating to couples-therapy, now promise to help meet such needs.

The concept of 'self-care' deserves consideration, especially in a world in which an increasing proportion of adults live alone. Activities such as eating, drinking, bathing, and grooming are socially necessary. People who cannot feed themselves or engage in other activities of daily living are considered disabled and require the assistance of other person. Grooming and manicuring services are often purchased in the market, suggesting that we should consider them productive activities when performed at home. Obesity, lack of exercise, and other health problems indicate that people do not always care for themselves as well as they should.

Institutional context

Care work that is done for pay clearly differs from that which takes place outside the market economy, if only because it is assigned an explicit market value. But how important is the distinction between paid and unpaid care work? The Marxian tradition has traditionally idealized production for use rather than exchange on the grounds that there is less separation between producer and consumer. No profit motive drives a wedge between the interests of owners and workers.

This aversion to commodification helps explain why some scholars argue that care should not be labelled work or labour, even if it is not exactly leisure.

But women often expect to receive a share of income earned by other household members in return for the care services they provide. Similarly, parents often expect to receive something in return for their transfers to children. The terms of these exchanges are not always the result of individual choices, but they are exchanges nonetheless, and not always equal ones (Folbre 1982). Family care givers sometimes feel exploited. They sometimes find it hard to persuade others to share their burden.

Some care researchers focus on unpaid care within the family or the community (Ward 1993). But the boundary between the family and the market is both variable and permeable, and care work often crosses it (Hochschild 2005; Zelizer 2005). Furthermore, not all non-market work involves direct care services. Housework activities such as vacuuming, doing laundry, mowing the lawn, or shopping involve little social or personal interaction.

As Table 6.1 illustrates, care services can take place in a variety of different institutional contexts on behalf of many different categories of people. Many forms of child and care of the elderly take place in the informal sector of the economy, paid for 'under the table' or deeply embedded in a family-like community network. Many paid care activities closely resemble unpaid care, and relationships of unequal power do not preclude mutual respect (Meagher 2002; Nelson and England 2002). Child care and elder care workers often form close personal relationships with their charges. Teachers get to know their students over the course of a year. Doctors and nurses develop long-term relationships with many of their patients.

Labour process

In this chapter, I define *direct* care services as those in which personal engagement and emotional connection are likely to affect the quantity or quality of services performed. I reserve the term *indirect* care services to describe other services that

Table 6.1 Examples of direct care work with different beneficiaries in different institutional contexts

	Children	*Elderly*	*Sick, Disabled*	*Adults (other than self)*	*Self*
Unpaid Family Work	breastfeeding, talking to, or playing with	feeding, bathing, comforting	feeding, bathing, comforting, administering medicine	counselling, nurturing	visiting doctor, exercising
Informal Market Work	nanny, babysitter, family day care provider	elder sitter, paid companion	home health care provider		
Paid Employment	child care worker, teacher pediatrician	elder care worker, gerontologist	nurse, nursing aide, doctor	counselor, nutritionist, yoga instructor	

are closely related to direct care, especially those that are likely to overlap with them – such as preparing and serving meals, or to be associated with being on call to provide care.

Harry Braverman used the term 'labor process' to call attention to the struggle between employers and workers over the exercise of skill and autonomy in paid employment (Braverman 1975). The labour process has often been defined in terms that seem more applicable to the production of goods than of services, with little attention to gender differences (Bowles and Edwards 1993: 45; Rogers 1999). But the term calls attention to the lived experience of work, and can encompass interactions between care managers, care providers, and care recipients in both paid and unpaid work activities.

Francesca Cancian and Stacy Oliker define caring as a combination of feelings and actions that 'provide responsively for an individual's personal needs or well-being, in a face-to-face relationship' (Cancian and Oliker 2000). This activity demands more than mere performance of emotional labour. Airline stewardesses are trained to make passengers feel welcome, reassured, safe, and willing to follow orders in the event of an emergency (Hochschild 1983). Likewise, sales personnel are instructed to behave in ways that will create some emotional resonance with customers – such as learning and using first names. What Cancian and Oliker describe is a process that involves actual, rather than merely performative emotional engagement.

The definition of care as a labour process in which emotional engagement plays an important role does not paint a bright line between what is care work and what is not. But it does provide a reasonable criterion for arraying different kinds of jobs along a continuum from those in which identity is irrelevant to those in which it is consequential. Parental care, perhaps the most person-specific direct care service, provides an archetype at one end of the spectrum. At the other end are paid care jobs that may involve person-specific knowledge and skills but only short-term engagement. (I disagree with Elisabetta Addis's (2003) description of care provided outside the household as not person-specific).

Implications for care recipients

Within the market economy, the offer of personal or family-like care services promises a commitment to high quality services. Advertising campaigns for hospitals and health insurance almost always include the word 'care'. Cigna, a major provider of health and retirement insurance, markets itself as 'a caring corporation'. Sheraton Hotel key card holders have featured the question 'Who's Taking Care of You?' (presumably, the hotel). What was once customer service at ATT Corporation is now called customer care.

Even an industry as seemingly impersonal as transportation uses this language. When I bought a Subaru in 2002 I received a letter welcoming me to the Subaru family. A prominent car rental company has the slogan 'Avis Cares'. In 2006, some Exxon gasoline pumps featured a 'We Care' slogan with a toll-free number that customers could call. The phrases 'we care', 'we care more', and 'we care about you completely' have all been trademarked (no one has yet trademarked the phrase 'we don't believe you really care').

Personal networks can provide information that improves the quality of all transactions in which the quality of services is difficult to ascertain (Dimaggio and Louch 1998; Granovetter 2005). Consumers (or clients, or patients, or students) seeking direct care services often hope for some degree of emotional engagement – at least enough to guarantee respect, affection, and concern:

> It may not matter who…picks up your rubbish bag in the street [but]it does matter who wipes your bum…and that ought to be the same person day in and day out because it's a very personal service and you have to trust that person.
>
> (Wistow *et al.* 1996: 29)

Most individuals interviewing a direct care provider for a job tending to their children or other family members will choose someone who they believe will have some affinity for the person to be cared for. Affinity does not necessarily imply close emotional bonding or invasive attachment. But for individuals who are disabled and truly dependent, the ideal caregiver is one for whom the needs of the care recipient are 'transparent' and take precedence over other demands (Kittay 1999).

Those who need care most are often those least able to exercise decision making power. Even competent adult consumers may not be the best judges of quality when purchasing services designed to increase their capabilities rather than meet immediate needs. Care that makes a recipient 'feel good' is not always the best form of care. A teacher's job is to educate students, not necessarily to make them happy. Doctors and nurses aim to improve health in the long run, not just comfort in the short run. Therapists try to help people learn to cope with their problems, not always to cheer them up.

Emotional engagement in the form of empathy or sympathy elicits helping behaviour (Batson 1990). Reported satisfaction with medical care is strongly related to the emotional content of interaction, and there is some evidence that health outcomes are also affected (Duffy 1992). Indeed, the positive effects of believing that one is being cared for may help explain so-called placebo effects in which patients report benefits from sugar pills or surgery that has not actually taken place.

Both parents and students often try to win the affection of teachers, recognizing that this may affect the level of effort that is forthcoming. Students benefit from developing their emotional intelligence – the sense when they need help from others and the ability to obtain such help, the ability to collaborate with others (Goleman 1995). Teachers try to develop these skills in their students, as well as those more easily measured on standardized exams.

Emotional engagement can enhance the beneficial effects of professional standards and cultural norms, helping protect dependents from abuse or neglect. But emotional engagement also has liabilities for care recipients or consumers because it limits the availability of substitutes. Even if parents are abusive, social workers may be hesitant to remove a child from the home for fear that separation will be even more harmful. The intensity of personal and emotional contact can make it difficult to even imagine substitutes. Money can't buy love, and love often requires face time, physical contact, interaction, engagement, visible commitment.

Conventional models of home production assume perfect substitutability between money and time, as if between any other two items in a choice set (Gronau 1977). In the real world, however, money and time are less than perfect substitutes. Wealthy parents can hire a nanny to take on some care responsibilities. But if they delegate too much to a nanny they may fail to develop meaningful or reciprocal relationships with their children. A husband who works overtime at the office can send his wife flowers and buy her jewellery to make up for the fact that he is never home for dinner. But such trade-offs often grow steep and wear thin.

The level of substitutability among purchased services and between family-provided and market-purchases services may reflect biological dictates. Young monkeys raised with ample food but no physical affection fare worse than those raised with insufficient food but ample nurturance. Infants who lack a stable relationship with a committed caregiver often fail to thrive (Hrdy 1999). The positive impacts of emotional connection on care recipients help explain why high turnover rates in childcare and elder care are worrisome. But many activities that we never imagined could be sold in the market are now available, suggesting that substitutability among providers of care services are shaped at least in part by social norms and economic pressures. Profound moral and philosophical questions also come into play: There are some things money should not buy, even if it can (Radin 1996).

Implications for care providers

Care providers also experience both an up and a down side to emotional engagement. Working in close proximity with individuals who often need their help creates or strengthens connections in unanticipated ways. Many workers 'acquire sentiment' for their clients, their fellow-workers, even their employers (Akerlof 1982). But the extent and intensity of the sentiment seem greater for those engaged in provision of direct care.

As one grandmother who became involved in caring for her grandson put it, 'I didn't expect this and I didn't want it, but my heart's involved now'. (Associated Press 2002) Paid caregivers often describe a similar process: 'I love them. That's all, you can't help it' (Stone 2000).

Emotional engagement can provide direct satisfaction, the feeling that one is doing something that is both enjoyable and worthwhile. Many ethnographic studies of care workers often emphasize this dimension of intrinsic reward, which clearly represents a form of psychic income. Even registered nurses who are dissatisfied with their working conditions report considerable job satisfaction (Buerhaus *et al.* 2006). On the other hand, the warm glow from providing care services does not always last. In many occupations, it tends to burn out.

Emotional attachment puts care workers in a vulnerable position, discouraging them from demanding higher wages or changes in working conditions that might adversely affect on care recipients. A parent of a small child represents an extreme case. Unless one parent enjoys cooperation from another parent who is willing to assume virtually complete responsibility, there is 'no exit' for the job (Alstott 2004). Exit from paid care jobs is far easier, but can nonetheless prove sticky. Childcare workers become attached to the toddlers they see every day. Nurses empathize with their patients. Teachers worry about their students. Evidence suggests that individuals in jobs requiring more intellectual skill get successively 'smarter' (Kohn and Schooler 1983). Similarly, in jobs requiring care, individuals may become more caring.

In a sense, care for others both requires and encourages less attention to self-interest. Grace Clement raises the possibility that the ethic of care may be 'less a creation of women than an unjust demand upon women, as it requires women to take care of men and men's interests at the expense of themselves and their own interests' (Clement 1996). As Eva Kittay puts it, 'by virtue of caring for someone who is dependent, the dependency worker herself becomes vulnerable' (Kittay 1999). Specialization in provision of care is costly. The time that women devote to the care of family members lowers their lifetime earnings and reduces their economic security (Rose and Hartmann 2004). Employed workers in caring occupations generally pay a penalty, earning less than workers with similar qualifications in occupations that are otherwise relatively similar (England *et al.* 1994; England *et al.* 2002).

Owners, employers, and managers are less likely to come into direct contact with clients or patients than are care workers. Therefore, they can generally engage in cost-cutting strategies without 'feeling' their consequences. They may even feel confident that adverse effects of their decisions on clients will be buffered by workers' willingness to sacrifice. Workers may respond to cutbacks in staffing levels by intensifying their effort or agreeing to work overtime. Emotional hostage effects can turn workers into prisoners of love, reluctant to walk out on strike or even to leave an occupation in which they know they are sorely needed.

Such buffering effects may, however, be short lived. Experienced nurses and teachers are often reluctant to make a career changes when they are close to retirement, but burnout may lower the effort they provide. Furthermore, deteriorating working conditions discourage the younger generation from entering these professions.

Direct care as a joint product

Many of the services that care workers provide are, in a sense, co-produced with consumers. The quality of an output such as health or skill often depends more on the relationship between provider and recipient than on the individual characteristics of either. Child care providers must cajole and convince children to cooperate. Teachers must motivate students to do their homework. Doctors and nurses, as well as elder care workers, must persuade patients to change their eating or exercise habits or to take medication. This motivational work may be as important to success in care provision as other, more easily measurable forms of skill.

The outputs of care work are often multidimensional. One aspect of teacher performance can be measured by changes in students' scores on standardized exams. But such measures do not capture the extent to which a teacher succeeds in instilling motivation or becoming an independent problem-solver. Likewise, hospital performance can be measured by the speed with which patients exit the hospital. Long run physical and mental health outcomes are far more difficult to isolate.

Peer effects also come into play. The number of other children and the type of behaviour they engage affects the quality of childcare services as much if not more than the credentials of the provider. A mentally healthy elderly person in a nursing home where a high percentage of residents suffer from dementia is likely to be adversely affected. Students learn from others students; selective schools and colleges can charge higher tuition than institutions with identical teaching staff in part because parents recognize the value of such peer effects (Winston 1999).

The central role of personal and social relationships in establishing care quality means that disruptions or discontinuities of care often have adverse consequences. Most studies of child care and elder care call attention to the negative effects of high turnover rates. Changing schools often lowers young children's chances of enjoying academic success. In many areas of the economy, consumers benefit from more choices. But if increased choices lead to increased disruption the benefits can be neutralized.

Care as a non-standard non-quite commodity

The emotional connections that characterize care services help explain why these services do not easily conform to standard economic assumptions: consumers lack sovereignty because both information and choices are restricted. Workers operate in a complex motivational environment in which wages may exercise less influence than working conditions. Table 6.2 illustrates the many possible combinations of consumer and worker characteristics in matrix format. The rows categorizing consumer needs convey the complexity of the demand side. The columns categorizing worker motivations convey the complexity of the supply side.

Cell number 1 represents the combination of standard assumptions for both consumers and workers. Exchanges of this type conform to the stylized consumer and worker featured in introductory economics textbooks. Put in more poetic terms, 'it's as if the buyer and the seller were in plastic bags' (Hyde 1983:10). At the opposite end of the diagonal, cell number 9 represents the combination of factors emphasized as important to direct care work. Care recipients need personal, emotionally attuned attention; care providers are intrinsically motivated to provide such attention. Here the buyer and seller are clearly touching one another. Between these two extremes lie a variety of permutations.

Table 6.2 Matrix illustrating important differences between direct care and other forms of work in terms of worker motivations and consumer needs

Needs of consumers	Motivation of workers		
	Primarily seeking pecuniary reward	*Motivated in part by obligation or sense of social expectation or hope of reciprocity*	*Also motivated in part by genuine affection and concern*
Certain of own impersonal needs	1. conventional transactions in idealized competitive market	2. many market transactions; some volunteer work, some family work such as housework	3. some market transactions, much volunteer work, some family work such as housework
Uncertain of own needs as a result of information problems	4. many transactions, esp. in health and education	5. many market transactions, esp. in health and education, much family work	6. some market transactions esp. health and education, some family work
Needing personal connection and emotional engagement	7. some transactions in market	8. many market transactions, especially in health and education; some volunteer and family work	9. direct care services in both market and family (paid and unpaid)

Sometimes consumers or recipients may need or long for services that are being provided only in return for a wage, but are not able to obtain these, as in cell 7. A child's feelings may be hurt if the new child care teacher doesn't remember her name. An elderly person may feel hurt that a home health care worker is in a hurry to accomplish her specified task and move on. A student in a large university class might want a word of personal encouragement, but realize that the instructor has no desire to give it. A patient in a clinic may be on the verge of revealing a personal problem, but decide that the doctor will not be interested in it.

On the other hand, sometimes consumers or recipients might be perfectly happy with completely impersonal services, while their service providers are not, as in cell 3. A child care worker who stays late to tend to a child whose parent has been delayed may feel hurt when no apology is offered. An elder care worker who has grown attached to a particular person may be fired because her attachment seems emotionally intrusive. A teacher who wants to motivate students to learn is put off when they ask 'will this be on the test?' A doctor who tries to change her patient's eating habits may be rebuked with a demand for medication that could solve the problem.

As these examples suggest, the interaction is complicated by the presence of third parties. Parents are typically paying for child care and education, not the children who receive it. Insurance companies are paying for health care and elder care, not those who directly need it. Wage earners are the direct providers of paid care services, but they work in environments largely shaped by owners and managers, who face very different incentives.

The other cells in the matrix represent combinations which conform neither to standard assumptions nor to the definition of direct care services. Consumers may simply lack the information that they need to make good choices (as in row 2); if workers in a bureaucratic organization are paid only to fulfill a narrowly prescribed function, as in column 1, they may not be motivated to provide that information. Workers may feel that they are striving to meet professional standards and social expectations, rather than just working for a wage, as in column 2. If consumers care only about the price they pay, as in row 1, they will feel under appreciated.

The matrix helps explain the limits of the traditional Marxist concept of 'commodification'. Any time a service is bought or sold it becomes, in technical terms, a 'commodity' (Radin 1996). The *American Heritage Dictionary* defines a commodity as 'something useful that can be turned to commercial advantage'. The assumption that all non-pecuniary need and motivation is stripped away is conveyed by the characteristics of cell 1. But the fact that many market exchanges fall outside of cell 1 illustrates the important point that such exchanges are not always impersonal or heartless.

Still, the unfortunate consequences of what has been termed commodification are poignantly illustrated by cell 7, in which a consumer or care recipient needs or wants something more than what is provided by paid worker. Consumers may also find themselves disappointed in cells 4, and 8, and workers may feel under utilized and alienated in cells 2, 3, and 6. We need a term to describe what happens when markets fail to establish the kinds of connections that individuals on either the demand side or the supply side would like to make – perhaps 'over-commodification'. Outside the market, we sometimes call such a mismatch disappointment or heartache.

Mixing and matching

Direct services represent cases of 'contested and incomplete commodification' (Jochimsen 2003: 148). In her beautiful exploration of cultural intersections between the intimate and the commercial, Viviana Zelizer argues that we should reject the presumption that these always represent separate, hostile worlds and the presumption that they are completely identical (Zelizer 2005). She argues instead for appreciation of the possibility of good matches between the two. This chapter makes a similar point in more analytical terms. We might define a 'good match' as one in which the needs of consumers and the motivations of workers complement one another.

This poses a problem of institutional design that is far more complex than the answer to a simply binary question such as 'family or market' or 'for love or for money?' As British researcher Clare Ungerson puts it, 'The social, political, and economic contexts in which payments for care operate and the way in which payments for care are themselves organized are just as likely to transform relationships as the existence of payments themselves' (Ungerson 1997:377).

Advances in institutional and behavioural economics offer some important insights into the impact of social institutions on the motivations of workers and the needs of consumers. Few individuals demand or supply care services in a spot market based only on immediate exchange. Almost all transfers of care services take place within the context of either explicit or implicit contractual arrangements. We need to pay closer attention to the ways in which the terms of these contracts are negotiated.

Acknowledgements

This chapter grew out of a presentation at the XVIII Workshop on Gender and Economics of the University International School of Economic Research at the University of Siena, July 5–7, 2005. I gratefully acknowledge the comments and criticisms of the organizers and participants.

References

Abel, E. K. and Nelson, M. K. (1990) 'Circles of Care: An Introductory Essay', in E. K. Abel and M. K. Nelson (eds) *Circles of Care. Work and Identity in Women's Lives*. New York: State University of New York Press. pp. 4–34.

Addis, E. (2003) 'Unpaid and Paid Caring Work in the Reform of Welfare States', in A. Picchio (ed.) *Unpaid Work and the Economy. A Gender Analysis of the Standards of Living*. New York: Routledge. pp. 189–223.

Akerlof, G. (1982) 'Labor Contracts as Partial Gift Exchange', *Quarterly Journal of Economics*, 97 (4): 543–570.

Alstott, A. (2004) *No Exit: What Parents Owe Their Children and What Societies Owe Parents*. New York: Oxford University Press.

Andreoni, J. (1989) 'Impure Altruism and Donations to Public Goods: A Theory of Warm-Glow Giving', *Economic Journal*, 100 (401): 464–477.

Associated Press (2002) 'Feds Study Grandparents as Caregivers', New York Times, 06/04/02.

Batson, D. C. (1990) 'How Social an Animal? The Human Capacity for Caring', *American Psychologist*, 45 (3): 336–346.

Bowles, S. and Edwards, R. (1993) *Understanding Capitalism. Competition, Command and Change in the U.S. Economy*. New York: Harper Collins.

Braverman, H. (1975) *Labor and Monopoly Capital. The Degradation of Work in the Twentieth Century*. New York: Monthly Review Press.

Bubeck, D. (1995) *Care, Gender, Justice*. Oxford: Clarendon Press.

Buerhaus, P. I., Ulrich, B. T., Norman, L. and Dittus, R. (2006) 'State of the Registered Nurse Workforce in the United States', *Nursing Economics Journal*, 24 (1): 6–12.

Cancian, F. M. and Oliker, S. J. (2000) *Caring and Gender*. Walnut Creek: Alta Mira Press.

Clement, G. (1996) *Care, Autonomy, and Justice. Feminism and the Ethic of Care*. New York: Westview Press.

Daly, M. (ed.) (2002) *Care Work: The Quest for Security*. Geneva: International Labour Organization.

114   *Nancy Folbre*

Dimaggio, P. and Louch, H. (1998) 'Socially Embedded Consumer Transactions: For What Kinds of Purchases Do People Most Often Use Networks', *American Sociological Review*, 63 (5): 619–637.

Duffy, J. R. (1992) 'The Impact of Nurse Caring on Patient Outcomes', in D. A. Gaut (ed.) *The Presence of Caring in Nursing*. New York: National League for Nursing.

England, P. and Folbre, N. (1999) 'The Cost of Caring', *Annals of the American Academy of Political and Social Sciences*, 561: 39–51.

England, P., Herbert, M. A., Kilbourne, B. S., Reid, L. L., Megdal, McCreary, L. (1994) 'The Gendered Valuation of Occupations and Skills: Earnings in 1980 Census Occupations', *Social Forces*, 73 (1): 65–99.

England, P., Budig, M. and Folbre, N. (2002) 'Wages of Virtue: The Relative Pay of Care Work', *Social Problems*, 49 (4): 455–473.

Filer, R. K. (1981) 'The Influence of Affective Human Capital on the Wage Equation', *Research in Labor Economics*, 4 (1981): 367–416.

Folbre, N. (1982) 'Exploitation Comes Home: A Critique of the Marxian Theory of Family Labor', *Cambridge Journal of Economics*, 6 (4): 317–329.

Folbre, N. and Goodin, R. (2004) 'Revealing Altruism', *Review of Social Economy*, 62 (1): 1–25.

Folbre, N. and Weisskopf, T. (1998) 'Did Father Know Best? Families, Markets and the Supply of Caring Labor', in A. Ben-Ner and L. Putterman (eds) *Economics, Values and Organization*. Cambridge: Cambridge University Press. pp. 171–205.

Fuchs, V. (1988) *Women's Quest for Economic Equality*. Cambridge: Harvard University Press.

Gardiner, J. (1997) *Gender, Care and Economics*. Basingstoke: Macmillan.

Gilligan, C. (1982) *In a Different Voice: Psychological Theory and Women's Development*. Cambridge: Harvard University Press.

Goleman, D. (1995) *Emotional Intelligence*. New York: Bantam.

Granovetter, M. (2005) 'The Impact of Social Structure on Economic Outcomes', *Journal of Economic Perspectives*, 19 (1): 33–50.

Gronau, R. (1977) 'Leisure, Home Production and Work—The Theory of the Allocation of Time Revisited', *Journal of Political Economy*, 85 (6): 1099–1123.

Himmelweit, S. (1999) 'Caring Labor', in R. Steinberg and D. Figart (eds) *The Annals of the American Academy of Political Science*, 561 (1): 27–38.

Hochschild, A. (1983) *The Managed Heart. Commercialization of Human Feeling*. Berkeley: University of California Press.

Hochschild, A. (2005) 'Rent-a-Mom and Other Services: Markets, Meanings, and Emotions', *International Journal of Work Organization and Emotion*, 1 (1): 74–86.

Hrdy, S. B. (1999) *Mother Nature: A History of Mothers, Infants, and Natural Selection*. New York: Pantheon Books.

Hyde, L. (1983) *The Gift. Imagination and the Erotic Life of Property*. New York: Vintage.

Jochimsen, M. (2003) *Integrating Caring Activities and Economic Science*. New York: Springer.

Kittay, E. F. (1999) *Love's Labor. Essays on Women, Equality, and Dependency*. New York: Routledge.

Kohn, M. L. and Schooler, C. (1983) *Work and Personality: An Inquiry Into the Impact of Social Stratification*. Norwood, New Jersey: Ablex.

Leira, A. (1994) 'Concepts of Caring: Loving, Thinking, and Doing', *Social Service Review*, 68 (2): 185–201.

Meagher, G. (2002) 'Is it Wrong to Pay for Housework', *Hypatia*, 17 (2): 52–66.

Nelson, J. A. and England, P. (2002) 'Feminist Philosophies of Love and Work', *Hypatia*, 17(2): 1–18.

Noddings, N. (1984) *A Feminine Approach to Ethics and Moral Education*. Berkeley: University of California Press.

Pollak, R. (2003) 'Gary Becker's Contributions to Family and Household Economics', *Review of Economics of the Household*, 1 (1): 111–141.

Radin, M. (1996) *Contested Commodities*. Cambridge, MA: Harvard University Press.

Rogers, J. K. (1999) 'Deskilled and Devalued. Changes in the Labor Process in Temporary Clerical Work', in M. Wardell, T. L. Steiger and P. Meiksins (eds) *Rethinking the Labor Process*. Albany: State University of New York Press. pp. 53–78.

Rose, S. J. and Hartmann, H. I. (2004) *Still a Man's Labor Market: The Long-Term Earnings Gap*. Washington, DC: The Institute for Women's Policy Research.

Stone, D. (2000) 'Caring by the Book', in M. H. Meyer (ed.) *Care Work. Gender, Labor, and the Welfare State*. New York: Routledge. pp. 89–111.

Tronto, J. (1987) 'Beyond Gender Difference to a Theory of Care', *Signs: Journal of Women in Culture and Society*, 12 (4): 644–663.

Ungerson, C. (1997) 'Social Politics and the Commodification of Care', *Social Politics*, 4 (3): 377.

Van Staveren, I. (2001) *The Values of Economics. An Aristotelian Perspective*. New York: Routledge.

Waerness, K. (1987) 'On the Rationality of Caring', in A. S. Sassoon (ed.) *Women and the State*. London: Hutchinson. pp. 207–234.

Ward, D. (1993) 'The Kin Care Trap: The Unpaid Labor of Long Term Care', *Socialist Review*, 23 (2): 83–106.

Winston, G. C. (1999) 'Subsidies, Hierarchy, and Peers: The Awkward Economics of Higher Education', *Journal of Economic Perspectives*, 13 (1): 13–36.

Wistow, G., Knapp, M., Hardy, B., Forder, J., Kendall, J. and Manning, R. (1996) *Social Care Markets: Progress and Prospects*. Buckingham: Open University Press.

Zelizer, V. (2005) *The Purchase of Intimacy*. Princeton, NJ: Princeton University Press.

7 Gender and household decision-making

Shelly Lundberg

Introduction

Families and households provide the context in which important non-market transactions between men and women take place. Partners in a marital or de facto union and their children generally co-reside and spend time together, and this proximity may yield benefits in the form of love, companionship, and sexual pleasure. Family members also pool resources to a greater or lesser extent; pooling permits the exploitation of economies of scale in household services and provides insurance in the face of individual income risks. Children and investments in children are often treated by economists as household 'public goods' valued by both parents, and other household-produced goods and services contribute to the comfort and health of all members and maintain their productivity. The contributions that men and women make to a joint family enterprise determine, to a large extent, the material wellbeing of adults and children. The gender division of labour in this family provisioning is also the principal element of distinct economic roles for men and women.

Economic analysis of the family has received substantial (and growing) scholarly attention since the work of Gary Becker in the 1970s, but the field still seems in its infancy, given the breadth and complexity of the subject matter. The organization of families and the economic roles they play have varied over time, space, and stage of market development. Give and take between men and women in families is multi-dimensional and evolves as adults age and children are born and achieve independence. However, gender specialization in economic activities within the family is widespread and has some common elements, in particular primary female responsibility for the care of children. That there is a link between a mother's commitment to her children and wholesale female disadvantage has been asserted by many family and gender analysts.

Households need not combine men and women and may include several generations, but the importance of heterosexual unions and resulting offspring as the archetypical economic family make this a logical place to start in exploring the significance of gender in the economics of the household. Though traditional models of the family treat a married couple with children as a single decision-making agent with unitary preferences, non-unitary models have allowed economists to investigate distribution within the household, including possible gender inequality, and to conceptually track individual men and women along a life-cycle path that includes transitions between family types.

My intention here is to focus on collective and bargaining models of a married/cohabiting couple/family and the role that gender per se plays in these models – in particular, what is the relationship between a gendered division of labour and the relative wellbeing of men and women? The simple versions of these models are well-known, but recent attempts to extend them to an intertemporal context have yielded new insights. In particular, the ability of men and women to enter into binding intertemporal agreements is key to maintaining a gendered division of labour. In the absence of complete contracts, individuals face incentives to act strategically that may impair efficiency and affect distributional outcomes: this general point has important implications in families. It also appears that extra-household factors such as social norms regarding appropriate gender roles and institutional constraints can play a role in both restricting and enforcing agreements between family members.

The family: changing economic paradigms

The traditional economic approach to modeling family behavior is now commonly known as the unitary model. The unitary model begins with a two-person household, consisting of a husband (m) and a wife (f), making joint decisions about consumption and time allocation. Samuelson (1956) shows that if the spouses agree to maximize a family social welfare function, subject to a pooled family budget constraint, then the family's expenditure pattern would look like the expenditure pattern of a utility-maximizing individual. This implies, conveniently, that family demands will possess all the standard properties of individual demand functions and depend only on prices and total family income.

Suppose that the joint utility of the couple depends upon consumption of a household public good, G, that is produced with inputs of the husband's and/or wife's time, l_m and l_f, and market goods c_m and c_f whose price is normalized to one. The husband and wife each possesses a time endowment of T, and devote all time not engaged in household production to market work at fixed wage rates w_i, for $i = m, f$. The unitary model assumes that the couple agrees to maximize $U(c_m, c_f, G)$ subject to the pooled budget constraint $c_m + c_f = y_m + y_f + w_m(T - l_m) + w_f(T - l_f)$ and the household production function $G = g(l_m, l_f)$. The household production function is often assumed to take the simple form $G = h_m l_m + h_f l_f$. The couple's demand for c_m, c_f and G, and their choices regarding time inputs into the production of G, will depend upon the price of his time and her time (and therefore upon individual wage rates), but on only the sum of their nonlabor incomes y rather than on individual incomes (y_m, y_f).

The unitary framework has been criticized on both conceptual and practical grounds. First, it departs from the economist's preferred methodological individualism and is unhelpful in examining the formation and dissolution of families and the distribution of resources within them. Second, empirical evidence has been accumulating that is inconsistent with unitary demands. Several alternatives have been suggested, including non-cooperative bargaining models (Lommerud 1997; Lundberg and Pollak 1994), cooperative bargaining models (McElroy and Horney 1981; Manser and Brown 1980; Lundberg and Pollak 1993), and a 'collective' approach that assumes couples jointly choose an efficient outcome on the utility-possibilities frontier (Chiappori 1988; 1992). What these approaches have in common is that they begin by assigning preferences to individual family members, rather than a 'consensus' utility function to the family as a whole. For the couple discussed on the previous page, a non-unitary model begins with individual preferences $U^m(c_m, G)$ and $U^f(c_f, G)$.[1] For our purposes, one implication of this paradigm shift is that it permits the analysis of gender inequality in a life-cycle context by maintaining individual identity within families.

Gender, bargaining power, and intrahousehold distribution

Threat points: alternatives matter

Gender does not play an explicit role in the early marital bargaining models, which present the joint decision-making problem of a household consisting of two agents denoted m and f. In McElroy and Horney, the couple plays a cooperative bargaining game with a Nash solution, maximizing a 'utility-gain product function' similar to:

$$N = [U^m(c_m, G) - T^m(y_m, y_f, w_m, w_f, h_m, h_f; \alpha_m)]$$
$$[U^f(c_f, G) - T^f(y_m, y_f, w_m, w_f, h_m, h_f; \alpha_f)] \tag{7.1}$$

where $U^k(c_k, G)$ is the marital utility of agent k as a function of home and market goods consumption and T^k is the threat point of individual k and represents the best that he or she could do outside the household. The indirect utility T of the agent k's best alternative is a function of wage rates, household productivity parameters, the (exogenous) non-market incomes of husband and wife, and a vector of shift parameters that reflect opportunities outside the marriage (α_k) such as remarriage market conditions.[2] In the cooperative bargaining framework of Manser and Brown (1980), the threat points are specified as the expected utility from search for a new partner.

Though the agents are identified as 'husband' and 'wife', in these 'divorce-threat' marital bargaining models the two agents are interchangable. Maximization of the Nash product function produces an equilibrium on the utility-possibility frontier that is symmetric with respect to the agents' threat points. However, the market and social alternatives available outside marriage may have a distinct gender dimension. A gender-biased shift in the expected wellbeing of divorced men and women – for example, an increase in the ratio of men to women in the remarriage market – will shift the threat points and change the relative utilities of married men and women, in this case to the advantage of women. If women face discrimination in the labour market, their potential earnings if divorced will be lower than those of their husbands and this will, *ceteris paribus*, reduce women's relative bargaining power (and their relative wellbeing) within marriage.

An alternative to the divorce threat approach is to postulate a fallback position for the couple that does not involve marital dissolution. Lundberg and Pollak (1993) present a model in which the threat points are defined by a non-cooperative game within the family. Husband and wife make voluntary contributions to household public goods, using income that they control independently. The outcome of this game is not neutral with respect to redistributions between husband and wife because they make contributions to separate public goods, to which they have been assigned exclusive responsibility by socially prescribed gender roles. In the 'separate spheres' equilibrium, therefore, the husband decides unilaterally how much he will contribute to household public good 1, and the wife decides on her contribution to good 2. These corner solutions ensure that the couple's threat point, and therefore the cooperative equilibrium, depends upon who controls income and other resources within the family, even if this differs from the distribution of resources that would ensue if the couple were to divorce. In formal terms, the Nash product function of the separate spheres model looks like (7.1), but the parameters α_i, which represent the conditions facing divorced partners, would be replaced by a vector δ_i, which characterizes the terms of a non-cooperative focal point for the married couple.

The 'collective' model of household decision making also assumes that family members are able to reach an efficient allocation of resources but, instead of following an axiomatic approach such as Nash bargaining, characterizes the family objective function as a weighted average of individual utilities: $\mu U^m + (1 - \mu)U^f$. The 'sharing rule' μ is in general a function of prices and individual incomes and, based on the intuition of the bargaining models, extra-marital conditions, so that $\mu = \mu(y_m, y_f, w_m, w_f, h_m, h_f, \alpha_m, \alpha_f)$. This framework generates some useful testable implications for the structure of household demands, but the role of gender in family decision making is more readily explored using bargaining models. The threat points, with their explicit alternatives-to-agreement interpretation, provide a mechanism for incorporating the different opportunities of men and women.

Sources of female disadvantage: a conventional view

Marital bargaining models have been used extensively during the past couple of decades to explore gender inequality. A World Bank report (2001) reviewed the literature and asserted that 'the evidence on determinants of intrahousehold resource allocation and investments makes a strong case for targeting interventions by gender—to promote gender equality and more effective development' (World Bank 2001: 163). Women, it is argued, have relatively poor prospects outside of marriage and experience limits on their ability to act independently within households, and therefore possess relatively little bargaining power within marriage. In some societies, restrictions on women's mobility, market work, ownership of property, and political activity are ubiquitous and provide a clear rationale for assertions that women are in a poor position in marital bargaining.

In wealthy societies, it is possible to argue that high rates of poverty in female-headed households are linked, through the divorce-threat bargaining framework, to unmeasured female disadvantage within married couple households. The proximate sources of gender inequality in this case are threefold: women have lower market wages than men, and therefore poorer earning prospects after divorce; women's post-divorce earnings must be shared with children, for whom they often have primary custodial responsibility; women have poor remarriage prospects relative to divorced men.[3] All of these factors reduce T^f relative to T^m in a fairly straightforward way, and therefore shift cooperatively-bargained marital utility along the utility-possibility frontier in a direction favourable to men.

Bargaining power discrepancies between men and women appear to emerge from a single source – the gender division of labour in the family and in particular the allocation of primary responsibility for the care of children to mothers. Potential market wages are reduced by lost experience and job tenure due to labour force withdrawals to care for children, by the double demands on working mothers, and by statistical discrimination by employers who infer job instability or reduced productivity from the maternal responsibilities, current or future, of their female employees. The maternal custody standard has been based, at least recently, on the mother's role as principal caregiver and the presumed benefits to children of maintaining this relationship. A woman's attractiveness in the marriage market is significantly reduced by the presence of children from a former partnership, and divorced men are much more likely to remarry than divorced women.

The implicit bargaining model of marriage that lies behind this analysis, however, is very much a sub-game, and takes as given the matching of individuals in marriage markets, premarital investments in home and market skills, and the sequence of negotiations over time in which a couple is likely to engage.[4] The importance of motherhood in generating systematic gender inequality is also influenced by institutions and policies that determine the property rights and resources of men and women (e.g. divorce laws, child support awards and enforcement), and which might reasonably be regarded as endogenous with respect to equilibrium family structure and functioning.[5] One key issue is how conventional patterns of gender specialization arise in equilibrium.

Gender specialization

Women in families tend to specialize in household production, including the care of children, and therefore face relatively poor alternatives outside their current partnership. In a bargaining or collective model of family decision making, this implies that women are disadvantaged in the intrahousehold distribution of resources. The traditional economic model that generates this scenario relies on a series of assertions about the gender division of labour: that specialization by family members is efficient, that task specialization should be assigned by gender, that women should be assigned to the household and men to market tasks and, finally, that individuals who specialize in household production necessarily face less attractive alternatives to cooperative bargaining with a partner.

Specialization by family members is efficient

The textbook model of marital gains to specialization and exchange is directly analogous to international trade models of comparative advantage and gains from trade. If a two-person family produces and consumes two types of output – market and non-market – and one family member is relatively more productive in one sector than the other, then at least one member will be completely specialized, and devote all of his or her time to either market or non-market production. This result does not follow directly from the model in the first section; we might expect to see an interior solution in the production of the household public good if $G = g(l_m, l_f)$ is characterized by decreasing marginal productivity of the two inputs. However, the standard assumption is that the household production times of the spouses are perfect substitutes, quality-adjusted, so that $G = g(h_m l_m + h_f l_f)$. Becker provides the justification:

> Since all persons are assumed to be intrinsically identical, they supply basically the same kind of time to the household and market sectors. Therefore, the effective time of different members would be perfect substitutes even if they accumulate different amounts of household capital.
>
> Becker (1981: 32)

Becker also emphasizes that the sexual division of labour depends not just on intrinsic (biological) differences but also on specialized investments in human capital, and that small amounts of market discrimination or biological differences can give rise to large differences in equilibrium comparative advantage.

The assumption that husbands and wives provide identical (quality-adjusted) inputs to household production is crucial to the efficient specialization result and to the 'tipping' equilibria in which small initial differences between men and women lead to very different allocations of time between home and market. If home production largely consists of childcare, and if there are advantages to joint production of childcare and other home-centered activities such as cooking and cleaning, this may not be unreasonable. A couple of refinements might lead us in the direction of an interior solution involving substantial inputs of both husband and wife's time to home production, however. One is the recognition that household production includes a diverse set of tasks requiring very different skills, including yard work and repair, accounting and bill-paying, cooking and shopping.[6] Even childcare involves many different activities – from sports coaching to clothes shopping – that become more varied as children mature. If time spent in household production is an aggregate of many different activities requiring different skills, then the argument that husbands and wives provide identical inputs becomes implausible, as does the rationale for extreme specialization. Second, the return to childcare may include not only physical and cognitive child outcomes, but also qualities such as parental attachment and social development to which both parents can make distinct contributions. This may be particularly true for couples with male children, since fathers are generally believed to play a unique role in the social and emotional development of boys.

Task specialization should be assigned by gender

Even if extreme specialization of family members in either market or household tasks is efficient, this does not necessarily imply that gender should be the basis for assigning individuals to the market or domestic sphere. Indeed, if individuals vary in innate skills or preferences that would predispose them to one set of tasks or the other, it could be argued that these individual propensities should determine who does what within the family, rather than a characteristic which may (or may not) be correlated with these propensities, such as gender. Several researchers have developed models in which gender task assignment serves as a coordinating device, either in the labour market or the marriage market, but which are neutral with respect to male and female roles.

Francois (1998) constructs a model of gender discrimination in the labour market that rests on the organization of men and women into two-person households where there are potential gains from trade if one person holds a 'good' efficiency-wage job and the other provides household services. Men and women are identical, but a discriminating equilibrium exists in which profit-maximizing firms prefer to hire members of one sex over members of the other, since household specialization reduces the wage that needs to be paid to ensure no shirking. The treatment of men and women, however, is completely symmetric, and either sex can be favoured in the labour market.

A more obvious role for gender as a coordination device emerges from early training in market or non-market tasks. If optimal specialization within marriage requires that one spouse specialize in market work and the other in household production, and if sector-specific skills investments are made prior to marriage, a coordination problem arises that can lead to a perfect correlation between sex and family roles (Echevarria and Merlo 1999; Engineer and Welling 1999; Hadfield 1999). That is, each individual will be better off if they marry someone with complementary skills but don't know who they will marry, other than that it will be someone of the opposite sex. Engineer and Welling (1999) show that with heterogeneous aptitudes for home and market work, there exist equilibria in which aptitude, rather than gender, determines training even if marital matching is random (i.e. on the basis of 'true love').

Women should stay home with the kids

It is customary to appeal to biology to explain why women should be assigned to home tasks and men to market work, given the potential gains to gender specialization: women are able to produce fewer children than men are and therefore follow a parenting strategy of intense investment in a few offspring. There is an extensive literature in biology, anthropology, and evolutionary psychology on the relationship between parenting and mating strategies and gender roles,[7] but intrinsic gender differences usually take a very simple form in economic treatments of the family.

Becker (1981: 37) emphasizes women's 'heavy biological commitment to the production and feeding of children' due to lengthy periods of gestation and lactation, and argues that it is easier to combine the care of older children with the production of new ones than with market activities. In a high-fertility regime in which household goods and services have few market substitutes and are time-intensive to produce, the relationship between childbearing and complete specialization in home work is compelling. Gender roles are further reinforced by sector-specific investments and the development of social norms and preferences that rationalize and support the separate spheres of men and women.[8] As fertility rates fall, and as household technology and marketization reduce the time burden of home production, the significance of the fixed maternal cost of children in explaining lifetime time allocation decreases. However, in the traditional model of specialization and exchange, only a minute difference between otherwise-identical men and women is sufficient to produce a gender-segregated equilibrium in market and home.[9]

Siow (1998) presents an alternative biological foundation for gender roles based on differential fecundity. Women are fecund for a smaller proportion of their lifetime than are men. A woman's probability of conception declines rapidly after she reaches her mid-30s, and menopause occurs at about age 50. Men experience a moderate age-related decline in fertility, but may continue to father children into old age. Siow argues that differential fecundity by itself has no implications for gender roles, but may interact with labour and marriage markets to generate an equilibrium in which young men work more hours in the market than their wives. The basic story is as follows: Young fecund women are scarce, and young men will compete with older divorced men for wives. If women prefer to marry men with higher wages, then young men will place more value on future labour income than his wife: it will allow him not only to buy consumption goods in the future, but also to compete for a young wife (and to have additional children) should his current marriage fail.

Staying home with the kids reduces relative bargaining power

If men and women invest in complementary skills, both before and during marriage, why should this systematically disadvantage women? The uncertain prospect of separation or divorce plays an important role in economic models of family bargaining. In Lommerud's (1989) model of the marital division of labour, spouses 'learn by doing' both market and domestic work, and there are positive returns to both sets of skills in case of divorce. In this case, the effect of a higher probability of divorce on specialization in marriage is ambiguous without further restrictions. It is usually assumed, however, that market skills have a much higher payoff after divorce than domestic skills, so that women who specialize in home production, absent post-divorce transfers, will be worse off than their former partners.

What is the source of this asymmetry? It is argued that some part of domestic skills is marriage-specific and has no value in single life or in subsequent relationships, and that parenting skills become obsolescent as a woman passes out of childbearing years. It seems clear that many domestic skills have a return in the market (cooking, childcare) but they are not generously remunerated (England and Folbre 1999). Investments in an individual's earning power, on the other hand, are equally valuable within and outside marriage, and so increase the relative value of an individual's threat point in a divorce-threat bargaining model. Baker and Jacobsen (2007) represent the relationship-specificity of investments in terms of the exchange possibilities outside of marriage for the goods produced.

In a bargaining model with an internal, non-cooperative threat point, there is still a useful distinction to be made between market earnings, which are privately appropriable in the case of domestic disagreement, and domestic work, which includes contributions to household public goods. The care of children or upkeep of the house produces goods which are non-excludable within the family, whereas control over a paycheck can be exclusively private. If, as in the separate spheres model, conventional gender roles determine the allocation of responsibilities in the non-cooperative equilibrium, this provides a mechanism whereby social norms can affect relative power and economic outcomes.

One way in which specialization in home production can increase the relative bargaining power of women is through a presumption that child custody will be awarded to the primary caregiver after divorce or separation. Customary custodial arrangements have varied, but for many years maternal custody was favoured as being 'in the best interests of the child'. To the extent that fathers continue to value control over and contact with their children after divorce, formal custody gives women considerable power, both during and after marriage. Many researchers have examined the relationship between divorced/separated parents and the impact of alternative custodial arrangements.[10]

To the extent that women continue to perform more household work than their partners, and to earn lower market wages as a result, simple non-unitary models of the family predict that they will receive a smaller share of household resources than they would in the absence of gender specialization. If specialization is efficient, however, there may be a conflict between individual actions that maximize total family resources and those that maximize individual utility. Within marriage, women can be compensated for actions that reduce their bargaining power. However, when premarital investments are made by agents cognizant of their effects on marital distribution, and when married couples are unable to enter into contracts that constrain their future behaviour, both men and women can engage in strategic behaviour that affects the gender division of labour.

Dynamic models and endogenous gender roles

Strategic investments

Gender-specific premarital investments can provide a way of coordinating the matching of individuals with complementary skills in the marriage market and thus, in the absence of substantial heterogeneity in individual aptitudes for home and market work, increase the wellbeing of both men and women. This analysis, however, abstracts from issues about distribution within the family.

Konrad and Lommerud (2000) assume that, though marital decisions are made cooperatively, educational investments that determine individual investments are made non-cooperatively (you can't bargain with someone you haven't met yet). Though marital decisions are constrained-efficient, individuals will invest too much in education compared to a first-best solution as a way to increase their bargaining power and share of resources in a future marriage. Vagstad (2001) extends this model to allow individuals to invest in both market and household production skills. Since complete specialization within marriage is efficient and couples achieve a constrained-efficient outcome, there will be a tradeoff between direct incentives to invest in household skills (increasing the productivity of your home time) and strategic incentives (avoiding being stuck at home). The marriage market effects of premarital investments are not analyzed in these papers, but Baker and Jacobsen (2007) develop the marriage market implications of a related model, and show how a customary gender division of labour may reduce the inefficiency of strategic investments, but at the cost of making one gender worse off.

Commitment

Strategic behaviour can also create inefficiencies in the time allocation decisions of married couples if current work affects future earnings opportunities, and if the spouses are unable to enter into a binding agreement concerning future behaviour. This is the standard holdup problem in a marital context, and can be illustrated with a simple 2-period model with and without intertemporal commitment.[11]

A two-person household, consisting of a husband (m) and a wife (f), makes decisions about consumption and time allocation over two periods, $t = 1, 2$. The utility of each individual i depends, as before, upon consumption of a household public good, G, and consumption of a private good, c_i. There is no altruism, in the sense of individual i's utility depending upon the consumption of individual j, no borrowing or saving, and no discounting. In period 1, husband and wife divide their time between market work at a fixed and common wage rate, w, and production of the household public good. In period 2, both spouses work in the market exclusively, at a wage rate that depends positively upon the amount of market work performed in period 1.

In period 1, we assume that the couple maximizes an objective function that is a weighted average of identical individual utilities, with the wife's utility having a weight μ.

$$W = U_1(c_{m1}, G) + U_2(c_{m2}) + \mu[U_1(c_{f1}, G) + U_2(c_{f2})] \qquad (7.2)$$

The public good is produced with inputs of husband and/or wife's time, $0 \leq l_i \leq 1$, such that $G = h_m l_m + h_f l_f$. Women are assumed to be more productive at home, so that $h_f > h_m$. Each individual's time endowment is normalized to one and all time not allocated to public good production is spent in market work, so that the household's budget constraint in the first period is:

$$c_{m1} + c_{f1} = w(2 - l_m - l_f) \qquad (7.3)$$

Second period wages are augmented by human capital acquired in first-period jobs, such that $w_i = w(\beta - l_i)$. Private consumption in the second period can be specified, without loss of generality, as private market income plus or minus a cash transfer between the spouses, so that:

$$\begin{aligned} c_{m2} &= w(\beta - l_m) - t \\ c_{f2} &= w(\beta - l_f) + t \end{aligned} \qquad (7.4)$$

If first period utility is strongly separable in the private and public goods, then:

$$U_1(c_{i1}, G) = u_1(c_{i1}) + \gamma(G) \qquad (7.5)$$

With commitment

We first assume that the couple is able to credibly commit in the first period to a level of interpersonal transfer in the second period, so that the household problem will be to maximize, with respect to first-period consumption, first-period household production, and the transfer:

$$\begin{aligned} W = &u_1[w(2 - l_m - l_f) - c_{f1}] + \gamma(h_m l_m + h_f l_f) + U_2[w(\beta - l_m) - t] \\ &+ \mu\left[u_1(c_{f1}) + \gamma(h_m l_m + h_f l_f) + U_2[w(\beta - l_f) + t]\right] \end{aligned} \qquad (7.6)$$

The first-order conditions yield:

$$u_1'(c_{m1}) = \mu u_1'(c_{f1}) \qquad (7.7a)$$
$$U_2'(c_{m2}) = \mu U_2'(c_{f2}) \qquad (7.7b)$$

When $\mu = 1$, (7.7b) ensures that the consumption levels of husband and wife in the second period will be equalized by a transfer $t^* = w(l_f - l_m)/2$. Given the public good production function, it is clear that interior solutions in both l_m and l_f will not be optimal – either the husband will fully specialize in market work, or the wife will specialize in household production, or both. The outcome of this problem is efficient; an optimal quantity of the household public good, G, will be produced in the first period, time allocation will reflect the husband's comparative advantage in market work and the wife's comparative (and absolute) advantage in household production, and income will be distributed within the household to equate the weighted marginal utilities of consumption.

Without commitment

Achievement of the efficient solution defined by (7.7) requires an enforceable intertemporal contract, privately negotiated between the husband and wife. Legal limits to the enforceability of such contracts within families are well-known. Weiss and Willis (1985) and Lommerud (1989) analyze, respectively, the ex post and ex ante effects of divorce on contracting within families. In Weiss and Willis, children are collective consumption goods to divorced parents. Within marriage, the public goods problem is avoided by 'mutual trust, altruism, and proximity', but after divorce the non-custodial parent is unable to monitor the custodial parent's expenditures on their own consumption and child consumption. Since divorce settlements cannot be conditional on child expenditures, voluntary transfers from the non-custodial parent will tend to be inefficiently low. In Lommerud, emotional ties are crucial to the enforcement of implicit marital contracts. The weakening of such ties with divorce implies that 'voice enforcement' of contracts between the (ex-)spouses is no longer feasible. In his model, the prospect of future divorce alters incentives to make marriage-specific investments through this enforceability constraint.

In dynamic bargaining models with investment, decisions made in one period can alter the relative bargaining power of individual family members in future periods. Several papers have shown that limited commitment in this situation can lead to inefficient allocations of household resources. Basu (2006) shows that, when the household's balance of power is endogenously determined and there is no intertemporal commitment (i.e. the division of family resources is renegotiated each period), then strategic considerations can lead to inefficient outcomes.[12] Lundberg and Pollak (2003) use a two-stage model of a married couple's location decision to show that marital decisions that affect future bargaining power need not be efficient unless the husband and wife can make binding agreements regarding their future actions.

The model above provides a simple framework for examining the role of contractual arrangements, the timing of marital investments, and the effect of these investments on the value of outside options in generating inefficient marital outcomes. An efficient solution requires that the couple commit in the first period to a transfer from husband to wife, t^*, in the second period. In general, the husband's promise to share market income equally (or in some agreed proportion) with his wife will not be legally enforceable, and renegotiation of individual control over family resources may occur, conditional on potential earnings in period two. If the expected value of the transfer is less than t^*, the allocation of time in the first period will change as well. If $t < t^*$, then $\mu U_2'(c_{f2}) > U_2'(c_{m2})$ and the marginal cost of wife's home production time will increase relative to the marginal cost of the husband's home production time (see Lundberg 2002). If both husband and wife are completely specialized in the efficient solution, a reduced transfer may leave both at a corner solution, but any change in time allocation will involve a reduction in the wife's home production or an increase in the husband's. Compared to the efficient solution, there will be less specialization in the equilibrium without intertemporal commitment. This leads to an increase in the implicit price of the public good. In general, an inability to commit to compensation for the partner who is the low-cost producer of the household public good reduces the equilibrium level of G below the socially-efficient level.[13]

A failure to commit to the optimal second-period transfer can be rationalized in a number of ways. If divorce occurs with some exogenous probability, p, between periods one and two, then the actual transfer will be determined by property division laws and court decisions, though it may be voluntarily augmented by the high-income spouse. Lommerud (1989) assumes, as a limiting case, that $t = t^*$ if the marriage remains intact, but $t = 0$ if there is a divorce. The model above predicts that, as the probability of divorce rises, production of the public good and specialization in the first period will fall.[14]

Alternatively, the couple may renegotiate in period 2, conditional on the earnings that the first period allocation has determined. If family agreements, implicit or explicit, cannot be legally enforced, the relevant question is not why a high-income husband would not comply with the ex ante optimal transfer to his wife, but rather why he would. If the second period division of family resources is renegotiated, it is necessary to specify what determines the ex post sharing rule. In an explicit bargaining model, possible fall-back positions for the husband and wife include divorce, or a non-cooperative equilibrium in which each spouse controls his or her own labour income. In either case, individual shares of total family income will depend upon individual market incomes, and the agreed transfer is unlikely to satisfy (7.7b).[15] This means that first period contributions to the household public good will decrease expected second period consumption, and implies that the family will be unable to achieve an efficient level of public goods production.

The problem here is that a credible promise to compensate public goods production in the first period with consumption in the second period cannot be made, and this reduces incentives to specialize in public goods production. Can credit markets make a difference? In general, the husband could compensate his wife for public goods production with a lump-sum transfer in the first period, possibly financed with a loan based on second-period earnings. This assumes consumer credit markets of unrealistic perfection – credit constraints resulting from the inadmissibility of human capital as collateral are likely to prevent the average husband from making a large enough transfer to a stay-at-home wife. Also, this mechanism requires the maintenance of individual control over assets between the first and second periods. Aura (2001) notes that when divorce is a possibility, intertemporal control of assets requires a common-law type property-division regime. Community property standards may prevent the couple from attaining an ex ante efficient allocation by restricting their ability to assign permanent property rights to assets.

Social norms, networks, and enforcement

One interesting feature of non-unitary models of household decision-making, particularly intertemporal models, is that customary gender roles, as expressed in social norms or in the operation of social networks, can play a formal role in determining the behaviour of individual couples. Gender norms can influence premarital investments by parents, the nature of focal point non-cooperative family equilibria, and the enforceability of marital agreements.

Baker and Jacobsen (2007) postulate a customary gender distribution of labour that determines skill acquisition and improves household efficiency, though it disadvantages one gender. They emphasize that the gender with the distributional advantage would resist changes in labour markets that make the other gender's skills more marketable. Lundberg and Pollak (1993) invoke customary gender roles as determinants of the 'separate spheres' non-cooperative equilibrium that provides the alternative to cooperative marital bargaining.

An important open question is the degree to which marital agreements concerning future compensation for investments in non-marketable household skills can be considered enforceable. In a model like Lommerud's where 'voice' enforcement of agreements within marriage is possible, limits to intertemporal commitment are caused by the possibility of divorce, so that divorce and property laws will affect equilibrium levels of specialization and gender roles within families. Renegotiation within intact marriages, however, presents a different set of enforceability problems. It is possible that community and extended family ties can enforce norms regarding the intrahousehold distribution of resources and ensure that high-earning husbands do not exploit the limited options of their wives later in the marriage. If the maintenance of cooperative behaviour in repeated games requires the ability to punish players for non-cooperative actions, the scope for such punishment may be limited within a single (aging) marriage. A social network of neighbours and relations (including grown children, who have intimate knowledge of family resources) may provide better enforcement of intrahousehold distributional norms. If such ties have weakened with increases in geographic mobility, this may also contribute to the increased reliance of women on their own market earnings.

If social ties can help to enforce marital agreements that are consistent with customary gender roles, they may also impede these agreements when economic conditions change. Sevilla-Sanz (2005) plausibly argues that very low fertility and marriage rates in countries with less-egalitarian gender norms can be explained by the constraints that these norms place on the ability of young men and women to credibly commit to an efficient household division of labour. As women's education levels and market wages have risen in Spain, Italy, and Japan, the market and household work performed by newly-married men and women should become more equal. However, if young men are unable to commit to a division of labour that is very different from that of their peers, marriage and childbearing will become relatively unattractive for women. In fact, marriage and fertility rates are higher in developed countries with more egalitarian attitudes towards gender roles.

Conclusion

Economic models of gender inequality begin with the division of labour in the family. Efficient specialization is implied by a home production function in which the time of men and women are quality-adjusted perfect substitutes, and the assignment of women to the home front rather than the market on the now-slender reed of the physical demands of childbearing. Economists, beginning with Becker, have postulated additional mechanisms such as sector-specific learning and marriage-market coordination that can leverage a small biological difference into an efficient separating equilibrium.

In simple static bargaining models, specialization has distributional conse-quences – women are disadvantaged by specialization in home production because it limits their command over resources outside the household. This disadvantage can be mitigated in a dynamic model of family decision-making, but the ability of men and women to make binding intertemporal commitments is crucial both to the distributional effects of specialization and the stability of an efficient allocation of individual effort within families. If men are unable to make credible promises to share future resources with the mothers of their children, then fewer women will be willing to marry, bear children, and stay home with them. Laws, institutions, and social norms may play important roles in facilitating (or inhibiting) the enforceability of intrahousehold agreements.

Acknowledgements

This chapter was originally presented as a lecture at the University of Siena International School of Economic Research, XVIII Workshop on Gender and Economics, 4–7 July 2005, Certosa di Pontignano, Siena, Italy. My thanks to Giedrius Blazys and Meredith Startz for helpful comments.

Notes

1 This specification rules out various forms of altruism, in which each spouse cares about the other's utility, or about the other's consumption of private goods, but few results are sensitive to this assumption.
2 McElroy and Horney include only the prices and parameters directly relevant to the individual agent as determinants of the threat point. However, in a model in which the household public good is identified as children, we wish to allow for transfers of time or money between divorced individuals and so include the resources of both agents in each threat point.

3 There is, of course, an adding-up constraint in marriage markets: the different remarriage prospects of divorced men and women in equilibrium are analyzed by Siow (1998).
4 Lundberg and Pollak (1993) show that the distributional implications of the separate spheres bargaining model depend upon the nature of marriage market adjustments.
5 McElroy (1990) called these determinants of bargaining power 'extrahousehold environmental parameters' or EEPs; Folbre (1997) suggests that they be termed 'gender-specific environmental parameters' or GEPs.
6 Stratton (2005) constructs measures of specialization by married and cohabiting couples in nine separate household activities, and finds that the degree of specialization is much greater than it appears to be with aggregated data, and that specialization increases with the duration of the relationship.
7 See, in particular, Trivers (1972).
8 Fuchs (1988) asserts that female economic disadvantage arises from the fact that they care more about children than men do.
9 Though it is unclear why ESPN doesn't tip the equilibrium in the other direction.
10 Edlund (2006), for example, treats marriage as the exchange of paternal custody for material support. Ermisch (2005) examines the effects of child support enforcement in a regime in which men pay for contact with their children. Some recent papers analyze the effects of ex ante custody arrangements on the distribution of marital surplus, investments in children, and divorce (Rasul 2006; Francesconi and Muthoo 2003).
11 This model is derived from Lundberg (2002), who analyzes the effects of family policy when marital commitment is imperfect.
12 In this paper, the objective function of the family 'agent' is a weighted average of the preferences of the husband and wife, and so changes over time as the balance of power in the household changes. This formulation suggests an interesting parallel between the inability of a household to make intertemporal commitments and the self-control problem of a hyperbolic-discounting individual (Laibson 1997), where a current 'self' is playing a game against future 'selves'.
13 The structure and intuition of this problem are very similar to the model of child labor in Baland and Robinson (2000). Inefficient child labor can arise, even when parents are altruistic, if children cannot commit to compensate their parents in the future for letting them go to school, rather than work.
14 In Lommerud's model, domestic human capital acquisition provides an alternative way to shift resources into the second period, and the effect of the divorce probability on the degree of specialization is ambiguous.
15 Evidence that control over income affects the distribution of resources within the family is surveyed in Lundberg and Pollak (1996). Lundberg, Startz, and Stillman (2003) show that the decrease in consumption spending at retirement appears to be a collective response to the changing relative bargaining power of husbands and wives when husbands retire.

References

Aura, S. (2001) *Uncommitted Couples: Some Efficiency and Policy Implications of Marital Bargaining*, working paper, IGIER/Bocconi University.
Baker, M.J. and Jacobsen, J.P. (2007) 'Marriage, Specialization and the Gender Division of Labor', *Journal of Labour Economics*, 25(4): 763–793.
Baland, J.-M. and Robinson, J.A. (2000) 'Is Child Labor Inefficient?' *Journal of Political Economy*, 108 (4): 663–679.
Basu, K. (2006) 'Gender and Say: A Model of Household Behavior with Endogenously-determined Balance of Power', *Economic Journal*, 116 (511): 558–580.

Becker, G.S. (1981) *Treatise on the Family*. Cambridge: Harvard University Press; Enlarged edition, 1991.

Chiappori, P.-A. (1988) 'Rational Household Labor Supply', *Econometrica*, 56 (1): 63–89.

Chiappori, P.-A. (1992) 'Collective Labor Supply and Welfare', *Journal of Political Economy*, 100 (3): 437–467.

Echevarria, C. and Merlo, A. (1999) 'Gender Differences in Education in a Dynamic Household Bargaining Model', *International Economic Review*, 40 (2): 265–286.

Edlund, L. (2006) 'Marriage: Past, Present, Future?' *CESifo Economic Studies*, 52 (4): 621–639.

England, P. and Folbre, N. (1999) 'The Cost of Caring', *Annals of the American Academy of Political and Social Science*, 561: 39–51.

Ermisch, J. (2005) *New Families, Child Support and Divorced Fathers' Contact with their Children*, working paper, ISER, University of Essex.

Engineer, M. and Welling, L. (1999) 'Human Capital, True Love, and Gender Roles: Is Sex Destiny?' *Journal of Economic Behavior and Organization*, 40 (2): 155–178.

Folbre, N. (1997) 'Gender Coalitions: Extrafamily Influences on Intrafamily Inequality', in L. Haddad, J. Hoddinott and H. Alderman (eds) *Intrahousehold Resource Allocation in Developing Countries: Models, Methods, and Policy*. Baltimore: Johns Hopkins University Press. pp. 263–274.

Francesconi, M. and Muthoo, A. (2003) *An Economic Model of Child Custody*, working paper, University of Essex.

Francois, P. (1998) 'Gender Discrimination without Gender Difference: Theory and Policy Responses', *Journal of Public Economics*, 68 (1): 1–32.

Fuchs, V. (1988) *Women's Quest for Economic Equality*. Cambridge, MA: Harvard University Press.

Hadfield, G.K. (1999) 'A Coordination Model of the Sexual Division of Labor', *Journal of Economic Behavior and Organization*, 40 (2): 125–154.

Konrad, K.A. and Lommerud, K.E. (2000) 'The Bargaining Family Revisited', *Canadian Journal of Economics*, Canadian Economics Association, 33 (2): 471–487.

Laibson, D. (1997) 'Golden Eggs and Hyperbolic Discounting', *Quarterly Journal of Economics*, 112 (2): 443–477.

Lommerud, K.E. (1989) 'Marital Division of Labor with Risk of Divorce: The Role of "Voice" Enforcement of Contracts', *Journal of Labor Economics*, 7 (1): 113–127.

Lommerud, K.E. (1997) 'Battles of the Sexes: Non-cooperative Games in the Theory of the Family', in I. Persson and C. Jonung (eds) *Economics of the Family and Family Policies*. London: Routledge. pp. 44–62.

Lundberg, S. (2002) 'Limits to Specialization: Family Policy and Economic Efficiency'. Available: http://csde.washington.edu/lundberg/pdfs/Limits to Specialization. pdf (accessed 21 January 2008).

Lundberg, S. and Pollak, R.A. (1993) 'Separate Spheres Bargaining and the Marriage Market', *Journal of Political Economy*, 101 (6): 988–1010.

Lundberg, S. and Pollak, R.A. (1994) 'Noncooperative Bargaining Models of Marriage', *American Economic Review Papers and Proceedings*, 84 (2): 132–137.

Lundberg, S. and Pollak, R.A. (1996) 'Bargaining and Distribution in Marriage', *Journal of Economic Perspectives*, 10 (4): 139–158.

Lundberg, S. and Pollak, R.A. (2003) 'Efficiency in Marriage', *Review of Economics of the Household*, 1 (3): 153–167.

Lundberg, S., Startz, R. and Stillman, S. (2003) 'The Retirement-Consumption Puzzle: A Marital Bargaining Approach', *Journal of Public Economics*, 87 (5): 1199–1218.

McElroy, M.B. (1990) 'The Empirical Content of Nash-Bargained Household Behavior', *Journal of Human Resources*, 25 (4): 559–583.

McElroy, M.B. and Horney, M.J. (1981) 'Nash-Bargained Household Decisions: Toward a Generalization of the Theory of Demand', *International Economic Review*, 22 (2): 333–349.

Manser, M. and Brown, M. (1980) 'Marriage and Household Decision-Making: A Bargaining Analysis', *International Economic Review*, 21 (1): 31–44.

Rasul, I. (2006) 'The Economics of Child Custody', *Economica*, 73 (289): 1–25.

Samuelson, P.A. (1956) 'Social Indifference Curves', *Quarterly Journal of Economics*, 70 (1): 1–22.

Sevilla-Sanz, A. (2005) *Social Effects, Household Time Allocation, and the Decline in Union Formation*, working paper, Congressional Budget Office.

Siow, A. (1998) 'Differential Fecundity, Markets, and Gender Roles', *Journal of Political Economy*, 106 (2): 334–354.

Stratton, L.S. (2005) 'The Degree of Intrahousehold Specialization in Housework and How Specialization Varies Across Couple Households', presented at *SOLE Annual Meetings*, San Francisco, June 2005.

Trivers, R.L. (1972) 'Parental Investment and Sexual Selection', in B.Campbell (ed.) *Sexual selection and the descent of man*. Chicago: Aldine Transaction. pp. 136–179.

Vagstad, S. (2001) 'On Private Incentives to Acquire Household Production Skills', *Journal of Population Economics*, 14 (2): 301–312.

Weiss, Y. and Willis, R. (1985) 'Children as Collective Goods and Divorce Settlements', *Journal of Labor Economics*, 3 (3): 268–292.

World Bank Policy Research Report, Engendering Development, January 2001.

Part 4
Labour market debates

8   Gender differences across Europe

Peter Dolton, Oscar Marcenaro-Guttierez and Ali Skalli

Introduction

The women of Europe face very different economic conditions depending on the country they live in. This has been known for some time but until recently we have not been able to look so comprehensively at how different these conditions are across countries. The advent of directly comparable data collected in the same way and asking the same questions now facilitates a much more rigorous examination of the labour market conditions faced by women in different countries of Europe. Such a descriptive analysis is central to an understanding of why the position of women vis-à-vis men is different in each country and what the implications are for legislative changes and policy initiatives.

In the last three decades, most OECD countries have experienced a continuous rise in educational enrolment rates for both men and women and the increase in educational investments has been faster for women than for men. In many countries women have also been outperforming men in terms of educational achievements in school and university examinations. At the same time in most countries there has been a higher rate of female participation in the labour market. This has been accompanied by a rising female – male relative wage. What is less well understood is how this process differs in different European countries.

In this chapter we do two things. We present an overview of the literature on gender wage differences in Europe to provide a perspective on the policy context for this latest research. Second, we use the best available comparative data to statistically describe the current differences faced by men and women in the different countries of Europe.

In what follows we will document how the men and women of Europe differ in their: working hours, labour force participation patterns, educational attainment levels and demographic age structure. We show how these patterns differ radically in different countries. With this socio-economic background context clear we then seek to analyse how the earnings of women and men compare in the different countries.

The contextual background to earnings differences for men and women must of course reflect the decisions they choose to make about participating in the labour market, how many hours they choose to work, and what educational qualifications they have. Any rigorous examination of the differences in earnings of men and women will attempt to 'net out' for these differences in any attempt to understand what residual discrimination there is in the labour market.

We begin our description by charting the rise in the female to male earnings ratio across different countries over the last 35 years. In what follows we clarify the extent of the pay gap by education and age as well as document the exact shape of the earnings distribution for men and women in each country. We also chart how earnings evolve over the life cycle for men and women in each European country and then seek to analyse how this pattern of life cycle earnings changes when you 'condition out' for all the demographic and structural differences of the position of women in each country.

The chapter is organised as follows. In the next section, we review the literature to assess the progress that has been made in measuring gender wage differentials as well as identifying their determinants. In section 2, we describe the data we use. Section 3 reports the results and highlights differences between age groups as well as between educational categories across Europe. The implications of our analysis provide our conclusions.

The received wisdom on gender wage differentials

There is a growing literature which attempts to make genuine cross country comparisons of the male-female wage gap and determine the extent of discrimination. Early attempts to make cross national comparisons of the gender pay were fraught with difficulty not least because of the non-comparable data sets used in different countries. An introductory chapter in the Joshi and Paci (1998) book attempts to make sense of the differences between countries by presenting the pattern of the overall female to male wage ratio and describing how the countries differ in terms of equal pay, equal opportunity legislation and child care arrangements. With the advent of good cross national data collection which basically uses the same questionnaire, it is now possible to make more meaningful comparisons. In Europe, several authors have used the European Community Household Panel (ECHP) to study the gender pay gap in a comparative perspective. Our task is to review the major recent contributions to this literature (both using the ECHP and different data) and explain what is already known, what is contentious and provide descriptive statistics of the position in Europe over the 1994–2001 period. Most of the studies reviewed in this section are summarised methodologically in Table 8.1 for ease of comparison. This table explicitly provides information on the objective pursued by each study as well as on the methodological difficulties they attempted to overcome.

The first study to use the ECHP data was by Rice (1999) who used the data up to the 1995 survey. She attempted to show how the position in each country was substantially different at different points in the earnings distribution – i.e. not just at mean earnings of men and women. She also argued that the legislation on equal pay and employment legislation and child care arrangements played a large role in this difference across countries. Further, she argued that variation in

Table 8.1 Summary of literature on inter-country comparisons of the gender wage gap

Authors	Data	Year/s	Countries included	Focus	Participation decision exclusion restrictions	Educational endogeneity	Occupation segregation	Decomposition method
Arulampalam et al. (2005)	ECHP	1995–2001	Austria, Belgium, Denmark, Finland, France, Germany, Ireland, Italy, Netherlands, Spain and UK	Quantile regression public/private sector differences	No	No	No	Bootstrap (Machado and Mata (2005))
Beblo et al. (2003)	ECHP	1998	France, Germany, Italy, Spain and UK	Self-selection into market work	Endogenous sample selection model by Lewbel (2002)	No	No	Oaxaca (1973)–Blinder (1973) and Juhn et al. (1991)
De la Rica et al. (2005)	ECHP	1999	Spain	Quantile regression	No	No	No	Oaxaca (1973)–Blinder (1973)
Gannon et al. (2005)	European Structure of Earnings Survey (ESES)	1995	Belgium, Denmark, Italy, Ireland, Spain, UK	Inter-industry wage differentials	No	No	No	No
Olivetti and Petrongolo (2005)	PSID and ECHP	1999	Austria, Belgium, Denmark, Finland, France, Germany, Greece, Ireland, Italy, Netherlands, Spain and UK	Simulation of wages for non-participants	Correction for participation decision using Johnson et al. (2000) and Neal (2004) approach (no exclusion restrictions)	No	Yes	Oaxaca (1973)–Blinder (1973)

(Continued)

Table 8.1 cont'd

Authors	Data	Countries included	Year/s	Focus	Participation decision exclusion restrictions	Educational endogeneity	Occupation segregation	Decomposition method
Pissarides et al. (2005)	ECHP	Canada, Denmark, Finland, Greece, Italy, Norway, Sweden, UK, Spain, Austria, Belgium, France, Germany, Ireland, Netherlands, Portugal, United States	1998	Women's employment patterns	Age, marital status, weekly hours in child care	No	No	Oaxaca (1973)–Blinder (1973)
Plasman and Sissoko (2005)	ESES	Belgium, Denmark, Ireland, Italy, Spain	1995	Role of occupational segregation	No	No	Yes	Oaxaca (1973)–Blinder (1973) and Brown, et al. (1980)
Rice (1999)	ECHP and Hungarian Household Panel	Denmark, France, Germany, Greece, Italy, Portugal, Spain, UK, Hungary	1995 (ECHP) 1994 (Hungarian Household Panel)	Impact of social policies	No	No	No	Juhn et al. (1991)
Weichselbaumer and Winter-Ebmer (2003)	Meta-Data	International (63 countries)	1960–1990	Review of empirical literature on gender wage discrimination	No	No	No	Oaxaca (1973)–Blinder (1973)

the collective bargaining arrangements and minimum wage legislation variation across countries played an important role in explaining these differences. In these respects she was following the arguments of Blau and Beller (1988), and Blau and Kahn (1992, 1996, 1997). However, it is not possible in the ECHP to provide any formal econometric identification of the role played by such forces in the determination of the changing size of the gender wage gap. This is because there is nothing to link the macroeconomic fluctuations and legislative changes with the microeconomic panel data on individuals. These problems are still faced by any empirical investigation of male-female wage differences using the ECHP.

An examination of the recent contributions to this literature shows that there are two main topics researchers are interested in. Some of the contributions focus on the selectivity issue. As argued by Olivetti and Petrongolo (2005), if selection into employment is non-random, then it makes sense to worry about the way in which selection may affect the resulting gender wage gap. In particular, if women who are employed tend to have relatively high-wage characteristics, low female employment rates may become consistent with low gender wage gaps simply because low-wage women would not feature in the observed wage distribution.

Other contributions aim to identify the parts of the wage distribution where the gender pay gap is the largest. The main objective in these studies is to examine whether the largest gap is observed at the bottom or at the top of the earnings distribution. The former case would suggest that women face greater difficulties than men in progressing from the lowest wages. This is often referred to as the 'sticky floor' phenomenon which is defined by Booth *et al.* (2003) as the situation arising where otherwise identical men and women might be appointed to the same pay scale or rank, but the women are appointed at the bottom and men further up the scale. Such a strategy can circumvent some discrimination laws, since the appointment rank is the same. The second characterization would suggest that women face obstacles which prevent them from reaching the highest wage levels. This is usually referred to as the 'glass ceiling' phenomenon and is defined as a situation where women, who are otherwise identical to men, can only advance so far up the pay ladder.

European studies include Blundell *et al.* (2004) who examine changes in the distribution of wages in the UK during 1978–2000, using bounds to the distribution of potential wages, in order to allow for the impact of non-random selection into work. Likewise, Albrecht *et al.* (2004) estimate gender wage gaps in the Netherlands having corrected for selection of women into market work according to Buchinsky's (1998) semi-parametric method for quintile regressions. They conclude that if all Dutch women were working full-time, the gender wage gap would be much higher. Beblo *et al.* (2003) show selection-corrected wage gaps for Germany using both the Heckman (1979) and the Lewbel (2002) two-stage selection models. The effect on wage gaps in Germany is, however, ambiguous as it depends on the estimation method used.

A number of recent studies have also taken a comparative perspective thanks to the use of the ECHP. Cholezas and Tsakloglou (2003), for instance, examine the difference in average expected earnings of males and females in ECHP countries.

The objective of their study is to investigate the trend over time of each component of the gender pay gap, comparing the 1994 and 2000 waves of the ECHP. Using the standard Oaxaca-Blinder (1973) decomposition, they show that the gender pay gap is widening in Belgium, Greece and Luxemburg and narrowing in the remaining countries. In particular, in 1994, Germany had the highest gap and Italy the lowest whereas in 2000, Luxemburg had the highest gap and Italy the lowest. They also show that differences in productivity favour women in most countries and that discrimination is the most important component of the gender pay gap, the greatest share being observed in 1994 in Italy and the lowest being observed in Luxemburg in 2000. Over time, the share of discrimination is decreasing in Belgium, France, Germany, Greece, Ireland and Spain and increasing in Denmark, Italy, Luxemburg, Portugal and the UK. The authors also account for selectivity into employment using the Neuman and Oaxaca (1998) approach. They show that discrimination is still the strongest source of the gender pay gap, the only exceptions being Italy, Belgium and Portugal in 1994 and Italy, Germany and Greece in 2000. Their results also suggest that failure to account for selectivity induces a negative effect on the measurement of discrimination.

A recent comparative study on the effects of selection on the gender pay gap is that by Olivetti and Petrongolo (2005). The authors' argument is that while correction for selection seems to have a sizeable effect, none of the previous studies uses data from southern European countries where employment rates are lowest and thus the selection issue should be most relevant. Actually, the authors use both the Panel Survey of Income Dynamics (PSID) for the US, and the ECHP. Their estimation strategy consists in recovering information on wages for those not in work following the approach of Johnson *et al.* (2000) and Neal (2004), which is based on wage imputation for the non-employed. They argue that such an approach has at least two advantages. First, it simply requires assumptions on the position of the imputed wage observations with respect to the median. Hence it does not require assumptions on the actual level of missing wages, as typically required in the matching approach. Second, it does not require arbitrary exclusion restrictions often involved in two-stage Heckman sample selection correction models.

Oaxaca-Blinder decompositions on actual and imputed distributions show that countries where the gender wage gap is not seriously affected by sample inclusion rules also have roughly unchanged gap decomposition across specifications. In countries where wage imputation affects the estimated wage gap, it is both characteristics and returns components that matter. In Ireland and southern Europe, women with lower labour market attachment have a higher wage penalty with respect to men because they have relatively poorer characteristics than women with higher labour market attachment and because they receive a lower remuneration for a given set of characteristics.

Olivetti and Petrongolo (2005) also use the decomposition technique used by Juhn *et al.* (1991) and by Blau and Kahn (1996) to quantify the contribution of cross-country differences in the wage structure to the explanation of the variation in the gender wage gap. This allows them to show that the contribution of characteristics relative to that of the wage structure is much stronger in southern Europe than elsewhere and that this effect is attenuated on the imputed wage distribution.

In addition to investigating the effects of selectivity on gender pay differentials estimates, a number of authors have endeavoured to locate the part of the wage distribution where the gender gap is the highest. These studies in general use quantile regression techniques to test for the sticky floor and/or the glass ceiling hypothesis. Country-specific studies of this type include the work by Albrecht *et al.* (2003) who use Swedish data for 1998 and show that the gender wage gap is increasing throughout the conditional wage distribution and accelerating at the top. They interpret this as evidence of a glass ceiling in Sweden. Likewise, de la Rica *et al.* (2005) use data from Spain for the year 1999 and conduct a similar analysis. They, however, stratify their sample by education group and find that the gender wage gap is expanding over the wage distribution only for the group with college/tertiary education. For the less educated groups, the wage gap is wider at the bottom than at the top. They thus conclude that, in Spain, there is a glass ceiling for the more educated, not for the less educated.

Other studies have addressed the same issue in a comparative perspective. The study by Arulampalam *et al.* (2005) uses 11 countries (out of the available 15 that are present) in the ECHP over the 1995–2001 period, and systematically compares them. The main objective of the study is to investigate the extent to which gender affects the location, scale and shape of the conditional wage distribution, and to examine whether or not these patterns differ across the public and the private sectors. The data suggest that for some of the countries, in both the public and private sectors, the average gender wage gap can be broken up into a gap that is typically wider at the top (glass ceiling) and occasionally also wider at the bottom (sticky floor). They also show that differences in returns account for a large part of the variation in the gender pay gap across the conditional wage distribution.

More specifically, a glass ceiling phenomenon is found in both the public and the private sectors in Denmark, Finland, Italy, France and the Netherlands. The sticky floor phenomenon is present in both sectors in Austria and France, in the Italian private sector and in the public sector in Belgium, Germany, Ireland and Denmark. Thus, the authors find the 'glass ceiling' and the 'sticky floor' to be a common but not systematic phenomenon in Europe in the sense that there is no clear pattern to the existence of gender pay gaps at either the bottom or the top of the wage distribution across different countries.

Most interesting are the various alternative explanations that are discussed by the authors. One possible interpretation of the glass ceiling phenomenon is the so-called taste-based explanation according to which women would prefer to work in family-friendly but low-wage jobs. This interpretation has been rejected by Albrecht *et al.* (2003) on the grounds that gender differences arise from differences in rewards even after controlling for occupation. An alternative explanation relates to parental leave and day-care policies, the objective of these being to provide women with incentives to participate but not to commit strongly to a career. Arulampalam *et al.* (2005) suggest that the case of Denmark supports this interpretation. However, they also note that a glass ceiling phenomenon is observed even in countries, like Italy for instance, where work-family reconciliation policies are very different from those adopted in Denmark. Among the alternative explanations they consider, is the idea that relatively high wages at the bottom of the wage distribution might make it very difficult for career-oriented women to hire household help or help with child care. Hence, women might be found in less-demanding jobs and thus fall substantially behind men towards the top of the distribution. However, while one would then expect the correlation between the magnitude of the glass ceiling and the dispersion of the wage distribution to be negative, the authors show it is statistically insignificant. Accordingly this explanation might also apply to gender differences in hierarchical labour markets and promotions. If promotion procedures favour men rather than women towards the top of the wage distribution, then the gender pay gap might be bigger towards the top. Booth *et al.* (2003) show how women do not do as well financially out of promotions as men. Landers *et al.* (1996) show, in their study of US law firms, how criteria for promotion like excessively long hours of work can exacerbate gender pay gaps towards the top of the lawyers' wage distribution.

Likewise, among the explanations of the sticky floor phenomenon which Arulampalam *et al.* (2005) consider, there is the idea that women towards the bottom of the wage distribution might have less bargaining power or are more likely to be subject to firms' market power, due perhaps to unobservable family commitments or social custom whereby the man's career takes precedence. Alternatively, it might also be the case that minimum wage compliance at the bottom may be unequal across genders, or trade unions might differentially represent the interests of their female members at the bottom of the wage distribution.

While a number of studies mentioned above conduct cross-country comparisons, it remains difficult to identify the relative importance of the sources of observed cross-country variation in the reported gender differentials in earnings. Obviously, such variation might be due to differences in the economic and institutional characteristics of the countries that are compared, but also to differences in the data sources or in the estimation strategies that are adopted in each specific study.

A means of assessing the relative explanatory power of each of these dimensions might consist in conducting a meta-analysis in which the results of the different studies are explicitly collated in a statistical analysis. While a number of meta-analyses have been conducted in different areas of economics, to our knowledge, the only study focusing on gender pay differentials is the one by Weichselbaumer and Winter-Ebmer (2002). It aims to assess the effect of (i) data characteristics; (ii) specification; and (iii) methodology on the reported estimates but also to examine the role of competition as well as of equal treatment laws as possible explanations of the cross-country variation of gender differentials in earnings. First, it is shown that the effect of data set restrictions on the estimated gaps is strong. To be more specific, male and female workers who have just entered the labour market earn more equal wages and the same is true for employees in the public sector. In addition, the wage differential is largest in low prestige occupations and this differential decreases as the status of the job rises. Also, the gap for married individuals is larger than for single people. Furthermore, ethnic minority men and women earn more similar wages than the majority group of a country. However, the study finds no such universal effects for variables pertaining to methodology, wage measurement and the inclusion of theoretically important variables. In particular, not surprisingly only the use of a gender dummy variable instead of the Oaxaca-Blinder decomposition, increased the estimated wage gap. In addition, if a study did not control for tenure, union status, or share of females in the occupation, this systematically increased the gender wage differential. Also of most relevance are Weichselbaumer and Winter-Ebmer's (2002) findings regarding the effect of economic environment and of equal treatment laws. Indeed, they show that not only do countries with a higher economic freedom (as measured by the Gwartney *et al.* index) have a lower gender wage gap than others, but also that ratification of international conventions supporting equal treatment of men and women also has a strong and significant impact on the gender wage gap.

An alternative approach consists of estimating the gender gap in earnings for several countries using a unique specification and comparable data. Cross-country variation in the estimated wage gaps is then explained by a number of economic and institutional characteristics. Examples of studies adopting such an approach include Blau and Kahn (2003) and Pissarides *et al.* (2005).[1]

Blau and Kahn (1996) and OECD (2002) use data from the International Social Survey Program (ISSP) and the ECHP, respectively, to study the effects of differences in the wage structure on the relative gender pay gap. Both use the decomposition technique developed by Juhn *et al.* (1991) to obtain measures of the wage gap, adjusted for between-country variations in the female/male differences in observed characteristics and in jobs held as well as in the extent of 'equal pay' for similar observed characteristics. The Juhn *et al.* decomposition technique is indeed seen as a means of solving the cross-country comparability problem as it consists of choosing one country as the benchmark and of using the entire wage structure for men in the reference country to evaluate 'gaps' in observed and unobserved characteristics by gender across different countries. However, one limitation of this approach is that it assumes that the estimated returns to observed characteristics do not differ by gender. Blau and Kahn (2003) attempt to overcome this problem by estimating gender-specific wage equations for each country and by using the observed characteristics of a reference country to evaluate cross-country differences in the wage gap.

These studies suggest there is a link between gender wage differentials and wage inequality. For instance, using data from 22 countries over the 1985–1994 period, Blau and Kahn (2003) find that more compressed male wage structures and lower female net supply are both associated with a lower gender gap in earnings. They also show that where collective bargaining coverage is high, the gender pay gap is low. These results mirror those of Rubery (1998) and Bettio (1988) who previously suggested that the extent of centralisation and wage setting unionisation raise women's relative pay.

The study by Pissarides *et al.* (2005) is specifically focused on European countries. Using the 1998 wave of the ECHP, the authors aim at primarily investigating the importance of adjusting for cross-country differences in patterns of female participation. But they also examine how likely country-specific institutions, such as employment protection policies, parental leave policies and product market regulation, are to explain cross-country differences in gender wage differentials. Their results could be summarised as follows. First, in line with previous studies, significant differentials in the pay of men and women remain in Europe, albeit not to the same extent as in America, a result which the authors relate to the lesser wage inequality in Europe. Like Blau and Kahn (2003), they also highlight a negative correlation between unionisation and the size of gender wage differentials.

Perhaps the most original result in the study by Pissarides *et al.* (2005) relates to the size of gender wage differentials in Mediterranean (Spain, Italy, Greece) countries. While the latter seem at first sight to be lower, compared to the rest of Europe, correction for the fact that female participation rates are lower and concentrated among more skilled women reveals that the gender pay gap in Mediterranean countries is actually close to that of other European countries.

Though not specifically focused on gender wage differentials, a number of other studies attempt to relate these to specific economic phenomena. Azmat *et al.* (2006) for instance study gender gaps in unemployment rates in OECD countries. They argue that while gender differences in participation behaviour have been given a number of plausible explanations, it still remains to explain why, once they have decided they want a job, women are less likely than men to be in employment in some countries, especially Mediterranean ones. They consider alternative explanations. First, it might be the case that women are less serious about getting work than men and that employers are thus less inclined to give jobs to women. Another possibility is the existence of a mismatch between the desires of the female unemployed in terms of jobs they like and the jobs that employers are offering. For instance, in some countries, women might be willing to work part-time when most offered jobs are full-time ones. These hypotheses find little support in the data, though it seems that discrimination against women may explain part of the gender gap in unemployment rates in Mediterranean countries.

Of specific interest to us here is the relationship between gender gaps in earnings and gender gaps in unemployment rates. While Blau and Kahn's (2003) argument about the negative correlation between the degree of wage compression and gender wage differentials would imply that where these are high, gender differentials in unemployment could be high as well, Azmat *et al.* (2006) find a positive but rather weak relationship between the two. This suggests that the decision to employ a man rather than a woman may not be based on a comparison of wages alone.

Another interesting study on the gender wage differentials is the one by Gannon *et al.* (2005) as it examines the link between these and inter-industry wage differentials. Using the 1995 European Structure of Earnings Survey for six EU countries (Belgium, Denmark, Italy, Ireland, Spain and the UK), the authors show that within each country, there are significant inter-industry wage differentials for both men and women and that their structure is quite similar across sexes and across countries. In addition, in all countries, more than 80 per cent of the gender wage gaps within industries are statistically significant but industries having the highest and the lowest gender wage gaps vary significantly from one country to another. Also most interesting is the result that there is a large cross-country variation in the proportion of within-country total variability of gender wage differentials that is explained by industry effects. This proportion varies between 0 per cent in Belgium and Spain, and 29 per cent in Ireland. Work by Plasman and Sissoko (2005) uses the same data to consider the role of occupational segregation in the variation in the gender pay gap across European countries. They suggest that occupational segregation plays the most important role in Belgium and Italy. They also consider the role of legislative changes and suggest that Belgium and Denmark could improve the efficiency of their wage equality policies. In turn they suggest that Spain could improve its policies on child care and institutions which would facilitate career break possibilities for women and that Ireland could improve its gender pay gap with more collective bargaining.

A further strand of the literature on international comparisons moves away from human capital explanations of the differences between men and women's pay. Rubery *et al.* (2005) suggest that 'gender audits' or 'gender mainstreaming' is an appropriate way to reduce the gender pay gap. The essence of their argument is that there should be a focus on policies to combat low pay and specifically to make minimum wage legislation more effective. They also discuss how to improve methods of pay bargaining and pay determination. The main thesis is that the structure of wages (inter-firm, inter-industry and inter-occupational differentials as well as internal labour market rules for wage progression) is largely influenced by institutional factors, specifically, pay bargaining and pay determination systems. Given persistent segregation, the same factors are bound to influence the size and variation of the gender gap.

The ECHP data

In the remainder of this chapter we use the full eight waves of the European Community Household Panel (ECHP) survey over the period 1994–2001. Despite the panel structure of the data, we simply pool the eight waves that are available to us and include year dummies in every specification we estimate.[2] The sample is restricted to salaried workers aged 16–64, working in the private or public sector, the self-employed being excluded. One advantage of these data is that we can perform cross-country comparisons using completely comparable data and also exploit the underlying information in terms of national economic and institutional differences. We have thus attempted to estimate common models for all the countries. There are, however, a few circumstances where we were unable to do so due to data restrictions and which we explain below.

Our basic earnings function uses the logarithm of individuals' average hourly wages as the dependent variable. Because of the panel structure of the data (and to facilitate international comparisons), these have been deflated using the series of year-specific Purchase Power Parity indices included in the data by Eurostat. The right-hand side of our wage equation includes education, age, job tenure, a dummy for foreign citizenship (national citizens being the omitted group), a dummy for private sector employment (public sector employees being the omitted group), a dummy for part-time work (full-time workers being the omitted group), a dummy for the married (single, divorced and widowed individuals being the omitted group), the number of children under 16 as well as year dummies (the first wave corresponding to the reference year).

A number of remarks are in order. First, we distinguish between three age groups: 16–30, 31–45 and 46–64 and conduct within-cohort analyses as well as analyses based on the pooled sample of all three cohorts. In the former case, age is included as a quadratic function. In the latter case, age is also included as a quadratic function but two further cohort dummies are included, the oldest cohort being the omitted group.

Second, the only education-related information available in the ECHP is individuals' highest qualification which only permits a distinction between 3 levels: Higher education, Upper Secondary education and Lower (rather than Upper) Secondary. However, in the ECHP an individual's highest qualification is only available when they enter the survey and the information is not updated. Therefore, for individuals who were already in the labour market at the time they entered the survey, we have assumed that their educational level has remained constant over the period when they are present in the panel. Those who were still attending school when they entered the survey have simply been deleted from the data. In no country has this proportion exceeded 2 per cent of our restricted sample. These data limitations are unavoidable and mean that we do not observe any educational attainment achievement after the individuals have entered the survey. This means that we cannot estimate the rate of return to earnings of educational qualifications achieved later in life.

Third, job tenure is inferred from the data as the survey year minus the year individuals started their current job. However, when the latter is more than 15 years prior to the survey year, it is coded in the data as '15 years before or earlier' so that its exact value is not known. We therefore set job tenure at 15 years for every individual who started her/his current job 15 years prior to the survey year or earlier, but we also constructed a dummy identifying these individuals and included it in addition to job tenure and its square. The coefficients on the latter two variables thus measure the average returns to job tenure when it is lower than 15 years. The coefficient on the high tenure dummy measures the average extra reward that is earned by individuals with more than 15 years of job tenure. Again, this is a regrettable limitation forced on us by the form of the available data.

Fourth, the foreign citizenship dummy could not be included for the UK as the number of foreign citizens turned out to be too low in this country. Finally, not all of the 13 countries entered the ECHP in 1994 so that all 8 waves are only available for 11 out of the 13 countries. Austria (1995) and Finland (1996) joined the survey later and for these two countries, the number of year dummies included has been adapted accordingly.

A new picture of gender wage differentials across Europe

The contextual background to comparisons of the relative wage position of men and women across Europe requires a careful analysis of the patterns of labour force participation, educational attainment, demographic age structure and working hours patterns which prevail in the different countries across Europe.

Raising female employment and more equitable wages are beneficial to the society as a whole. When more of a country's population is trained and put into productive use, competing for jobs and for markets worldwide, the better are the country's chances that it will advance technologically and grow faster with benefits for everyone.

Bringing more women into the labour force increases GDP through the introduction of new activities and through the recording of activities that were hitherto unrecorded and protected from taxation and regulation. It thus corrects a distortion in the tax system – that market activities are taxed but home activities are not – and in the process increases the tax base, which should make it easier for governments to manage their finances.

Women made important advances in labour markets across most of the countries of Europe. The participation rate is now higher, the degree of segregation is lower and the female/male raw wage ratio has been rising slowly across most countries in Europe. In addition the distinctions between the activities of single and married women are not as sharp as they used to be.

The relevant issues to an assessment of the position of women across Europe are:

(i) How many women have jobs?
(ii) How many are willing to work full-time or part-time or to work more and how many are not?
(iii) How well qualified are they relative to their male counterparts?
(iv) What jobs do they have – and are they segregated into particular occupations?

As we explained, one of the main conditioning factors which must be taken into account in inter-country comparisons of earnings is the socio-demographic structure of the population specifically with respect to age, educational background, working hours and female participation patterns. Figure 8.1 shows simply what the difference in the demographic structure of the male and female population is across Europe. The share of young people (aged 16–30) in the country is as high as 43.7 per cent for men in Ireland and as low as 27.9 per cent for men in Belgium. Likewise the fraction of the population in each country who are from the older generation (aged 46–64) is as small as 28.2 per cent for men in Ireland and as much as 39.4 per cent for women in Greece. This difference in the age structure in each country will be reflected in the wage gap decompositions. It is clear that the gender pay gap will be higher for older people than younger people. We can see this indirectly in Figure 8.2 as for most countries the ratio of female to male earnings has been rising and hence older women will be less well off relative to men than younger women.

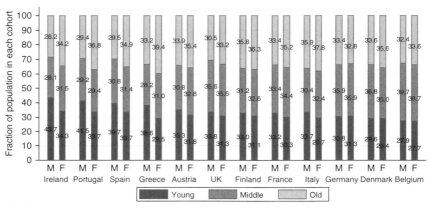

M=Male
F=Female

Figure 8.1 Demographic age structure between young, middle and old age cohort across
Europe.
Source: Author's own calculations from ECHP 1994–2001.

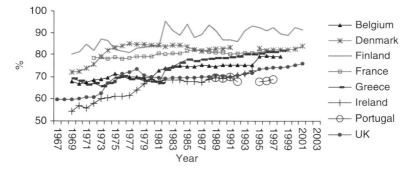

Figure 8.2 Joshi and Paci (1998) figure updated for the countries considered in our
estimates (ratio female hourly wages: male hourly wages).

Figure 8.3 illustrates one of the most important elements of diversity in Europe.
If we wish to explain earnings variation, a key element in this is the amount of
human capital which is present in each country. The ECHP does not measure this
entirely satisfactorily but this simple classification of Lower Secondary, Upper
Secondary and Higher education is sufficient to show up the diversity which exists
in Europe. In the ECHP sample participation in Higher education is lowest in
the southern European countries like Portugal (5.6 per cent to 7.8 per cent) and
Italy (6.5 per cent to 8.0 per cent). Higher educational participation is highest
in the UK, Denmark, Germany, Finland and Belgium. It is also noticeable that in
some countries the gap between male and female Higher educational participation

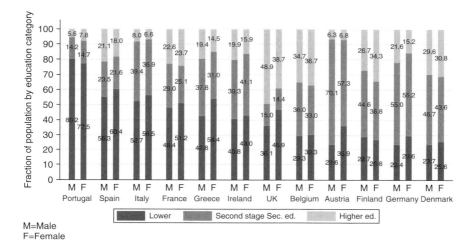

M=Male
F=Female

Figure 8.3 Educational level achieved by country.
Source: Author's own calculations from ECHP 1994–2001.

is large – e.g. in the UK this gap is 10 per cent whereas in other countries there is little difference in the gender participation rates. Indeed, in other countries, women go to college with a higher frequency than men; namely, Austria, France, Belgium even if this difference is less than or equal to 2 per cent. The difference in educational attainment across countries is not confined to the highest level of education. Figure 8.3 also shows us that there are wide differences across countries at the secondary level of education. In Portugal and the UK secondary education is the highest qualification for around 14 per cent of men and women whereas the corresponding proportion in Austria, Germany, Denmark and Finland is over 40 per cent. Indeed in Austria this figure is 70 per cent for men and 57 per cent for women. It is clear that the training and apprenticeship systems in these northern European countries endow a substantial fraction of people with an intermediate level of qualification which is missing in other countries like the UK. Furthermore, differences in the fraction of men and women educated to this level within a country could play an important role in the gender pay gap.

Figure 8.4 illustrates the heterogeneous pattern of female participation in the labour market across different European countries. In the Mediterranean countries of Greece, Spain, and Italy full time work among women aged between 16–64, is low at between 20 per cent and 24 per cent. In contrast full-time working is much more prevalent in the northern European countries of Denmark, Finland, UK and Germany at up to nearly 50 per cent. Part-time working is also less common in the Mediterranean countries. These facts are clearly very much part of the explanation of why relative female earnings differ so much across countries as the group of women who select themselves into work in Greece, Spain and Italy are very different to those who choose to work in northern European countries.

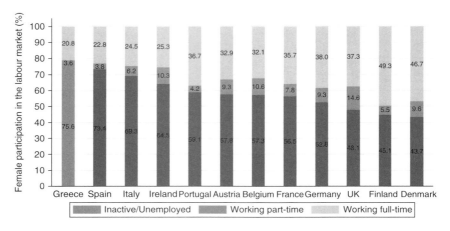

Figure 8.4 Labour force participation of women in Europe by country.
Source: Author's own calculations from ECHP 1994–2001.

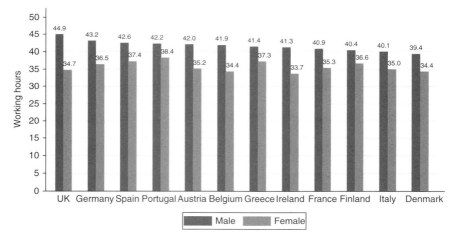

Figure 8.5 Male and female average working hours by country.
Source: Author's own calculations from ECHP 1994–2001.

Economic theory would suggest that those women with the highest earning potential are the ones observed to be working in the Mediterranean countries whilst many less well qualified women may still be drawn into work in the Northern European countries.

Figure 8.5 shows the pattern of working hours for 'full-time' men and women across the ECHP countries. Men in the UK work the longest, 44.94 hours on average whilst women in Ireland work the shortest hours – 33.72 hours on average. The biggest gap in hours of work between men and women within a country are to be found in the UK with men in the country working, on average, over 10 hours more than their female counterparts. The smallest gap within a country is to be found in Denmark where full time women work only 5 hours less per week. It is clear that there are substantial differences in work patterns in different European countries and that they are partially explained by cultural factors. Notwithstanding the causes of this variation – it will have consequences on the average rate of pay per hour which is earned and its distribution.

We now turn our attention to how wages differ in each of the countries that we have data for. Detailed information on the aggregate female to male wage ratios across time for each country is limited. We use the data reported in Joshi and Paci (1998)[3] and have updated it wherever possible. Figures 8.2 and 8.6 show the

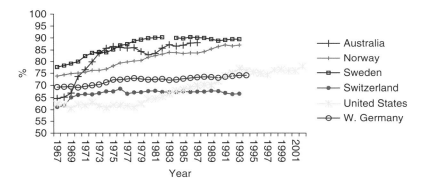

Figure 8.6 Countries not considered in our estimates (Ratio female hourly wages: male hourly wages).

Source: U.S. Bureau of Labor Statistics (http://www.bls.gov/cps/wlf-databook.htm) for United States and ILO Yearbook of Labour Statistics for the other countries.

Note: The series plotted in Figure 8.6 refer mainly to gross hourly earnings in non-agricultural activities, but due to data shortcomings the above figure was based on the following data across countries:

Australia: Only full time workers, adult, nonmanagerial employees.
Belgium: Manufacturing and construction.
Denmark: Manufacturing and construction.
Finland: Manufacturing.
France: Manufacturing and nondomestic services.
Greece: Manufacturing.
Ireland: Manufacturing.
Norway: Manufacturing.
Portugal: All industries.
Sweden: All industries.
Switzerland: Includes family allowances paid by the employer.
United States: Weekly earnings and only for full time workers.
United Kingdom: All industries, includes overtime.
West Germany: Pre-Germany reunification territory.

steady upward rise in the female to male wage in most OECD countries over the 1967–2003 period. Most countries had a female average wage which was between 54 and 72 per cent of the male average wage in 1967. This has steadily risen so that in most countries this ratio is more like 75 per cent to 85 per cent. The pattern shows clear discontinuities in certain countries at definite points in time or structural breaks in the series which may well be induced by legislative change. In the UK this break occurred in 1975 but in Greece this discontinuity came in 1981 and in Belgium in 1995. In some countries there has been a rapid rise in this ratio over a few years, e.g. Australia between 1967 and 1975 and Denmark between 1970 and 1977. But in other countries the rise has been much more gradual – for example Germany, Switzerland, Norway and Sweden. Figure 8.6 shows no sign that the improvement in this ratio is falling off.

Figure 8.7 looks at this same ratio using the ECHP data over the years 1994–2001. Here we see that the ratio has been much more static and hardly rising at all in most countries (with the possible exceptions of Italy and Finland). The reason for the apparent contradiction with the data in Figures 8.2 and 8.6 is that the ECHP data used in Figure 8.7 relates to a cohort of the same individuals and hence we would not expect to see the same improvement in this ratio amongst the same people in different years as we would expect to see over different people in different years.

Figure 8.8 presents the most basic information relating to the size of the overall 'raw' gender wage gap in each country based on the ECHP data. The largest gaps

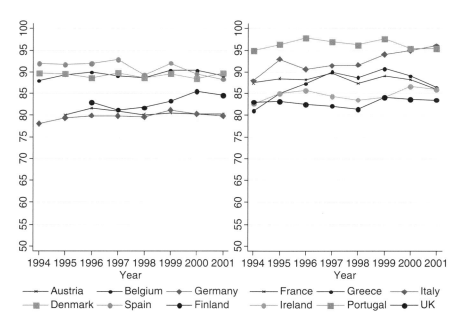

Figure 8.7 Relative female/male wage rate 1994–2001 by country.
Source: Author's own calculations from ECHP 1994–2001.

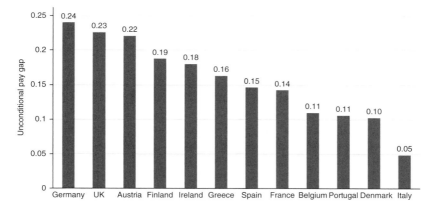

Figure 8.8 Total unconditional gender pay gap by country.
Source: Author's own calculations from ECHP 1994–2001

are to be found in Germany, the UK and Austria – all well above the 20 per cent mark. The smallest gap by some margin is in Italy with 5 per cent. The other countries cluster at around 10 per cent (Denmark, Portugal and Belgium) and around 15 per cent (Greece, Spain and France). This figure shows the sizeable variance in the gap which remains to be explained by the data. Some of this variance can be attributed to observable differences in human capital, demographic structure or female participation patterns but much remains unaccounted for. In what follows we will decompose this gap and attempt to explain the variance in it across countries.

Figures 8.9 and 8.10 examine the pattern of the raw gender wage gap across countries by level of education (in Figure 8.9) and by age cohort (in Figure 8.10). Figure 8.9 shows that in some countries the wage gap is largest for the more highly educated – notably Greece, Portugal and Spain. But in other countries the pattern is reversed with the least educated experiencing the largest gap – notably Austria, Denmark, France, and Germany. In the remaining countries there is no significant difference in the education groups or the intermediate group with just secondary education experiences the biggest gap.

Figure 8.10 shows that the raw gap is largest for the young rather than the old in every country except Portugal in which those with intermediate education experience the lowest gender wage pay gap.

Figure 8.11 provides a new take on the gender pay gap by positioning the average female wage at the appropriate point of the male wage distribution for each country. To a large extent this provides an inverse ordering than that given in Figure 8.6 on the total raw pay gap. But the subtle difference is that Figure 8.11 takes account of the shape of both the male and female wage distributions in a very crude way. Broadly speaking the countries in which women fare the best are

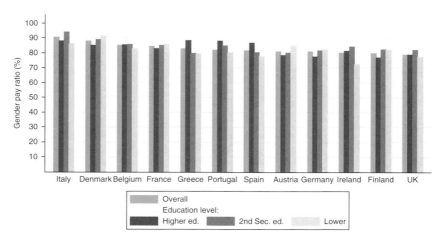

Figure 8.9 Gender pay ratio (unconditional) by country and education level.
Source: Author's own calculations from ECHP 1994–2001.

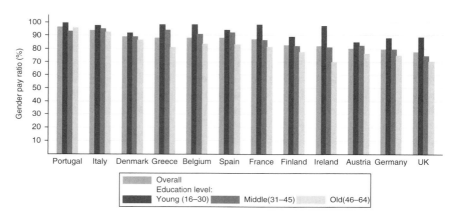

Figure 8.10 Gender pay ratio (unconditional) by country and age group.
Source: Author's own calculations from ECHP 1994–2001.

those in which the pay gap is smallest, notably Italy, France and Denmark. The countries in which women fare the worst are Austria, UK and Germany.

Further exploring the theme of the wage structure differences within countries between men and women we can graph what the overall frequency distribution of wages looks like for men and women in each country and examine the structure of the age-earnings profile within each country by gender. We do this respectively in Figures 8.12 and 8.13. In several countries the overall frequency distribution looks very similar for men and women – for example Portugal, Italy, Spain. This is

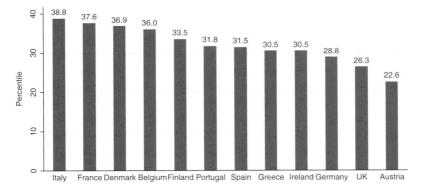

Figure 8.11 The percentile ranking of the median women's earnings in the male earnings distribution by country.
Source: Author's own calculations from ECHP 1994–2001.

in turn reflected in the age-earnings profile for these countries where there is not much difference in the unconditional profile for men and women by age. It should be remembered that these are the countries in which the female participation rate is relatively low and so those women who are working are a much more self-selected group – with presumably much higher earnings potential. In sharp contrast, several other countries have a clear difference in Figure 8.13 in the age-earnings profile between men and women, notably the UK, Ireland, Denmark, Germany, France, Austria and Finland. This is reflected in their frequency distributions in Figure 8.12. Although many countries have a fairly steep age-earnings profile in the early years of the life cycle (notably the UK, Ireland, Belgium, France, Denmark, Germany) this is not where the most significant differences between men and women within a country are to be found. These figures also show us quite clearly that the male-female gap grows with age in some countries like Belgium, France, but remains relatively constant in other countries like the UK and Germany.

In the analysis so far and in particular in Figure 8.12 and 8.13 the structure of the wage distribution has been taken as given and no attempt has been made to look at the distribution of earnings conditional on characteristics and hence assess the effect of gender on earnings allowing for the possibility of different experience, education and other endowments. This we do in the most straightforward way in Figure 8.14. What we do here is to estimate an earnings regression separately for men and for women with all the conditioning factors that we have data for in the ECHP. We then estimate the predicted wage schedule by age holding all other factors constant – i.e. conditioning out for all observable differences between men and women. The resulting plots give us an idea of the conditional age-earnings profile by gender and this reveals the real difference between men and women as they age when all the standard factors like education and experience have been allowed for. Such an analysis is instructive as it tells us where the differences

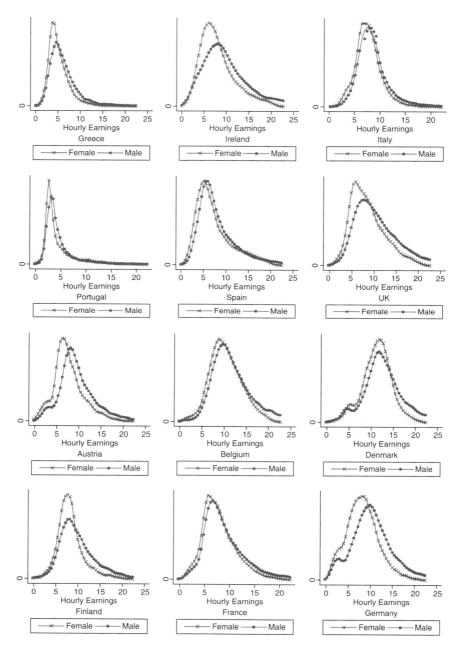

Figure 8.12 Raw wage frequency distribution by gender by country.
Source: Author's own calculations from ECHP 1994–2001.

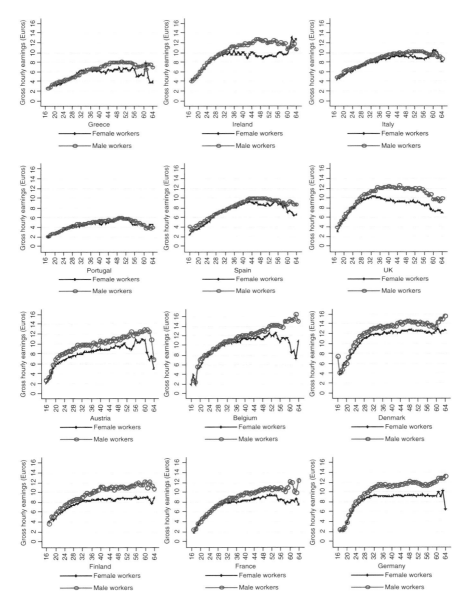

Figure 8.13 Age-earnings profile by gender by country.
Source: Author's own calculations from ECHP 1994–2001.

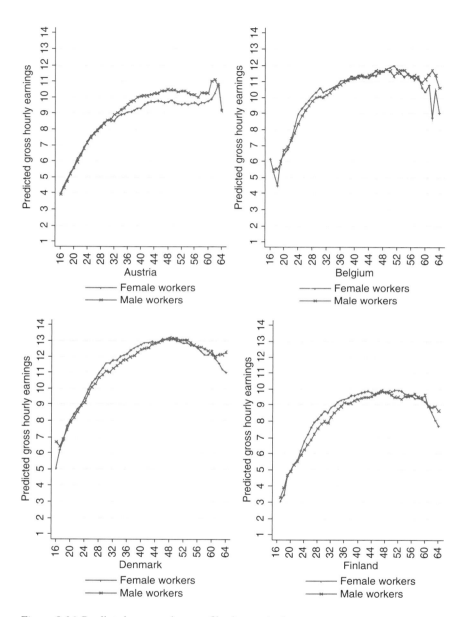

Figure 8.14 Predicted age-earnings profiles by gender by country.
Source: Author's own caculations from ECHP 1994–2001.

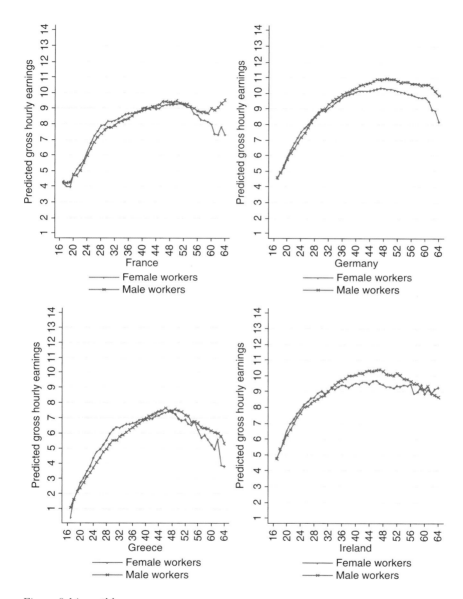

Figure 8.14 cont'd

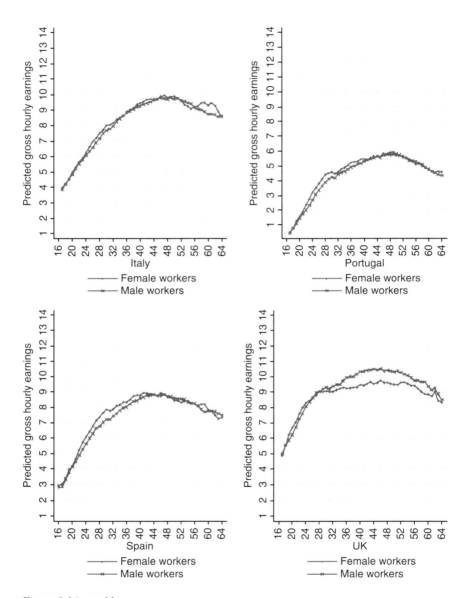

Figure 8.14 cont'd

are between men and women across the whole spectrum of their lives. This is in sharp contrast to the standard decomposition at the mean which just presents a limited view of male-female earnings comparisons. The plots in Figure 8.14 show us the diversity between countries. For Italy and Portugal there is relatively little difference between the pay of working women and men. The position is similar in Spain although working women earn more than men over the 24–40 age range. A similar pattern of early female advantage is observed in Denmark, Finland, Belgium, Greece and France – but in all these countries men earn more in the late part of their lives in their fifties and sixties. In Austria, Germany, Ireland and the UK we observe that women never earn more than men and for long periods in their lives earn considerably less. It is this considerable gap over a large part of their working lives that contributes to the overall size of the gender pay gap that we saw in these countries in Figure 8.8.

Conclusion

Just like a number of other comparative studies, our results show that there are significant differences in the extent as well as in the structure of the gender pay gap across EU member countries. This suggests that although the equal treatment target should be common to all countries, the means of achieving it should be country-specific. One value added of our analysis is the light it sheds on the importance of designing specific policies for the different countries, depending on which group of female workers is the most likely to face discrimination. Our study explored at least five dimensions to identify such groups.

First, the structure by age of discrimination related wage differentials suggests that in some countries anti-discrimination policies should first target old rather than young workers, although the extent of wage discrimination in old ages is likely to reflect the cumulative discriminatory effect which took place all along working careers.

Second, whether anti-discrimination policies should target relative appreciation of women's salaries or relative depreciation of men's salaries is another important issue. Again, our results suggest that it is only in some countries that discrimination mean underpayment of women.

Third, occupational segregation is an important factor in understanding gender wage differentials. However, there are countries where occupations employing the highest shares of women are also occupations where the extent of wage discrimination is the largest, the opposite being true in the other countries.

Fourth, the structure of the gender wage differential also differs according to whether women work part- or full-time. In comparison to female full-time workers, those working part-time are more likely to be better endowed (in terms of individual characteristics) than their male counterparts. In addition, in most countries, the extent of wage discrimination is larger among part-time workers than among full-time employees. This suggests that in these countries the higher is the fraction of female part-time workers, the more anti-discrimination policies should be targeted towards this group of workers.

Last but not least, our results also highlight sometimes significant differences in the extent of wage discrimination by educational group. In particular, there are countries where wage discrimination is more important among the highly educated than among the least educated. In such countries, anti-discrimination policies should therefore not focus exclusively on the low educated.

Notes

1 See also Kidd and Shannon (1996) for a comparison of Australia and Canada and Edin and Richardson (2002) for a comparison of Sweden and the US.
2 Polachek and Kim (1994) discuss alternative methods of estimating the gender wage gap with panel data and show that the role of individual unobserved heterogeneity can be very high when panel methods are used. The problem with this approach is that there is no clear way of distinguishing between the role of individual unobserved heterogeneity and the discrimination faced by women in the labour market. The problems of using the panel features of the data are also compounded in the case of an unbalanced panel. It is for these reasons that we opt for using the simplest models in this chapter. A further justification for pooling the data is that we wish to estimate the average size of the gender wage differences over the 1994–2001 period and we do not attempt to model the course of individual wage growth or the life-course trajectory of wages as it is doubtful whether we have enough data to identify this dynamic process.
3 See Joshi and Paci (1998: 16), Figure 1.2.

References

Albrecht, J., Bjorklund, A. and Vroman, S. (2003) 'Is there a Glass Ceiling in Sweden?' *Journal of Labor Economics*, 21 (1):145–177.
Albrecht, J., van Vuuren A. and Vroman, S. (2004) *Decomposing the Gender Wage Gap in the Netherlands with Sample Selection Adjustment*, IZA Discussion Paper no. 1400.
Arulampalam, W., Booth, A. and Bryan, M. L. (2005) *Is there a glass ceiling over Europe? Exploring the gender pay gap across the wages distribution*, ISER Working Paper no. 25.
Azmat, G., Güell, M. and Manning, A. (2006) 'Gender gaps in Unemployment Rates in OECD Countries', *Journal of Labor Economics*, 24 (1): 1–37.
Beblo, M., Beninger, D., Heinze, A. and Laisney, F. (2003) *Measuring Selectivity-Corrected Gender Wage Gaps in the EU*, ZEW Discussion Paper no. 03–74.
Bettio, F (1988) *The Sexual Division of Labour*. Clarendon Press: Oxford.
Blinder, A.S. (1973) 'Wage Discrimination: Reduced Form and Structural Variables', *Journal of Human Resources*, 8 (4): 436–465.
Blau, F. and Beller, A. (1988) 'Trends in Earnings Differentials by Gender, 1971–81', *Industrial and Labor Relations Review*, 41 (4): 513–529.
Blau, F. and Kahn, L. (1992) 'The Gender Earnings Gap: Learning from International Comparisons', *American Economic Review*, 82 (2): 533–538.
Blau, F. and Kahn, L. (1996) 'Wage Structure and Gender Earnings Differentials: An International Comparisons', *Economica*, 63 (250): S29–S62.
Blau, F. and Kahn, L. (1997) 'Swimming Upstream: Trends in the Gender Earnings Differential in the 1980s', *Journal of Labor Economics*, 15 (1): 1–42.
Blau, F. and Kahn, L. (2003) 'Understanding International Differences in the Gender Pay Gap', *Journal of Labor Economics*, 21 (6): 106–144.
Blinder, A.S. (1973) 'Wage Discrimination: Reduced Form and Structural Variables', *Journal of Human Resources*, 8 (4): 436–465.
Blundell, R., Gosling, A., Ichimura, H. and Meghir, C. (2004) *Changes in the Distribution of Male and Female Wages Accounting for Employment Composition Using Bounds*, CEPR DP no. 4705.
Booth, A., Francesconi, M. and Frank, J. (2003) 'Glass Ceilings and Sticky Floors', *European Economic Review,* 47 (2): 295–322.

Brown, R., Moon, M., and Zoloth, B. (1980) 'Incorporating Occupational Attainment in Studies of Male-Female Earnings Differentials', *Journal of Human Resources*, 15 (1): 3–28.

Buchinsky, M. (1998) 'The Dynamics of Changes in the Female Male Distribution in the USA: A Quantile Regression Approach', *Journal of Applied Econometrics*, 13 (1): 1–30.

Cholezas, I. and Tskloglou, P. (2003) *'Gender Earnings Gap: Evidence from the ECHP'*, mimeo.

Commission of the European Communities (1993) *Employment in Europe*, Luxembourg.

Edin, P. A. and Richardson, K. (2002) 'Swimming with the Tide: Solidarity Wage Policy and the Gender Earnings Gap', *Scandinavian Journal of Economics*, 104 (1): 79–67.

Gannon, B., Plasman, R., Rycx, F. and Tojerow, I. (2005) *Inter-Industry Wage Differentials and the Gender Wage Gap: Evidence, from European Countries*, IZA Discussion Paper no. 1563.

Gwartney, J., Lawson, R., Park, W. and Skipton, C. (various years) *Economic Freedom in the World*, Frasier Institute, Vancouver BC.

Heckman, J. (1979) 'Sample Selection Bias as a Specification Error', *Econometrica*, 47 (1): 153–163.

Johnson, W., Kitamura, Y. and Neal, D. (2000) 'Evaluating a Simple Model for Estimating Black-White Gaps in Median Wages', *American Economic Review*, 90 (2): 339–343.

Joshi, H. and Paci, P. (1998) *Unequal Pay for Women and Men*. Cambridge MA: MIT Press.

Juhn, C., Murphy, K. and Pierce B. (1991) 'Accounting for the Slowdown in Black-White wage convergence' in M Kosters (ed.) *Workers and their Wages*. Washington DC: AEI Press.

Juhn, C., Murphy, K. and Pierce B. (1993) 'Wage inequality and The Rise in the Returns to Skill', *Journal of Political Economy*, 101 (3): 410–442.

Kidd, M. P. and Shannon, M. (1996) 'The Gender Wage Gap: A Comparison of Australia and Canada', *Industrial and Labour Relations Review*, 49 (4): 729–746.

Landers, R. M., Rebitzer, J. B. and Taylor, L. J. (1996) 'Rat Race Redux: Adverse Selection in the Determination of Work Hours in Law Firms', *American Economic Review*, 86 (3): 329–348.

Lewbel, A. (2002) 'Selection Model and Conditional Treatment Effects, Including Endogenous Regressors', mimeo, Boston College.

Machado, J and Mata, J. (2005) 'Counterfactual Decomposition of Changes in Wage Distributions Using Quantile Regression', *Journal of Applied Econometrics*, 20 (4): 445–465.

Neal, D. (2004) 'The Measured Black-White Wage Gap among Women is too Small', *Journal of Political Economy*, 112 (S1): S1–S28.

Neuman, S. and Oaxaca, R. L. (1998) 'Wage Decompositions with Selectivity-corrected Wage Equations: A Methodological Note', *Journal of Economic Inequality*, 2 (1): 3–10.

OECD (2002) 'Women at Work: Who are they and How are they Faring?', *OECD Employment Outlook*. Paris: OECD. pp. 61–125.

Oaxaca, R. (1973) 'Male-Female Wage Differentials in Urban Labour Markets', *International Economic Review*, 14 (3): 693–709.

Olivetti, C. and Petrongolo, B. (2005) *Unequal Pay or Unequal Employment? A Cross-Country Analysis of Gender Gaps*, CEP Discussion Paper no. 711.

Pissarides, C., Garibaldi, P. Olivetti, C., Petrongolo, B. and Wasmer, E. (2005) 'Women in the Labour Force: How Well is Europe Doing?' in T. Boeri, D. del Boca and C. Pissarides (eds) *Women at work: an Economic Perspective: A report for the Fondazione Rodolfo Debenedetti*, Oxford University Press.

Plasman, R. and Sissoko, S. (2005) 'Comparing Apples and Oranges: Revisiting the Gender Wage Gap in an International Perspective', mimeo, Universite Libre de Bruxelles.

Polachek, S. and Kim, M. (1994) 'Panel Estimates of the Gender Earnings Gap', *Journal of Econometrics*, 61 (1): 23–42.

de la Rica, S., Dolado, J. J. and Llorens, V. (2005) *Ceilings and Floors: Gender Wage Gaps by Education in Spain*, IZA Discussion Paper no. 1483.

Rice, P. (1999) *Gender Earnings Differentials: The European Experience*, World Bank Working Paper no. 8.

Rubery, J (ed) (1998) *Equal Pay In Europe? Closing the Gender Wage Gap*, ILO Studies Series. London: Macmillan and New York: S. Martins.

Rubery, J., Grimshaw, D. and Figueiredo, H. (2005) 'How to close the Gender Pay Gap in Europe: Towards the gender mainstreaming of pay policy', *Industrial Relations Journal*, 36 (3): 184–213.

Weichselbaumer, D. and Winter-Ebmer, R. (2002) *The effects of markets, politics and society on the gender wage differential: A meta-analysis*, Working Paper, University of Linz.

9 Occupational segregation and gender wage disparities in developed economies

Should we still worry?

Francesca Bettio

Questions arising from secular trends

Take a century-long view and think how best to summarize the change in the position of women in employment vis-à-vis men in industrialized countries. The chances are that you will come up with two very popular indicators, namely, the degree of occupational segregation and the gender wage gap. In order to illustrate secular trends in these indicators, take two mature economies sufficiently different in their development paths, state vs. market balances, levels of female employment and gender cultures. Your choice may well fall on the USA and Italy. Mine did, and Figures 9.1 and 9.2 contrast the trend in occupational gender segregation and in the female to male ratio in earnings over the past hundred years in these two countries. Although the respective patterns are different, they tell a similar and sufficiently clear story until the 1980s, namely, that women's earnings rose considerably relatively to men's only when segregation visibly weakened. Since the 1980s, however, the relation has de-coupled for Italy, with segregation (probably) diminishing and relative earnings barely growing, although they have remained fairly high.

The numbers behind the trends in Figures 9.1 and 9.2 are inevitably controversial on several grounds, e.g. the juxtaposition of annual and hourly series to reconstruct trends in earnings, or the choice of a relatively 'crude' index – the Index of Dissimilarity (ID) – to capture change in segregation over time.[1] Precision and sophistication must often be traded for comparability and continuity in such exercises, and this is no exception. However, before these difficulties prompt us to dismiss the insights arising from the above figures, let us return to the case of Italy and illustrate the bare numbers with two snapshots taken more than a century apart. The first is archive material from a renowned wool mill in Northern Italy – the Sella Company – and dates back to around 1880. The second dates to 1992 and is taken from the administrative records of a large public hospital in Rome. Both detail the allocation of men and women across occupations, rank occupations by skill, and record occupational earnings. Both are fairly representative of similar concerns in their time and country and are examples of relatively good job opportunities for women (see Tables 9.1 and 9.2).

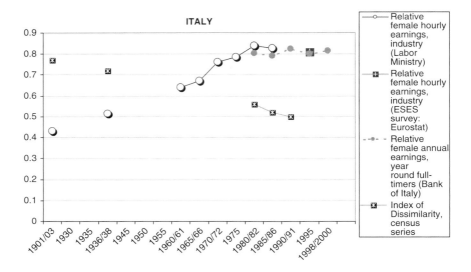

Figure 9.1 Occupational segregation and the gender pay gap, 1901–2000.
Sources: 1st series: Bettio (1988: p. 104 and Table 5.9); 2nd series: Structure of Earnings Survey, Eurostat; 3rd series: own calculation on microdata from the Bank of Italy Household Survey on Income and Wealth: outliers were removed with STATA standard procedure; 4th series: Index of dissimilarity, census occupational data adjusted for the number of occupations using 235 occupational categories as the reference size. Following Anker (1998), the adjustment factor is 0.061*ln(235/X)*100 where X is the actual number of categories.

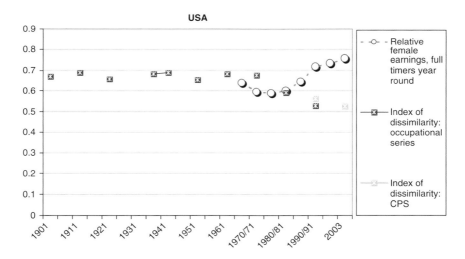

Figure 9.2 Occupational segregation and the gender pay gap 1901–2003.
Sources: 1st series: Blau *et al.* (2006: Table 5.6); 2nd series: Gross (1968: Table 2) and Jacobs (2003), 3 digit classification with between 300 and 400 categories; 3rd series: Blau *et al.* (2006: Table 5.5).

Table 9.1 Occupations and pay at the wool Sella plant, Italy around 1880

	Adult men		Adult women	
	Occupations	Hourly earnings (Male labourer=100)	Occupations	Hourly earnings (Male labourer=100)
Skilled				
	Foreman*	473.7		–
	Washing	235.9	Embroidering	114.4
	Spinning	205.4	Weaving	109.0
	Chemical burring	200.6	Warping	103.0
Semi-skilled				
	Folding and checking	143.1	Carding**	86.2
	Beating and oiling	143.1	Cloth Mending	85.6
	Dyeing	114.4	Grading	80.2
	Carding**	114.4	Spotting	71.3
	Milling and raising	114.4		
Unskilled				
	Labourers	100.0	Purging	57.5

Sources: Reconstructed from Ministero per l'Agricoltura, l'Industria e il Commercio 'L'industria della lana' (1895: 46–49) *Annali di Statistica*, serie 4, no. 84, 59; Castronovo V. (1964: 592) L'industria laniera in Piemonte nel secolo XIX', Archivio Economico dell'Unificazione Italiana, serie 2, vol. 9, Torino: ILTE.
Notes
*Data for foremen do not refer to the Sella plant but are representative of wool firms between 1880 and 1885;
**Men and women were allocated to different stages of carding.

Segregation was practically total at the Sella plant, where women were employed across the skill spectrum, barring foremen, but were paid between 48 and 70 per cent of what men earned at a broadly comparable skill level (the overall wage ratio would be lower than 50 per cent because of overrepresentation towards the bottom). Since hours of work differed little between men and women,[2] it is difficult to resist the implication that segregation played an independent part in keeping women's pay low.

More than a century later, at the Italian hospital, women were also found across the skill spectrum, excluding top management (not recorded in Table 9.2), but segregation was far from total. Moreover, within each occupation the female share was thinner at the top of the grading scale, but the across-occupations pattern was not consistent, since, for example relatively fewer women were present in the lowest paid occupational group – manual workers – than in the highest paid group – doctors. Gross annual earnings for women relative to men in the hospital ranged from a minimum of 88 among lower-skilled technicians to a maximum of 111 among intermediate-skilled doctors, with skill and pay grading within occupations

Table 9.2 Occupations and pay of women and men: public hospital, Italy, 1992

Occupation	Skill grade	Share of female employees	Relative gross annual earnings for women, (men=100)
Full-time doctors			
	11	0.09	95
	10	0.32	111
	9	0.37	102
Other professionals			
	11	0.00	—
	10	0.50	93
	9	0.67	103
	8	0.00	—
Nurses			
	7	0.07	110
	6	0.65	97
	5	0.65	88
Physiotherapists			
	7	1.00	—
Technicians			
	7	0.25	93
	6	0.00	88
Administration			
	7	0.00	—
	6	0.41	99
	4	0.33	95
Manual and technical workers			
	6	0.18	104
	5	0.00	—
	4	0.18	110
	3	0.42	91
All		0.47	90

Source: Bettio (1998: Table 2).

largely reflecting seniority. Thus, in spite of the fact that four occupational groups out of seven – nurses, physiotherapists, manual workers and technicians – could still be considered 'segregated' on most criteria, and in spite of the fact that women were systematically scarce at the top of each group, the implications for women's wages were less dramatic: overall, women earned 90 per cent of what men did. Admittedly, the relative position of women in an Italian public hospital during the early 1990s was especially favourable thanks to a compressed wage scale, employment security and the equalizing effect of seniority pay. The underlying story, however, echoes that shown by Figure 9.1, namely that the relation between segregation, as conventionally understood or measured, and the gender wage gap had not only weakened but may have changed.

Is there still a link between occupational segregation and gender pay discrimination? And can we continue to equate gender occupational segregation indiscriminately with gender inequality in industrialized countries? How does economic theory aid understanding of the ways in which the relationship between segregation and the gender wage gap has evolved over time? Should de-segregation remain a first-order priority for the further integration of women in mature market economies, or should policy be focused elsewhere?

In what follows I shall use these questions as threads to organize a review of the theoretical and empirical debate on segregation. I begin in the following section (section 2) illustrating how mainstream economic theories have recently been revisited to the effect of acknowledging that segregation may imply discrimination, a conclusion that heterodox theories have shared from the outset. In section 3, I discuss recent evidence on the actual importance of segregation for the gender pay gap and, more broadly, for gender equality in mature market economies. I conclude in section 4 by advocating a shift of policy towards selective rather than indiscriminate de-segregation and a shift of research attention from the wage gap to the intra-household gap in earnings and employment between partners.

Theories: quietly converging

Perhaps *the* main theoretical divide among economists centres on whether and how segregation implies discrimination. Before re-examining this divide, let us clarify the concepts. Employment segregation by sex is the disproportionate concentration of women (men) in the relevant employment category. Segregation by occupation (which I shall also sometimes refer to as segregation *tout court*) has received the closest theoretical and empirical attention, partly because it is often seen as the root cause of all segregation (by firms, industry or even type of contract). The issue held centre stage in the 1970s and early 1980s within and outside economics in what we would now call the 'gender studies' field. I would argue that at that time segregation had an even greater stage presence than discrimination. Unlike the latter, which requires proof, occupational segregation is itself proof that women and men behave and/or are treated differently in the labour market. By evoking a distinction between 'intrinsically feminine' and 'intrinsically male' categories, analysis of occupational segregation provides an ideological battleground that extends well beyond economics and sets those convinced that gender differences should be recognized and valued against those persuaded that women are as good as men but need to show it before it may be wise to stress specific differences.

Employment discrimination is generally viewed as leading to wage discrimination or as deriving from the same causes. It therefore makes sense to focus on wage discrimination, which is largely understood by economists as persistent wage disparities between clearly identifiable labour segments (groups) with *equal* productivity *potential* (Cain 1986). 'Equality' here implies that (group) differences in preferences or attitudes are allowed to exist if they do not interfere with labour market outcomes. 'Potential' implies that discriminatory processes may take place in the labour market but may also precede labour market entry, for instance because they are driven by ideology, religion, jurisdiction or all of these.

Table 9.3 Segregation and discrimination: classifying theoretical approaches

	Historical debate	*Post 1990s additions*
Occupational segregation:		
Implies wage discrimination	Overcrowding	Pollution theory
	Restrictive practices	Hierarchical discrimination
	Dual labour markets and statistical theory	Marriage market theory
	Dual labour market and class divisions	
	Patriarchy	
	Socialisation	Identity Theory
Does not imply or prevents wage discrimination	Socialisation	Identity theory
	Taste discrimination	
	Human capital	
	Compensating wage differentials	

Table 9.3 identifies the main theoretical explanations, distinguishing between what I call the 'historical' debate in the 1970s and the 1980s, and the recent debate. I shall only briefly summarize the terms of the historical debate, given that the literature offers numerous reviews (Chiplin and Sloane 1976; England 1982; Hartman and Reskin 1986; Cain 1986; Anker 1997; Blau *et al.* 2006: Chapters 5–7), while I shall spend more time on recent and less well-known contributions.

In the historical debate, explanations that did not assume perfectly competitive markets – this being a rather standard assumption before the 'new microeconomics' of asymmetric information took over – generally saw discrimination as being caused by segregation or as occurring via the latter. Lack of competition was viewed as taking different forms, from restricted access to entry to more general processes of labour-market segmentation. And the underlying reasons for segregation ranged from the influence of institutions, to patriarchy, to class.

The analytical core of most explanations invoking entry barriers in order to account for segregation can be traced back to Bergmann's model (1974), where women are overcrowded into a limited number of occupations, and overcrowding depresses their wages relative to men, independent of the respective attributes or attitudes. Restrictive practices or legal bans can be seen as belonging among such crowding mechanisms. In most developed market economies, bans and restrictions may be regarded as things of the past, but some of that past is sufficiently recent to exert influence still today.[3] Moreover, the lifting of a legal ban does not guarantee that covert opposition disappears. May (this volume) maintains that some of the arguments used in the past to justify barriers to entry to higher education are still used today to justify the resilient segregation of school/university curricula. Most feminist economists involved in the historical debate agreed with Bergman that these restrictions were expression of patriarchy (Hartman and Reskin 1986), but some viewed them differently. For example, it was argued that restrictive practices were implemented selectively by unionized male workers in order to protect high-paying occupations against deskilling (Rubery 1978).

However widespread they may have been in the past, restrictive practices and legal bans may be viewed as specific and sometimes contingent obstacles to an otherwise competitive market. In the understanding of radical, institutional and some feminist economists, the labour market is segmented rather than competitive, and segregation is a facet of widespread segmentation rather than the outcome of specific barriers to entry. Segmentation theory does not (or does not entirely) share the marginal productivity view of wages, since wages are co-determined by market and institutional mechanisms. But it is nevertheless compatible with the concept of discrimination outlined above. In the classic version of the *dual labour market* theory (Doeringer and Piore 1971), for example, skill specificity gives rise to a primary segment of jobs/firms where employment and wage outcomes are the result of practices, norms and routines ensuring that firms internalize the benefits of training since they cannot avoid internalizing the costs. In this setting, any sorting mechanism that assigns one group of workers a lower probability of accessing the primary sector – and higher wages – may cause discrimination. This is the case, for example, when the sorting mechanism is statistical discrimination whereby women are found to be less predictable than men with regard to employment continuity (higher variance), and employers fail to select them for primary segment jobs even if their average discontinuity is no higher than that of their male counterparts (Phelps 1972; Aigner and Cain 1995).

For radical Marxists the division between primary and secondary labour segments ensues from class interest rather than from skill specificity, and wages are the outcome of class bargaining, not institutional routines. Dividing workers in order to undermine their bargaining power is therefore rational for employers, and the prevailing ideology can be used to differentiate occupations and wages across segments, independently of actual productivity (Bowles and Gintis 1977).

According to feminists, the allocation of women to secondary jobs/firms/sectors originates primarily if not entirely from patriarchy, and may take the form of legal, ideological or union-prompted barriers to entry, as noted. However, these need not be the only or even the main mechanisms at work. In my own version (Bettio 1988), the mechanisms are more subtle. Women, I argue, have lower reservation wages than men because of differential income roles in the family, i.e. they are potentially 'cheaper'. At the same time, the value of a given occupation to the organization (firm or other) is strongly influenced by the 'damage potential' of any interruption or misconduct (including low effort) on the part of the employee – often referred to as 'responsibility'. A production line manager can cause more damage than a line worker; a fork-lift truck driver in a ceramic firm of some thirty years could cause more damage than any single worker in charge of testing tiles for wholeness and sorting them. Differing damage potentials justify efficiency wage differentials across occupations, i.e. wage premiums that reflect the characteristics and location of the job and not necessarily the productivity potential of the incumbent workers. In this setting, allocation of 'cheaper' supplies (women) to lower damage-potential jobs is a possible equilibrium solution which is stabilized and legitimized by the prevailing social stratification, patriarchy in particular.

This explanation is compatible with widespread evidence that women have been preferentially allocated to labour-intensive occupations, especially in the past (horizontal segregation), and that they still find it more difficult to climb job ladders (hierarchical segregation).

Economists tend to take preferences as given. But if discrimination operates at the level of preference formation then it cannot be attributed solely to labour market mechanisms. One distinction widely debated among radical and feminist economists was in-market vs. pre-market discrimination, and it rested on the notion of socialization borrowed from sociology. 'Socialisation' is the term used to indicate that sex is a fundamental organizing principle in any society and that women and men are brought up with different preferences and different attitudes: dolls for little girls and toy cars for little boys is an all too familiar example. Socialisation thus defined is a very general explanation of occupational segregation, but it is not clear whether it can account for discrimination as previously defined. Why, in fact, should women's preferences or attitudes or skills be valued less, systematically or even on average? (note that a similar objection applies to the theory of equalizing wage differentials). Many sociologists would answer that social stratification by sex goes hand in hand with undervaluation of women's work, or, at least, has done so in the past (England 2004). Historical examples of feminization of occupations followed by decreasing wages can be cited in support of this assertion, e.g. in the well-known case of bank telling in the USA (Strober and Arnold 1987). Support also comes from laboratory experiments showing that lower social evaluation may result in lower remuneration (Eckel, this volume). It is however a thorny question as to whether this socially shared undervaluation of attributes and skills which is sometimes referred to as 'societal discrimination' amounts to labour-market discrimination as previously defined.

One way to answer this question has been to draw a distinction between pre-market and in-market discrimination, with the former broadly corresponding to a socially-shared (and implemented) undervaluation of women's skills and attributes, and the latter being closer to the definition adopted here. Some argued, however, that in-market and not pre-market discrimination is at work for those skills acquired by women as part of their informal training to be good housewives and carers. These are emotional skills that may be exploited in jobs involving public relations (PR) or care-related occupations; dexterity, patience or visual precision, which are often exploited in manufacturing; organisational skills and a multi-tasking ability; and so on. Since socialisation and informal learning ensure the reproduction of these skills, employers can afford not to pay for them (Phillips and Taylor 1980; Elson and Pearson 1981). If we are willing to accept that, unlike female occupations, those dominated by men are intensive in skills primarily acquired on the job or via formal education, rather than through socialisation, systematic undervaluation of female skills by employers lowers female wages and constitutes discrimination.

As noted, none of the above explanations subscribe to the view that markets are fully or even largely competitive. On the other side of the theoretical divide, where markets are fully competitive, it is accepted that tastes are socially constructed and that they may even give rise to segregation but, if anything, the latter is seen to prevent discrimination rather than implying it. In Becker's (1957) taste discrimination model(s), segregation is a way out of discrimination in that it enables 'prejudiced' employers fully to indulge their taste for men (or white workers) without a loss of profits due to their unwillingness to hire equally productive but cheaper women (or black workers). The theory of compensating wage differentials (Rosen 1986) and human capital theory (Mincer and Polachek 1974) also rule out discrimination in the presence of segregation: in the former case, occupational choices by women may reflect characteristics that they are willing to pay for with a wage penalty, e.g. a flexible work schedule; in the latter, women end up in occupations requiring less qualifications/experience because of lower investment on their part, and hence lower productivity. In turn, lower investment in human capital ultimately reflects the biological comparative advantage that women have in care work.

The divide in the historical debate was thus fairly clear-cut, with 'mainstream' explanations on the side of 'inconsequential' segregation, radical, feminist and Marxist explanations on the other, and sociological explanations sitting uneasily in the middle. Criticism has been directed at all sides, but while some explanations have gained more popularity than others, no single explanation has emerged as clearly superior (Arrow 1973; England 1982; Cain 1986; Anker 1997; Holzer and Neumark 2006; Blau *et al.* 2006).

Partly in response to criticism and partly as a reaction to changing trends in segregation, some recent studies have built on the original ideas to provide novel or refined explanations. Not surprisingly, these new attempts have mainly targeted the two most popular mainstream explanations, namely human capital and Becker's 'taste' model(s). It is more surprising that most new attempts, even those fully part of the neoclassical tradition, end up by agreeing with the radical strand in the historical debate which argues that segregation can or does imply discrimination, at least on a temporary basis.

Pollution theory

In order to account for continuing de-segregation and re-segregation, Goldin (2002) re-positions Becker's original model in a market context where asymmetric information and signalling matter – as in the theory of statistical discrimination – and where the process of social change is sticky. Select a characteristic that is relevant to productivity (from physical strength to some sort of specific knowledge/education). Call it C and assume that occupations differ in the minimum requirement of C. Suppose also that C is distributed in the same way among men and women, and that the distribution has median value F.[4] Assume that the distribution of C for men is fully known while only the median value of C for women is common knowledge. Assume further that women are late-comers to the labour market (i.e. they enter it when only men are working), that men derive prestige as well as earnings from a given occupation, and that prestige is higher the higher the C requirement. Finally, consider occupation H: 'society' knows that occupation H requires exactly H value of C and that the median value of C for women is F, where $F < H$. Now suppose that there is technological change and that society can only infer whether technology has reduced the C requirement in occupation H from indirect information, principally the gender composition of the workforce. If a woman is hired, society will infer that, since her median endowment of C is $F < H$, the probability that there has been downgrading in C is higher than 50 per cent: the occupation will therefore lose prestige, even if there has been no downgrading. Men will thus oppose women's entry or demand monetary compensation for it. Employers will eventually overcome men's opposition by, for example, creating two occupations with equivalent C requirements but sex typed 'female' and 'male' (and paid equally!).

However, the solution of creating two distinct and completely segregated occupations takes time, and in the meantime women will be crowded into occupations requiring values of C below the female median. Discrimination will therefore take place during the adjustment lags and may be reinforced by feedback effects: if male workers infer the value of C for women from the occupational distribution of the latter at any point in time, then adjustment lags will lead to underestimation of the 'true' value, thus reinforcing opposition to women's entry.

Given that occupational segregation by sex is such a complex phenomenon that it is virtually impossible for any single theory to comprehensively account for it, Goldin's pollution theory does remarkably well, as the many and different examples cited in her paper testify. It accounts for re-segregation as well as de-segregation in the context of technological change, a regular finding of case studies in this area. It points to a relatively neglected factor in explanation of why segregation decreases over time, namely greater knowledge about women's characteristics and behaviour as they are progressively integrated into the labour force. Last but not least, it is sufficiently flexible to allow for the fact that segregation may imply discrimination or may protect women from it.

At the same time, the endeavour to stick to the (neo)classical view of competitive markets while injecting some realism into it (imperfect information and laggard adjustment processes) results in an account that may not be equal to the task. Are we really prepared to believe that a phenomenon as widespread and persistent as segregation derives from the fact that the productive potential of women is less-known than that of men? Or that, in any given occupation, segregation is only a temporary phenomenon which will disappear when employers overcome workers' opposition?

Identity theory

Personal identity, rather than (temporary) lack of information, is the key to explaining persistence and change in segregation in Akerlof and Kranton's contribution (2000). Identity affects the cornerstone of economic modelling – the utility function. Utility is made to depend on own and other people's actions, but it also includes a vector of prescriptions and a function – '*I*' for Identity - whose value depends on both individual's characteristics and assigned social categories. Woman (man) is arguably the most important of such categories, and like other social categories it can be chosen to a (very) limited extent. In Akerlof and Kranton's model, the identity function with 'woman' as its argument – 'I(woman)' – measures the social status of being a woman, and its value is higher, the closer the correspondence between the characteristics of the woman and the 'ideal' female characteristics. Ideal characteristics and ideal behaviour are indicated by a vector of prescriptions.

One important property of these functions is that one person's utility can be influenced by other people's actions, e.g. if a man wears a dress and a dress is a symbol of female identity, this may be a threat to the identity of other men (externality). To see the difference from standard utility maximization, assume that men and women can choose between occupations F and M, earning utility V if they enter their preferred occupation, zero otherwise. In standard models, a woman would maximize her utility by choosing her preferred occupation regardless of what other women or men do. In identity theory, prescriptions specify that women should choose occupation F, men occupation M. Any woman choosing M is not a 'true woman', and this non-conformity causes her to lose utility in amount I_s because of the loss of self-identity. Non-conformity on her part also entails a reduction in the utility (I_o) of the men in M, who may feel that their manhood is threatened by women working alongside them, and may respond by not cooperating. Non-cooperation has a cost c for the male co-worker but induces a further loss of utility L for the non-conforming female 'intruder', as well as productivity losses for the employer. Depending on the relative magnitudes of V, I_s, I_o, c and L there are four possible outcomes: non-conforming women do not enter occupation M regardless of what men do; they are deterred from entry by men's non cooperative response; men do not respond; or do respond but do not succeed in deterring women. As in Goldin's model, moreover, employers may forestall men's response by resorting to segregation, i.e. by creating female and male occupations that are substantively similar but made to look different by using gender identity rhetoric.

Akerlof and Kranton credit their identity theory with providing the microfoundations for Becker's model of taste discrimination. I would argue that it also provides the microfoundations for the construct of 'societal discrimination' that I reviewed earlier. Furthermore, identity theory allows for the fact that policy can influence outcomes by influencing the cost of the response, e.g. a fine on restrictive practices may discourage men's non cooperative response. Policy and politics also influence prescriptions, e.g. when legal bans are removed. By explicitly modelling the role of policy and politics, therefore, the theory calls for examination of trends in segregation to be made in light of political changes, and not only with reference to labour market change. In particular, the authors credit the feminist movement for decisively contributing to the unprecedented decrease in segregation that took place in the USA in the 1970s and 1980s. Feminism was successful, the authors suggest, because it purposely undermined the association between gender and occupations.

However, the theory hardly improves our understanding of how segregation and discrimination are related. For example, there are no reasons within the model why male occupations should be systematically better paid. Moreover, in real life, the re-segregation of new occupations occurs just as frequently as the de-segregation of existing ones, but the model does not inform us how social prescriptions are formed with respect to re-segregation. In short, identity may suffer from the same shortcoming as preferences, i.e. exogeneity with respect to economic and social change.

Segregation and the marriage market

Admittedly, change in society's prescription is generally a sticky process. If we take up Badgett and Folbre's suggestion (2003), stickiness is reinforced by the way the marriage market interacts with the labour market. Taking a feminist perspective, the authors offer fresh arguments in favour of one of the criticisms often brought against human capital theory, namely that feedback effects may actually introduce discrimination into this framework via underinvestment (Coute and Loury 1993). In other words, to the extent that women 'infer' from segregation that they may expect to find employment primarily in low-skilled occupations, they may end up by under-investing regardless of the time that they plan to spend in the labour force.

Badgett and Folbre reason as follows. Given socially prescribed associations between occupations and gender, non-conforming individuals – men and women – may lose attractiveness to prospective partners, and thus find it more difficult to secure one. Since women depend on the partner's income more than men do, marriage market penalization may induce them to underinvest in the human capital needed to enter male occupations ('earnings specific human capital' in the authors' terminology, to distinguish it from other human capital). This gives rise to (self-inflicted) discrimination, although the latter originates from marriage, not the labour market.[5]

Formally, assume that the partner's share of combined income is exogenous, that income is pooled, and that there is no initial discrimination in the labour market. The combined income on which either partner can count (G) can be expressed as:

$$G = g(E_o) + P(E_o)g(E_s) \tag{9.1}$$

where $g(E)$ is the earnings function of human capital theory, P is the probability of finding and retaining a partner, and the subscripts o and s stand for own and spouse, respectively. The hypothesis of marriage market penalization implies that P is a function of one's own investment in human capital E_o. If social norms are such that prospective partners value men's gains in earnings more than women's, G is greater if he invests than if she invests. To see this, differentiate G with respect to her or his human capital and obtain two terms. The first term – $\delta g (E_o)/\delta E_o$ – measures own returns to human capital and is the same for him and her if there is no discrimination in the labour market. The second term – $[\delta P\,(E_o)/\delta E_o]\,g\,(E_s)$ – is lower for her because of the undervaluation of her additional earnings induced by social norms, or because additional investment in human capital is associated with entry into a male-dominated occupation. Overall, therefore, G increases more if 'own' means 'his' investment.

Hierarchical theory

Badgett and Folbre's account rationalizes the vertical dimension of segregation, i.e. under-representation of women at the top of the pyramid of occupational earnings. Baldwin *et al.* (2001) prefer to view this pyramid as strictly mirroring a hierarchical command chain. In view of increasing evidence that the vertical/hierarchical component of segregation is especially resistant to change (see next section), Baldwin *et al.* conflate the human capital hypothesis and Becker's theory into a model that equates segregation with hierarchical segregation and allows for (self-inflicted) discrimination. In their fully competitive market world, occupations are ranked in terms of the human capital they require, with wages strictly compensating for investment in human capital; unlike in Becker's model, however, individuals are allowed to vary in ability. Because workers vary in their ability to acquire the human capital needed to climb up the occupational ladder, the most able workers enjoy wage 'rents', i.e. their net return from investment in human capital is positive. The male workers populating this world have a positive taste for discrimination against women in supervisory positions but are willing to trade money for the disutility of having women managing them.

If the distribution of ability and the numbers in employment are the same for men and women, complete segregation can prevent discrimination, as in Becker: women supervise women and men supervise men. If the numbers differ and women are fewer (e.g. because of housework) some women will have to manage men, but only the most capable of them will be able to devote part of the wage rents they earn in apical occupations to compensate for workers' distaste. Given technology (which determines the amount of human capital along the occupational ladder) the extent of this compensation depends on the strength of taste discrimination, the number of men supervised, and the (male) occupational wage level, as follows:

$$W_s p = L_m W_l \delta \tag{9.2}$$

where the subscripts m, l and s stand, respectively, for man, labourer (workers under supervision) and supervisor, W is wage, L units of labour, δ is the discrimination coefficient and p the female supervisor's wage penalty expressed as a fraction of a male supervisor's wage. Employers are indifferent between hiring women or men as supervisors provided the above equality is satisfied.

Two key predictions of the model are that the wage gap exists at each rung of the occupational hierarchy, and that the share of women in occupation j relative to that of men (over the respective totals) declines as one moves up the occupational ladder. Unlike in Becker's model, moreover, discriminatory outcomes are compatible with long-run competitive equilibrium since it is women, not employers, who use their rent to pay the full cost of discrimination.

Some answers from empirical research

To my knowledge, none of these recent explanations have been tested to a conclusive extent, if one disregards the evidence cited in support by the respective authors. As happened earlier during the historical debate, empirical and theoretical research on segregation pursue parallel paths and do no frequently meet. Beset by the scarcity of data able to combine the detail of single case studies with the representativeness of survey records, quantitative research on segregation by sociologists and statisticians has often been dominated by issues of measurement rather than theory, while remaining at the margin of the broader research on wage differentials conducted by economists.[6]

However, if we stick to basic and shared theoretical questions, measurement and theory enter into dialogue. The strongest message from the theories I reviewed is that, yes, discrimination is a probable, if not systematic, outcome in the presence of segregation. Thus questions that empirical research must address are to what extent this is borne out by recent evidence and what its order of magnitude is. A related finding of the theoretical review is the importance of vertical/hierarchical segregation rather than segregation per se, which prompts a more general question about which components of segregation matter most for gender pay inequality.

The final question raised by the theory concerns the direction and pace of change in segregation. Although there is no single theoretical contribution to the historical or recent debate that directly addresses this complex issue, most of the studies reviewed imply that the phenomenon should weaken as female participation increases, albeit via a complex balance of de-segregation and re-segregation. Within the human capital approach, for example, household appliances and fertility decline should concur in reducing women's comparative advantage in household production, which is at the core of gendered occupational choices. Where the explanation pivots on the secondary income role of women, as in several feminist accounts, increasing female participation ought to bring with it lower levels of segregation insofar as 'she' moves from a secondary to a primary income role. Progressive integration into the labour force should also improve knowledge about women's characteristics and behaviour, thus eroding the mechanisms implied by statistical discrimination or by pollution theory. Insofar as it subverts stereotypes, the political emancipation of women may be an independent factor of erosion, as in sociological theories of job stereotyping, or in identity theory. The expectation is therefore consistent across theoretical perspectives that segregation should weaken with increasing female participation (more women and more full-time women in the labour force).

At the same time, there is evidence of resistance to further change in the division of labour within households,[7] which raises the possibility that developed economies may be approaching a lower bound to de-segregation. Let me start from this possibility. Anker's world-wide study on segregation (1998) has gained notoriety because of the sheer scope of its coverage. For the 32 countries in the ILO database observed between 1970 and 1990, Anker finds that de-segregation (measured by the decline in the Index of Dissimilarity) advanced, on average, at the pace of 2.4 per cent points in the 1970s and 2.6 in the 1980s, although some countries showed persistent re-segregation (Asian countries) or very limited change (Transition economies). His recent update (Anker *et al.* 2003) indicates that similar trends prevailed in the 1990s, with de-segregation clearly advancing at a pace of around 3 per cent, except in Asia and transition economies. OECD countries, in particular, are reported to have de-segregated at values between 3 and 3.8 per cent in these three decades. However, the figures for the 1990s concern only 4 countries, as opposed to 16 for earlier years,[8] and the trend that they reveal is not uniformly supported by other studies. Jacobs (2003), Fortin and Huberman (2002) and Finzi (2005) confirm that segregation has declined in the USA, Canada and Switzerland in the current decade, while I find that the average, unweighted change in the Dissimilarity Index for 9 European countries between 1992 and 2000 is close to zero (see Table 9.4).

Table 9.4 Recent trends in occupational segregation in Europe and North America

Countries	Index of Dissimilarity					
	1980–1	*1990–2*	*1995*	*1997*	*2000*	*2003*
Austria			0.51	0.59	0.58	
Belgium			0.54	0.56	0.55	
Germany			0.55	0.56	0.56	
Denmark		0.61	0.62	0.56	0.56	
Spain		0.55	0.54	0.55	0.55	
Finland				0.62	0.62	
France		0.55	0.56	0.57	0.56	
Greece		0.50	0.53	0.53	0.52	
Ireland		0.51	0.51	0.51	0.55	
Italy		0.49	0.49	0.48	0.48	
Netherlands		0.54	0.53	0.53	0.53	
Portugal		0.52	0.54	0.54	0.58	
Sweden*				0.60	0.58	
UK		0.57	0.56	0.55	0.54	
EU(9) average		0.54	0.54	0.54	0.54	
Switzerland	0.63	0.58			0.56	
Canada	0.57			0.42		
USA		0.56				0.52

Sources: EU countries: own calculation, European Labour Force Sample Survey, 146 occupational categories excluding agriculture; Switzerland: Finzi (2005: Table 3:based on census data); Canada: Huberman and Fortin (2002: S23; based on 250 census occupational categories); USA: Blau (2006: Table 5–5; based on CPS data).

One gains the overall impression from these studies that if there is a floor to de-segregation, mature market economies show no clear signs of having reached it yet. At the same time, the controversial evidence for de-segregation in Europe over the past decade suggests that the phenomenon is not linearly related to women's integration into the labour force. This is confirmed by Anker's cross-section and time-series investigation of the association between the Index of Dissimilarity and the female share of the non-agricultural labour force. By means of regression analysis Anker finds that changes in ID and in the female share of the non-agricultural labour force correlate negatively on a time-series base. But he also finds that cross-section data yield a negative relation only in those countries where women are a minority in the labour force (below one third, e.g. in Middle-Eastern countries). For countries where women make up more than 35 per cent of the entire labour force, further integration has meant more segregation!

This latter finding that segregation and women's employment tend to correlate positively for developed countries is shared by other European studies, suggesting that the correlation is driven, amongst other things, by the role of the public sector in 'marketizing' feminized care work or in offering provisions that disproportionately attract women to public-sector occupations (employment security, leave provisions, tolerance of absenteeism and so on). Typical occupations in health care, long-term care or public child care, but also the ongoing feminization of the judiciary in several European countries, are all cases in point and are compelling examples of how segregation has often protected or even fostered female employment (Bettio 2002, Emerek *et al.* 2002).

If, then, segregation *can* be 'good' for women's employment, is it consistently 'bad' for their pay? This brings us back to the question of how far recent empirical evidence supports the contention that segregation is an important vehicle of gender pay discrimination or, more generally, gender pay inequality. As well documented in the essay by Dolton *et al.* (this volume), pay discrimination is usually equated in empirical research with the net wage gap between male and female workers, i.e. the residual wage gap that obtains in the estimation of wage equations after controlling for individual differences like schooling or age. However, if discrimination is both pre-market and in-market, or if feedback effects are large, this residual may underestimate discrimination.[9] For example, if women underinvest in their own capital because they anticipate discrimination or because of how the marriage market operates, then individual qualifications are themselves the result of discrimination, and controlling for such qualifications does not prevent underestimation. Still unresolved, therefore, is the issue of whether the net or the entire gap should be used. I shall consider both types of approaches.

In the conclusion to his 1998 study, Anker definitely equates segregation with restricted access to jobs, hence with employment discrimination, but refrains from conducting thorough analysis of the consequences on pay. Nevertheless he concludes that '... the most important occupations for women represent poor jobs in terms of pay, status, decision-making authority and career opportunity' (Anker 1998: 411).

His conclusion contrasts with the findings of recent analyses that use individual data from household surveys and focus on Europe and the USA. Dolado *et al.* (2002) verify for EU15 countries and the USA the sign and the strength of the correlation between indexes of segregation broken down by age and educational level and the respective 'net' wage gap, i.e. the Oaxaca-Blinder residual from standard, Mincerian wage equations. Using the European Community Household Panel (ECHP henceforth) for Europe and the Current Population Survey for the USA, they find that the correlation is positive but low and not significant, although significance increases when the Scandinavian countries are dropped from the estimation (the latter are known for having higher segregation and a lower pay gap). Pissarides *et al.* (2003) combine various sources of microdata, including the ECHP, and conduct a somewhat different exercise for European countries. For 11 countries observed between 1980 and 1998 they first estimate a wage gap on the basis of a fairly standard set of individual characteristics, correcting for selectivity. They then regress the wage gap thus netted of personal characteristics on a set of variables accounting for institutional differences among countries as well as for segregation. For the latter variable they obtain a negative sign (more segregation decreases the gap) but no statistical significance. The exercise by Pissarides *et al.* very closely follows that by Blau and Khan (2001), who examine 22 countries over the 1985–1994 period and find that segregation and the 'net' wage gap are positively correlated but the correlation does not reach the conventional significance.

Different results are yielded by matched employee–employer data. These data are not readily available, but they have the advantage of recording the wage gap at progressively finer levels of aggregation: industry, establishment, occupation, down to the within-establishment job level, or 'job-cell' as it is called in this literature. Most of these studies find that segregation between occupations, firms and industries accounts for a large share of the overall gender wage gap. This finding was first born out by Groshen (1991) who used a large matched data set for the USA spanning from 1974 and 1983, and found that the gender gap at job-cell level contributed very little (a maximum of 6 per cent) to the aggregate gap, while segregation between occupations, establishments, and industries explained practically the entire gap. Adopting a rather simple methodology for analysis, but using a very accurate and large data set collected between 1970 and 1990, Meyersson *et al.* (2001) also find that in Sweden the gender gap within the same job-cell was negligible around 1990 (between 1 and 5 per cent), whereas segregation between occupations, establishments and industries accounted for the largest shares of the overall gap.

Unlike Meyersson *et al.*, Bayard *et al.* (2003) as well as Amuedo-Dorantes and De la Rica (2006), estimate the impact of segregation, controlling for personal and (some) institutional characteristics. Bayard *et al.* find for the US in 1990 that job cell segregation – which they attribute to direct discrimination (different pay for exactly the same job) or to differences in skill/responsibility/rung between men and women within the same occupation – remains important since it accounted for between one fourth and one half of the overall gender wage gap. They also find that the estimated effect of segregation between occupations, establishments and industries is large, but not as large as implied by Groshen (1991) or Meyersson *et al.* (2001): altogether, it explained around a third of the wage gap at the highest level of occupational breakdown and for the whole sample. Amuedo-Dorantes and De la Rica (2006: Table 5) also find for Spain that the within cell component of segregation is large as it accounted for 22 per cent of the gender wage gap in 1995 and 53 per cent in 2002. However, the estimated impact of segregation between occupations, establishments and industries varied considerably with the year of the survey, ranging between one tenth and one half of the gender wage gap.[10]

Overall, analyses of matched employee-employer data appear to restore the importance of segregation for the wage gap that analyses based on employee-only data seem to question. However, the estimated order of magnitudes varies, sometimes sensibly, depending on the year, type of data and methodology. Also, the link with discrimination is not so clear. For example, if we refer to the studies that control for individual characteristics and institutional factors, can we infer that the estimated impact of segregation on the wage gap provides an upper bound for discrimination? Or is this the case only for within job cells segregation since here we can rule out major unobserved differences in job content, environment or other? Uncertainty about the estimated order of magnitude on the one hand, and about the precise link with discrimination on the other hand, continues to thwart any attempt to draw precise conclusions from existing evidence on this point.

Another line of inquiry investigates the relative importance of different components of segregation by distinguishing between the vertical and the horizontal dimensions. As noted, some analyses using matched employee-employer data interpret within cells differences in women's and men's wages as reflecting direct discrimination or unobserved segregation by skill/responsibility within the same occupation. Like before, refer to hierarchical segregation as the uneven distribution of different groups of workers along the rungs of the within-occupations job/skill scale. Even if occupations are less sharply defined than in matched employee-employer, it is likely that the within-occupation wage gap reflects hierarchical segregation. Fortin and Huberman (2002) take this view. They analyse census data between 1961 and 1997–8 and decompose the total gap in earnings into the part that originates from differences in male and female earnings within a detailed occupation class, and the part that arises from differences in the distribution of men and women across occupational classes. They find that, while the overall gap decreased consistently over time, the within-occupational class component grew in percentage terms, accounting for almost two thirds of the total by 1997–8. They interpret these findings as evidence of the growing importance of hierarchical segregation (Fortin and Huberman 2002: 23).

I focus specifically on hierarchical segregation (Bettio 2002), exploiting the fact that the ECHP – my source of data – allows one to distinguish among supervisory, intermediate and bottom positions within each of the 18 occupations reported. By way of a simple counterfactual exercises for 1996, I simulate the impact on relative earnings of redistributing women across occupations and positions in such a way as to reproduce the male employment pattern, while assigning women and men their actual wages within each occupation and position. I find that the inter-occupational redistribution would actually increase the gender gap by more than two per cent points in four countries, decrease it by at least the same amount in five, while exerting a marginal impact either way in the remaining four. Redistribution between occupational category and at the same time up the hierarchical ladder has a more definite, positive effect on female relative earnings, decreasing the gender gap in 8 out of 13 countries while leaving it practically unaffected only in Italy and Germany. In the vast majority of cases the overall improvement is entirely or mainly attributable to redistribution up the hierarchical ladder. The order of magnitude is low – the impact of the hierarchical re-distribution decreases the raw wage gap in amounts comprised between 2 and 16 per cent of the raw wage gap – but this may also reflect a relatively gross occupational breakdown.

Economists view hierarchical within-occupations segregation as a facet of vertical segregation. Across disciplinary boundaries, however, there is no consensus on what constitutes vertical segregation apart from the idea that 'vertical' captures the extent to which men and women are asymmetrically distributed among the rungs (positions) of within-occupation scales (in which case it coincides with hierarchical segregation), or are assigned different ranks in a given occupational ordering. Sociological research understands vertical segregation in this latter sense and uses it to measure the extent of labour market inequality.

Blackburn and Jarman (2005) choose earnings and occupational prestige to assess the inequality implications of gender segregation. Using the Somer's D statistics[11] they decompose overall segregation (measured by ranking occupations by the share of women) into a vertical component obtained by ranking occupations in terms of male pay or prestige, and a residual, orthogonal component that is equated to horizontal segregation. By means of a very detailed occupational breakdown for Canada the USA and the UK in the 1990s, they find that when the ranking criterion is male pay rates both vertical and horizontal segregation positively contribute to reducing women's relative wage, the relative contribution of the vertical component being about half that of the horizontal component. When the ranking criterion is occupational prestige, vertical segregation appears actually to benefit women, probably reflecting the higher prestige of white-collar occupations, where women predominate. They also find that overall segregation correlates strongly and *positively* with measures of gender empowerment for the 32 countries in the ILO database used by Anker (see above). They take all these findings as implying that overall segregation is weakly or inversely associated with gender labour-market inequality, depending on the choice of inequality indicators.

Bridges (2003) proposes a measure based on the likelihood ratio chi-square statistics in order to decompose vertical and horizontal segregation. In his case the ranking criterion is the within-occupation share of workers reporting yearly earnings above the country's median value. Using the International Social Survey Programme (ISSP) data on 22 countries between 1996 and 1997 with a limited but just adequate number of occupational categories – 19 ISCO88 occupations – Bridges finds that, for the average country, the vertical component accounts for less than half of overall segregation if Somer's D is used, but rises to 60 per cent if his own index is used instead. By means of regression he also finds evidence that the vertical component tends to gain weight as GDP increases. He takes his findings to imply that overall segregation should no longer be equated with inequality, because it hides both 'invidious' (unfair) and 'non invidious' components.

In fact, the notion that segregation is not always 'bad' for women is not new, as noted above. But there is more than this in the findings that I have reviewed in this section. First is the overall suggestion that the balance between the 'pros' and 'cons' of segregation may no longer, or not consistently, be in favour of the cons. Second, there is growing consensus that in order to address the 'cons', it is advisable to target within-occupations rather than between-occupations mobility. This in turn amounts to removing at least part of the blame for wage inequality or discrimination from the gender stereotyping of occupations.

Policy priorities in need of revision

To conclude, economists and sociologists seem to agree that it makes increasingly less sense to consider segregation as a unitary phenomenon. As discussed earlier, recent economic theorizing separates out the hierarchical component of segregation supported by evidence on the practical relevance of the latter for the gender pay gap. Sociological theorizing has revitalized the distinction between vertical and horizontal segregation, or between the invidious and non-invidious components, in order to document the conflicting relation with labour market inequality.

It is equally important, however, to distinguish segregation within occupations from that between occupations, firms or industries, although many theoretical explanations still lump all of them into the same phenomenon. Such distinctions matter for policy reasons. If priority is to be given to the within-occupation hierarchical component, then comparable worth policies may be less appropriate. Or if, as emerges from some studies, between-firms segregation is more important than segregation across occupations, then attention should focus on the institutional process of wage bargaining. Finally, if occupational dimensions other than pay are important – sociologists have stressed prestige, but I would add job security, e.g. in public-sector jobs – then indiscriminate efforts to de-segregate may not maximize women's welfare.

As sociologists point out, moreover, clear identification of the positive implications of segregation – alongside the negative or risky aspects – helps put the debate about inequality and segregation on a less ideologically charged basis. I would venture even further. The fight to fully integrate women into the labour force has often been legitimized by the quest for equality and justice: hence the emphasis on segregation and discrimination understood as 'involuntary' inequality. However, exclusive attention to (in)equality may not only be misleading – as was discussed above – it may also be inadequate. Compare the (gross) income gap for European

Table 9.5 Relative earnings for women and the partners gap

Country	Share of couples where she earns at least 40% of combined earnings , 2001	Women's hourly earnings in percentage of male earnings (private sector only), 2002
Greece	29.0	74.5
Spain	23.1	75.0
Netherlands	26.9	76.4
Ireland	28.7	73.7
Italy	32.7	81.2
Austria	30.7	73.6
Germany	34.4	74.4
France	35.3	83.4
Portugal	40.3	80.3
UK	38.3	69.7
Belgium	41.5	82.9
Finland	55.4	82.0
Sweden	62.1	84.7
Denmark	68.8	80.0

Sources: 1st column of data: ECHP 8th wave, own calculations; 2nd column: Eurostat, Structure of Earnings Survey.
Notes
* Difference between men's and women's average gross hourly earnings as percentage of men's average gross hourly earnings (for paid employees at work 15+ hours).

countries with the intra-household partners' gap in earnings (Table 9.5). The latter is measured as the share of couples where she earns at least 40 per cent of combined earnings, and values range from 23.1 per cent in Spain to 68.8 per cent in Denmark, the unweighted average being barely 39.3 per cent. That is, the disparities measured by the partners gap are of a much large order of magnitude, since this statistic cumulates the wage gap with the gap in labour market participation and in hours worked.[12]

Precisely because disparities in earnings between partners also reflect individual employment choices, they cannot be taken as a meaningful indicator of individual inequality. So far, in fact, they have been investigated in connection with inter-family inequalities, e.g. to ascertain whether increasing female employment leads to larger income dispersion across families. I would argue, however, that the partners gap provides a more comprehensive indicator of the extent to which women are actually integrated into the labour market than does segregation or the hourly wage gap. If the earlier feminist explanations of segregation that pivot on the distinction between primary and secondary earner still retain some validity, persistence of a partners gap may itself help segregation to persist. And if the household bargaining approach is correct, the same gap perpetuates an unbalanced division of labour within households (Couprie 2007; Frieberg and Webb 2005). The time has perhaps come, therefore, to de-emphasize the issue of segregation in research and policy on women's labour-market positions in developed countries, while giving a larger role to the formation and distribution of earnings at household level.

Notes

1 The index of dissimilarity is defined as $ID = \frac{1}{2}\sum_i \left| \frac{M_i}{M} - \frac{F_i}{F} \right|$ and can be interpreted as the proportion of men (women) who would need to change occupation to obtain symmetrical distributions of the sexes across occupations (Duncan and Duncan 1955). Despite widespread criticisms it is the most widely used measure of overall segregation and is practically the only option to carry out comparison across countries and over time using existing research. The literature on alternative measures is extensive, see for example Hakim (1992); Blackburn *et al.* (1995), Grusky and Charles (1998); Fluckiger and Silber (1999); Emerek *et al.* (2002); Bridges (2003).
2 Note that physical strength would provide, at best, a partial explanation of the wage gap (Bettio 1988:132–135).
3 For example, women were first allowed into the Italian judiciary in 1963, and since then have made extremely rapid inroads. However, their share is still below 40 per cent, because low turnover slows down the replacement of incumbents (ASDO 2006). To take other well-known examples for Italy, women were allowed to join the police force in the 1980s and the army in 1999.
4 Asymmetric distributions complicate but do not change the basic predictions of the model.
5 In the authors' view, supply side factors may partly compensate for stereotyped demand, but are less important. For example a female engineer may have a lower probability of finding a partner because her non-conforming choice of occupation renders her less attractive to men, but the pool of men to draw from is larger exactly because most engineers are men.
6 Measurement of segregation is a research field on its own, one too large and complex to be summarized here. See footnote 1 for selected references. Some recent contributions are reviewed in this section.
7 Among recent studies stressing that husbands' involvement in housework and care work is still low compared to their wives' see Couprie (2007) for the UK. Friedberg and Webb (2005) stress change but also continuity in the household division of labour in the US.
8 Unweighted average values for the ID75 Index, i.e. the ID Index standardized to 75 occupational categories: (Anker 1998: Table 13.1; 2006: Table 5).
9 The Oaxaca decomposition separates the part of the wage gap due to personal characteristics from a residual attributed to discrimination (see Dolton *et al.*, this volume). Suppose there are feed-back effects, so that a woman chooses not to invest in job-specific training because she anticipates resistance to her promotion, regardless of her training. This will not be counted towards discrimination in the Oaxaca decomposition.
10 Note that segregation between establishments (Spain) or industries (USA) is found to contribute to the wage gap more than segregation between occupations.
11 Given two bivariate data pairs $(X1, Y1)$ and $(X2, Y2)$, Somers' D parameter DYX is the difference between the corresponding conditional probabilities, given that the X values are ordered.
12 This is implicitly recognized by a strand in the literature that I have deliberately neglected here, namely analysis of segregation in employment contracts, like part-time, temporary and so on. I would argue, in fact, that the processes generating segregation in employment contracts differ in important respects from those that lead to or sustain occupational stereotyping by sex, but it is the latter that has been and remains central to the debate on gender employment segregation.

References

Aigner, D.J. and Cain, G.G. (1995) 'Statistical Theories of Discrimination in Labor Markets' in O. C. Ashenfelter and K. F. Hallock (eds) *Labor Economics*, vol. 4, Aldershot: Elgar; Brookfield, Vt.: Ashgate.

Akerlof, G.A. and Kranton R.E. (2000) 'Economics and Identity', *Quarterly Journal of Economics*, 115 (3): 715–753.

Amuedo-Dorantes, C. and De la Rica, S. (2006) 'The Role of Segregation and Pay Structure on the Gender Wage Gap: Evidence from Matched Employer-Employee Data for Spain', *B.E. Journals in Economic Analysis and Policy: Contributions to Economic Analysis and Policy*, 5 (1): 1–32.

Anker, R. (1997) 'Theories of Occupational Segregation by Sex: An Overview', *International Labour Review*, 136 (3): 315–339.

Anker, R. (1998) '*Gender and Jobs. Sex Segregation of Occupations in the World*', Geneva: ILO.

Anker, R., Melkas, H. and Karten, A. (2003) *Gender Based Occupational Segregation in the 1990s*, Declaration Working Paper no. 16, Geneva: ILO.

Arrow, K. J. (1973) 'The Theory of Discrimination' in O.C. Ashenfelter and K.F. Hallock (eds) *Labor economics*, vol. 4, Aldershot: Elgar; Brookfield, Vt.: Ashgate.

Assemblea delle donne per lo sviluppo e la lotta all'esclusione sociale (ASDO) (2006) 'Donne in politica', Rapporto di Ricerca, Roma: ASDO. Available:http://www. donnepolitica.org/Docs/RappRic.pdf (Accessed 31 May 2007).

Badgett, M.V.L. and Folbre, N. (2003) 'Job Gendering: Occupational Choice and the Marriage Market', *Industrial Relations*, 42 (2): 270–298.

Baldwin, M. L., Butler, R. J. and Johnson, W. G. (2001) 'A Hierarchical Theory of Occupational Segregation and Wage Discrimination', *Economic Inquiry*, 39 (1): 94–110.

Bayard, K., Troske, R., Hellerstein, J. and Neumark, D. (2003) 'New Evidence on Sex Segregation and Sex Differences in Wages from Matched Employee-Employer Data', *Journal of Labor Economics*, 21 (4): 887–922.

Becker, G. (1957) 'The Economics of Discrimination', Chicago: University of Chicago Press.

Bergmann, B.R. (1974) 'Occupational Segregation, Wages and Profits When Employers Discriminate by Race or Sex', *Eastern Economic Journal*, 1 (1–2): 103–10.

Bettio, F. (1988) 'The Sexual Division of Labour: The Italian Case', Oxford; New York; Toronto and Melbourne: Oxford University Press, Clarendon Press.

Bettio, F. (1998) 'Health Services' in Rubery J. (ed.) *Equal Pay in Europe? Closing the gender wage gap*, ILO Studies, New York: St. Martin's Press; London: Macmillan.

Bettio, F. (2002) 'The Pros and Cons of Occupational Gender Segregation in Europe', *Canadian Public Policy*, 28, Supplement: S65–84.

Blackburn, R. and Jarman, J. (2005) *Gendered Occupations: Exploring the Relationship between Gender Segregation and Inequality*, GeNet ESRC Gender Equality Network, University of Cambridge Working Paper no. 5. Available: http://www.genet.ac.uk/ workpapers/GeNet2005p5.pdf (Accessed 31 May 2007).

Blackburn, R., Siltanen, M. and Jarman, J. (1995) 'The Measurement of Occupational Gender Segregation: Current Problems and a New Approach', *Journal of the Royal Statistical Society: Series A (Statistics in Society)*, 158 (2): 319–31.

Blau, F.D., Ferber, M. and Winkler, A.E. (2006) *The Economics of Women, Men and Work*, Upper Saddle River: Pearson.

Blau, F.D. and Kahn, L.M. (2001) 'Understanding International Differences in the Gender Pay Gap', *Journal of Labor Economics*, University of Chicago Press, 21 (1): 106–144.

Bowles, S. and Gintis, H. (1977) 'The Marxian Theory of Value and Heterogeneous Labour: A Critique and Reformulation', *Cambridge Journal of Economics*, 1 (2): 173–192.

Bridges, W.P. (2003) 'Rethinking Gender Segregation and Gender Inequality: Measures and Meanings', *Demography*, 40 (3): 543–568.

Cain, G.G. (1986) 'The Economic Analysis of Labor Market Discrimination: A Survey', in O.C. Ashenfelter and R. Layard (eds) *Handbook of Labor Economics*, vol. 1, Amsterdam; Oxford and Tokyo: North-Holland; New York: Elsevier Science.

Chiplin, B. and Sloane, P. (1976) *Sex Discrimination in the Labour Market*, London: Macmillan.

Couprie, H. (2007) 'Allocation Within the Family: Welfare Implications of Life in a Couple', *The Economic Journal*, 117 (516): 287–305.

Coute, S. and Loury, G. C. (1993) 'Will Affirmative Action Policies Eliminate Negative Stereotypes?', *American Economic Review*, 85 (5): 1220–1240.

Doeringer, P. and Piore, M. (1971) *Internal Labour Markets and Manpower Analysis*. Lexington, MA.: D.C. Heath and Co.

Dolado, J.J., Felgueroso, F. and Jimeno, J.F. (2002) 'Recent Trends in Occupational Segregation by Gender: A Look across the Atlantic', in A. Argandona and J. Gual (eds) *The Social Dimensions of Employment: Institutional Reforms in Labour Markets*, Cheltenham, U.K. and Northampton, MA.: Elgar; Williston, VT.: American International Distribution Corporation.

Duncan, O.D. and Duncan, B. (1955) 'Residential Distribution and Occupational Stratification', *The American Journal of Sociology*, 60 (March): 493–503.

Elson, D. and Pearson, R. (1981) ' "Nimble Fingers Make Cheap Workers": An Analysis of Women's Employment in Third World Export Manufacturing', *Feminist Review*, 2 (7): 87–107.

Emerek, R., Figueiredo, H., González, M.P., Gonäs, L. and Rubery, J. (2002) 'Indicators on Gender Segregation', in J. Rubery, D. Fagan, D. Grimshaw, H. Figuereido and M. Smith (eds) *Indicators on Gender Equality in the European Employment Strategy*, EGGE – EC's Expert Group on Gender and Employment, Manchester: University of Manchester. Available: http://ec.europa.eu/employment_social/employment_analysis/gender/indic_gender_equal_in_ees.pdf (Accessed 31 May 2007).

England, P. (1982) 'The Failure of Human Capital Theory to Explain Occupational Sex Segregation', *Journal of Human Resources*, 17 (3): 358–370.

England, P. (2004) *Does Bad Pay Cause Occupations to Feminize, Does Feminization Reduce Pay, and How Can We Tell with Longitudinal Data?*, Dept. of Sociology, Stanford University: Stanford, mimeo.

Frieberg, L. and Webb, A. (2005) *The Chore Wars: Household Bargaining and Leisure Time*, Charlottsville, VA: Department of Economics, University of Virginia, mimeo.

Finzi, I. (2005) 'Formazione e Segregazione Occupazionale', Dati Statistiche e Società (collana USTAT), 4. Available: http://www.ti.ch/DFE/USTAT/PUBBLICAZIONI/dati_societa/default.asp?sigla_collana=DSS&numero_volume=2005-4 (Accessed 31 May 2007).

Fluckiger, Y. and Silber, J. (1999) *The Measurement of Segregation in the Labor Force*. Heidelberg: Physica.

Fortin, N.M. and Huberman, M. (2002) 'Occupational Gender Segregation and Women's Wages in Canada: A Historical Perspective', *Canadian Public Policy*, 28, Supplement: S11–39.

Goldin, C. (2002) *A Pollution Theory of Discrimination: Male and Female Differences in Occupations and Earnings*, National Bureau of Economic Research, Inc: NBER Working Paper no. 8985.

Groshen, E.L. (1991) 'The Structure of the Female/Male Wage Differential: Is It Who You Are, What You Do, or Where You Work?', *Journal of Human Resources*, 26 (3): 457–472.

Gross, E. (1968) 'Plus Ca Change…? The Sexual Structure of Occupations over Time', *Social Problems*, 16 (2): 198–208.

Grusky, D.B. and Charles, M. (1998) 'The Past Present, and Future of Sex Segregation Methodology', *Demography*, 35 (4): 497–504.

Hakim, C. (1992) 'Explaining Trends in Occupational Segregation: the Measurement, Causes and Consequences of the Sexual Division of Labour', *European Sociological Review*, 8 (3): 127–152.

Hartman, H.I. and Reskin, B.F. (1986) *Women's Work, Men's Work*, Washington, D.C.: National Academy Press.

Holzer, H. and Neumark, D. (2006) 'Affirmative Action: What Do We Know?', *Journal of Policy Analysis and Management*, 25 (2): 463–490.

Jacobs, J. A. (2003) 'Detours on the Road to Equality: Women, Work and Higher Education', *Context*, 2 (1): 32–41.

Meyersson, M.E.M., Petersen, T. and Snartland, V. (2001) 'Equal Pay for Equal Work? Evidence from Sweden and a Comparison with Norway and the U.S.', *Scandinavian Journal of Economics*, 103 (4): 559–583.

Mincer, J. and Polachek, S. (1974) 'Family Investment in Human Capital: Earnings of Women', *Journal of Political Economy, Part 2,* 82 (2): S76–108.

Phelps, E.S. (1972) 'The Statistical Theory of Racism and Sexism', *American Economic Review*, 62 (4): 659–661.

Phillips, A. and Taylor, B. (1980) 'Sex and Skill': Notes Towards a Feminist Economics', *Feminist Review*, 6: 79–88.

Pissarides, C., Garibaldi, P., Olivetti, C., Petrongolo, B. and Wasmer, E. (2003) *Women in the Labor Force: How Well is Europe Doing*, Report, Annual European Conference of the Fondazione Rodolfo De Benedetti, Milano: Fondazione Rodolfo De Benedetti.

Rosen, S. (1986) 'The Theory of Equalizing Differences' in O.C. Ashenfelter and R. Layard (eds) *Handbook of Labor Economics*, Amsterdam, Oxford and Tokyo: North-Holland; New York: Elsevier Science.

Rubery, J. (1978) 'Structured Labour Markets, Worker Organisation and Low Pay', *Cambridge Journal of Economics*, 2 (1): 17–36.

Strober, M.H. and Arnold, C.L. (1987) 'The Dynamics of Occupational Segregation Among Bank Tellers', in C. Brown and J. A. Pechman (eds) *Gender in the Workplace,* Washington, D.C.: Brookings Institution.

Watts, M. (1998) 'Occupational Gender Segregation: Index Measurement and Econometric Modelling', Demography, 35 (4): 489–96.

10 The transition from a planned to a market economy

How are women faring?

Marina Malysheva and Alina Verashchagina

Introduction

It is almost two decades since market-oriented reform was launched in the Former Soviet Union (FSU), several years later than in Central and Eastern Europe (CEE). One commonly acknowledged fact regarding gender is, as Paci (2002) put it, that *transition*[1] *has not been gender neutral*. The underlying idea is that men and women may differ in their ability to handle the uncertainty inherent in a market economy.

In this chapter, we investigate different dimensions of market-oriented reforms that have caused a deterioration or improvement in the relative position of women in the labour market. Our aim is to contribute to an economic policy agenda sensitive to gender issues, given that the latter were ignored for at least a decade after the start of reform, being overshadowed by 'more important' goals. The most evident effect of this inadequate consideration of gender for sustainable development was a decline in female labour force participation as well as the segregation of women into low-paid jobs, often accompanied by a widening of the gender pay gap (Brainerd 2000; Jurajda 2005). This is actually the opposite of what was happening during the same time period in most mature market economies (see Blau *et al.* 2006; Dolton *et al.* this volume).

The downturn in economic development experienced by most transition countries during the 1990s (EBRD 2000) was certainly counterproductive to the provision of equal opportunities for men and women. The question arises how this may have affected the welfare of women in Eastern Europe and how they are faring now, after almost two decades of reform. Unlike existing studies, which concentrate on the labour market position of women in the context of emerging market economies, we also look at their position within the household.

We investigate the effects of labour market liberalization by looking first at the traditional measures of women's well-being represented by their relative wages, labour force participation, educational attainments, etc. Despite the fact that the overall picture seems quite promising, we can distinguish two patterns of reforms, which are represented by CEE on the one hand and the CIS[2] on the other, with the latter group of countries having proved less able to sustain gender-balanced societies. We shall draw attention to several facets of reform that are still understudied, namely: female participation in the informal sector of the economy, and international migration. We argue that both issues should be a matter of concern for economic policy makers because they signal a potential worsening of women's well-being in the transition countries.

The chapter is structured in three main sections. We first describe some stylized facts about gender in transition. Evidence on various characteristics of female attachment to the labour market is presented on the largest possible number of countries, including several mature market economies as a term of comparison. We then sketch the analytical framework used in the available literature to address gender issues in transition, followed by a survey of the available empirical findings. Finally, we highlight several under-researched topics that should be part of a future research agenda.

Stylized facts about gender in transition

In this section, we introduce some stylized facts with which to begin investigating whether transition from a planned to a market economy has increased or reduced gender differences in the labour market. The existing literature has mainly focused on wage differentials, returns to education and their evolution over time. Here we start with female labour force participation, which has been shrinking in the transition countries, in clear contrast to the trends prevailing in mature market economies, and with obvious side-effects on all aspects of women's lives.

Employment and unemployment practices

A well-known feature of socialist systems was their ability to integrate women almost fully into the economy (Atkinson and Micklewright 1992). As Table 10.1 shows, in the early 1990s the share of active women in the female population aged over 15 stood at around 60 per cent in Eastern Europe: a level which, as documented by the UN (1991), was higher than anywhere else at that time.

The very high female labour force participation rates that had been previously attained dropped considerably just after the start of transition. The reduction was larger in CEE countries than in those that had constituted the FSU. The reason was that many state-owned enterprises in the latter group of countries had resorted to the practice of so-called labour hoarding in order to prevent mass unemployment and withdrawal from the labour market (Koumakhov and Najman 2000; Namazie 2003). In other words, people were kept employed, but they only worked a short day (or a short week) and were paid a minimum wage. Labour hoarding often went together with wage arrears (Earle and Sabirianova 2002, Lehmann and Wadsworth 2007), when that scant pay due to workers was also delayed, sometimes for several months.[3] This certainly affected the effort that people put into their main jobs and also induced them to search for additional sources of income. Combining several jobs at once, or doing casual work, became the normal practice – more so for men, who appeared to cope with the situation better.[4]

Table 10.1 Economic activity rates

Country		1990	1995	2000	2005
Armenia	F	61	36.2	45.3	–
	M	72	51.3	54.8	–
Azerbaijan	F	–	–	43.4	43.5
	M	–	–	49.5	49.2
Belarus	F	–	54.9	52.7†	45.3
	M	–	59	65.7†	45.5
Bulgaria	F	50.3	47.9	44.7	44.8
	M	59.7	56.8	56.2	55.8
Czech Republic	F	60.8†	52.3	51.6	50.5
	M	72.9†	71.4	69.3	68.5
Estonia	F	60.6	53.6	51.4	53.3
	M	77.1	71.3	66.4	65.7
Georgia	F	–	–	55	55.9
	M	–	–	74.7	73.5
Hungary	F	46.3	40.3	41.7	43
	M	64.5	57.1	58.5	58.1
Kazakhstan	F	62.3†	–	–	–
	M	78.2†	–	–	–
Kyrgyzstan	F	58.6	–	56.8	–
	M	74.5	–	68.6	–
Latvia	F	64.1†	–	49	51.1
	M	77.5†	–	65	65.6
Lithuania	F	60.2†	55.1	55	51.1
	M	74.7†	72	66.5	63.4
Moldova	F	61.6†	–	56.3	47.5
	M	74.9†	–	63.9	50.2
Poland	F	–	51.1	50.1	47.2
	M	–	66.5	64.2	62.4
Romania	F	54.9	60.4	58.2	48.1
	M	67.2	74.4	71.2	62.7
Russian Federation	F	61†	48.4	48.3	–
	M	77.4†	63.3	61.1	–
Slovakia	F	59.7	51.2	52.3	51.1
	M	73	68.5	67.9	68
Slovenia	F	54.1†	52.1	51.4	52.5
	M	67.7†	65.8	63.8	65.3
Tajikistan	F	–	–	–	–
	M	–	–	–	–
Ukraine	F	–	57.1	50.7	57
	M	–	69.1	64.4	67.9

Source: Own calculations using Gender Statistics Database [http://www.unece.org/stats/gender/].

Note
F-female, M-Male. Rates are calculated for all the population over 15. Data are from Labour Force Surveys unless otherwise specified: † Kazakhstan, Latvia, Lithuania, Moldova and Russia 1990: data refer to 1989 population censuses; Belarus 2000: data refer to the population census of 1999, for other years – official estimates; Slovenia and Czech Republic 1990: data refer to 1991 population censuses.

Labour market adjustment in Central Europe took a rather different course (Rutkowski and Scarpetta 2005). There, unemployment rates reached double-digit figures very soon after the start of reform. The decision of firms to shed redundant labour put all workers at risk, including women, who after losing their jobs experienced greater difficulties in returning to work, and thus often abandoned the labour market altogether. Thus labour force participation reduced considerably from the previous high levels of about 60 per cent[5] for women and close to 80 per cent for men to about 50 per cent for women and 60 per cent for men (UNIFEM 2006). This was still high compared to the participation rates of women in some Western European countries, where female participation rates ranged from below 40 per cent in Mediterranean countries to around 60 per cent in Scandinavian countries (European Commission 2006). The latter group of countries is similar to the US, where female participation in the labour market was high already in the 1980s (50 per cent) and has increased up to the current figure of 60 per cent (Blau *et al*. 2006).

Women in the East also fared comparatively worse than men in terms of unemployment, which, as known, rose at the beginning of the 1990s from the practically non-existent level experienced before. The unemployment statistics for the transition countries should, however, be treated with caution.[6] The only source of information, especially for the early 1990s, is often the official rates based on registered unemployment, which tend to underestimate the true levels. This is evident when alternative data become available, like Population or Household Surveys. Nevertheless even early statistics gave rise to the idea that women are more subject to unemployment than men. In fact, women tend to register as unemployed more often,[7] which is indicative of a different perception on their part of unemployment and of the related risks. Moreover, Stefanova Lauerova and Terrell (2007) provide empirical evidence in support of the hypothesis that women have lower job-finding rates once they become unemployed and are therefore more subject to long-term unemployment. This is generally true, as can be seen from Table 10.2. In addition to that, returning to employment for women is often associated with a decrease in the quality of the job (see Acemoglu 2001 and Layard 2004 on 'good' and 'bad' jobs).

Employment segregation

Vertical and horizontal gender segregation are economic phenomena that persist in mature market economies (see Bettio, this volume). In the post-communist countries, prior to transition, men and women were more or less equally present in different spheres of life, apart from politics (Brainerd 2000). Moreover, strategic occupations in the healthcare sector, such as physicians, became feminized much earlier in the East, and the share of women remains higher among professional engineers, an occupation that still resists change in the West. The prevailing view in the literature, albeit based on rather scarce evidence (Katz 1997), is that on the eve of transition occupational segregation in Eastern Europe was lower than in developed market economies (for discussion see Brainerd 2000, Maltseva and

Table 10.2 Unemployment rates

Country		Unemployment rate				Long-term unemployment rate*			
		1990	*1995*	*2000*	*2005*	*1990*	*1995*	*2000*	*2005*
Albania'	F	10.9	14.8	19.3	–	–	74.7	90.7	–
	M	8.4	11.6	14.9	–	–	71	88.6	–
Armenia'	F	–	15.2	15.7	12	–	53.2	75.4	–
	M	–	4.7	8	4.6	–	57	70.1	–
Belarus'	F	–	3.5	2.4	2	–	17.9	16.7	–
	M	–	2.2	1.7	1	–	11.7	6.2	–
Bulgaria	F	22†	15.8	15.9	–	52.3	68.6	56.7	61.1
	M	20.9†	15.5	16.7	–	52.6	63.2	57.3	58.8
Czech Republic	F	–	4.8	10.5	9.8	–	1.4"	49.8	53.7
	M	–	3.4	7.4	6.5	–	0.9"	47.2	52.1
Estonia	F	0.7	8.9	12.7	7.1	–	26.7"	42.7	59.9
	M	0.6	10.5	14.5	8.8	–	35.6"	48.3	48.2
Hungary	F	–	–	5.6	7.4	–	50.8	44.7	43.4
	M	–	–	7	7	–	57.4	50.1	46.6
Kyrgyzstan	F	–	–	–	9.1	–	10	30.2	–
	M	–	–	–	7.4	–	8.5	30.2	–
Latvia	F	–	19.8	13.2	8.8	–	58.3	58.1	42.8
	M	–	20.7	15.2	9	–	58.4	57.6	48.8
Lithuania	F	–	13.9†	14	8.4	–	–	45.9	53.6
	M	–	14.2†	18.8	8.2	–	–	50.6	51.3
Moldova	F	–	–	7.2	6	–	–	56.1	–
	M	–	–	9.7	8.7	–	–	63.5	–
Poland	F	14.9†	14.7	18.1	19.1	34.3	43.7"	50.2	59.3
	M	12.2†	12.1	14.4	16.6	32	36.3"	41.6	56.1
Romania	F	–	8.6	6.4	6.4	–	47.9"	53.9	52.3
	M	–	7.5	7.8	7.8	–	46.2"	49.8	59
Russian Federation	F	5.2'	9.2	9.4	7	–	–	48.8	–
	M	5.2'	9.7	10.2	7.3	–	–	37.1	–
Slovakia	F	–	13.8	18.6	17.2	–	55.2	55.2	71.5
	M	–	12.6	18.9	15.5	–	51.4	54.2	72.3
Slovenia	F	–	7	7.1	7	–	48.7	59.8	46.3
	M	–	7.7	6.4	6	–	56.7	62.8	48.4
Ukraine	F	–	4.9'	11.6	6.8	–	–	–	–
	M	–	6.3'	11.6	7.5	–	–	–	–

Source: Own calculations using UNECE Gender Statistics Database.

Note
F-female, M-Male. Rates are calculated for all the population over 15.
*'Long-term unemployment' refers to people who are unemployed for 12 months and more. 'Long-term unemployment rate' stands for the percentage of long-term unemployed in total number of unemployed.
† Bulgaria 1990: data refer to 1993; Lithuania 1995: data refer to 1997; Poland 1990: data refer to 1992.
Data from Labour Force Surveys unless otherwise specified: 'For Albania, Armenia, Belarus, Russian Federation (1990) and Ukraine (1995) registered unemployment rates are reported.
"For Czech Republic, Estonia, Poland and Romania 1995: data refer to 1997.

Roshchin 2006). Newell and Reilly (1996) also claim that vertical rather than horizontal segregation contributed most to the female wage disadvantage (this may have been the case in mature western economies as well). In fact, at present few women occupy top managerial positions (Roshchin and Solntcev 2006), and they are still largely under represented in politics (UN 2006).

Reforms have brought about a considerable redistribution of the labour force from sectors of so-called material production (industry) to the service sectors, including those sex-typed female ones that are now becoming the lowest-paid, causing a feminization of poverty. Table 10.3 provides evidence on the change in the composition of employment in different sectors of the economy across the transition countries. The growth of the service sector has been accompanied by a large reallocation of women to it from both industry and agriculture. This is the case of most of the countries presented in Table 10.3. Here it is important to distinguish between instances where the service sector is largely privatized which is the case for CEE, and the opposite one of overwhelming state control, which is more typical of CIS. A privatized service

Table 10.3 Employment by sector and gender

Country		Sector	Percentage of males and females within sectors				Female/male distribution between sectors			
			1990	1995	2000	2005	1990	1995	2000	2005
Armenia	F	Agriculture	42.5	26	41.6	–	15.5	23.4	40.6	–
		Industry	42.3	44.4	35.6	–	36.3	27.5	13.9	–
		Services	57.7	55.1	54.5	–	48.2	49.1	45.5	–
	M	Agriculture	57.5	74	58.4	–	19.8	47.3	47.5	–
		Industry	57.7	55.6	64.4	–	46.7	24.4	20.9	–
		Services	42.3	44.9	45.5	–	33.4	28.4	31.6	–
Bulgaria	F	Agriculture	–	40.2	37.6	35.7	–	10.6	10.6	6.9
		Industry	–	39.5	38.8	39.3	–	30.5	27.2	28.8
		Services	–	53.6	53.6	52.7	–	58.8	61.9	64.2
	M	Agriculture	–	59.8	62.4	64.3	–	13.9	15.3	10.8
		Industry	–	60.5	61.2	60.7	–	41.1	37.5	38.9
		Services	–	46.4	46.4	47.3	–	44.9	46.9	50.3
Czech Republic	F	Agriculture	–	36.5	31.7	30.7	–	5.5	3.7	2.8
		Industry	–	32.3	30.2	29	–	30.8	27.5	26.5
		Services	–	54.3	53.9	54	–	63.7	68.7	70.7
	M	Agriculture	–	63.5	68.3	69.3	–	7.4	6.1	4.9
		Industry	–	67.7	69.8	71	–	50.5	48.7	49.4
		Services	–	45.7	46.1	46	–	42	45.1	45.7
Estonia	F	Agriculture	34.8	36.7	31.5	33.6	14.3	7.8	4.6	3.5
		Industry	41.2	37.5	35.3	36	32	26.6	23.9	24.2
		Services	61	57.1	59.1	60.3	53.7	65.7	71.6	72.4
	M	Agriculture	65.2	63.3	67.9	67.2	25.2	12.5	9.6	7.2
		Industry	58.8	62.5	64.7	64	42.7	41.4	42.4	44
		Services	39	42.9	41	39.7	32.2	46.2	47.9	48.7

(Continued)

Table 10.3 cont'd

Country		Sector	Percentage of males and females within sectors				Female/male distribution between sectors			
			1990	1995	2000	2005	1990	1995	2000	2005
Hungary	F	Agriculture	–	25.7	23.7	24.9	–	4.7	3.3	2.6
		Industry	–	33.7	33.1	29.9	–	24.8	25	21.2
		Services	–	52.6	54.2	55.6	–	70.6	71.7	76.1
	M	Agriculture	–	74.3	76.4	75	–	10.7	8.8	6.7
		Industry	–	66.3	66.9	70.1	–	38.8	41.4	42
		Services	–	47.4	45.8	44.4	–	50.5	49.8	51.3
Moldova	F	Agriculture	–	–	49.6	51.8	–	–	49.8	40.3
		Industry	–	–	37.3	37.6	–	–	10.2	11.5
		Services	–	–	57.5	58.2	–	–	40	48.2
	M	Agriculture	–	–	50.4	48.4	–	–	52	41.1
		Industry	–	–	62.7	62.4	–	–	17.7	20.9
		Services	–	–	42.5	41.8	–	–	30.3	37.9
Poland	F	Agriculture	–	45	43.9	42.8	–	22.5	18.3	16.6
		Industry	–	29.7	27.6	26.2	–	21	19	17.1
		Services	–	56.4	55.8	55.4	–	56.6	62.7	66.2
	M	Agriculture	–	55	56.1	57.2	–	22.7	19.1	18
		Industry	–	70.3	72.4	73.8	–	41	40.5	39
		Services	–	43.6	44.2	44.6	–	36.2	40.4	43
Romania	F	Agriculture	–	52.7	49.4	46.4	–	46.2	45.6	33.1
		Industry	–	36.1	37.4	36.9	–	24.3	21.1	24.8
		Services	–	47.2	49.9	51.3	–	29.5	33.4	42.2
	M	Agriculture	–	47.3	50.6	53.5	–	35.3	40.4	31.6
		Industry	–	63.9	62.6	63.1	–	36.6	30.6	35.2
		Services	–	52.8	50.1	48.6	–	28	29	33.2
Russian Federation	F	Agriculture	–	–	39.1	38.8	–	–	11.7	8
		Industry	–	–	37	35.2	–	–	21.7	21.2
		Services	–	–	56.4	58.1	–	–	66.5	70.7
	M	Agriculture	–	–	60.9	61.2	–	–	17.1	12.3
		Industry	–	–	62.9	64.8	–	–	34.7	38.1
		Services	–	–	43.6	41.9	–	–	48.2	49.6

Source: Own calculations using UNECE Gender Statistics Database.

sector tends to be associated with an improvement in the wage position of women (Giddings 2002, for Bulgaria), while overwhelming state control may imply a disproportionate concentration in lower-paid service jobs (Pastore and Verashchagina 2007a).[8]

The empirical evidence on the effect of occupational segregation on wages is rather mixed. Ogloblin (1999) finds that it accounts for about 80 per cent of the gender wage gap in Russia, while Jurajda (2003) claims that it only accounts for one third in the Czech Republic and Slovakia. Moreover, in his recent study Jurajda (2007) points out that in the mid-1990s predominantly female occupations paid more (compared to jobs with a low or more or less equal share of female workers) to both men and women in Eastern Germany. At the same time, no relationship was found between the occupation-specific concentration of women and wages in West Germany.

Wages and the gender wage gap

To sum up, on average, the broad trends discussed so far, fewer women are in employment compared with the pre-transition period, while more of them are in unemployment or are likely to work in feminized, service sector occupations. How does all this reflect on trends in female wages and the gender wage gap (GWG)?

The dominant view in the literature is that the gender wage gap has been stable or declining in the transition countries (see, among others, Newell and Reilly 2001, for a number of post-communist countries in CEE and the FSU; Adamchik and Bedi 2003, for Poland; Munich *et al.* 2005, for the Czech Republic; Joliffe and Campos 2005, for Hungary). The gap is documented as standing at about 20 per cent, which is broadly comparable to the values reported for mature market economies (see Blau *et al.* 2006; and Dolton *et al.* this volume). The 20 per cent figure, however, is primarily based on evidence from CEE, and the picture changes as one moves further to the East (Table 10.4).

Brainerd (2000) was the first to point out that, while the GWG has diminished in CEE, it has increased in Russia and Ukraine. More recent studies reveal some variations. Ganguli and Terrell (2005) find an extremely high GWG in the Ukraine (about 40 per cent) already at the beginning of the 1990s, which, however, had decreased to 34 per cent by 2003. Kazakova (2007) explains the flattening of the GWG in Russia (after a 10 per cent increase from about 35 to 45 per cent during the 1996–2000 period) as being the result of a decrease in wage arrears.

Decomposition of change in the GWG over time suggests that in the CIS the marked widening of the wage distribution that took place in the early 1990s penalized women – as exemplified by the well-known cases of Russia and Ukraine. At the same time, Pastore and Verashchagina (2007a) find that, despite the relatively stable inequality pattern, the GWG has recently widened in Belarus, where it is driven instead by change in observed individual characteristics and their rewards (see Juhn *et al.* (1991) for the decomposition technique). Despite the presence of other relevant characteristics, the question arises as to why the widening wage gap may go together with the very high and increasing educational attainments of women in the FSU countries (UNIFEM 2006). Is it a sign of over education, or perhaps of large-scale under-utilization of human capital?

Educational attainments

This brings us to the issue of education. The educational attainments of women in post-communist countries were already very high on the eve of transition, this being a heritage from the Soviet education system. Figure 10.1 gives an idea of education levels by gender at the beginning of the 1990s in selected countries for which comparable data are available. The fact that education was financed by the

Table 10.4 The gender wage gap across countries

GWG		1995	2000	2005
Albania	Total	–	31.1†	–
Armenia	Total	51.9†	48.1†	44.3
Bulgaria	Total	–	24.2	–
Czech Republic	Total	22.8†	26.7	–
	Primary and lower secondary	30.6	30	–
	Upper secondary	21.9	27.3	–
	Tertiary	26.8	36.8	–
	Not stated	19.9	24.6	–
Georgia	Total	–	38.7	50.9
Hungary	Total	19.9	19.5	11.2
Kazakhstan	Total	–	38.5	–
Kyrgyzstan†	Total	26.7	32.4	–
Latvia†	Total	21.5	21.2	18.1
Lithuania	Total	27.9†	18.3	17.6
Poland	Total	–	20†	–
	Primary and lower secondary	–	27	–
	Upper secondary	–	17.9	–
	Tertiary	–	34.2	–
Romania†	Total	21	16.5	–
Slovakia	Total	–	25	–
	Primary and lower secondary	–	26	–
	Upper secondary	–	22.5	–
	Tertiary	–	35.2	–
	Not stated	–	–	–
Slovenia	Total	14.1†	13.3†	–
	Primary and lower secondary	17	19.5	–
	Upper secondary	12.3	14.7	–
	Tertiary	19.2	22.1	–
Tajikistan	Total	35.2†	56.8	–
Ukraine	Total	19.9	29.1	29.1

Source: Own calculations using UNECE Gender Statistics Database.

Note
'The GWG is defined as the percentage that the difference between average monthly earnings of male and female employees makes with respect to the average monthly earnings of male employees'.
† Albania: 2000 refers to October 1998; Armenia: 1995 refers to 1997, 2000 refers to 1999; Czech Republic 1995: data refer to 1996; Kyrgyzstan: enterprise-level data, refer to November of each year; Latvia: data refer to first quarter of each year and 1995 refers to 1996; Lithuania: 1995 refers to January; Poland 2000: data refer to 1999; Romania: data refer to October of each year; Slovenia: 1995 – data refer to 1996, instead 2000 refer to 1999; Tajikistan: December of each year, 1995 refers to 1996.

state provided women with high chances of access to it. This tendency still holds, and females outnumber males in university attendance in countries like Russia, Belarus and Kazakhstan (Baskakova 2004; Paci 2002).[9]

At the same time, there is an alarming tendency for women to be pushed out of free into fee-paying education (Baskakova 2004). This is especially worrisome considering that private educational establishments are not always credited with

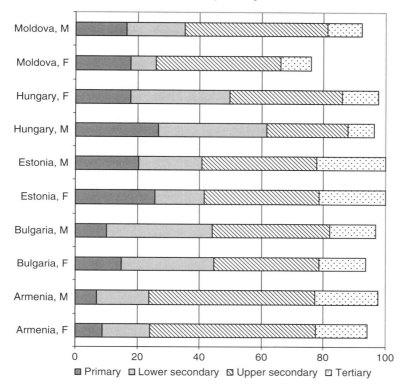

Figure 10.1 Educational attainments, 1990.
Source: Own calculation using UNECE Gender Statistics Database.

high standards (Vanags and Hansen 2005). However, relative standards of private and public education may be country specific. The cause for concern may be that the higher enrolment of girls at private schools may weaken the role that their attained education plays in a market economy during the job search. In fact, the proportion of unemployed women with university or professional-college education amounts to 40 per cent in Russia, whereas the corresponding share for men is about 25 per cent (Baskakova 2004).

A possible threat to gender equality in the sphere of education is the differentiation of professional training by sex, which is eventually likely to favour employment segregation. There are traditionally 'female' dominated colleges and universities, for example in teaching and medicine. The choice of the future profession by girls depends considerably on prejudices in society and in the family concerning what is 'appropriate' work for women, but also on the extent to which the society is traditional. Overall, with the necessity to pay for education and at the same time very limited access to credit, female specialization is becoming increasingly a matter of family rather than personal choice.

Attitudes towards gender roles

Thus far we have focused on traditional economic indicators: employment, unemployment, wages and educational attainments. Together these can be taken as indicative of women's aspirations in regard to the labour market, but they do not provide information on the level of welfare that women experience. This is influenced by achievements both at work and in the family. Apparently, women tend to place increasing emphasis on their professional success, which is reflected in a change in their life strategies. We observe a constant increase in the age of first marriage[10] (Figure 10.2) in parallel with a dramatic decline in fertility rates (Figure 10.3). And we may expect that the absolute and the relative effort that women put into domestic as opposed to market activities also matters for their fulfilment (Kahneman *et al.* 2004). This balance, however, depends on the availability of equal pay and equal opportunities law provisions, on services for childrearing, on the ease of access, extent and duration of paid maternity leave and so on (Table 10.5).[11]

This section considers three indicators of the commitment of women to non-market work: (a) the share of part-time work; (b) the time spent in the household and (c) the attitude towards gender roles. Part-time work is a proxy for the availability in a country of employment contracts that favour the reconciliation of work and family via flexibility of working times. In the US and Western Europe about 30 per cent of female employment is part-time (Bureau of Labor Statistics 2005; European Commission 2006), which gives an idea of the importance of this type of contract. Table 10.6 shows that in all transition countries the share of part-time work is much below the EU average. More importantly, there is a widespread tendency for the share of part-time over total employment to reduce further.[12]

In principle, the low share and further reduction in part-time work may be a consequence of the increased availability of measures supporting child-rearing: when women have such support they are better able to take on full-time work.

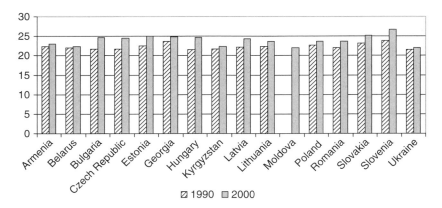

Figure 10.2 Age of women at first marriage.
Source: Own calculation using UNECE Gender Statistics Database.

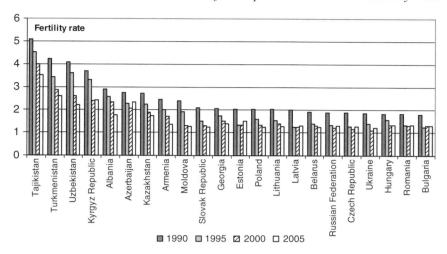

Figure 10.3 Fertility rates.
Source: Own calculation using World Development Indicators on-line database
[http://devdata.worldbank.org/dataonline/].

Table 10.5 Maternity leave duration and related benefits

Country	Maternity leave benefits, as of 2004		
	Length of maternity leave	*Percentage of wages paid in covered period*	*Provider of coverage*
Azerbaijan	126 days	100	Social security
Belarus	126 days	100	Social security
Bulgaria	135 days	90	Social security
Czech Republic	28 weeks	69	Social security
Estonia	140 days	100	Social security
Hungary	24 weeks	Pre-natal (min. 4 weeks): 70. Then flat rate	Social security
Kazakhstan	126 days	–	Employer
Kyrgyzstan	126 days	100	Social security
Latvia	112 days	100	Social security
Lithuania	126 days	100	Social security
Moldova	126 days	100	Social security
Poland	16 weeks	100	Social security
Romania	126 days	85	Social security
Russian Federation	140 days	100	Social security
Slovakia	28 weeks	55	Social security
Slovenia	105 days	100	Social security
Ukraine	126 days	100	Social security
Uzbekistan	126 days	100	Social security

Source: Calculation on Table A9 from The World's Women 2005 (UN 2006).

Table 10.6 Part-time employment of women (% of total employment)

Country	1995	2000	2004
Bulgaria	1	0.9	2.5
Czech Republic	10.3	9.1	8.3
Estonia	9.7	10.9	10.7
Hungary	4.3	4.9	6.3
Latvia	12.3†	12.7	13.2
Lithuania	11.5†	10.4	10.4
Moldova	–	2.6	–
Poland	13.3	13.4	14
Romania	19.4	18.6	11.2
Russian Federation	–	9.5	–
Slovakia	3.7	3	4.2
Slovenia	6.7	7.8	10.9
Ukraine	–	3.5	–

Source: Own calculations on UNECE Gender Statistics Database.

Note
Here 'part-time' stands for persons who perform paid work for less than 30 hours per week.
Data from Labour Force Surveys unless otherwise specified:
† Latvia 1995: data refer to 1996; Lithuania 1995: data refer to 1997.

However, other indicators suggest that the explanation of the reduction in part-time work is different in the case of the transition countries. To verify this, Figure 10.4 provides measures of the time spent in market work and in the household across a number of the EU and transition countries. It is evident that women in the transition countries devote more or roughly the same amount of time to paid work as in the EU countries, but they spend much more time in unpaid family work, so that the combined work load is massive. One possible interpretation for this evidence is that the reduction in public welfare and social services is forcing many women to take on unpaid work. At the same time, the low income of spouses and the increasing cost of living is compelling them not to decrease their effort in market work (for details see Vannoy *et al.* 1999).

Analytical framework

The evidence just reviewed suggests that, despite a considerable reduction in female labour force participation from a very high level in the pre-transition period, the double-breadwinner family model still prevails in most of the countries under consideration. At the same time, the manifest change in women's life strategies[13] is challenging for researchers, who have inquired into whether transition will eventually change the established view on gender roles. The first issue that the literature has addressed is the causes of reduced female labour force participation during transition. This section attempts to provide an analytical framework in which to consider this shift, which, as was noted before, went in the opposite direction to the trend observed in mature market economies.

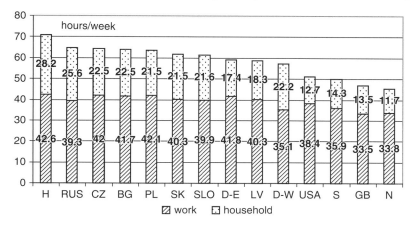

Figure 10.4 Time spent on paid work and unpaid work in the household.
Source: Own calculation on the basis of ISSP (2002) [http://www.issp.org/].

Note
Countries are H – Hungary, RUS – Russia, CZ – Czech Republic, BG – Bulgaria, PL –
Poland, SLO–Slovenia, SK–Slovakia, LV – Latvia, D-E/D-W – Germany – East/ West,
USA, S–Sweden, GB – Great Britain, N – Norway.

Transition has led to a liberalization of wage-setting mechanisms, although wage
fixing, minimum wages and unemployment benefits are instruments widely used
to hinder the operation of market forces. According to the conventional wisdom,
liberalization should eventually reduce discriminatory differences by gender in the
labour market (Becker 1957), and the empirical evidence seems to confirm this
across a number of countries (Weichselbaumer and Winter-Ebner 2007).[14]

Based on labour-supply considerations, one would think that during the period
of market-oriented reform the reduction in the gender pay gap, as well as increased
returns to education, should have led to increasing participation of women
relatively to men.[15] This was not the case, however, even though the fact that
part-time employment rates tended to remain rather low suggests that women's
labour force attachment remained high.

A very simple graphical representation of the impact of reform on female
labour force participation is provided in Figure 10.5. Several factors are at work.
Assuming homogeneous labour, changes in the female labour market position
may have been initially driven by a reduction in the labour demand (D) which in
turn induced a leftward shift of the labour supply (S) curve.[16] Final employment
(N) and wage (W) outcomes depend, however, on demand and supply elasticities.
Compare two situations differing with respect to labour supply elasticity for women
(panel a) of Figure 10.5. In line with evidence from section 1, the first situation
exemplifies the FSU countries, where labour hoarding was the usual practice and
led to a relatively rigid supply; the second describes the pattern of the CEE, where
the elasticity of supply was higher. Depending on labour supply elasticity and the

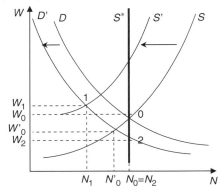

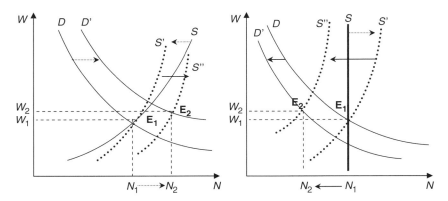

Figure 10.5 Female labour market in mature and emerging market economies

relative size of the reduction in supply in response to a drop in labour demand, the wage level may increase or decrease. If liberalization and privatization go together with restructuring and the creation of new jobs, then labour demand will take over and start improving the relative position of women. In many countries this has implied the development of the service sector with a high share of female workers employed in it (see Table 10.3). If instead little restructuring takes place, workers are trapped in old, inefficient jobs. In the case of labour hoarding, this situation is characterized by scant decline in participation rates, if any at all, with the consequent reduction in wages. The two scenarios lead, respectively, to equilibrium 1 and 2 in panel a of Figure 10.5 and can roughly describe the observed trends in CEE versus the FSU.

Note that the simplifying assumption made earlier about homogeneous labour may not hold; or it may become too restrictive in the context of a market economy.

We assume that a market economy allows for more a heterogeneous composition of the labour force in terms of tastes for work. Swaffield (2007) has empirically proved that attitudes exert a significant effect on female wages. Hence we consider it important to shed some light on how, for example, the change in labour market attachment may have affected the positions of women.

Blau and Kahn (2006), in their study on the US, document not only a rightward shift of the labour supply of married women, but also a decline in their wage elasticities, which makes the labour supply curve steeper. Illustrating this is the shift of the female labour supply curve from S to S'' in panel b of Figure 10.5, where S' stands for the change in the labour supply elasticity. With an increasing demand for labour, this maintains women's relative wages more or less unchanged, as at equilibrium points E_1 and E_2 in the same figure.[17]

To return to the emerging market economies, we would expect there to be a change in the slope together with a shift of the labour supply curve. Although the direction of change is the opposite to the one described above, we now observe an increase in elasticity together with a leftward shift of labour supply curve (from S to S'' in panel c of Figure 10.5). There is scant empirical evidence on the elasticity of the labour supply for the transition countries. Saget (1999) finds a very high and positive elasticity (+1.82) of female labour supply with respect to wages in Hungary already in the year 1992. Paci and Reilly (2006) calculate wage offer elasticities for a range of transition countries in Europe and Central Asia. Although no clear pattern emerges from their study, the values range from as low as 0.33 for Bulgaria in 1995 to as high as 1.99 for Serbia in 2001.[18]

The expectation would be that the rigid labour supply, as represented by the vertical line, has become more sensitive to the level of wages. This may be explained by change in the employment regime from one that obliged everybody to work to one that imposes no such constraint, but causes the labour supply curve to bend downwards and at the same time shift backwards. The resulting increase in the elasticity of supply could, however, be partly offset by a change in the composition of female labour, whereby the high-paid and more motivated and thus more rigid female component remains in work, while the low-paid and presumably less-motivated component quits work. The final impact on wages depends on which of these counterbalancing forces prevails and on how much the labour supply curve shifts to the left.[19]

The idea of the changing skill composition of the working female population was first addressed in a study by Hunt (2002) on East Germany. She claims that a general cause of the declining gender pay gap in that country was a sample selection mechanism operating via the reduction in female participation rates. Almost half the female relative wage growth was the result of disproportionate exits from employment of low-paid women. This means that the causality chain is exactly the opposite to that commonly hypothesized: it was not that the reduced gender pay gap and increased female wages caused increasing female participation; rather, that reduced female participation yielded an apparent reduction in the gender pay gap and an increase in the average wage for women.

Assuming that the process described in Figure 10.5 is correct, what were the determinants of this change and what was the role of welfare state retrenchment? A number of studies, reviewed below, have tested the hypothesis that employment reduction was random or, rather, distributed in an asymmetric way against low-skilled, low-motivated women. The common procedure followed to test this hypothesis is to estimate returns to education corrected for sample selection bias (Heckman 1979).

For various reasons, the studies in the literature are not uniform in terms of either their methodology or their results. Beyond methodological differences and the large variety of instrumental variables used, two main strands of enquiry can be identified. On the one hand, some studies (Ogloblin 1999, for Russia; Orazem and Vodopivec 2000, for Estonia and Slovenia; Jolliffe 2002, for Bulgaria) have found that, when detected, sample selection mechanisms do cause a reduction in returns to education whose actual size differs across countries. On the other hand, there are cases where sample selection has not been detected (Saget 1999) or has proved to be highly sensitive to the type of instruments used for the analysis (Pastore and Verashchagina 2007b). Although it is reasonable to assume that low-skilled and low-motivated women may have withdrawn from the labour market, it may be equally true that, due to a lack of opportunities, highly-educated and motivated women, too, have quit work. In fact, the high percentage of unemployed women with university degrees who are potential drop-outs, suggests that this possibility should not be ruled out. In what follows we address other explanations of what might be driving the change in female labour force participation in the transition countries.

Directions for future research

In order to assess the change in gender roles over transition, one may draw on surveys specifically designed to address the issue.[20] Figure 10.6, constructed using the 1994 and 2002 waves of the International Social Survey Programme, shows that in 1994 an overwhelming share of people in all transition countries agreed or strongly agreed with the statement that: 'Men's job is work and women's job is household'. This share fell dramatically in 2002, although the traditional way of thinking still prevailed. Ironically, in the available set of countries, the highest percentage of respondents who want see women dedicate their lives to the family is in Belarus, which also has one of the highest rates of female labour force participation (Pastore and Verashchagina 2007b). 'Having the woman back in the family' seems like an unattainable dream. The natural question to ask at this point is whether the decline in female labour force participation can be considered a 'good' or 'bad' thing, given the very high level attained in the past.[21]

In our view, a cause for concern regarding change in participation is the shift of many women to the informal economy.[22] Although numerous studies have addressed this issue, it is still a grey area. It is difficult to obtain the relevant data, and the existing evidence is rather contradictory. Some authors claim that women are more prone to end up in the informal sector because this is compatible with

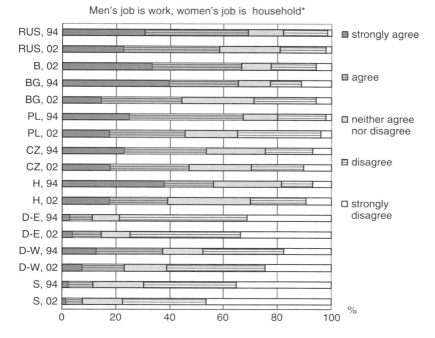

Figure 10.6 Cross-country differences in attitude towards the role of men and women.
Source: Own calculation on the basis of the International Social Survey Program data (1994 and 2002) [http://www.issp.org/].

Note
Countries are RUS – Russia, B – Belarus (only 2002), BG – Bulgaria, PL – Poland, CZ – Czech Republic, H – Hungary, D-E/D-W – East/Germany – East/West, S – Sweden.

child-rearing and household activities (in fact this is the case of many developing countries, see ILO 2007). Others find that men are more widely represented as informal workers (for a survey of the literature see Losby *et al.* 2002).

According to ILO (2002), the overall share of people involved in the informal sector is lower in the transition than in the developing countries, with figures ranging from about 5 per cent for Ukraine to more than 20 per cent for Slovakia. At the same time, whilst in Slovakia men are more 'at risk' of informal employment (with one in every four working men being involved, against one in every ten working women), in Russia men and women are equally represented in the informal sector; if anything, the female share is higher in rural areas (see Table 10.7). In 2001 informal employment represented the only source of income for more than 90 per cent of persons employed in the informal sector in Russian cities (and for about 60 per cent in rural areas).[23] The situation was even worse in countries like Georgia or Kyrgyzstan, where the majority of people employed in informal sector – men or women – relied on it as their main source of income in cities and in rural areas (ILO 2002).

Table 10.7 Persons employed in the informal sector: selected transition countries, urban and rural areas, latest available year

Country	Year	Total/ Urban/ Rural	Number (1000s)			Women per 100 men	Total employment (%)		
			Total	*Men*	*Women*		*Total*	*Men*	*Women*
Georgia	1999	Urban	73.4	53.2	19.1	36	14.2	20.7	7.4
		Rural	29.9	20.4	9.5	47	3.1	4.3	1.9
Kazakhstan	1995	Total	1069				11.7		
		Urban	662.4				11.9		
		Rural	406.6				11.4		
	1996	Urban	962.7				17.3		
Kyrgyzstan	1994	Total	140				8.2		
	1999	Total	194.1	118.8	75.3	63	24.9	28.5	20.8
	1999	Urban	139.0	84.2	54.8	65	29.4	32.8	25.3
	1999	Rural	55.1	34.6	20.5	69	18.0	21.6	14.1
Turkmenistan	1999	Total	126.4				6.8		
Latvia	1996	Total	122.3				17.2		
	1999	Total	157.8				18.2		
	1999	Urban	127.2				18.2		
		Rural	30.6				18.1		
Poland	1998	Total	1166	817	349	43	7.5	9.5	5.0
Russian	2001	Total	8179	4236	3853	89	12.6	12.9	12.3
Federation	2001	Urban	4525	2403	2122	88	9.2	9.6	8.8
		Rural	3654	1924	1730	90	23.8	23.2	24.5
Slovakia	1994	Total	362	276.3	85.7	31	17.6	23.2	9.9
	1999	Total	450	343.5	106.5	31	23.0	30.5	12.9
Ukraine	1997	Urban	755.9	345.4	420.5	122	4.9	4.5	5.3

Source: Own calculation on the basis of ILO Compendium of official statistics on employment in the informal sector.

Note
National definitions of the informal sector have been used to construct the table, for details see ILO http://www.ilo.org/public/english/bureau/stat/download/compmeth.pdf

Besides taking up employment in the informal sector, women have responded to the lack of suitable jobs by searching for work outside the home country. Female emigration from Eastern Europe has increased substantially in recent decades (UNFPA 2006), and the number of female international migrants was generally higher than that of men in 2000 in the region under consideration.[24] As reported by the UN (2006, Table A5), in the year 2000 the number of international migrant women per 100 men was 115 in Russia, 133 in Romania, and 147 in the Czech Republic.

In many cases, women who migrate accept positions which do not correspond to their qualifications. As documented by Yarova (2006), about 37 per cent of Ukrainian women working in Italy as care givers for elderly people have university degrees; 56 per cent of them worked as specialists before migration. Owing to the difference in the level of incomes across countries, performing low-skill jobs still enables them to earn much more than in their previous employment, even in higher-rank positions. Upon re-entry, women often lose social standing, also switching to completely different jobs often related to some kind of trade or small business activity. Although their financial contribution to the families is crucial, it is difficult to estimate the benefits and costs of implementing this strategy, which would require consideration of individual, household, and above all country levels. Several attempts have nevertheless been made, including those by UNFPA (2006) and Szczepaniková *et al.* (2006) with a special focus on Central and Eastern Europe.

Migration may be a risky strategy, with falling victim to human trafficking being the worst of the possible outcomes. This is one of the most lucrative businesses today (after the sale of weapons and drugs), with its roots in poor countries, including those in transition. The scale of the phenomenon is astonishing: more than 100,000 persons are trafficked from the FSU and 75,000 from CEE every year (UNFPA 2006: 45).

As they dream of making better lives for themselves, many women become easy prey for human traffickers, mainly for the purpose of sexual exploitation (Kligman and Limoncelli 2005). This is particularly worrying, because even if these women manage to escape from the criminal network, their psychological state as well as reproductive health have been irrevocably damaged.

It is widely believed that trafficked women generally come from the lowest social-ranking families and from poor, low-educated backgrounds. As recent studies reveal, however, this is not, or not consistently, the case. Lack of opportunities in a home country together with a lack of information concur to making the risk of trafficking uncomfortably high (for more detailed investigation of the risk factors involved in trafficking from Eastern Europe see Bettio *et al.* 2007; Malysheva and Tyuryukanova 2001). Further investigation is required to reconstruct the profile of victims of trafficking in order to understand the forces behind demand and supply in this business, which involves an ever-increasing number of women from the transition countries.

Overall, gender and related issues have been widely underestimated in the post-communist world (Malysheva 2001; 2006), partly because of the lack of women in high decision-making positions and politics (UN 2006). Women's share of parliamentary seats in 2000 ranged from as low as 5 per cent in Ukraine to 10 per cent in Hungary and Russia and 13 per cent in Moldova, up to 'peaks' of 20 per cent in Poland (for comparison, Germany records 32 per cent: see UN, 2006, Table A10). This is of great importance, considering the dramatic change in the behaviour of women; a change that should be first understood and then taken into account when implementing economic policy at the state level.

The transition countries have imported behavioural models from the market economies at an even faster pace than might have been expected. As a result, women in emerging market economies, like their Western counterparts, tend to feel more self-sufficient and autonomous; they allocate time differently than in the past and invest more in their careers. They also tend to postpone marriage and maternity.

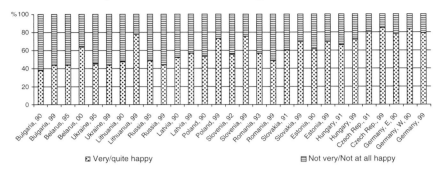

□ Very/quite happy   ⊟ Not very/Not at all happy

Figure 10.7 Subjective well-being of women*
Source: Own calculation on the basis of European Values Study [http://www.gesis.org/
Datenservice/zacat.htm].

Note
*Here defined as response to the question: 'Taking all things together would you say you
are: (1) Very happy; (2) Quite happy; (3) Not very happy; (4) Not at all happy'.

Their values and attitudes are changing and becoming more differentiated. Some
women are more concerned to achieve professional self-fulfilment, while others,
low-motivated, look for a successful marriage that will enable them may be
not to work at all. Since the stigma of being out of the labour force has been
removed, this has become one of women's life-strategies, and it contributes to
reducing female labour force participation. Arguably, all this represents a wider
choice set for women after decades of an excessive double burden of paid and
unpaid work.

A different way to address the question of whether or not lower female
participation is desirable is to introduce concepts like subjective well-being and
happiness into economic theory, as proposed by the economics of happiness
(see Kahneman and Krueger 2006). This introduces an alternative perspective, suggesting that policies should target the degree of people's satisfaction with their lives. However, the existing evidence does not afford a clear
answer.

Figure 10.7 traces the change over time in subjective well-being as reported
by women in transition countries, first at the beginning and then at the end of the
1990s. Russia and Ukraine show up as the worst cases, where the percentage of
women who feel not quite or not at all happy increased over time despite starting
from some of the highest levels in the region (over 50 per cent). At the same
time several smaller countries (like Belarus, Lithuania, Slovenia) have undergone
remarkable improvement in this respect.

Understanding what makes women happy would be a major step forward.
However, we have not sought to answer the question in this survey, our aim being
instead to stimulate discussion.

Conclusion

This chapter has undertaken a survey of the literature on change in the labour market position of women in a wide range of transition countries. Women are generally known to be at a disadvantage in situations of risk and uncertainty. This was less the case in the centrally planned economies, but it fully materialized with the introduction of the market economy, causing a dramatic change in women's life strategies. The main factors driving this change are increasing opportunities in the labour market and change in gender roles within the household.

We started by analysing a series of stylized facts, focusing on employment practices, wages and the gender wage gap, segregation and educational attainments. The countries considered divide into two large groups, respectively the CEE and the FSU. Partly owing to geographical proximity to the European Union, the former group of countries are apparently converging to a Western pattern of female labour force participation. The latter group continues to record comparatively high female activity rates, but on closer inspection this is largely the result of state intervention. One clear example of state intervention with this effect is labour hoarding, which in the long run does not enhance the competitiveness of women in the labour market and may even cause a widening of the gender wage gap. On the eve of reforms, extensive state control was justified by a deep economic recession, but the inertia with which some of the countries have implemented market reforms has not created a stimulating environment. Rather, it has encouraged women to adhere to the old and inefficient employment practices, thereby perpetuating inertia in a cultural tradition that ultimately assigns household and family duties – i.e. non-market work – primarily to women.

We have paid especial attention to the issue of shrinking female labour force participation and proposed an analytical framework to explain past and recent trends observed during transition. In our reconstruction, both the leftward shift in the female labour supply and the rise in the elasticity of labour supply with respect to wages has originated from, on the one side, the liberalization of wage setting mechanisms and, on the other, increasing budget constraints for both firms and households which have depressed labour demand. A comparatively stronger labour market in CEE has translated this leftward shift into lower participation rather than into lower wages, whereas labour hoarding practices have had the opposite effect in the FSU countries. At the same time, the empirical evidence suggests that the GWG has narrowed in CEE, while it has remained high or increased in the CIS. Segregation may be another potential sign of deteriorating female labour market positions.

High educational attainment is still the main advantage of women in the transition countries. But the lack of decently paid jobs prevents them from fully benefiting from such attainment, and often pushes them towards the informal sector or induces them to migrate. We have highlighted these outcomes as signalling a risk of decreasing well-being for women. The feminization of international migration has proceeded side by side with an increasing incidence of human trafficking; and a social matter of concern is that trafficking mainly involves sexual exploitation. In search of better lives, Eastern European women have become more easily the victims of this lucrative business.

We concluded the survey by discussing the evidence on change in the subjective well-being of women in transition countries. The picture that emerged was a rather mixed one, and we did not find evidence of a clear association between women's happiness and the change in gender roles, or a lack of it. We believe that change in attitudes and values may be a painful process, one that also depends on the country-specific context, and that it can affect all spheres of life. In our view, analysis of what is driving this change, and what its long-term implications are, requires further research.

Acknowledgements

We are very grateful to the participants at the ISER 2005 summer school on *Gender and Economics* at the University of Siena for the stimulating environment that they created, and for the comments and suggestions that we received. Special thanks are due to the organizers for the opportunity they provided us to present this research. We are particularly indebted to Francesca Bettio for her guidance, inspiration and support for this work. All possible errors, however, are our responsibility alone.

Notes

1 Overall about a quarter of the world's population experienced a move from centrally-planned to market economy in the late 1980s–early 1990s. The reform process labeled 'Economic Transition' is thought to be concluded in some countries but not in others, like the block of the FSU. Although this chapter deals mainly with the cases of prolonged transition, the conclusions drawn are likely to be valid for other economies that have undergone similar types of reform.

2 CIS stands for the Commonwealth of Independent States, which is a successor of the FSU. It includes all the previous members except for the Baltic States, namely: Armenia, Azerbaijan, Belarus, Georgia, Kazakhstan, Kyrgyzstan, Moldova, Russia, Tajikistan, Turkmenistan, Ukraine and Uzbekistan.

3 Labour hoarding and wage arrears were common practices in all the countries of the FSU throughout the 1990s. It is now slowly disappearing, but is still attracting the attention of many researchers that have analysed the determinants and consequences of this phenomenon (e.g. Lehmann and Wadsworth 2007; Gerry *et al.* 2004; Boyarchuk *et al.* 2005). They generally conclude that women and men suffered equally from late payments (Kazakova 2007).

4 Many non-standard forms of employment emerged as a consequence of this demand for additional income, which remains an understudied issue (Roshchin and Razumova 2002; Brown *et al.* 2006, are few exceptions), especially in connection with the informal sector (Bouev 2001).

5 Note that we refer to participation rates calculated for the whole female population aged over 15.

6 The registration procedures of the employment services in the CIS countries have a negative influence both on the incentives for the unemployed to register and on the objective opportunities gained by those who register. This has resulted in fewer people

seeking the status of unemployed and in an apparent decrease in official unemployment statistics, as compared to the actual number of unemployed. It is not by chance that in practically all CIS countries that collect sufficiently reliable unemployment statistics, total unemployment is several times higher than registered unemployment. Between 2000 and 2005 (the overall unemployment figure exceeded that for registered unemployed in Kazakhstan – 3.5 times, in Russia – 4–7 times, in Armenia – 25 times, in Georgia – 35–40 times.

7 The unemployment rates in Table 10.2 were calculated based on the definition of unemployed as persons who during the reference period were: (a) without work – i.e. were not in paid employment or self-employment; (b) were available for paid employment and (c) were seeking work – i.e. had taken specific steps in a specified reference period to seek paid employment.

8 It is worth noting that the opposite is often the case in Western Europe, where public sector employees are not necessarily worse off in terms of pay.

9 In 2006, 48 per cent out of the total number of 1200 candidates who visited the QS World MBA Tour in Moscow were women. For comparison: in 2005 their share was 34 per cent, in 2003 – 28 per cent. However, further investigation for Russia (see http://www.topmba.com/) highlights that women themselves are placing limits on their career development. They have lower payment expectations, more modest status ambitions. Russia and most CIS countries lack a tradition of career planning, and few educational establishments have qualified career centres. Very often women graduate without any strategic vision about their future.

10 It is still considerably lower than in Western European countries.

11 Table 10.5 sheds some light on the amount of social support provided to women during their maternity leave. It is important to keep in mind that wages from the main job have rather different purchasing power across countries, and scarce earnings often push people to search for additional sources of income, often in the informal sector. For example, wages from the main job make up only about 70 per cent of the total monthly labour incomes in Russia (Roshchin and Razumova 2002).

12 We do not imply that this reflects women's taste for work; rather, a lack of opportunities to find a suitable part-time work.

13 The process of economic transition in CEE and the FSU countries is drastically changing the working profiles of women, who are re-assessing their lifetime decisions about when and whether to seek gainful employment, to start a family and to participate in tertiary education. Privatization of state-owned enterprises (Paci and Reilly 2006), or the simple process of liberalization of wage setting mechanisms and a general weakening of the employment protection legislation (Brainerd 2000; Munich *et al.* 2005) in the labour market fuel these changes.

14 However, as discussed in section one, resistance to market forces gave rise to different patterns of change of the GWG in the FSU countries, depending on starting conditions on the eve of reform.

15 The evidence discussed in the first section suggests that the GWG was increasing in countries which were more prone to hinder the working of market forces. As for returns to education, there is ample evidence that they were on the rise in transition countries.

16 The leftward shift was expected, since under the system of central planning everybody was employed and firms starting to adopt new forms of production and management schemes wanted to get rid of redundant workers.

17 In fact the GWG in the US has been stable at about 20 per cent since the mid-1980s (see Blau *et al.* 2006).

18 The results of the few available studies seem to be very much country-specific, due to the type of data used, but also methodology applied, and thus deserve further investigation.

19 For the sake of simplicity here we do not consider the change in the elasticity of demand, although we could view labour hoarding as sustaining a rigid labour demand that was bound to decrease following the process of reform.
20 Three waves of the International Social Survey Programme (ISSP 1988, 1994 and 2002: http://www.issp.org/) were aimed at tracing the change in family structure and gender roles in different parts of the world, including some of the transition countries.
21 Kornai (1992, Ch. 10) provides a suggestive explanation of why this was the case everywhere under communist regimes. As he puts it, the socialist system had a preference for labour intensive production processes in order to facilitate extraction of the entire possible surplus from manpower and at the same time to maintain social and political control. In this type of system, working was almost a duty, rather than a right. This was true independent of gender.
22 Economic activities undertaken without official statistical registration.
23 According to the recent estimates, at the end of 2004 about 11.5 million people in Russia (17 per cent of employed population) were involved in the informal sector (6/5.5 million of men/women). For about 7 million of them this was the only source of income (Population Survey on Employment Issues (2005); see also Khotkina 2006). Interestingly, despite the high involvement of Russian women in the informal economy, incomes generated in this sector do not appear to affect significantly their formal job participation (Kolev 1998). However, this finding by Kolev may be driven by the type of data he used, which is not specifically designed to study the issue (RLMS).
24 Except for Central Asian countries, where cultural traditions may prevent women from being mobile.

References

Acemoglu, D. (2001) 'Good Jobs versus Bad Jobs', *Journal of Labor Economics*, 19 (1): 1–21.
Adamchik, V.A. and Bedi, A.S. (2003) 'Gender Pay Differentials during the Transition in Poland', *Economics of Transition*, 11 (4): 697–726.
Atkinson, A. and Micklewright, J. (1992) *Economic Transformation in Eastern Europe and the Distribution of Income*. Cambridge: Cambridge University Press.
Baskakova, M.E (ed.) (2004) *Gender Inequality in Modern Russia Through the Mirror of Statistics*. URRS: M.:Editorial.
Becker, G. (1957) *The Economics of Discrimination*. Chicago: University of Chicago Press.
Bettio, F., Nandi, T. and Verashchagina, A. (2007) *Risk factors of falling into human trafficking in Eastern Europe*, mimeo.
Blau, F.D., Ferber, M.A. and Winkler, A.E. (2006) *The Economics of Women, Men and Work*, 5th Edition. Essex: Pearson Prentice Hall.
Blau, F.D. and Kahn, L.M. (2006) '*Changes in the Labor Supply Behavior of Married Women: 1980–2000*', IZA DP 2180.
Bouev, M. (2001) *Labor Supply, Informal Economy and Russian Transition*, William Davidson Institute WP No. 408.
Boyarchuk, D., Maliar, L. and Maliar, S. (2005) 'The Consumption and Welfare Implications of Wage Arrears in Transition Economies', *Journal of Comparative Economics*, 33 (3): 540–567.
Brainerd, E. (2000) 'Women in Transition: Change in Gender Wage Differentials in Eastern Europe and FSU', *Industrial and Labour Relations Review*, 54 (1): 139–162.
Brown, J.D., Earle, J.S, Gimpelson, V., Kapeliushnikov, R., Lehmann, H., Telegdy, Á., Vantu, I., Visan, R. and Voicu, A. (2006) 'Non-standard Forms and Measures of

Employment and Unemployment in Transition: A Comparative Study of Estonia, Romania and Russia', *Comparative Economic Studies*, 48 (1): 435–457.

Bureau of Labor Statistics (2005) Women in the Labor Force: A Databook. Available: http://www.bls.gov/cps/wlf-databook2005.htm (Accessed 10 May 2007).

Earle, J.S. and Sabirianova, K.Z. (2002) 'How Late to Pay? Understanding Wage Arrears in Russia', *Journal of Labor Economics*, 20 (3): 661–707.

EBRD (2000), Transition report 2000: Employment, Skills and Transition, London.

European Commission (2006) Employment in Europe, report. Available: http://ec.europa.eu/employment_social/employment_analysis/employ_2006_en.htm (Accessed 10 May 2007).

Ganguli, I. and Terrell, K. (2005) *Wage Ceilings and Floors: The Gender Gap in Ukraine's Transition*, IZA DP No. 1776.

Gerry, Ch. J., Li, C.A. and Kim, B.-Y. (2004) 'The Gender Wage Gap and Wage Arrears in Russia: Evidence from the RLMS', *Journal of Population Economics*, 17 (2): 267–288.

Giddings, L. (2002) 'Changes in Gender Earnings Differentials in Bulgaria's Transition to a Mixed-Market Economy', *Eastern Economic Journal*, 28 (4): 481–497.

Heckman, J. (1979) 'Sample Selection Bias as a Specification Error', *Econometrica*, 47 (1): 153–162.

Hunt, J. (2002) 'The Transition in East Germany: When is a Ten-point Fall in the Gender Pay Gap Bad News?', *Journal of Labor Economics*, 20 (1): 148–169.

ILO (2002) compendium of official statistics on employment in the informal sector. Available: http://www.ilo.org/public/english/bureau/stat/download/compmeth.pdf (Accessed 10 May 2007).

ILO (2007) *Global Employment Trends for Women*, March.

Jolliffe, D. (2002) 'The Gender Wage Gap in Bulgaria: A Semiparametric Estimation of Discrimination', *Journal of Comparative Economics*, 30 (2): 276–295.

Jolliffe, D. and Campos, H.F. (2005) 'Does Market Liberalization Reduce Gender Discrimination? Econometric evidence from Hungary, 1986–1998', *Labour Economics*, 12 (1): 1–22.

Juhn, C., Murphy, K. and Pierce B. (1991) Accounting for the Slowdown in Black White Wage Convergence, in Marvin H. Kosters (ed.) *Workers and Their Wages: Changing Patterns in the U.S.* Washington DC.: American Enterprise Institute Press: pp.107–143.

Jurajda, Š. (2003) 'Gender Wage Gap and Segregation in Enterprises and the Public Sector in Late Transition Countries', *Journal of Comparative Economics*, 31 (2): 199–222.

Jurajda, Š. (2005) 'Gender Segregation and Wage Gap: an East-West Comparison', *Journal of the European Economic Association*, 3 (2–3): 598–607.

Jurajda, Š. and Harmgart, H. (2007) 'When do female occupations pay more?', *Journal of Comparative Economics*, 35 (1): 170–187.

Kahneman, D. and Krueger, A.B. (2006) 'Developments in the Measurement of Subjective Well-Being', *Journal of Economic Perspectives*, American Economic Association, 20 (1): 3–24.

Kahneman, D., Krueger, A.B., Schkade, D., Schwarz, N. and Stone, A. (2004) 'Toward National Well-Being Accounts', *American Economic Review*, 94 (2): 429–434.

Katz, K. (1997) 'Gender, Wages and Discrimination in the USSR: A Study of a Russian Industrial Town', *Cambridge Journal of Economics*, 21 (4): 431–452.

Kazakova, E. (2007) 'Wages in a Growing Russia. When is a 10 per cent rise in the Gender Wage Gap Good News?', *Economics of Transition,* 15 (2): 365–392.

Khotkina, Z. (2006) 'Employment in Informal Sector', *Population*, 1 (31): 107–108.

Kligman, G. and Limoncelli, S.A. (2005) 'Trafficking Women After Socialism: From, To, and Through Eastern Europe', *Social Politics*, 12 (1): 118–140.

Kolev, A. (1998) *Labour Supply in the Informal Economy in Russia during Transition*, CEPR DP 2024.

Kornai, J. (1992) *The Socialist System. The Political Economy of Communism*. Oxford: Oxford University Press.

Koumakhov, R. and Najman, B. (2000) *Labor Hoarding in Russia: Where Does it Come From?*, William Davidson Institute WP No. 394.

Layard, R. (2004) *Good Jobs and Bad Jobs*, LSE, CEP Occasional Paper No.19.

Lehmann, H. and Wadsworth, J. (2007) 'Wage Arrears and Inequality in the Distribution of Pay: Lessons from Russia', *Research in Labor Economics,* 1 (26): 125–155.

Losby, J.L., Else, J.F., Kingslow, M.E., Edgcomb, E.L., Malm, E.T. and Kao, V. (2002) Informal Economy Literature Review. Available: http://www.ised.us/doc/Informal%20Economy%20Lit%20Review.pdf. (Accessed 10 May 2007).

Maltseva, I.O., Roshchin S.Y. (2006) *Gender segregation and Mobility on the Russian Labour Market*. Moscow: Higher School of Economics.

Malysheva, M. (2001) *Contemporary Patriarchy*. Moscow: Academia Publishing House,.

Malysheva, M. (2006) 'Gender Issues of Globalization', *Russia in Globalizing World*. Moscow, Institute on Population Studies.

Malysheva, M. and Tyuryukanova, E. (2001) *Women, Migration and State*. Moscow: Academia Publishing House.

Munich, D., Svejnar, J. and Terrell, K. (2005) 'Is Women's Human Capital Valued More by Markets than by Planners?', *Journal of Comparative Economics*, 33 (2): 278–299.

Namazie, C.Z. (2003) *Why Labour Hoarding may be Rational: A Model of Firm Behaviour during Transition*, CASE paper 69, May.

Newell, A. and Reilly, B. (2001) 'The Gender Pay Gap in the Transition from Communism: Some Empirical Evidence', *Economic Systems*, 25 (4): 287–304.

Newell, A. and Reilly, B. (1996) 'The Gender Wage Gap in Russia: Some Empirical Evidence', *Labour Economics*, 3 (3): 337–356.

Ogloblin, C. (1999) 'The Gender Earnings Differentials in the Russian Transition Economy', *Industrial and Labour Relations Review*, 52 (4): 602–627.

Orazem, P.F. and Vodopivec, M. (2000) 'Male-Female Differences in Labour Market Outcomes during the Early Transition to Market: The Case of Estonia and Slovenia', *Journal of Population Economics*, 13 (2): 283–303.

Paci, P. (2002) 'Gender in Transition', World Bank, Washington D.C.

Paci, P. and Reilly, B. (2006) *Does Economic Liberalization Reduce Gender Inequality in the Labour Market? The Experience of the Transitional Economies of Europe and Central Asia*. Washington D.C.: World Bank.

Pastore, F. and Verashchagina, A. (2007a), *'When Does Transition Increase the Gender Wage Gap? An Application to Belarus'*, IZA DP.

Pastore, F. and Verashchagina, A. (2007b) *'On Female Labour Force Participation and their Job Remuneration in Transition: An Application to Belarus'*, mimeo.

Population Survey on Employment Issues (2005) *Federal Service on State Statistics*, Moscow.

Roshchin, S. and Razumova, T. (2002) *Secondary Employment in Russia. Labour Supply Modelling*, EERC working paper No. 02/07.

Roshchin, S.Y. and Solntcev, S.A. (2006) *Who Overcomes "Glass Ceiling": Vertical Gender Segregation in Russian Economy*. Working paper WP4/2006/03. — Moscow: State University — Higher School of Economics.

Rutkowski, J. and Scarpetta, S. (2005) *Enhancing Job Opportunities: Eastern Europe and the Former Soviet Union.* Washington D.C.: World Bank.

Saget, C. (1999) 'The Determinants of Female Labour Supply in Hungary', *Economics of Transition*, 7 (3): 575–591.

Stefanova Lauerova, J. and Terrell, K. (2007) 'What Drives Gender Differences in Unemployment?', *Comparative Economic Studies*, 49 (1): 128–155.

Szczepaniková, A., Čaněk, M. and Grill, J. (eds) (2006) *Migration Processes in Central and Eastern Europe: Unpacking the Diversity,* Prague: Multicultural Center Prague. Available: http://aa.ecn.cz/img_upload/79a33131c9c4293e0fcefb50bfa263ef/Migration_Processes_in_CEE_MKC.pdf (Accessed 3 January 2008).

Swaffield, J.K. (2007) 'Estimates of the Impact of Labour Market Attachment and Attitudes on the Female Wage', *The Manchester School*, 75 (3): 349–371.

UNFPA (2006) A Passage to Hope: Women and International Migration. On-line: <http://www.unfpa.org/swp/2006/pdf/en_sowp06.pdf>. Accessed 10.05.07.

UNICEF (1999) 'Women in Transition', Innocenti Social Monitor Regional Report, no. 6, ICDC, Florence, Italy.

UNIFEM (2006) *The story behind the numbers: Women and Employment in Central and Eastern Europe and the Western commonwealth of Independent States.*

United Nations (1991) The World's Women 1970–1990: Trends and Statistics. New York: UN.

UNIFEM (2006) The World's Women 2005. *Progress in Statistics*, New York: UN.

Vanags, A. and Hansen, M. (2005) The Private Sector in Higher Education in the Baltic States and Belarus: Permanent Feature or Transition Phenomenon? Online: <http://www.cerge-ei.cz/gdn/regional_research_competition/>. Accessed: 10.05.07.

Vannoy, D., Rimashevskaya, N. and Malysheva, M. (1999) *Marriages in Russia. Couples during the Economic Transition.* Westport, CT.: Praeger Publishers.

Weichselbaumer, D. and R. Winter-Ebner (2007) 'The effects of competition and equal treatment laws on gender wage differentials', *Economic Policy*, 22 (50): 235–287.

Yarova, O. (2006) 'The Migration of Ukrainian Women to Italy and the Impact on Their Family in Ukraine' in A. Szczepaniková, M. Čaněk. and J. Grill (eds) *Migration Processes in Central and Eastern Europe: Unpacking the Diversity*, Prague: Multicultural Center Prague. Available: http://aa.ecn.cz/img_upload/79a33131c9c4293e0fcefb50bfa263ef/Migration_Processes_in_CEE_MKC.pdf (Accessed 3 January 2008). pp. 38–41.

Part 5

Lessons from the laboratory

11 The gender gap

Using the lab as a window on the market

Catherine Eckel

Introduction

Labour market studies reveal that women's earnings are lower than men's, even after correcting for job characteristics and worker characteristics. Although that difference has diminished over the last 30 years (e.g. Bergmann 1996: 37), a significant difference in earnings is found in virtually every study that has been conducted. In a meta-analysis, Weichselbaumer and Winter-Ebner (2005) report that recent studies show a total wage gap of around 30 per cent and residual wage gaps averaging just under 20 per cent. In this chapter I selectively review evidence from experimental studies with an eye to evidence that might suggest possible explanations for the wage gap.[1]

Laboratory experiments are not a substitute for empirical studies of labour market choices and outcomes, but rather complementary. The advantage of the lab is that particular elements of preferences or behaviour can be isolated and examined separately, controlling for all (or most) possible confounds. This cannot be done in the field, where preferences and behaviours are found in combinations that are hard or impossible to separate. Of course like any other methodology the lab also has limitations, which must be acknowledged and examined. However, lab experiments are an important element of the economist's toolkit that can be brought to bear for better understanding important economic phenomena such as the gender gap. The lab can act as a window on the market.

Who is economic man, and what is he doing in our models?

Economic man is a simple agent who maximizes his utility. He cares only about his own happiness. Of course this doesn't exclude his caring about the happiness of others – that is to say, others' consumption can be an argument in his utility function – but only to the extent that it makes him happy to do so. Economic models (game theoretical models among them) use him as a building block, and he most commonly appears in his simpler guise as an agent who cares only about his own consumption. Keep in mind, however, that no one really believes in him, not even economists: he is a simplifying approximation, as is true of all useful theoretical building blocks. Models where he lives often do a very good job of predicting aggregate behaviour in a wide variety of settings, particularly those involving competition such as a market with many buyers and sellers. But he turns out not to be such a useful approximation in other settings.

Economic man is useful in another way. In a recent essay directed at political scientists, Schotter (2006) argues that building models based on rational economic man is very useful because it allows the careful exploration of the implications of assumptions, thereby separating logical 'wheat' from intuitive 'chaff'. He says, '[p]eople get confused by the rational choice methodology when they believe that the results of the theorems proven in this fashion are correct predictors of human behavior. Mature thinkers understand that this is not true' (Schotter 2006: 500). A great deal can be learned from theory that is 'strong and wrong'.

To illustrate, let us make a small detour through the history of experimental economics. The earliest experiments on competitive markets were conducted by Vernon Smith in the early 1960s, and strongly supported the economic man model (see Smith 1991). In these experiments, subjects are given costs and values that reproduce in the lab the familiar upward-sloping supply and downward-sloping demand schedules associated with the standard classroom version of the supply/demand model. For example, a seller might be told that his cost is $3 per unit, and that his earnings will be the selling price of any units he sells less the $3 cost; a buyer will be told her value is $10 and her earnings equal $10 less the purchase price of any units she buys. Trading occurs using a double auction institution where both buyers and sellers call out prices, and trades occur when an offer to buy or sell is accepted. These markets work as predicted by models of supply and demand. Prices and quantities rapidly converge to equilibrium values.

A parallel branch of experimental economics tests game theoretic models of interactions among smaller groups of people. Here the economic man model does not do so well. It is more difficult to find self-interested behaviour in games where the payoffs to others are known, where there are potential gains to cooperation with an associated incentive to free ride on others' efforts. Though monetary incentives affect choices, subjects in these experiments are clearly more other-regarding in their behaviour than naïve game theory will allow. On the other hand, since cooperation allows subjects as a group to capture more of the experimenter's money, it is difficult to justify labelling the behaviour as outside rationality. By their behaviour, which Vernon Smith might term 'ecological rationality', they succeed in increasing aggregate earnings and efficiency (Smith 2003).

Thus we see that economic man is a powerful, but limited creature. As an inhabitant of economic models, he does a pretty good job of capturing the behaviour of subjects in the lab in some settings – those involving competition – but not in others, those involving gains to cooperation. In an early encounter in my career, a somewhat hostile colleague suggested that economic man might be a reasonable approximation to the motivation and behaviour of men, but certainly was not a good model of the behaviour of women. (Actually she said it was a good model of 'aging white men', but there's no need to single them out.) Nevertheless, one might reasonably ask, 'Is economic man the same as economic woman?'

As economists, what do we know about the economic progress of women? Women earn about two thirds of what men earn for full-time employment. Even within a profession and rank, women earn 10–15 per cent less than men. Only 2 per cent of Chief Executive Officers of Fortune 500 firms are women (as of 2006). Studies show that women academics publish less than their male counterparts in every field, including those dominated by women such as library science. Perhaps as a consequence, women are less likely to be granted tenure. In economics (in the US) specifically, women make up about 30 per cent of assistant professors, 15 per cent of associate professors, and 8 per cent of professors, and this pattern has been in place for some time. The Committee on the Status of Women in the Economics Profession of the American Economic Association collects data on the academic advancement of women academic economists. Their most recent survey shows that women continue to lag men in their progress toward higher academic ranks. While women earned 20 per cent of PhDs awarded in economics in the 1980s and 25 per cent in the 1990s, only 8.3 per cent of full professors in PhD granting departments are women (see Committee on the Status of Women, 2007).

These observations suggest that there is something different about economic women. Women may earn less than men for many reasons: we focus on three that are particularly amenable to isolating and testing in laboratory experiments.[2] First, women may have different preferences. In particular, as suggested by mountains of research in psychology and sociology, women may be more altruistic and cooperative, and less interested in competition, than men.[3] Second, women may be perceived differently, and this difference in perceptions may be reflected in the expectations of others. The female stereotype (cooperative, nurturing) may affect others' beliefs about their preferences or performance in such a way that earnings are affected.[4] Finally, women may be treated differently from men. They may be presented with different opportunities, or offered different wages. That is, women may be the objects of unfavorable discrimination. This is not unrelated to the first two – that is, differences in treatment may arise because of perceived difference in preferences, but may also be related to the perceived social status of women. All economic agents act within a social structure, and status hierarchies are an important influence on behaviour.

In this chapter I examine each of these aspects in the context of laboratory experiments. I ask, do women and men earn different wages because of differences in their preferences, because of differences in the way others perceive them, or in the ways they are treated by others within a social context? We ask these questions by examining differences in the behaviour of women and men in several different experimental settings, most of which have implications for more than one of these factors.

Measuring preferences

Women's preferences may differ from men's in many ways, three of which are examined here: altruism, risk aversion and competition. Preferences in these areas could be relevant for women's behaviour and earnings in the work place. The challenge for the economist is to design experiments that measure preferences so as to accurately capture and isolate these differences.

Traditionally, preferences have been measured using survey questions. However, recent methodological developments in experimental economics have focused on developing experiments that provide behavioural measures of preferences. The survey approach is to develop questions that ask subjects to report their own attitudes, or alternatively, their past behaviour. Experimentalists put people in a situation where their preferences can be revealed by the subjects' own choices. Economists are inherently suspicious of self-reported survey measures because the subjects have no incentive to report correctly, and may have an incentive to distort reported preferences.

For example, suppose that as a researcher you want a measure of your subjects' altruism – the extent to which they are willing to share resources with others. You could develop a questionnaire asking what they would do in hypothetical situations, or what they have done in the past. Asking someone if they are altruistic is likely to give a biased measure, as subjects want to appear to be a 'good' person to others – the experimenter or other subjects – or even to themselves.[5] Since the cost of misrepresentation is low, subjects may distort the answers to the questions without penalty. Furthermore, 'wishful thinking' can result in subjects distorting their answers even to themselves. To illustrate the point, consider reports of voting behaviour. Survey measures of voting behaviour (answers to the question, 'Did you vote in the previous election?') consistently produce voting levels that are far higher than actual recorded voting behaviour. If you as an experimenter ask your subject, in essence, 'Are you altruistic?', what do you think the answer will be? Experiments, on the other hand, involve monetary incentives. Subjects are put in a situation where, in order to answer 'yes' to the question posed, they must give up resources. As a result, misrepresentation of preferences becomes costly.

Experimentalists have gone to some trouble to eliminate any observer effect or experimenter demand in their designs. Care is taken to use neutral language in instructions, and to ensure that subjects' decisions cannot be observed by each other. Some experiments study the effect of observation directly, to try to gauge the impact of being observed on subjects' decisions. Hoffman *et al.* (1994) introduce a 'double blind' protocol that removes the possibility that a decision can be observed by the experimenter, in a very transparent way. They show that this protocol makes subjects behave in a more self-interested manner. Haley and Fessler (2005) find that very subtle cues (eye-like images on the instruction form) increase cooperation; this is confirmed by Bateson *et al.* (2006) who find, in a field experiment, that posting an image with eyes significantly increases the rate at which people pay for their coffee in a break room. Given how strong the effects of observation are on behaviour, experimentalists are careful to eliminate, or at least control for, the extent of observability.

In designing games to measure preferences, economists' view of preferences as described by a utility function suggests a measurement strategy. Altruism is the tradeoff between one's own and others' payoffs, so any task that measures this tradeoff should be adequate. Economists think of risk aversion as the result of diminishing marginal utility and the attendant curvature of the utility function. Any task that reveals the shape of the utility function should serve the purpose. However, despite the apparent simplicity of the strategy, it turns out that there is some art involved in designing the games that subjects play, whether they be with other counterparts or against nature, in order to capture particular aspects of preferences.

For example, the earliest studies of gender differences in cooperation used the two-person prisoner's dilemma, or multi-person games with similar incentive structures such as social dilemma games, with mixed results. Eckel and Grossman (1998) point out that these games confound two possible differences in preferences: altruism and risk aversion. The cooperative strategy in these games is also the risky alternative: cooperation risks a really low payoff. If women are both more altruistic and more risk averse, then any gender difference would depend on the tradeoffs implicit in the parameters of the game. These games do not succeed in isolating altruism, and so do not make good measures.[6]

Altruism

The most popular game in use for isolating and measuring altruism is the dictator game, which was first developed as economists tried to understand puzzling results from studies of two-person bargaining (Kahneman *et al.* 1986; Forsythe *et al.* 1994). Its use as a measure of preferences, rather than for testing theory, came later (e.g. Eckel and Grossman 1996). The dictator game is the simplest possible two-person bargaining game. Indeed, it is not a game at all (since there is no strategic element to the decision), but rather an allocation task.

In this experiment, the first mover is endowed by the experimenter with an amount of money. She is given the opportunity to pass (donate) some of her endowment to another person, the second-mover. The second mover doesn't actually get to move, but rather is a passive recipient of whatever the first mover decides to send.

When women and men participate in these experiments, they behave differently. Figure 11.1 shows the distribution of choices by women and men in a dictator game experiment conducted by Eckel and Grossman (1998). Women and men dictators were recruited separately to participate in the experiment. All subjects were matched randomly with an anonymous second mover chosen from a mixed group of student second movers who were recruited to a separate room. The experiment was 'double blind' (Hoffman *et al.* 1994), ensuring that the experimenter did not know who had made what decision. In this setting, women gave on average $1.60 from a $10 endowment, while men gave only $0.82 to their assigned counterparts.

These results are confirmed in a couple of other settings. When the anonymous counterpart was replaced by a reputable charity, the American Red Cross, women again gave more than men. In Eckel and Grossman (2003) we report experiments designed to examine the effect of different endowments distributed by the experimenter ($4, $6 and $10) and different ways of subsidizing charitable giving.[7]

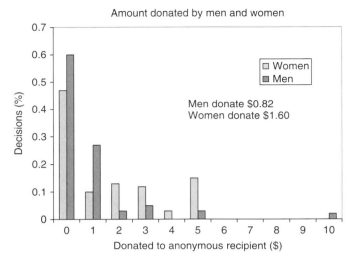

Figure 11.1 Altruism in the dictator game (anonymous counterpart).
Source: Eckel and Grossman (1998).

Across all of the treatments, women gave about 20 per cent more than men.
For example, from a $6.00 endowment, women gave $3.11 and men $2.63; from
a $10.00 endowment, women gave $5.34 and men $4.52. In a similar protocol
designed to study giving to Hurricane Katrina victims, subjects completed a series
of allocation decisions that varied the endowment ($10, $20 and $50) and the rate
of subsidy, women gave on average an additional 10% of their endowments (Eckel
et al. 2007).

This result is not always confirmed. For example, in a study that uses tokens
and varies the exchange rate between tokens and money for the sender and the
receiver, Andreoni and Vesterlund (2001) find that while women try to equalize
payoffs, men are concerned with efficiency. Women are more generous at a 1/1
exchange rate and for exchange rates that favour the dictator, but men are more
generous when the exchange rate favours the recipient in the game, suggesting
that men value efficiency in addition to fairness.

Gender differences in altruism can be inferred from their behaviour in a second
game: the ultimatum game. Here women's behaviour also supports the idea that
they may be more cooperative and altruistic than men. In this game, an amount of
money is provisionally allocated to a pair – a proposer and a responder. The
proposer, the first mover in the game, offers a division of the amount to the
responder. If the responder agrees, the money is divided as planned; if she rejects
the offer, both players earn zero.

Figure 11.2 shows the distribution of offers from same-gender pairings in
ultimatum game experiments where the stakes are $5.00, as reported in Eckel
and Grossman (2001).[8] Each column shows the proportion of all offers at that
level, and the lighter part of the column represents the offers that were rejected.

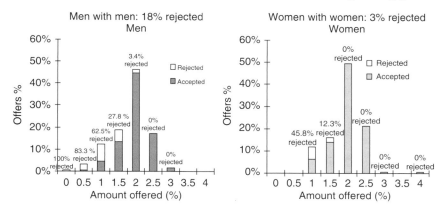

Figure 11.2 Men and women play ultimatum (same gender groups).
Source: Eckel and Grossman (2001).

The figure indicates that as proposers, offers by women to women are about the same on average as offers by men to men. It is also apparent from the figure that, for any offer level, women matched with women are less likely to reject than men matched with men. For every possible offer level lower than the 50/50 split, women accept that offer with a higher probability than men. (At 50/50 or above, all offers are accepted). Men are willing to forego a substantial share of the pie to punish what they see as unfair or unacceptable offers. Men reject 28 per cent of the offers of $1.50/$5.00, for example, while women reject 12 per cent of offers at that level. Women either have different perceptions about what is a fair offer, or are less willing to punish unfair offers by rejection. Compounding the two effects, when men are paired to play ultimatum, 18 per cent of offers are rejected; when women play women, only 3 per cent are rejected.

In the chapter we include opposite-gender pairings in the analysis as well and show that women's offers are more likely to be accepted by both men and women. It is as if both women and men assume that, if an offer comes from a woman, it must be 'fair' in some sense. A presumption that women are fairer in their offers may drive this higher acceptance rate for women's offers, illustrating the importance of beliefs in driving behaviour.

The two main results in this section – that women give more to an anonymous counterpart in a dictator game, and are more likely to accept offers in the ultimatum game – and support the idea that women are more altruistic than men. If the lab is a window on the market, then greater altruism implies lower demands in a bargaining context, and willingness to accept lower offers may also carry over to employment settings.

In addition, the fact that women's offers are more likely to be accepted illustrates the importance of beliefs in determining behaviour. While we did not elicit beliefs or perceptions explicitly, it seems that subjects perceived offers from women to be fairer and responded accordingly. Another possibility is that people anticipated lower offers from women, and so, pleasantly surprised, accepted them. Further research is needed to tease out the role of expectations in this game.[9]

While the advantage of the lab is the degree of control it gives over the decision context and incentives, external validity is always a concern. A labour market negotiation is a much more complex situation than the one in the lab. This points to the advantage of the lab – that a single element of preferences can be isolated and examined – but also its limitation. Using a decision-based measure of preferences also leaves unexamined the underlying feelings or attitudes that might motivate women's greater generosity and willingness to accept less. It is important to recognize that many motives are possible. Women may accept less because they feel they deserve less, for example, or because it is the 'norm' for women to receive a lower share, and not because they are more caring about others per se. In this case, we can only say that behaviour in the lab is consistent with the observed outcome in labour markets, but cannot conclude that the same forces are at work without further study.

Risk aversion

A second area where preferences may be relevant for labour market outcomes is attitudes toward risk. Like cooperation, gender differences in risk aversion have been much studied in fields outside economics. In most situations, greater risk taking by men is well documented (Byrnes *et al.* 1999).

In markets, a willingness to take on risk is traditionally associated with greater rewards. For example, in labour markets, CEO contracts for women contain smaller performance-based components than men, resulting in higher – though more variable – average earnings for men (Chauvin and Ash 1994). Considerable evidence exists that women's investment portfolios differ from men's (e.g. Sunden and Surette 1998). One reason that has been suggested for this difference is that women may receive different investment advice than men, a notion supported by a survey reported in Money magazine that found that male investors are treated better by their brokers than female investors. The survey notes that brokers spend more time with men, and offer them higher return investment options (Wang 1994).

Bajtelsmit and Bernasek (1996) catalogue a number of reasons why women might invest differently from men, including income differences, wealth differences, and differences in the investment opportunities presented to women. Interestingly, women brokers do not choose more risk-averse portfolios than their male counterparts although the flow of investment monies to female-managed funds is lower (Atkinson *et al.* 2003). Some evidence even suggests that female brokers outperform males (Kim 1997). Of course, even if women were to choose less-risky portfolios, this is not necessarily a bad thing. Higher risk is not always good: Barber and Odean (2001) present evidence that male day-traders' overconfidence leads them to make decisions that are too risky, exhibiting trading that is overly aggressive and damages portfolio returns. The relationship between gender and decisions over risky outcomes can also be explored in the lab.

As with altruism, experimental games have been developed to measure the degree of risk aversion. These experiments are shaped by economist's views of preferences over risky alternatives. Economists summarize preferences by assuming a function that assesses the value (utility) of all possible consumption alternatives – a domain-general utility function. The function is assumed to be increasing in income, but at a declining rate. This diminishing marginal utility of money implies that the expected value of a gamble will be preferred to the gamble: $100 for sure is preferred to a 50/50 chance of 0 and $200, since the marginal utility of the additional $100 is less than the utility of the first $100. This view of preferences suggests that any game that reveals the curvature of the utility function will provide a measure of risk aversion.[10]

Many different experimental tasks have been developed to do this measurement (a discussion of the alternatives is available in Eckel and Grossman 2006). We prefer a simple experimental task, where subjects choose their most preferred alternative from among a set of possible gambles. In our protocol, subjects are presented with a set of simple gambles with equal chances of a high or low payoff. Each subject then plays out his chosen gamble by rolling a die, and is paid in cash the resulting earnings – either the high or the low amount.

Figure 11.3 shows the way in which we present the task to subjects. Each circle represents a gamble that is a 50/50 chance of a high or low amount, as shown in each circle, and the subject chooses his most preferred gamble by marking it with an X. Thus subjects make a decision based on the information given here. All the gambles are simple even-odds chances of winning the high or the low amount. The subjects' job is to choose the one they would like to play.

Figure 11.4 shows the properties of the gambles. The left panel describes the gambles, showing the gamble number and the high and low payoffs, and the right

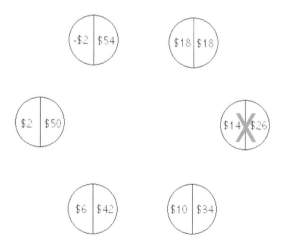

Figure 11.3 Risk game protocol. Each circle represents a gamble with equally-likely high and low payoffs.

Subjects choose most preferred among 6 gambles with 50/50 odds.

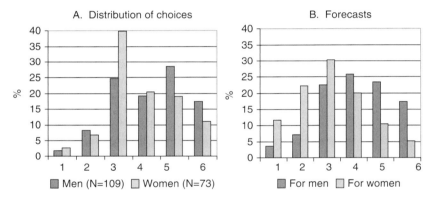

Gamble	Low	High
1	18	18
2	14	26
3	10	34
4	6	42
5	2	50
6	-2	54

Figure 11.4 Gambles for risk protocol.

Figure 11.5 University students' forecasts exaggerate choice differences.

panel graphs the risk and return of each, with the vertical axis indicating the expected payoff, and the horizontal axis the risk, measured by standard deviation. Risk aversion can be represented by upward sloping indifference curves in this space, with steeper curves indicating greater aversion to risk. A highly risk averse person will have very steep indifference curves, and maximize utility by choosing gamble 1. A risk neutral person will choose gamble 5 (or 6). Risk loving persons will choose gamble 6. Figure 11.5A shows the distribution of choices by men and women in the standard population of university students. Figure 11.6 shows high school students, for comparison. In both populations, women choose less risky gambles on average.

In some of our experiments, we add another stage to the protocol. After making their own choices, subjects have to guess what the others did. Each person is asked to stand while the others in the room guess which gamble that person chose.

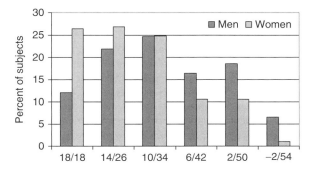

Figure 11.6 High school women are more risk averse.
Source: Eckel *et al.* 2005.

A correct guess earns an additional dollar. These guesses are then forecasts of the subjects' choices and can be used to analyze perceptions about the risk attitudes of others. Figure 11.5B shows the distribution of forecasts. We see that the forecasts also show greater risk aversion for women, but the differences are exaggerated. The guesses are based on stereotypes that tend to magnify observed differences by gender. This result shows how perceptions of people's preferences are based on – and biased by – stereotypes.

In a third experiment (Eckel 2007b) we further examine stereotyping by allowing each subject to act as a financial advisor, and choose a portfolio (in the form of one of the 50/50 gambles) for the other subjects.[11] In this experiment we see a similar gender difference in choices, but the financial advisor's choices show a much larger gender difference. The advisors make substantially less-risky choices for their female compared with their male clients. Gender plays an important role in how the clients are treated by the financial advisor.

What are the implications of these patterns of behaviour for labour markets? If women are more risk averse, then they will choose compensation packages that tradeoff higher for more stable, but lower, wages. As with the previous experiments, one must of course be cautious about generalizing results from the lab to the field, but the results are consistent with lower earnings for women. In a simple matching model with two equally-productive types of agents, Vesterlund (1997) shows that small differences in risk aversion can lead to an equilibrium outcome with lower wages for the more risk-averse type. Risk averse agents are at a disadvantage when negotiating a wage, as they have lower reservation wages. In equilibrium, the risk averse type faces a lower wage distribution, even though the distribution of productivity is equal across groups. This model illustrates that risk aversion alone can account for lower wage distributions for women.

Competition aversion

A third set of experiments addresses yet another possible difference in the preferences of women and men: attitudes toward competition. Psychologists have documented differences in competitiveness among children. Girls tend to avoid competition, while boys enjoy it, and boys but not girls do better when there is competition (see Maccoby (1998) and Rhoads (2004) for many examples.) The experiments described below serve to legitimize this finding for economists. These experiments test the theory that men have a taste for competition that women do not share, and explore the possibility that this preference drives differences in wages. The experiments look at how competition affects performance, and examines whether women and men choose competitive situations equally.

The first study in this agenda is a laboratory labour experiment where women and men are paid to solve mazes (Gneezy *et al.* 2003). The study compares work performance under two types of compensation: a piece rate, where workers are paid by the maze, and a winner-take – tournament where only the highest producer is paid. Women work about the same under the two schemes, while men work significantly harder for the tournament payment. This result spurred additional studies.

Two studies allow women and men to choose their preferred compensation rate. In the first, Gupta *et al.* (2005) again use mazes and find that men are more likely to choose tournament rates: 60 per cent of men against 34 per cent of women choose the tournament rate. They also measure subjects' risk attitudes, and find that choices are related to measured risk attitudes, with more risk averse subjects choosing piece rates.

A criticism of the studies I've described is the possibility that men are just better at solving mazes, so that women are rational in their decision not to go for the tournament rate. Niederle and Vesterlund (2007) are careful to choose a task where women and men perform the same under piece and tournament rates – solving easy math problems. Here again, men are more likely to choose the tournament, with 73 per cent of men and 35 per cent of women choosing the tournament. This effect remains after controlling for subjects' measured ability as well as their own beliefs about theirs and others' abilities; thus the result is due only in part to the greater confidence – indeed overconfidence – of men. Men sacrifice earnings in this game because low-ability men choose the tournament, but women lose more and so earn less than men because high-ability women shy away from the tournament.

An aversion to competition is consistent with lower earnings for women. This choice may be based in part on beliefs about skill levels. If the belief that women are less skilled is held by both women and men, then men will choose to compete too often and women too seldom, driving the differences in earnings seen in the experiment. In addition, if this revealed preference not to compete transfers from the lab to the field, then it is likely to affect earnings.

To summarize the results thus far, we showed that, in the lab, women are more altruistic and more risk averse on average than men. In addition, women dislike competition, and respond less to competitive incentives. Others believe women are more altruistic and risk averse, and at least in the case of risk aversion, those beliefs exaggerate the gender difference in choices. Overconfidence or underconfidence about ability can also play a role in whether someone chooses to compete. Taken together, this cluster of preference differences is consistent with lower offers and lower negotiated wages for women. Perceptions of greater altruism, risk aversion and lower ability also can contribute to differences in the way women and men are treated in negotiations.

Social status

We now turn to a discussion of an additional factor that might affect earnings: social status. We refer to status as a persons' '...ranking in a social hierarchy that is socially recognized....' (Ball *et al.* 2001). This is an area where sociologists and social psychologists are far ahead of economists, with the development of status characteristics theory (e.g. Berger *et al.* 1977). People who are recognized as having higher status are deferred to and receive superior treatment by others. Individuals interact in many status hierarchies, some of which are defined narrowly and involve expertise in a particular area (basketball or physics, for example), and some of which are broad and recognized widely – like gender. Differential treatment can result in higher earnings by higher-status individuals. In most societies, men have higher status than women (see Ball (2007) for a discussion of status in economics more broadly).

Lab experiments are useful for studying status, allowing status to be isolated from other factors. Naturally occurring status is problematic because the status cannot be considered apart from any expertise that gives rise to it. That is, a high status person may be favoured solely because their expertise is valuable. In Ball *et al.* (2001) we test whether status alone can affect behaviour. We create status hierarchies artificially in the lab, by rewarding with gold stars half of the subjects in a market experiment.

As described in the first section, in market experiments, sellers are given costs and buyers are given values. Bids and offers are called out, and a 'pit boss' collects bids and offers until an agreement is reached and a trade occurs. Profits are price less cost for sellers, and value less price for buyers. In the status experiment, all the sellers have the same cost and all the buyers have the same value, with equal numbers on both sides of the market. This structure creates a market that has a range of possible equilibrium prices; any common price between the cost and value. The subjects with stars are seated on one side of the market and those without on the other. For example, all the buyers, but not the sellers, might have stars in one session, with the opposite arrangement in another session.

In these experiments subjects on the star side of the market systematically earn about 15 per cent more than those on the side that failed to earn stars. Additional treatments have led us to believe that the difference in earnings is caused partially by changes in the behaviour of the people with stars, and partially by changes in the way the starred subjects are treated by others.

In the chapter, we report the results of a follow-on experiment, where instead of stars facing no-stars, men are on one side of the market and women on the other. In these sessions, men's behaviour is much like the starred subjects (though they compete more aggressively against each other at the beginning), and women like the unstarred. In the last half of the experiment, the men earn significantly more than the women.

To assess the role of beliefs about each other on the market outcome, after the experiment, subjects rated their side of the market and their counterparts on the other side on several simple scales designed to elicit their perceptions of the cleverness, aggressiveness, powerfulness and deservingness of both sides of the market. We found gender differences in the ratings, in addition to the earnings differences. Women rated themselves as significantly less clever and powerful, though equally aggressive and somewhat more deserving than the male subjects' ratings of themselves. The subjects also rated each other. Women rated their male counterparts as more clever and powerful than the men rated themselves. These ratings are further evidence of a perceived status differential. This experiment suggests that perceived differentials in status may affect behaviour in such a way that men receive higher wages than women.[12]

Linking games to consequences

What can we conclude from the experiments? One way to interpret the results is to note that people bring their histories and social contexts with them when they come into the lab. Our subjects operate in the world with identities – characteristics that are observed by others and their own self-images – and those identities affect their behaviour and the way others interact with them. Individuals differ in their preferences – altruism, risk, competition – and those preferences are (on average) different for women and men. In addition, people are aware of the identities of others, and condition their own beliefs and behaviour on what they can observe about other people. The way a person interacts with a counterpart depends on what they observe about that person, and the perceptions of the counterpart that are founded on what can be observed. Thus differences in outcomes are affected by both the preferences of a decision maker, and the way that decision maker is perceived and treated by others. In a status hierarchy, people of higher status may earn more in part because of their own behaviour and in part because they are imitated and deferred to by others.[13]

Evidence in support of this kind of differential treatment and its consequences can be seen in many domains. A series of carefully controlled experiments show clearly that doctors offer systematically different treatment options to women (Schulman *et al.* 1999). Men are offered more aggressive, risky treatments and women safer, less invasive procedures. Financial advisors offer different alternative investments based on their perceptions of customers (see Bajtelsmit and Bernasek 1996). In experiments we observe something similar; as experimental financial advisors choose more risk averse gambles for women (see Eckel 2007).

Babcock and Laschever (2003) argue that women negotiate differently from men, and that this difference has consequences for earnings. The book got its start when Babcock, then dean of the Heinz School of Public Policy at Carnegie Mellon University, noticed that her female students earned significantly lower starting salaries than the male students, prompting further study. She found that, when presented with an initial offer, male students asked for more, whereas the women tended to treat the offer as take-it-or-leave-it, and didn't ask. Women are also less likely to ask for a raise, and expect their contributions to be recognized, acknowledged and rewarded without having to ask. When requested to take on additional tasks without compensation, women are less likely to say no. A follow on study showed that women were punished if they negotiated more aggressively or refused uncompensated assignments (Bowles *et al.* 2007).

Despite decades of earning PhDs in large numbers, women's advancement in academia has been unexpectedly slow. The comments of the Harvard President Lawrence H. Summers asserting that women's slow advancement was due to their inferior aptitude for math and science led to some strongly worded responses. In *Why So Slow,* Virginia Valian describes the slow advancement as resulting from '1000 paper cuts', small disadvantageous perceptions, evaluations, or actions that have a large cumulative effect.[14] Many of these paper cuts are due to stereotypes of women and the ways in which women's accomplishments are evaluated by others. It is well known that stereotypes bias perceptions and perceptions drive the many evaluations that are so critical to academic advancement.

Valian cites two types of studies that I found most troubling. The first is the CV studies where raters evaluate the CVs that have women's, men's or ambiguous (initials) names on them. When a CV has a woman's name on it, it is evaluated lower than if the same CV has a man's name. The second involves the content and perception of letters of recommendation. Letters for men include superlatives such as 'best' and assessments of characteristics like 'talented', 'creative'; letters for women are much more likely to say that the woman works hard or is 'a pleasure to work with'. Both of these are very important for the recruitment and advancement of women.

NSF's Advance Program has taken this research seriously in funding proposals to 'transform' institutions. Among many other things, these grants to institutions supported the development of materials to help educate search committees about 'gender schemas' – unconscious hypotheses about gender differences that guide everyone's – men and women's – perceptions and actions. Awareness of the effect of unconscious stereotyping can help search committees do a better job of recruiting first-rate faculty. These materials are bursting with relevant research results, including: blind auditions increase the proportion of women who secure orchestral positions; if women are more than 25 per cent of an applicant pool or work group, their performance is judged more positively; university faculty are more likely to want to hire 'Brian' rather than 'Karen', with identical application packages; women awarded post-docs in a prestigious program have 2.5 times the accomplishments (publications, grants) of men, etc. (see the Advance program portal, www.advance-portal.net, for examples of such materials).

Economists may be particularly skeptical of the sort of claim made by Valian and others. Our belief in rationality and in markets interferes with our ability to believe this kind of research. Economic theories of wage determination convince us that earnings are the result of an equilibrium process that rewards productivity. There is no room in competitive markets for 'perceptions' and 'stereotypes' to affect wages. In the standard argument, if one type of person is under-rewarded relative to their productivity, some enterprising firm will bid them away, earning supernormal profits in the process. It seems that economists may be blinded by their own theories, and missing something important in the process.

One way to sell the evidence to economists is by appealing to the plethora of equilibria produced by many game-theoretic models. In a world with multiple equilibria, perceptions and stereotypes can act as equilibrium selection devices, along the lines of the status markets investigated by Ball *et al.* (2001). Preferences may differ, but beliefs based on stereotypes can be dangerously self fulfilling in such a world.

What about economic man?

What, then, about economic man? Economic agents clearly pay attention to social elements when making their decisions. Economic agents are not anonymous, as are the 'maximizing monads' (McCloskey's term) of game theory. Agents condition behaviour on the characteristics of others. But that is not to say that incentives are unimportant. Perhaps what we need is a model that we might call 'economic man plus'.

Two approaches seem particularly fruitful. First, the standard model can be modified explicitly to incorporate elements of social preferences. There has been considerable progress in this direction, with models incorporating inequality aversion, reciprocity, and intentions. This in turn has led to an avalanche of additional experiments that are designed to test the relative performance of the models, giving some indication of the appeal of this approach.[15] A second approach has been to model beliefs, learning and the development of expectations. This also has been a very fruitful avenue for research, with models that explicitly take into account beliefs and learning, and experiments that test them.[16] Because people differ in their characteristics, beliefs, and preferences, it is important that modeling also allow for heterogeneity. In addition, it is likely that the environment also plays a part in determining when and how social preferences, stereotyping and beliefs play a role in the outcome – the allocation of resources, wages, prices, etc. An ongoing dialogue among economists in different fields – experiment, theory and empirics – as well as among social scientists is needed.

Acknowledgements

This chapter is based on a lecture I presented at the workshop on Gender and Economics, sponsored by the University of Siena, which took place at the beautiful Certosa di Pontignano outside Siena. My thanks go to the faculty and students who participated in the workshop for their questions and insights, and especially to Francesca Bettio for her encouragement and inspiration. The research described here was funded by the John D. and Catherine T. MacArthur Foundation, Network on Preferences and Norms; the National Science Foundation; and the Aspen Foundation.

Notes

1 Croson and Gneezy cover much of the same territory as this chapter in their recent comprehensive survey (2007).

2 Gender differences have been the subject of experimental investigations in economics for some time. One of the earliest studies by Rapoport and Chammah (1965) explored variations of the Prisoner's Dilemma game.

3 Differences in the behaviour of women and men in psychology and sociology predates the study of gender differences in economics, and extensively documents the differences. An overview of this work, which covers differences in ability, personality, leadership styles, aggression, competitiveness, etc., can be found in Rhoads (2004), Low (2000), and Maccoby (1998) among many others.

4 Claude Steele is known for his work on 'stereotype threat', showing that activating a performance stereotype can significantly damage the performance of African American subjects (Steele and Aronson, 1995). Something similar is likely to affect the performance of women in situations where they believe they are being judged as women (Dar-Nimrod and Heine 2006).

5 In economics classes or among economics majors, the bias may go the other way. Economists make a mistake, I believe, when they train their students to recognize opportunities to free ride and label free riding as 'rational', thereby encouraging bad behaviour. Indeed, Frank *et al.* (1993) present evidence that economists are more selfish, and that the result is partly due to selection (more selfish people are attracted to economics) and partly due to exposure to the economic man model. It is likely, then, that students are more selfish in economics class and perhaps in economics experiments than elsewhere.

6 In addition to the games reported here, gender differences in public goods games (which are social dilemma games) and trust games have received a great deal of attention. These are described in the excellent survey by Croson and Gneezy (2007).

7 In this experiment subjects make multiple decisions involving different parameters (endowments, subsidy rates, etc.), and at the end of the experiment one decision is chosen at random for payment.

8 In this experiment, people are seated across from each other in groups, with a set of proposers facing a set of responders. They know they are matched with a person in the other group, but not precisely who. In this way we can reveal the gender or race of the recipient by using all male or all female (or all black or white) persons in a group. Note that the M/M and F/F groups shown here are the most extreme, with M/F and F/M groups in between.

9 In Eckel (2007a) I review several studies that focus on eliciting beliefs and examining how beliefs affect behaviour in somewhat different experimented games.

10 Psychologists have developed measures that vary across domains (e.g. Weber *et al.* 2002).

11 In this experiment, each subject first makes his own decision. Then each subject acts as a financial advisor, and chooses a portfolio for each of the other subjects in the room. Finally one person is chosen at random and their choices are implemented for all subjects, and determine everyone's payoffs.

12 Kumru and Vesterlund (2005) investigate the effect of status differentials on charitable giving using a similar protocol, and find that if high status subjects donate first, lower-status second movers imitate them and give more, resulting in higher total giving.

13 Mobius and Rosenblat (2006) find a similar result for beauty, which is a status characteristic. In their study, attractive persons earn more. In telephone interactions, where subjects don't see each other, attractive persons still earn more, but not as much as in face-to-face interactions. Thus they earn more in part because they behave differently and in part because they are treated differently.

14 See also a similar argument by Cole and Singer (1991).

15 There are so many research papers in this area now that it is impossible to cite them all, but as an example, an important paper by Fehr and Schmidt (1999) has more than 1400 citations using Google Scholar.
16 As with social preferences, this area has many researchers. The work of Al Roth and his colleagues on learning models, and the work of Charles Holt and Tom Palfrey and their coauthors on the 'quantal response equilibrium' are examples.

References

Andreoni, J. and Vesterlund, L. (2001) 'Which is the Fair Sex? Gender Differences in Altruism', *Quarterly Journal of Economics*, 116 (1): 293–312.

Atkinson, S.M., Baird, S.B. and Frye, M.B. (2003) 'Do Female Mutual Fund Managers Manage Differently?', *The Journal of Financial Research*, 26 (1): 1–18.

Babcock, L. and Laschever, S. (2003) *Women Don't Ask: Negotiation and the Gender Divide*. Princeton, NJ: Princeton University Press.

Bajtelsmit, V.L. and Bernasek, A. (1996) 'Why Do Women Invest Differently than Men?', *Financial Counseling and Planning*, 7: 1–10.

Ball, S. (2007) 'Status and Economics', in S.N. Durlauf and L.E. Blume (eds) *The New Palgrave Dictionary of Economics*. 2nd edition, Basingstoke and New York: Palgrave Macmillan.

Ball, S., Eckel, C., Grossman, P. and Zame, W. (2001) 'Status in Markets', *Quarterly Journal of Economics*, 116 (1): 161–181.

Ball, S., Eckel, C. and Heracleous, M. (2005) *'Risk Preferences and Physical Prowess: Is the Weaker Sex More Risk Averse, or Do We Just Think So?'*, Unpublished manuscript, Virginia Tech.

Barber, B.M. and Odean, T. (2001) 'Boys Will Be Boys: Gender, Overconfidence and Common Stock Investing', *Quarterly Journal of Economics*, 116 (1): 261–292.

Bateson, M., Nettle, D. and Roberts, G. (2006) 'Cues of Being Watched Enhance Cooperation in A Real-World Setting', *Biology Letters*, 2 (3): 412–414.

Berger, J., Fisek, M.H., Norman, R.Z. and Zelditch, M. (1977) *Status Characteristics and Social Interaction: An Expectation-States Approach*. New York: Elsevier.

Bergmann, B.R. (1996) *In Defense of Affirmative Action*. New York: BasicBooks.

Bowles, H.R., Babcock, L. and Lai, L. (2007) 'Social Incentives for Gender Differences in the Propensity to Initiate Negotiations: Sometimes It Does Hurt to Ask', *Organizational Behavior and Human Decision Processes*, 103 (1): 84–103.

Byrnes, J., Miller, D.C., Schafer, W. D. (1999) 'Gender Differences in Risk Taking: A Meta Analysis', *Psychological Bulletin*, 125 (3): 367–383.

Chauvin, K.W. and Ash, R.A. (1994) 'Gender Earnings Differentials in Total Pay, Base Pay, and Contingent Pay', *Industrial and Labor Relations Review*, 47 (4): 634–649.

Cole, J.R. and Singer, B. (1991) 'A theory of limited differences: Explaining the productivity puzzle in science', in H. Zuckerman, J. R. Cole, and J. T. Bruer (eds), *The Outer Circle: Women in the Scientific Community*. New York: W. W. Norton and Company. pp. 277–323.

Committee on the Status of Women, Winter 2007 newsletter. Available: http://www.cswep.org/newsletters/CSWEP_nsltr_Winter2007.pdf (accessed 8 May 2007).

Croson, R. and Gneezy, U. (2007) *Gender Differences in Preferences*, Unpublished manuscript, University of California, San Diego.

Dar-Nimrod, I. and Heine, S.J. (2006) 'Exposure to Scientific Theories Affects Women's Math Performance', *Science*, 314 (5798): 435.

Eckel, C.C. (2007a) 'People Playing Games: The Human Face of Experimental Economics', *Southern Economic Journal*, 73 (4): 840–857.

Eckel, C.C. (2007b) 'Gender and Financial Advice in the Lab' Unpublished manuscript, Dallas: University of Texas.

Eckel, C.C. and Grossman, P.J. (1996) 'Altruism in Anonymous Dictator Games', *Games and Economic Behavior*, 16 (2): 181–191.

Eckel, C.C. and Grossman, P.J. (1998) 'Are Women Less Selfish Than Men?: Evidence from Dictator Games', *The Economic Journal*, 108 (448): 726–735.

Eckel, C.C. and Grossman, P.J. (2001) 'Chivalry and Solidarity in Ultimatum Games', *Economic Inquiry*, 39 (2): 171–188.

Eckel, C.C. and Grossman, P.J. (2003) 'Rebates Versus Matching: Does How We Subsidize Charitable Contributions Matter?', *Journal of Public Economics*, 87 (3–4): 681–701.

Eckel, C.C. and Grossman, P.J. (2006) '*Forecasting Risk: An Experimental Study of Actual and Forecast Risk Attitudes*', Unpublished manuscript, University of Texas at Dallas.

Eckel, C.C., Grossman, P.J. and Milano, A. (2007) 'Is More Information Always Better? An Experimental Study of Charitable Giving and Hurricane Katrina', *Southern Economic Journal*, 74 (2): 388–411.

Eckel, C., Grossman, P., Johnson, C., Rojas, C. and Wilson, R. (2005) *Time, Risk and Pro-Social Preferences in Adolescents: The Houston Schools Project*. A report to the Network on Preferences and Norms, John D. and Catherine T. MacArthur Foundation.

Fehr, E. and Schmidt, K.M. (1999) 'A Theory of Fairness, Competition, and Cooperation', *Quarterly Journal of Economics*, 114 (3): 817–868.

Forsythe, R., Horowitz, J.L., Savin, N.E. and Sefton, M. (1994) 'Fairness in Simple Bargaining Experiments', *Games and Economic Behavior*, 6 (3): 347–369.

Frank, R.H., Gilovich, T., Regan, D.T. (1993) 'Does Studying Economics Inhibit Cooperation?', *Journal of Economic Perspectives*, 7 (2): 159–171.

Gneezy, U., Niederle, M. and Rustichini, A. (2003) 'Performance in Competitive Environments: Gender Differences', *Quarterly Journal of Economics*, 118 (3): 1049–1074.

Gupta, N.D., Poulsen, A. and Villeval, M-C. (2005) '*Male and Female Competitive Behavior: Experimental Evidence*', IZA Discussion Paper 1833.

Haley, K.J. and Fessler, D.M.T. (2005) 'Nobody's Watching? Subtle Cues Affect Generosity in An Anonymous Economic Game', *Evolution and Human Behavior*, 26 (3): 245–256.

Hoffman, E., McCabe, K., Shachat, K. and Smith, V.K. (1994) 'Preferences, Property Rights and Anonymity in Bargaining Games', *Games and Economic Behavior*, 7 (3): 346–380.

Kahneman, D., Knetsch, J. and Thaler, R. (1986) 'Fairness and the Assumptions of Economics', *Journal of Business*, 59 (4 Part 2): S285–S300.

Kim, J. (1997) 'If You Don't Believe This, Read it Again: Women Fund Managers Outdo Men', *Money*, 26 (11): 25–26.

Kumru, C. and Vesterlund, L. (2005) '*The Effects of Status on Voluntary Contribution*', Working Paper, University of Pittsburgh.

Low, B.S. (2000) *Why Sex Matters: A Darwinian Look at Human Behavior*. Princeton, NJ.: Princeton University Press.

Maccoby, E. (1998) *The Two Sexes*. Cambridge, MA.: Harvard University Press.

Mobius, M. and Rosenblat, T. (2006) 'Why Beauty Matters', *American Economic Review*, 96 (1): 222–235.

Niederle, M. and Vesterlund, L. (2007) 'Do Women Shy Away from Competition? Do Men Compete Too Much?', *Quarterly Journal of Economics*, 122 (3): 1067–1101.

Rapoport, A. and Chammah, A. M. (1965) 'Sex Differences in Factors Contributing to the Level of Cooperation in the Prisoner's Dilemma Game', *Journal of Personality and Social Psychology*, 2 (6): 831–838.

Rhoads, S. E. (2004) *Taking Sex Differences Seriously*. San Francisco: Encounter Books.

Schotter, A. (2006) 'Strong and Wrong: The Use of Rational Choice Theory in Experimental Economics', *Journal of Theoretical Politics*, 18 (4): 498–511.

Schulman, K. A., Berlin, J. A., Harless, W., F. Kerner, J. F., Sistrunk, S., Gersh, B. J., Dubé, R., Taleghani, C. K., Burke, J. E., Williams, S., Eisenberg, J. M., Escarce, J. J. and Ayers, W. (1999) 'The Effect of Race and Sex on Physicians' Recommendations for Cardiac Catheterization', *New England Journal of Medicine*, 340 (8): 618–626.

Smith, V.L. (1991) *Papers in Experimental Economics*. New York: Cambridge University Press.

Smith, V.L. (2003) 'Constructivist and Ecological Rationality in Economics', *American Economic Review*, 93 (3): 465–508.

Steele, C.M., and Aronson, J. (1995) 'Stereotype Threat and the Intellectual Test Performance of African Americans', *Journal of Personality and Social Psychology*, 69 (5): 797–811.

Sunden, A. E. and Surette, B. J. (1998) 'Gender Differences in the Allocation of Assets in Retirement Savings Plans', *American Economic Review*, 88 (2): 207–211.

Vesterlund, L. (1997) *'The Effects of Risk Aversion on Job Matching: Can Differences in Risk Aversion Explain the Wage Gap?'*, Unpublished manuscript, University of Pittsburgh.

Wang, P. (1994) 'Brokers Still Treat Men Better than Women', *Money*, 23 (6): 108–110.

Weber, E.U., Blais, A.-R. and Betz, N.E. (2002) 'A Domain-Specific Risk-Attitude Scale: Measuring Risk Perceptions and Risk Behaviors', *Journal of Behavioral Decision Making*, 15 (4): 263–290.

Weichselbaumer, D. and Winter-Ebmer, R. (2005) 'A MetaAnalysis of the International Gender Wage Gap', *Journal of Economic Surveys*, 19 (3): 479–511.

12 The gender effect in the laboratory

Experimenter bias and altruism

Alessandro Innocenti and Maria Grazia Pazienza

Introduction

The finding that people care about others' utilities or payoffs is very common in experimental economics.[1] Despite the self-seeking behaviour assumption of mainstream economics, there are also many formal models which seek theoretically to explain why individuals make sacrifices in order to increase the utilities or payoffs of others.[2] The gender variable has been taken into account to predict altruistic behaviour in social environments. According to the conventional view, women are more socially-oriented than men (Eckel and Grossman 1998). This difference would justify the introduction of gender differences in economic models. Recent laboratory work supports this position. There is evidence that men and women exhibit different propensities to trust and to reciprocate. This finding can be attributed to the fact that women have more other-regarding preferences than men (Innocenti and Pazienza 2006).

This result has significant implications for the theory that non-selfish behaviour may be based on the expectation of reciprocity (Rabin 1993; Levine 1998). In this light, gender may signal how altruistic other players may be, and hence increase the propensity to trust. However, the hypothesis that women may be perceived by others as potentially less selfish than men is difficult to test in the laboratory, because subjects' expectations are usually investigated by means of self-assessment questionnaires that may be biased by the tendency of respondents to answer question in a socially desirable fashion. In this chapter we take a different approach by reporting study of this issue by means of an actual experiment which checks whether the presence in the laboratory of a male or a female experimenter affects individual behaviour. According to the concept of experimenter bias, laboratory data may be influenced by the supposed expectations of the person collecting the data. Our test was intended to investigate if the gender of the experimenter would induce changes in experimental subjects' propensity to trust and to reciprocate and if these changes would be motivated by their perceptions of gender differences in altruism.

The chapter is organized as follows. The next section describes the object of our experiment and surveys the background literature. The experimental design is illustrated in the third section and the results are presented and discussed in the fourth section. The last section draws some conclusions.

Experimental purpose

Our experiment tests the trust game, also known as the investment game. This game is played by two players, who are paired off anonymously and respectively named the 'sender' and the 'responder'. The sender is given a certain amount of money and told that he or she can keep the entire amount or send some or all of it to the responder. Any money passed from the sender to the responder is tripled by the experimenter and then given to the responder. The responder can keep the entire amount or give some or all of it back to the sender. When the sender receives the amount returned by the responder the game ends.

This game-theoretical framework gives a simple measure of the propensity to trust, which is the proportion of the initial endowment sent by the sender, and to reciprocate, which is the ratio between the amount returned and the amount received by the responder. The backward induction solution of the game predicts that the responder will not send any money back. Anticipating the responder's decision, the sender will not send any money to the responder.

Results from earlier experiments are inconsistent with the standard game theory prediction. Table 12.1 provides a summary of previous results on the trust game.

Even if there are significant variations across tests, the backward induction prediction is refuted.[3] Other studies examine gender differences in the trust game. Table 12.2 summarizes these experimental results.

Men generally exhibit greater levels of trust and lower levels of reciprocity than women do, even if the difference between genders is not always statistically significant.

A possible explanation of these results can be couched in terms of altruism. It can be argued that trust and trustworthiness depend on different factors. Trust is usually perceived as an investment in the trustee's reliability, and consequently as a decision dependent on risk attitude or on the perception of vulnerability to the action of others. Trustworthiness seems to be better explained by institutional, psychological or moral factors, such as social distance or inequality aversion, and it is justified by ethical values. However, it is quite evident that both trust and reciprocity may be the result of altruistic preferences. If utility increases in other individuals' utility or consumption, the truster may find it rational to trust even if they do not expect the trustee to be trustworthy. Similarly, the trustee may exhibit reciprocity without any economic incentive to reciprocate.

To detect the effect of altruism, Cox (2002; 2004) proposes an experiment that discriminates between transfers resulting from trust or trustworthiness and transfers resulting from altruistic preferences. Cox's findings show that subjects are also driven by altruistic preferences. His conclusion is that utility should not be assumed to be independent of other individuals' payoffs, and altruistic preferences should be included in the rational model of economic behaviour.

Table 12.1 Experimental results on the trust game

	Berg et al. (1995)[b]		Buchan et al. (2000)[b]		Schwieren and Sutter (2003)	Burks et al. (2003)[b]			Chaudhuri and Gangadharan (2003)
	No history	Social history	Only US	All		Single role	Both roles, no prior	Both roles, prior	
Trust[a]	51.6	53.6	49	67	65.7	65.0	65.2	47.3	43.3
Reciprocity[a]	30.1	40.2	22	37	37.6	43.6	25.9	17.1	17.5

Notes

[a] Trust = Average fraction sent (Amount sent/Initial endowment); Reciprocity = Average fraction returned (Amount sent back/Amount received).

[b] In the social history treatment by Berg et al. (1995) subjects were given a summary of the no history treatment results as part of the instructions. Buchan et al.'s (2000) international experiment tested the trust game in China, Japan, Korea and the United States. Burks et al. (2003) compared three treatments: the first (single role) in which subjects played either the sender or responder role, the second (both roles, no prior) in which subjects played both roles but they did not know it before sending, and the third (both roles, prior) where subjects knew that they had played both roles before any decisions were made.

Table 12.2 Experimental results on gender differences in the trust game

	Ashraf et al. (2003)		Buchan et al. (2004)		Chaudhuri and Gangadharan (2002)		Cox (2002)		Croson and Buchan (1999)	
	Men	*Women*	*Men*	*Women*	*Men*	*Women*	*Men*	*Women*	*Men*	*Women*
Trust[a]	47	41	74	61	53	34	64	53	63	63
Reciprocity[a]	27	26	24	32	15	20	40	40	28	37

Note
[a] Trust = Average fraction sent (Amount sent/Initial endowment); Reciprocity = Average fraction returned (Amount sent back/Amount received).

We replicated Cox's experiment by highlighting gender differences and modifying the information given to the subjects (Innocenti and Pazienza 2006). Our test showed that women exhibit a higher degree of altruism than men do, for both trust and reciprocity, but the difference between genders in the degree of altruism is greater for trustworthiness than for trust. This result supports the hypothesis that women's higher propensity to reciprocate compared with men is motivated by a greater degree of altruism.

Experiments of this kind test trust and reciprocity in a double blind laboratory environment, where each participant is assured that neither the experimenter nor the other participants are able to attribute individual choices to individual subjects. This condition is imposed to minimize the effect of experimenter bias[4] whereby the experimenter's acts may unconsciously convey to the subjects how they should behave in relation to some characteristics of the design, so that they consequently produce biased results. Another case is participant bias, also known as 'demand characteristics', which applies to experiments in which participants act in ways they believe correspond to what the experimenter wants. Thus, if participants modify their spontaneous behaviour to match the real or presumed aims of the experimenter, the results are also biased. These sources of bias are differentiated by the fact that the former explicitly relates to some specific act or characteristic of the experimenter, while the latter refers generically to the experimental design, but it is not always easy to discriminate between them.

What matters most is that in both cases some features of the laboratory environment may induce subjects to change their choices in order to comply with the experimental purpose. Once the experimenter has become aware of this effect, data interpretation must be revised in order to evaluate the laboratory findings correctly.

The very robust experimental result that subjects prefer fair to maximized payoffs has been also attributed to the influence of the experimenter's observation. Hoffman *et al.* (1994) and Bolton and Zwick (1995) term this effect the 'anonymity hypothesis', and they give two reasons for it. The first relates to the subjects' participation in future experiments. If the experimenter's presumed aim is to find evidence against self-seeking behaviour, a subject's preference for fair payoffs may increase his or her probability of being recruited again by the same experimenter. The second reason is ethical in nature: subjects may be concerned with the experimenter's judgement and believe that he or she does or does not disapprove of maximized choices. Both arguments can be criticized. Experimenters usually prefer inexperienced to experienced subjects so that they can gain better control over learning processes. The beliefs held by experimenters about economic or moral principles are not easily predictable by the participants in experiments.

Orne (1962) offers another explanation:

> The subject's performance in an experiment might almost be conceptualized as problem-solving behavior; that is, at some level he sees it as his task to ascertain the true purpose of the experiment and respond in a manner which will support the hypotheses being tested. Viewed in this light, the totality of cues which convey an experimental hypothesis to the subject become significant determinants of subjects' behavior.
>
> (Orne 1962: 778).

Experimenter bias may be important because subjects are greatly concerned to view their performance as meaningful. During the experiment, they constantly wonder about what the experimenter is trying to test, and any cue that enables them to answer this question may influence their behaviour. If the design incorporates explicit suggestions as treatment variables, the data interpretation is unbiased. Otherwise, expectations about the supposed experimental purpose may affect the subjects' behaviour and consequently distort the results.

The observable characteristics of the experimenter may be among these cues. Indeed, the experimental purpose can also be inferred from his or her gender. For instance, if the design informs the subjects of their counterparts' gender, the presence of a female experimenter may cause the subjects to believe that the experiment is related in some way to discrimination against women.

Although experimental research is increasingly focused on the gender issue, we are not aware of laboratory tests that seek to analyse the effect of experimenter bias across gender differences.[5] The purpose of our experiment was to provide evidence on this issue by testing three different treatments of the trust game. In the first two treatments there were a female and a male experimenter respectively, while in the third treatment we adopted a double blind procedure.

Our test followed almost the same design as in Berg *et al.* (1995), but introduced two variants: first, we imposed that each subject would play the roles of both sender and responder; second, when participants played as senders, they were informed about the gender of the responder with whom they had been paired off.[6] This latter variation served two purposes. First, it enabled us to test the relevance of gender pairing in bilateral relationships. This has been analysed experimentally by Sutter *et al.* (2003), who find that cooperation between players is lower when bargaining partners have the same gender than when they have the opposite gender. Second, it was intended to focus the subjects' attention on the gender variable. In this way, an explicit signal about the experimental purpose was conveyed to all subjects, each of whom acted as both sender and responder. If they conjectured that the purpose of the experiment was to study gender differences in trust and reciprocity, we expected their behaviour to be affected by the experimenter's gender.

Specifically, our conjecture was that, in the double blind treatment, subjects would exhibit behaviour significantly different from that in the other two treatments. In addition, we expected subjects to change their behaviour significantly in relation to the experimenter's gender. Taking up Orne's (1962) suggestion, we presumed that the subjects would try to guess the experimental purpose. Our hypothesis was that the presence of the female experimenter, differently from that of the male experimenter, would induce subjects to believe that the experimental purpose was in some way related to non-selfish behaviour. We thus conjectured that, because women were perceived by the experimental subjects as more altruistic than men, the female experimenter would induce an increase in the degree of altruism in all subjects. The subjects' attempt to conform to the supposed experimental purpose should have had two effects. First, the senders who were informed of the paired responder's gender would increase the degree of trust in women in the female treatment in comparison with the other treatments, because trust is mainly understood to be an economic investment in the trustee's reliability. Second, responders who did not know the paired sender's gender would reciprocate subjects of both genders more in the female than in the male treatment because reciprocity is mainly motivated by altruism, and because the gender effect was not relevant for responders in our experimental design.

Experimental procedures

The experiment was carried out in the spring of 2004. We submitted the trust game to 94 subjects: 46 women and 48 men. They were undergraduate students in economics from the University of Siena and in political sciences from the University of Florence, recruited from first and second year courses through notices posted on the web pages and around the campuses of the two universities.

The experiment was run manually. The participants were paid according to the euros earned. There was no participation fee.

We ran three treatments. The only difference between the first and the second treatment was that a female and a male respectively played the role of experimenter.[7] It was made clear to the subjects that in these treatments only the experimenter was able to attribute individual choices to individual people. However, anonymity between subjects was guaranteed. The third control treatment adopted a double blind procedure.

Table 12.3 presents the number of participants for each session and treatment.

In the female and male treatments, subjects were first identified by numbers. These numbers were randomly assigned and determined the pairings of senders and responders. Then each subject was directed to an isolated desk so that they could make their decision privately. At the desk subjects received written instructions. The first part of the instructions was read aloud by the experimenter of the pertinent gender. The second part contained a short questionnaire, which was answered at the end of the experiment.

When the experiment began, the subjects were given a large unmarked envelope which contained the money to be invested (5 euros, which could be transferred

Table 12.3 Number of participants per treatment by gender

Session	Treatment	Participants (Female + Male)
1	Female experimenter	8 + 6
2	Female experimenter	7 + 9
3	Male experimenter	7 + 9
4	Male experimenter	8 + 8
5	Double blind	8 + 8
6	Double blind	8 + 8
Total		46 + 48

in steps of half units), a card marked with the identification number, and a small envelope marked with a circle that was either pink or blue. Subjects were asked to remember their numbers. The correspondence between each number and each participant remained unknown to the other participants but not to the experimenter, and this was made clear to the participants. The subjects were also informed that if the circle was pink (blue), the person to whom they were to send money was a female (male). In this way, the sender knew the responder's gender but the sender's gender remained unknown to the responder.

Senders decided how many euros to keep and how many euros they wanted to send to their partner by inserting them in the small envelope. The experimenter collected the small envelopes, privately recorded the amount sent, tripled it and placed the tripled money into the same envelope for delivery to the appropriate responder. Responders then opened their envelopes and decided how much of the money received they would return to the sender. The experimenter again collected the envelopes, recorded the amounts returned and gave the envelopes back to the senders. Subjects were informed in the written instructions that they would be playing the roles of both sender and responder, but also that the responder with whom they were paired as sender would not be their sender when they played the role of responder.

In the double blind treatment, the design had to assure the participants that the experimenter was unable to attribute individual choices to individual subjects, and to avoid giving any hint about the experimenter's gender. The subjects were gathered in a room where two undergraduate students, a male and a female previously instructed to play the role of monitors, gave them instructions to read privately. When the experiment began, the subjects were given a large unmarked envelope containing 5 euros, a smaller envelope, and a numbered identification card. The small envelope was marked with a pink or a blue circle. As in the previous treatments, the subjects were informed that the coloured circle on the small envelope identified the gender of their paired responder. Moreover, they were asked to remember their numbers. The correspondence between these numbers and the identities of the subjects remained unknown to the experimenters, to the monitors and to the other participants at all times, and this was made clear to the participants.

Once senders had decided how much money to send to their partners in the small envelopes, they had to insert the identification cards in the smaller envelopes. Moreover, each subject had to write the letter F, if female, or the letter M, if male, on the identification card. The sealed envelopes were collected in a closed urn and taken by the monitor to the experimenters in another room. After recording the amount sent and tripling it, the experimenters marked each larger envelope with the number identifying a responder of the appropriate gender. The envelopes in the closed urn were delivered by the monitor to the subjects' room. At this time, subjects were called one at a time by the monitor. Once called, a subject had to privately choose the envelope with her or his identification number from the urn placed on an isolated desk. Having decided how much of the money received to return to the sender, subjects sealed their envelopes. The monitors again collected the envelopes, and took them to the experimenters' room, where the experimenters recorded the amounts returned and gave the envelopes back for distribution to senders by the same procedure used before. When the experiment was over, all subjects left the room without revealing their identities.

To summarize, our variations with respect to the reference design by Berg *et al.* (1995) were the following:

1   All subjects played both roles (sender and responder), and they knew this before any decision was made.[8]
2   Senders were informed of their responder's gender, but responders did not know their sender's gender.
3   Only the third treatment was double blind, whereas in the first and in the second treatment, the experimenter (but not the subjects) was able to attribute individual choices to individual subjects, and this was made clear to the subjects.

Results

Our experiment was intended to verify the effect of experimenter bias by testing three hypotheses.

Hypothesis 1: Subjects' behaviour in the double blind treatment would be significantly different from that in the other two treatments, in which the experimenter was able to associate each participant with his or her choices.
Hypothesis 2: In the female treatment, senders would exhibit a higher level of trust in women than they did in the other two treatments.
Hypothesis 3: In the female treatment, responders would exhibit a higher degree of reciprocity than in the male treatment.

Our discussion of the experimental findings addresses the question of whether men and women make different choices across the three treatments, first for trust, and then for reciprocity.

Table 12.4 Trust per treatment by sender's gender

Treatment	Female experimenter		Male experimenter		Double blind		Total	
Sender's gender	Mean	StdD	Mean	StdD	Mean	StdD	Mean	StdD
Women	43.3	35.4	39.3	22.2	32.5	23.8	38.3	27.4
Men	28.0	27.0	24.1	18.4	39.4	27.2	30.4	24.8
Total	35.7	31.9	31.3	21.4	35.9	25.4	34.3	26.3

Table 12.4 presents senders' behaviour in the three treatments across gender.

Contrary to earlier experimental evidence (see Table 12.2), on average the women in our experiment show a higher degree of trust than men, but the difference between the two means (38.3 and 30.4) is not significantly different from zero. However, the order between genders is reversed in the double blind treatment, the results of which conform to the previous experimental findings. The lack of anonymity seems to represent a 'social cue' that influences men and women differently. Experimenter's observation increases women's and decrease men's propensity to trust.

Inspection of the difference among treatments shows that, on average, the value of trust is higher in the female treatment than in the male treatment (35.7 vs. 31.3). Both women and men trust more in the female treatment, and the difference in the fraction of the amount sent between women and men is not significant using either a t-test (with a t-value of 0.04 and a p-value of 0.97) or a Wilcoxon rank sum test (with a z-value of 911 and a p-value of 0.63).

Figure 12.1 summarizes data on trust with box plots reporting the median of the data distribution, and the interquartile range to measure the data dispersion. The dispersion of data, which is higher in the female experimenter treatment, explains why the mean differences are not statistically significant. Nevertheless, the figure shows that the difference between the men's and the women's median values is greater than the difference between the corresponding average values.

In our design, senders were informed of their paired responder's gender in order to emphasize the effect of experimenter bias. Table 12.5 presents the average values of trust by responder's gender. In the aggregate, senders trust men (35 per cent) slightly more than women (33 per cent), but the difference between the two average values is not significant and the medians are nearly identical (Figure 12.2). In the male and in the female experimenter treatments, senders exhibit a higher degree of trust in men than in women, while in the double blind treatment the reverse is the case. Also to be noted is that there is no gender pairing effect, because the degree of trust is quite similar across pairs of the same gender and of opposite gender.

The box plots depicted in Figure 12.2 show that the amount of money sent to both men and women is more dispersed in the female experimenter treatment than in the other two treatments.

These findings partially support our conjectures on sender's behaviour. In conformity with our first hypothesis, trusting behaviour exhibits systematic differences

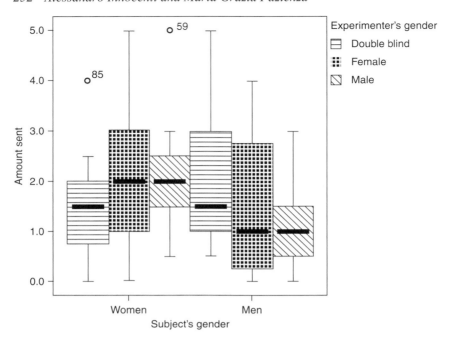

Figure 12.1 Distribution of trust per treatment and sender's gender.

Table 12.5 Trust per treatment by responder's gender

		Treatment			
		Female experimenter	*Male experimenter*	*Double blind*	*Total*
		Total (N = 94)			
	Women	30.7	26.7	41.9	33.3
Responder's gender	Men	40.7	35.3	30.0	35.2
	Total	35.7	31.3	35.9	34.3
		Male senders (N = 48)			
	Women	21.2	21.0	50.0	30.0
Responder's gender	Men	35.7	28.6	28.7	30.9
	Total	28.0	24.1	39.4	30.4
		Female senders (N = 46)			
	Women	41.4	38.0	33.7	37.5
Responder's gender	Men	45.0	40.0	31.2	38.8
	Total	43.3	39.3	32.5	38.3

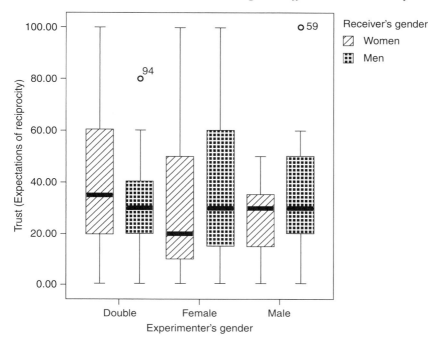

Figure 12.2 Distribution of trust per treatment and responder's gender.

between the double blind and the other two treatments. However, experimenter's presence influences the men and the women differently: it increases the degree of trust of women and decreases that of men. This result may be due to a presumed greater sensitivity of women to changes in the laboratory environment[9] (Croson and Gneezy 2004). We also find evidence of a difference in trusting behaviour between the female and the male treatments. However, the presence of the female experimenter increases the degree of trust in subjects of both genders, and not just in women as predicted by our second hypothesis, which is consequently rejected.

We next turn to the analysis of responders' choices. Table 12.6 shows the degree of reciprocity measured by the average fractions returned by responders.

The strongest pattern of behaviour is that in which the presence of the female experimenter induces subjects of both genders to reciprocate more than in the other treatments. This result is confirmed by Figure 12.3, which presents the median values and the interquartile range of the distribution in the three treatments.[10]

The median values in the male experimenter treatment and in the double blind treatment are quite similar and significantly lower than in the female experimenter treatment. Statistical tests also corroborate this difference for the average values. Table 12.7 shows that both the *t*-test and the Wilcoxon test are significant at 95 per cent.

The box plots in Figure 12.4 show that male responders show a markedly lower degree of reciprocity in the male experimenter treatment. This effect is reinforced by the fact that the median value is zero.

Table 12.6 Reciprocity per treatment by responder's gender

	Treatment							
	Female experimenter		Male experimenter		Double blind		Total	
Responder's gender	Mean	StdD	Mean	StdD	Mean	StdD	Mean	StdD
Women	27.3	27.0	21.0	17.9	20.4	20.8	22.6	21.5
Men	30.9	22.6	9.7	17.7	18.9	19.4	19.0	21.1
Total	29.1	24.4	15.2	18.4	19.7	19.8	20.8	21.3

Note
Reciprocity = Average fraction returned (Amount sent back/Amount received)

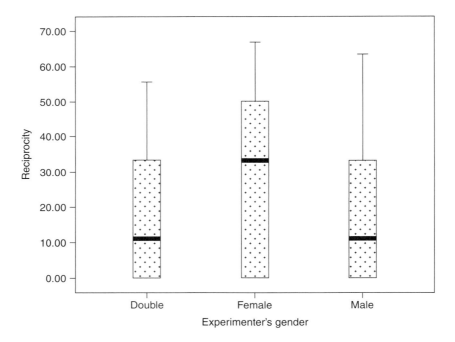

Figure 12.3 Distribution of reciprocity per treatment.

The propensity to be 'fairer' in the female experimenter treatment is also confirmed by statistical analysis of men's behaviour.[11] Table 12.8 shows that the presence of a female experimenter induces male subjects to reciprocate significantly more than in the other two treatments, using either a *t*-test or a Wilcoxon rank sum test.

These findings support our third hypothesis. In the female treatment, responders' behaviour exhibits a higher propensity to reciprocate. According to the interpretation proposed, experimenter bias is effective only for the treatment in which the

Table 12.7 Statistical tests for reciprocity among treatments

t-test for equality of means	N	Mean	Mean diff.	T	Sig. (2-tailed)
Female experimenter treatment	24	29.12			
Male experimenter and double blind treatments	59	17.44	−11.67	−2.32	0.02

Wilcoxon test	
Wilcoxon *W*	2289.5
Z	−1.95
Sig. (2-tailed)	0.052

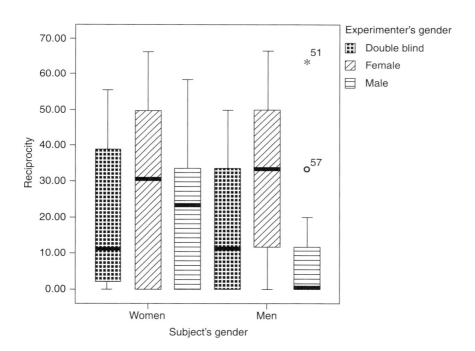

Figure 12.4 Distribution of reciprocity per treatment by subject's gender.

signal used to infer the experimental purpose is perceived by subjects as more evident, that in our case is the presence of the female experimenter.

Conclusion

This chapter has analysed the experimenter bias effect in a test on gender differences. It has assumed that experimental subjects seek to discover the true

Table 12.8 Statistical tests for reciprocity among treatments (men only)

t-test for equality of means	N	Mean	Mean diff.	T	Sig. (2-tailed)
Female experimenter treatment	12	30.92			
Male experimenter and double blind treatments	30	14.30	−16.62	−2.44	0.02
Wilcoxon test					
Wilcoxon W	563.5				
Z	−2.35				
Sig. (2-tailed)	0.02				

purpose of the experiment and may modify their spontaneous behaviour in order to confirm the experimenter's expectations. The gender of the experimenter may produce this bias if gender differences are explicitly considered as treatment variables.

We tested the trust game by differentiating subjects' information: trusters were informed of their paired trustee's gender, but trustees did not know their paired truster's gender. We observed behaviour in three different treatments: the female treatment and the male treatment, conducted respectively by a female and a male experimenter, and the double blind treatment, where complete anonymity among subjects and between subjects and experimenter was guaranteed.

Our findings show that:

(i) there is significant evidence of difference in trusting behaviour between the double blind and the other two treatments;
(ii) the presence of the female experimenter increased the degree of trust in subjects of both genders, although not in a statistically significant way;
(iii) the presence of the female experimenter significantly increased the propensity to reciprocate of male and female subjects.

We interpret these results as generally confirming the importance of experimenter bias. In our interpretation, experimenter bias is effective when subjects receive a signal clear enough to convey a specific experimental purpose. The presence of the female experimenter was perceived by the subjects as evidence that the experiment's purpose was to corroborate the hypothesis of other-regarding behaviour. This conjecture increased the subjects' propensity to be altruistic and consequently improved both trust and reciprocity.

Finally, our experiment supports the hypothesis that women are perceived by others as potentially less selfish than men. If altruism is enhanced by the assessment of how altruistic others are in return, the gender variable may be a useful signal to implement non-selfish behaviour.

Acknowledgements

The financial support of the University of Siena and the MIUR is gratefully acknowledged. We thank Francesco Lomagistro for valuable research assistance.

Appendix

Translation of the instructions

A. Female and male experimenter treatments

This is an experiment in the economics of decision-making. The Ministry of University and the University of Siena have provided funds to conduct this research. The instructions you are about to read are self-explanatory. If you follow them closely and make appropriate decisions, you can earn an amount of money that will be given to you in cash at the end of the experiment. If you have any question, please raise your hand and the experimenter will come to you and answer your question.

In this experiment, each of you will be paired with a different person. You will not be told who these people are either during or after the experiment, nor will they be told who the others are. The only information you will have is the gender of the person with whom you are paired. The experimenter will be in charge of the envelopes as explained below. In addition, they will verify that the instructions have been followed as they appear here.

Each person will be given 5 euros and will have the opportunity to send in an envelope, some, all or none of 5 euros to the person with whom they have been paired. The amount sent will be tripled. For example, if you send an envelope that contains 2 euros, the envelope will contain 6 euros when it reaches the paired person. If you send an envelope that contains 4 euros, the envelope will contain 12 euros when it reaches the paired person. The paired person will then decide how much money to send back to you and how much money to keep.

Each person will play both roles in the experiment. Each of you will be paired with two people. In one pair, you will be the person who decides how much of the 5-euros to send to another person, who will receive the amount sent tripled by the experimenter. In the other pair, you will be the person who receives the amount sent by another person and tripled by the experimenter, and you will decide whether to send back some, all or none of the amount received to the sender. So each of you will make two decisions. However, the important thing to bear in mind is that you are not paired with the same person as sender and responder. Rather, you are paired with two different people.

The remainder of these instructions will explain exactly how the experiment will be run. It is structured so that no one except the experimenter will know the personal decisions of the subjects. Since your decision is private, we ask you not to tell anyone about your decision during, or after, the experiment.

The experiment will be conducted as follows: a number of large unmarked envelopes have been placed in a box. Each of these envelopes contains 5 euros, a card marked with an identification number that you are asked to remember, and a smaller envelope marked with a circle, which will be coloured pink or blue. The experimenter will hand one person at a time an unmarked envelope from the box. Once a person has an envelope, he or she will privately open the unmarked envelope and place as many euros in the smaller circled envelope as she/he wants, keeping the rest. Examples: (1) put 2 euros in the smaller envelope and keep 3 euros; (2) put 4 euros in the smaller envelope and keep 1 euro. These are examples only; the actual decision is up to each person.

It is important to bear in mind that the person who receives the amount you send will be a female if the smaller envelope is marked with a pink circle, and he will be a male if the smaller envelope is marked with a blue circle. This process will continue until everyone has made his or her decision.

Once everyone has made their decisions, the experimenter will collect all the larger, unmarked envelopes, and return them to the box. Note that each returned envelope will look exactly the same.

After all the envelopes have been put in the return box, the experimenter will then privately, one at a time, take the smaller envelopes out of the larger envelopes, record on a sheet of paper the number of the identification card and the amount of money inside the smaller envelope. The experimenter will then triple the amount of money in the smaller envelope and place the smaller envelope back into the larger envelope. At this point, the experimenter will transfer the envelopes to the return box.

The experimenter will then give to each person, one at a time, an unmarked envelope from the box. Each of you will privately open the larger envelope and must decide how many euros to leave in the smaller envelope. The person keeps the remaining euros. The smaller envelope should then be placed in the larger envelope. When everyone has had the opportunity to make his or her decision, the experimenter will collect the larger envelopes and return them to the box. The experimenter will then privately, one at a time, open the larger envelopes and record how much is in the smaller envelope. After recording how much was in the smaller envelope, the experimenter will put the smaller envelope in the larger envelope, and will replace them in the return box.

Then the experimenter will choose one person at a time to go to the box marked 'return envelopes' to retrieve the smaller envelope with the appropriate identification number marked on it. You should not open your envelope yet. This process will continue until everyone has retrieved his or her envelope and returned to his or her seat. When everyone is finished, the experimenter will ask if everyone has retrieved the correct envelope. If everyone has taken the correct envelope, the experiment is finished. If, however, an envelope has ended up with the wrong person, then the experimenter will collect all the smaller envelopes again, and the process will be repeated until everyone has the correct envelope.

Before leaving the room, everyone will be asked to fill out a short questionnaire. At the top of the questionnaire, you will be asked for the card identification number. Please do not forget to include this information. Once you have finished the questionnaire, you will be asked to put it in the box placed at the back of the room.

Please raise your hand if you have any questions regarding how the experiment will proceed.

B. Double blind treatment

This is an experiment in the economics of decision-making. The Ministry of University and the University of Siena have provided funds to conduct this research. The instructions you are about to read are self-explanatory. Two of us have been chosen as monitors and will check that the instructions have been followed as they appear here. However, they will not answer any questions during this experiment. If you have any doubts, you should read back through these instructions. Now that the experiment has begun, we ask that you do not talk at all. If you follow these instructions closely and make the appropriate decisions, you will earn an amount of money that will be given to you in cash at the end of the experiment.

In this experiment, each of you will be paired with a different person. You will not be told who this person is either during or after the experiment, nor will they be told who the others are. The only information you will have is the gender of the person with whom you are paired.

Each person will be given 5 euros and will have the opportunity to send in an envelope, some, all or none of the 5 euros to the person whom she/he is paired. The amount sent will be tripled. For example, if you send an envelope that contains 2 euros, the envelope will contain 6 euros when it reaches the paired person. If you send an envelope that contains 4 euros, the envelope will contain 12 euros when it reaches the paired person. The paired person will then decide how much money to send back to you and how much money to keep.

Each person will play both roles in the experiment. Each of you will be paired with two people. In one pair, you will be the person who decides how much of the 5-euros to send to another person, who receives the amount sent tripled by the monitors. In the other pair, you will be the person who receives the amount sent by another person and tripled by the experimenter, and you will decide whether to send back some, all or none of the amount received to the sender. So each of you will make two decisions. However, the important thing to bear in mind is that you are not paired with the same person as sender and responder. Rather, you are paired with two different people.

The remainder of these instructions will explain exactly how the experiment will be run. It is structured so that no one, including the experimenters and the monitors, will know the personal decisions taken by the subjects. Since your decision is absolutely private, we ask you not to tell anyone about your decision during, or after, the experiment.

The experiment will be conducted as follows: a number of large unmarked envelopes have been placed in a box. Each of these envelopes contains 5 euros, a card marked with an identification number that you are asked to remember, and a smaller envelope marked with a circle, which will be coloured pink or blue. Then monitors will call one person at a time to go to the isolated box placed in the front of the room. Each person will take an unmarked envelope from the box and will return to his or her isolated desk.

Once a person has an envelope, he or she will privately open the unmarked envelope and write on the identification card the letter F if he is a female or the letter M if he is a male. Please do not forget to include this information. Then each person will place as many euros in the smaller circled envelope as they want, keeping the rest. Examples: (1) put 2 euros in the smaller envelope and keep 3 euros; (2) put 4 euros in the smaller envelope and keep 1 euro. These are examples only; the actual decision is up to each person. It is important to bear in mind that the person who receives the amount you sent will be a female if the smaller envelope is marked with a pink circle and a male if the smaller envelope is marked with a blue circle. This process will continue until everyone has made his or her decision.

Once a person has made a decision, he or she will put the smaller envelope and the identification card in the larger envelope. Then the monitors will call one person at a time to go to the isolated box. Each person will put the larger envelope into the box. Note that each returned envelope will look exactly the same, and neither monitors nor anyone else will be able to attribute individual choices to individual subjects.

After all the envelopes have been put in the return box, the monitors will then privately, one at a time, take the smaller envelopes out of the larger envelopes, record on a sheet of paper the letter and the number written on the identification card and the amount of money inside the smaller envelope. The monitors will then triple the amount of money in the smaller envelope, place the smaller envelope back into the larger envelope, and write an identification number on the larger envelope. At this point, the monitors will transfer the envelopes to the return box.

The monitors will then call one person at a time to go to the isolated box to retrieve the larger envelope with his or her identification number marked on it. You should not open your envelope yet. This process will continue until everyone has retrieved his or her appropriate envelope and returned to his or her seat. When everyone is finished, monitors will ask if everyone has retrieved the correct envelope. If everyone has taken the correct envelope, the experiment will continue. If, however, an envelope has ended up with the wrong person, then the monitors will call one person at a time again and the process will be repeated until everyone has the correct envelope.

Then each of you will privately open the larger envelope and must decide how many euros to leave in the smaller envelope. The person keeps the remaining euros. The smaller envelope should then be placed again in the larger envelope. When everyone has had the opportunity to make his or her decision, the monitors will call again one person at a time. Each person will return the larger envelopes to the box. The monitors will then privately, one at a time, open the larger envelopes and record how much is in the smaller envelope. After recording how much is in the smaller envelope, the monitors will put the smaller envelope in the larger envelope, and will replace back in the return box.

Then monitors will call one person at a time to go to the box marked 'return envelopes' to retrieve the smaller envelope with the appropriate identification number marked on it. You should not open your envelope yet. This process will continue until everyone has retrieved his or her envelope and returned to his or her seat. When everyone is finished, monitors will ask if everyone has retrieved the correct envelope. If everyone has taken the correct envelope, the experiment is finished. If, however, an envelope has ended up with the wrong person, then the monitors will collect all the smaller envelopes again and the process will be repeated until everyone has the correct envelope.

At this time, you should take all your belongings and leave the building. When everyone in the room has left, the experiment is over, and the monitors will be paid for their participation.

Notes

1 Ledyard (1995) and Schram (2000) survey the experimental evidence on subjects deviating from own-payoff-maximizing behaviour.

2 See Fehr and Schmidt (2005) for a survey.

3 Abbink *et al.* (2000), Cox (2001) and Cox *et al.* (2002) obtain analogous results by testing the moonlighting game. In this game, the sender can choose whether they want to give the responder part of their endowment or take up to half the endowment from the responder. The amount given by the sender is tripled by the experimenter. The responder then decides whether they want to give or take money from the sender.

4 It is only recently that experimental economists have analyzed this problem. In particular, Hoffman *et al.* (1996) argue that the subjects' degree of social distance from the experimenter may affect their behaviour, especially because it gives rise to expectations of reciprocity. See also Bolton and Zwick (1995).

5 Ortmann and Tichy (1999) sought to deal with the experimenter bias problem by jointly conducting a test on gender differences in the prisoner's dilemma. However, the physical presence of two experimenters, one male and one female, did not eliminate the possibility that one of the two experimenters would be perceived by the participants as the leading one. For example, the person who reads the instructions aloud is presumably considered to be conducting the experiment.

6 We did not inform the responders about their sender's gender in order to differentiate factors influencing reciprocity and trust. If subjects, when they played as responders, did not know the gender of their paired sender, their decision to reciprocate could be considered to depend only on the amount of money received and on the experiment's perceived purpose.

7 The authors acted separately as the experimenters for the two treatments. In each session, there was also an assistant of the same gender as the experimenter.

8 Burks *et al.* (2003) made the same assumption in their third treatment, which they termed 'both roles, prior'. Chaudhuri and Gangadharan (2002) also made this assumption to test gender differences (see Table 12.1).

9 In a survey on gender differences in the laboratory, Croson and Gneezy argue that

   this variance (gender difference) can be explained by a differential sensitivity of men and women to the social conditions in the experiment. Research from psychology suggests that women are more sensitive to social cues in determining appropriate behavior than are men. (…) Participants of both genders are likely maximizing an underlying utility function, but the function that men use is less sensitive to the conditions of the experiment, information about the other party, and (even) the other party's actions, than the function that women use.

(Croson and Gneezy 2004:19).

10 If the responder is sent nothing by the paired sender, he or she is excluded from computation as a missing case.
11 The amount of money received from the paired sender and the percentage of money sent back to the paired sender was positively correlated with the Spearman's correlation coefficient of 0.46 (0.576 for women and 0.372 for male), which was significant at the 0.01 level in all cases.

References

Abbink, K., Irlenbusch, B. and Renner, E. (2000) 'The Moonlighting Game: An Empirical Study on Reciprocity and Retribution', *Journal of Economic Behavior and Organization*, 42 (2): 265–277.

Ashraf, N., Bohnet, I. and Piankov, N. (2003) '*Is Trust a Bad Investment?*', KSG Working Papers, RWP03–047.

Bacharach, M., Guerra, G. and Zizzo, D. (2001) '*Is Trust Self-Fulfilling? An Experimental Study*', Economics Discussion Paper No. 76, University of Oxford.

Berg, J., Dickhaut, J. and McCabe, K. (1995) 'Trust, Reciprocity, and Social History', *Games and Economic Behavior*, 10 (1): 122–42.

Bolton, G.E. and Zwick, R. (1995) 'Anonymity versus Punishment in Ultimatum Bargaining', *Games and Economic Behavior*, 10 (1): 95–121.

Buchan, N.R., Rachel, T.A., Croson and Johnson, E.J. (2000) '*Trust and Reciprocity: An International Experiment*', Discussion paper, University of Wisconsin-Madison, University of Pennsylvania and Columbia University.

Buchan, N. R., Croson, R.T.A. and Solnick, S. S. (2004) '*Trust and Gender: An Examination of Behavior, Biases, and Beliefs in the Investment Game*', Working paper, University of Pennsylvania.

Burks, S., Carpenter, J. and Verhoogen, E. (2003) 'Playing Both Roles in the Trust Game', *Journal of Economic Behavior and Organization*, 51 (2): 195–216.

Chaudhuri, A. and Gangadharan, L. (2002) '*Gender Differences in Trust and Reciprocity*', Discussion paper, Wellesley College and University of Melbourne.

Chaudhuri, A. and Gangadharan, L. (2003) '*Sending Money in the Trust Game: Trust or Other Regarding Preferences*', Discussion paper, Wellesley College and University of Melbourne.

Cox, J.C. (2001) '*On the Economics of Reciprocity*', Discussion paper, University of Arizona.

Cox, J.C. (2002) 'Trust, Reciprocity, and Other-Regarding Preferences: Groups vs. Individuals and Males vs. Females', in R. Zwick and A. Rapoport (eds), *Advances in Experimental Business Research*, Boston: Kluwer Academic Publishers.

Cox, J.C. (2004) 'How to identify trust and reciprocity', *Games and Economic Behavior*, 46 (2): 260–81.

Cox, J.C., Sadiraj, K. and Sadiraj, V. (2002) '*Trust, Fear, Reciprocity, and Altruism*', Discussion paper, University of Arizona and University of Amsterdam.

Croson, R. and Buchan, N. (1999) 'Gender and Culture: International Experimental Evidence from Trust Games', *American Economic Review*, 89 (2): 386–91.

Croson, R. and Gneezy, U. (2004) '*Gender Differences in Preferences*', Working paper, Wharton School, University of Pennsylvania.

Eckel, C.C. and Grossman, P.J. (1998) 'Are Women Less Selfish than Men: Evidence from Dictator Experiments', *The Economic Journal*, 108 (448): 726–35.

Eckel, C.C. and Grossman, P.J. (2000) 'The Difference in the Economic Decisions of Men and Women: Experimental Evidence', in C. Plott and V. Smith (eds), *Handbook of Experimental Results*. New York: Elsevier.

Fehr, E. and Schmidt, K.M. (2005) '*The Economics of Fairness, Reciprocity and Altruism – Experimental Evidence and New Theories*', Discussion Paper No. 66, GESY, University of Mannheim.

Hoffman, E., McCabe, K., Shachat, K. and Smith, V.L. (1994) 'Preferences, Property Rights, and Anonymity in Bargaining Games', *Games and Economic Behavior*, 7 (3): 346–80.

Hoffman, E., McCabe, K. and Smith, V.L. (1996) 'Social Distance and Other-Regarding Behavior in Dictator Games', *American Economic Review*, 86 (3): 653–60.

Innocenti, A. and Pazienza, M.G. (2006) 'Altruism and Gender in the Trust Game', *Labsi Working Papers*, No. 5/2006.

Ledyard, J.O. (1995) 'Public goods: a survey of experimental research', in J. Kagel and A. Roth (eds) *The Handbook of Experimental Economics*. Princeton: Princeton University Press.

Levine, D.K. (1998) 'Modeling Altruism and Spitefulness in Experiments', *Review of Economic Dynamics*, 1 (3): 593–622.

Orne, M.T. (1962) 'On the social psychology of the psychological experiment: with particular reference to demand characteristics and their implications', *American Psychologist*, 17 (8): 776–83.

Ortmann, A. and Tichy, L.K. (1999) 'Gender differences in the laboratory: evidence from prisoner's dilemma games', *Journal of Economic Behavior and Organization*, 39 (3): 327–39.

Rabin, M. (1993) 'Incorporating Fairness in Game Theory and Economics', *American Economic Review*, 83 (5): 1281–1302.

Schram, A. (2000) 'Sorting Out the Seeking: Rents and Individual Motivation', *Public Choice*, 103 (3–4): 231–58.

Schwieren, C. and Sutter, M. (2003) '*Trust in cooperation or ability? An experimental study on gender differences*', Discussion paper 2003–10, Max-Planck Institute zur Erforschung von Wirtschaftssystemen.

Sutter, M., Bosman, R., Kocher, M. and van Winden, F. (2003) '*Experimental evidence of the importance of gender pairing in bargaining*', Discussion paper 2003–27, Max Planck Institute.

.

Part 6

Institutions matter

13 Gender and the political economy of knowledge

Ann Mari May

Introduction

The importance of increased levels of education in improving the status of women throughout the world is well established. Higher levels of education are associated with lower birth rates, higher incomes, and greater autonomy for women. In fact, it has been argued that education is a fundamental prerequisite for empowering women in all spheres of society (Lopez-Claros and Zahidi 2005: 5).

In the last third of the twentieth century, women have made particularly significant strides in many countries. For example, UNESCO reports that women's share of enrollment in higher education in Switzerland rose from 3 per cent in 1985 to 43 per cent in 2000 and in France, women's share of enrollment increased from 50 to 55 per cent. Women's share in Latin American colleges and universities over the same time period rose from 43 to 47 per cent in Chile, and 44 to 54 per cent in El Salvador. In India, women's share has risen from 30 to 39 per cent.[1] While certainly not universal, this trend towards gender balance in student enrollment is remarkably similar in a large number of industrialized countries throughout the world.[2]

The increase in the participation of women as students is now beginning to reach the highest levels of educational attainment. The Nordic Research Board (NORBAL) reports that women received 46 per cent of doctoral degrees awarded by universities in the Nordic and Baltic countries in 2005 – up from 28 per cent in 1990 (NORBAL 2005: 3). In the United States, in 2002, for the first time in American history, more American women than American men received doctorates from US universities (Hoffer *et al.* 2003).

The increase in representation of women as students in higher education has not, however, produced a proportional increase in the representation of women as faculty. For example, in 2000, women constituted only 4.4 per cent of faculty at Austrian universities, 11 per cent of faculty at German universities, 12 per cent in Swedish universities, and 10 per cent in UK universities (Zimmer 2003: 9). In 1995, UNESCO reported that in Norway and Canada women constituted only 21 per cent of faculty, and in the US only 31 per cent of faculty (UNESCO 2005).

While some countries, such as Sweden, Canada, and Norway, have implemented programmes to increase the representation of women faculty, these programmes

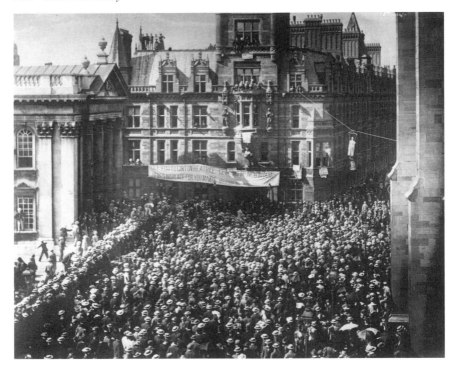

Figure 13.1 Students protest the introduction of women at Cambridge University, 1897.

have often been strongly criticized by male faculty and thrown out by (mostly male) courts. In 1995, the Swedish government created 32 posts at full professor level, the so-called Tham professors, especially for women. Men were allowed to apply but would only be given the job if there were no qualified women. But in 2000, the EU Supreme Court turned down the Tham proposal, and the program is currently under debate in Sweden (Jordansson 1999). In 2000, the University of Oslo implemented a plan to improve gender diversity among faculty by reserving 12 full or associate professorships for female candidates. However, in January 2003 the European Free Trade Association Court ruled it illegal for the University of Oslo to reserve faculty positions for women.[3]

In describing the reaction of academics in Norway to the call for gender equality in higher education, Ms. Tove Beate Pedersen, head of the Secretariat for Women's Studies and whose job is to work with female recruitment said, 'We have experienced stronger and more sophisticated resistance than we had expected. Vigilance and additional resources are necessary in order to increase female recruitment, and to integrate female perspectives and interests more effectively in academic life' (Ministry of Children and Family Affairs, Norway 2000).

The history of men's opposition to women's participation in higher education has been remarkably consistent across cultures and through time. From male students in Cambridge in 1897 protesting the presence of women students, to male faculty in the first years of the twenty-first century opposed to governmental attempts to redress the paucity of women as faculty, equity for women in higher education has seldom been uncontroversial.

Today higher education, like other sectors in society, remains gender segregated. Women continue to occupy the lowest ranks, work at the least prestigious institutions, and receive the lowest pay and least job security. As Jerry Jacobs has pointed out, in the US, while women have attained access to higher education more or less on a par with their male counterparts, they fail to benefit in terms of outcomes on par with men (Jacobs 1996: 154). Worldwide, while women have increasingly been accepted as consumers in the seminaries of learning, they continue to be marginalized and excluded as colleagues or writers of the canon – particularly at the research institutions from which the canon emerges. Their desire to participate as full citizens in the institutions of higher learning is often met with resistance.

This essay examines the institutions responsible for knowledge production, focusing on gender and the political economy of knowledge. We begin with an examination of gender politics and the higher learning through the controversy that came to be known as the *querelle des femmes* – the quarrel of the women. Through the *querelle des femmes*, we examine what is at stake in the higher learning and begin to consider the strategies that have been employed to maintain the patriarchy of knowledge. These issues are given formal theoretical consideration through the work of Thorstein Veblen. Engaging with and expanding the framework established by Veblen's *The Theory of the Leisure Class* (1899), we will examine higher education as an institution and consider the ways in which the social construction of gender is used to signify and maintain power relationships within higher education.

By examining higher education as an institution that responds not only to the internal imperatives of the agents involved in the production of knowledge, but also as an institution influenced in various ways by the broader culture, we gain insight into the reasons for women's limited inclusion and marginalization within the higher learning. Moreover, a more complete understanding of the higher learning as an institution allows us to better develop strategies for promoting a more equitable higher learning.

The 'Woman Question' and the higher learning

In 1895, when women students from Smith College gathered on the day before commencement to celebrate Ivy Day, it was a ceremony rich with symbolism. Women students, dressed in white and carrying roses, led a parade through campus, which ended with the planting of ivy as a symbol of their lifelong connection to the college (Smith College Archives 2006). This sanguine picture masks another reality of women's other lived experiences in the higher learning – an experience evidenced most clearly by the photograph of Cambridge students taken in 1897 and found at the beginning of this essay. In this photograph, male university students are found protesting the presence of women students who were allowed merely to take classes but not to graduate with degrees.

The experience of women at Cambridge was not unlike the experience of women at hundreds of universities throughout the world. As 'intruders' into the halls of ivy, women have been seen as a threat to the status of institutions, restricted in their use of facilities such as libraries and laboratories, constrained in their choice of courses, assumed to be lacking in intelligence and analytical skills, and told that their desire for equal treatment was a 'bid for power' and that they were 'never satisfied' (Tullberg 1998).

In Europe, the controversy over women and knowledge came to be known as the *querelle des femmes* or quarrel of the women – a centuries-long debate begun in the 1400s about equality of the sexes. In the nineteenth century, as biology surpassed prudence as the fashionable rationale for women's exclusion, debates about women's suitability for higher education came to be known as the 'Woman Question'. This debate continues today, with many of the same arguments being used to rationalize women's absence as producers of knowledge along with new arguments more suited to a market economy (May 2006). Yet, within the current debate remain the concerns raised over six centuries ago regarding the psychology of patriarchy and the gender politics of knowledge production.

Querelle des Femmes

While women today have an easier time being accepted as consumers than as colleagues, their role in the higher learning has long been contested and their access to knowledge production has been controversial for centuries. The debate, originating in the writings of Christine de Pizan and carried on by numerous women for over 400 years, represented an attempt to investigate and rebut the misogynistic view of women's inferiority constructed and reconstructed through 3,000 years of western culture. This misogyny permeated intellectual, religious, legal, and medical notions, as well as social and familial relations, during the European Middle Ages. The origin of this debate is worth examining because it tells us much about the psychology of patriarchy and the gender politics of knowledge production. Moreover, it foreshadows many of the arguments used to rationalize women's exclusion and limit their participation, strategies employed to preserve the patriarchy of knowledge, and difficulties that women would face in exercising their voice. Both Pizan's critique of patriarchal culture in *The Book of the City of Ladies*, and her treatment as a woman writer, present important lessons on the patriarchy of knowledge (Kelly 1982).

Pizan's critique of patriarchal culture found in *City of Ladies*, begins with the narrator reading the works of male authors from Aristotle to Matheolus. At first absorbing the view of women's inferiority espoused by 'solemn scholars', the narrator then emerges from the 'anguish' of 'despising [herself] and all womankind' to articulate 'a recognition of the man-made, misogynous nature of that claim' (Pizan [1431] 1982: 4–5 and Kelly 1982: 14). With the help of three allegorical women – Reason, Rectitude, and Justice – the narrator learns to reject the authority of 'grave dons, learned men, and men of sense', instead learning to explore women's experiences as authoritative in themselves (Astell 1730: 74).[4]

Demonstrating that education is central to identity, Pizan encourages women to educate themselves, not merely for practical reasons of administration of their household, but for more profound reasons as well: that they might come to see the authoritative view of men as non-authoritative (Pizan [1431] 1982: 153–4). As Pizan points out in the *Epistre au Dieu d'Amours*, 'if women had written the books we read, they would have handled things differently, for women know they have been falsely accused'.[5]

Although the *querelle* used allegory, history, and empiricism to refute the claim of women's inferiority, the defense of women often focused on the psychology of men. In particular, these early feminists noted the importance of male competitiveness, explaining how men denigrated women out of fear that women would be found equal or even superior to them (Drake [1696] 1970: 11–20).[6]

The City of Ladies makes the argument for women's education and literacy, as Susan Schibanoff points out, recognizing that 'as long as literacy remained an almost exclusively male prerogative, those token women who were allowed to attain this privilege did so at the risk of, among other things, their own identities' (Schibanoff 1983: 325). This view of the importance of access to knowledge recognizes the importance of the right of women to make knowledge claims, not merely to access the knowledge claims of men. In other words, women must have access to knowledge not merely to learn the canon, but to write the canon as well.

The City of Ladies provides us with an understanding of the why access to knowledge production is essential for women in terms of their identity, but the personal experience of Christine de Pizan as a writer also offers valuable insights on the costs of exercising voice and bears witness to the strategies that have been employed to preserve the patriarchy of knowledge. As a writer, Pizan was able to make a living for herself and her family, something few women of her time could do (Bell 1976: 175). However, she was allowed to do so only insofar as she wrote with a voice that was, as Schibanoff points out, 'conventionally male-identified in subject, form, and genre' (Schibanoff 1983: 324).

In her early career, Pizan wrote largely uncontroversial poems and was able to function as a writer without significant criticism. However, when Pizan briefly attacked Jean de Meun for his antifeminist poem, *The Romance of the Rose*, she was marginalized by powerful men. Pizan was soon made aware of the 'term of her tenuous condition' by three men who rose to de Meun's defense and who, according to Schibanoff, 'reminded Christine that her male privilege was honorary and that they could and would demote her to female status if she persisted with her perverse feminist accusations against their "beloved master"' (Schibanoff 1983: 325).

The critique of Pizan first took the form of mild rebuke. The authors express surprise that Pizan would offer such an inappropriate attack. Suggesting that she must have been put up to it by others, the authors discount her critique and minimize her independence of thought. When Pizan persisted, she was met with sexist insults as her opponents labeled her a 'typically impassioned, arrogant, willful, foolish, and ignorant woman' (Schibanoff 1983: 325). In the end, her opponents excluded her altogether from their company. As Schibanoff so aptly describes it, 'as a woman, she had proved herself to be unexceptional, hence unacceptable' (Schibanoff 1983: 325).

Identity, agency, and the patriarchy of knowledge

It is indeed revealing that the first, and perhaps most profound, lesson in *The City of Ladies* concerns identity and its construction. The construction of identity is particularly important in that it so strongly influences agency – the ability of individuals to act within a context of being affected by institutions and history. While many modern discussions of the importance of education have focused on its pecuniary influence, the effect of education on agency is of profound concern as well. As Amaryta Sen and Martha Nussbaum have pointed out, education adds not only to *human capital* but to *human capability*, enabling women to exercise their legal rights as well as to strengthen their political and civic engagement (Sen 1999; Nussbaum 2000).

It is this relationship between identity and agency that lies at the heart of the patriarchy of knowledge and reveals, in a very fundamental way, the reciprocal relationship that exists between the patriarchy of knowledge and other patriarchal institutions in society. Higher education is particularly important as an institution in playing a pivotal role in shaping identity and generating constructions of reality that help rationalize inequalities and ultimately frame capabilities. Higher education, in this sense, both creates identity and offers a potent mechanism either for change or for maintenance of the status quo and is thus a crucial institution in society. While it is often argued that the 'real world' has little in common with the higher learning, there is, in fact, a subtle and important relationship between the institution of the higher learning and other institutions in society.[7]

While scholars from a variety of disciplines examine the role of higher education in society, few have offered as provocative a look at the higher learning – a look that integrates important insights on women and the higher learning – than the economist and social philosopher Thorstein Veblen (May 1998). Veblen viewed the institution of higher learning in a way that later philosophers of science might refer to as the sociology of knowledge tradition. These philosophers, from Thomas Kuhn (1962) to Paul Feyerabend (1988), view the creation of knowledge as a social process that takes place in communities of scholars who are influenced by personal, social, and political values of the larger community. However, these later philosophers of science often failed to examine the gendered nature of socially situated knowledge. For example, they argued that science is often influenced by the agendas of those who fund research, but they failed to identify the ways in which the metaphors and conceptual frameworks used in science were themselves gendered. In other words, they were sensitive to the politics of knowledge claims but not the gender politics of such claims.

Extending a gendered lens to the sociology of knowledge tradition, feminist philosophers of science such as Helen Longino (1990) and Sandra Harding (1986; 1991) and others have shed light on the gendered nature of these communities and the ways in which perspective is determined by the location of the scholar. According to these scholars, women are often misrepresented in science because they are under-represented in science. Moreover, as Harding has pointed out, failure to recognize that observation involves subjective perceptions that are shaped by community and experience of the knower, limits our understanding. According to Harding,

> Knowledge claims are always socially situated, and the failure of the dominant groups critically and systematically to interrogate their advantaged social situation and the effect of such advantages on their beliefs leaves their social situation a scientifically and epistemologically disadvantaged one for generating knowledge.
>
> (Harding 1993: 54)

These feminist philosophers of science provide valuable insights on gender and knowledge production which, along with the insights of the political economist Thorstein Veblen, provide a useful framework for examining gender and the political economy of knowledge production. Veblen's insights found in *The Theory of the Leisure Class*, *The Higher Learning in America*, and in his little read *The Nature of Peace*, offer a unique view of the higher learning as an institution embedded in and impacted by society and a view in which gender is integral. They provide, as well, a provocative foundation for our examination of women and higher education today.

Veblen and the political economy of knowledge

As Veblen pointed out, institutions distribute power, and institutions of higher learning are no exception. While popular conceptions often explicitly argue or tacitly assume that higher education is a meritocracy in which the best ideas simply 'bubble to the top', Veblen views the higher learning as an institution that distributes power (much like any other institution), is preoccupied with status maintenance (probably more than other institutions), is influenced by the values and imperatives of society, and occupies a critical position in manufacturing opinion. Veblen remains one of the few economists to provide an integrated view of the role of higher education that explicitly incorporates gender in his analysis in more than a trivial manner. In fact, from the introductory chapter of *The Theory of the Leisure Class* to his concluding chapter on the higher learning, there is little in Veblen's work that does not reflect a recognition of gender.

It is noteworthy that the introduction of Veblen's most famous work begins with a discussion of the emergence of the sexual division of labour – a distinction that Veblen saw as invidious. In the transformation from primitive savagery to barbarism – from largely peaceable to consistently warlike society – Veblen argues that the division of labour emerged in such a way that men were associated with activities such as war, hunting, sports, and devout observances, while women 'held those employments out of which industrial occupations proper develop in the next advance' (Veblen [1899] 1998: 4). Thus, for Veblen, the modern distinction between industrial and non-industrial reflects the barbarian distinction between exploit and drudgery – a distinction that coincides with the difference between the sexes and one in which those employments classified as exploit are considered 'worthy, honorable, and noble', while those considered drudgery are thought to be 'unworthy, debasing, [and] ignoble' (Veblen [1899] 1998: 15).

In barbarian society, class distinctions emerge, bringing distinctions between a leisure and working class and an emphasis on ownership and pecuniary emulation. While every civilization cultivates esoteric knowledge that is considered to have intrinsic value apart from material considerations, the development and refinement of this esoteric knowledge 'in its incipient phase' is a leisure-class occupation undertaken by men (Veblen [1899] 1998: 367). Although the pursuit of knowledge is taken by many to be an unadulterated search for 'truth', it is itself a reflection of the 'habits of thought' of the learned class who are, according to Veblen, 'great sticklers for form, precedent, gradations of rank, ritual, ceremonial vestments, and learned paraphernalia generally' (Veblen [1899] 1998: 367).

Veblen applies to the institution of higher learning the same framework of evolutionary change that he applies to other institutions. This broader framework is one in which institutions themselves, as well as institutional change, are presumed to reflect both ceremonial or backward-looking habits of thought related to stratified structures of status, as well as instrumental or technological values. Hence, the institution of the higher learning reflects both ceremonial and instrumental values in the internal structure or the habits and rituals of those who make up the corporation of the higher learning as well as the activities of those involved in the 'matter of fact' activities of disinterested enquiry. Moreover, the higher learning reflects the influence of the broader culture, or what Veblen, at the turn of the twentieth century, called the pecuniary drift of the market system. For Veblen, the higher learning is a cultural artifact emanating from two impulsive traits of human nature – the instinct of workmanship and idle curiosity, and behaviour that is, in a variety of ways and at various developmental stages, influenced by ceremonial behaviour and the drift of pecuniary culture.

While the origin of the higher learning is rooted in the priestly and leisure class, there came to be a distinction between esoteric and exoteric knowledge, the former 'comprising such knowledge as is primarily of no economic or industrial effect and the latter comprising chiefly knowledge of industrial processes of nature phenomenon which were habitually turned to account for the material purposes of life' (Veblen [1899] 1998: 367). Hence, the search for and preservation of esoteric knowledge constitutes the primary activities of those institutions associated with higher learning, while, in time, the existence of exoteric knowledge has come to be associated with what Veblen sometimes calls lower learning. However, in both institutions, ceremonial values are present to some degree.

It was, of course, in the late nineteenth and early twentieth centuries that the advent of the market system, or what Veblen called the drift of pecuniary culture, began to exert its influence on the higher learning. Veblen speaks of the influence that emanates from the imperatives of a pecuniary culture that seeks, for example, to fit youths for careers in commerce. This motive drives the curriculum to prepare students to engage in the mechanics of commerce as well as to shape their values so that they appreciate, rather than question, existing arrangements. More to the point, according to Veblen, the purpose of higher learning is increasingly to fit youths of the leisure class for the 'consumption of goods, material and immaterial, according to a conventionally accepted, reputable scope and method' (Veblen [1899] 1998: 370).

The drift of pecuniary culture directs a variety of activities so as to avoid the drop in enrollment and loss of goodwill in genteel circles and leads to the growth of a variety of 'student activities' that Veblen sees as 'sideshows to the main tent' (Veblen [1918] 1918: 74). Hence the growth in scholastic accessories – collegiate sports, fraternities, clubs, and exhibitions, all of which reflect the pandering of the corporation of learning to the business culture. The businesslike mentality of the corporation of learning and the resulting expansion of undergraduate education for that purpose, leads to the degradation of the higher learning and is decried because of its deleterious effect on the pursuit of knowledge. While even the sagacious Veblen could not have imagined the degree to which the growth of scholastic accessories would envelop the higher learning in the late twentieth century, it is perhaps his view of women and the higher learning that was most prescient.

Women and higher learning

As a by-product of the priestly and leisure class, the higher learning was taboo to women. Those few women who read widely, were allowed to exercise their new found voice to the extent that it did not challenge the patriarchy of knowledge. Yet by the mid-nineteenth century, women began to test this convention and call for admission into the halls of ivy both in Europe and in the US. By the 1860s, women students were already studying medicine in Paris. At the University of Zurich, one of the first universities to admit women as students, women they were enrolled as early as 1867. By the 1870s, women were admitted into women's colleges in the UK. Also by that time Sweden and Denmark opened their doors to female students (Mazón 2003: 14–15).

In the US, although women's colleges began in the 1830s, it was the decline in male enrollment during the Civil War along with passage of the Morrill Act that spurred coeducation in the postwar years. The Morrill Act created a system of land grant colleges and universities, often in sparsely populated states – colleges and universities that could ill afford to forgo the potential revenue from female students. It was the rise of these new coeducational state universities that put increasing pressure on existing universities to admit women students thus raising the spectre of women as faculty. In a very real sense then, the drift of pecuniary culture put pressure on state funded universities to open as coeducational. Women who were often viewed as unnecessary in established private schools, were increasingly viewed as necessary sources of revenue for fledging colleges in the west and mid-west.

When Veblen published *The Theory of the Leisure Class* in 1899, the University of Chicago where he taught, was coeducational, also retaining women on the faculty; yet, schools such as Harvard were notorious in their refusal to admit women. For Veblen, the attitude of schools towards women represented a measure of the degree to which these institutions departed from their priestly and leisure-class prerogatives and embraced the values of a modern or matter-of-fact standpoint (Veblen [1899] 1998: 375). Moreover, Veblen saw the reluctance of institutions to embrace women as a ceremonial vestment – a demonstration of class-worthiness and status. As Veblen puts it:

> ... the highest and most reputable universities show an extreme reluctance in making the move. The sense of class worthiness, that is to say of status, of a honorific differentiation of the sexes according to a distinction between superior and inferior intellectual dignity, survives in a vigorous form in these corporations of the aristocracy of learning.
>
> (Veblen [1899] 1998: 376)

Veblen's observation that the preservation of male domination should be viewed as a form of status maintenance was not missed on women activists at the time. Women were often well organized and set about targeting particular institutions such as Harvard in the US and Cambridge in England, to gain admittance for women most certainly with the knowledge that if prestigious institutions were to open their doors to women, other universities would emulate them (Walsh 1977; Tullberg 1998). Moreover, women in the US travelled to Europe to gain degrees when unable to do so in the US, often hoping to pressure universities in the US to open their doors to women.

In addition to noting concerns that the mere presence of women would 'be derogatory to the dignity of the learned craft', Veblen points out that, to the extent that women were allowed the privilege of admission to the higher learning, it was felt that they should be constrained to acquire knowledge only in those areas that conduce 'immediately to a better performance of domestic service' or to the 'quasi-scholarly and quasi-artistic, as plainly come in under the head of a performance of vicarious leisure' (Veblen [1899] 1998: 376). That is, the ultimate purpose of education for women is to support the activities of her ultimate role in life – marriage and family.

That a particular type of education would be supported for women was true at the University of Chicago as well as elsewhere in the nineteenth century. In the same year that Veblen published *The Theory of Leisure Class*, Charles Eliot, noted president of Harvard, would argue that coeducation was 'not possible in highly civilized communities', but women's colleges might be useful in encouraging religion and as schools of manners for young girls (Eliot 1874: 50–52). Therefore, while Harvard would offer 'as many years as they wish of liberal culture in studies which have no direct professional value, to be sure, but which enrich and enlarge both intellect and character', the education of women should be different than that of men in that 'their lives are different and their education should be different ... Their education should take account of the life which is before them ...' (Eliot 1874: 53).

Likewise, even those few women who were able to secure degrees in areas not thought to be feminized *per se*, would find that their career advancement was to be attained only by abiding by this convention of separate spheres. For example, while Veblen was at the University of Chicago, not a single woman in the fields of Political Science, Economics, Anthropology, History, Psychology, or Sociology began her career as a junior faculty member and became promoted to full professor (Freeman 1969: 2). As Jo Freeman points out in her study of the University of Chicago during this period, Sophonisba Preston Breckinridge, who had received a doctoral degree in 1901 in the Department of Political Science and Economics and received her Doctor of Law in 1904, would find that she would be hired in neither law nor political economy. Her first appointment would be Assistant Professor in the Department of Household Administration. For her part, Edith Abbott, who taught sociology for six years without promotion, transferred to one of the so-called 'women's departments' where she later became Dean of the School (Freeman 1969: 2).

The containment of women to the domestic sphere and to those areas of knowledge that serve to aid the performance of vicarious leisure was to be accomplished in subtle ways and, as we have seen, some rather not so subtle ways. However, the way that Veblen defines how these 'feminine' and 'unfeminine' fields are determined is both curious and compelling and may go far in understanding yet today in what areas women's work has been accepted and in what areas it is likely to be marginalized and forgotten. Specifically, Veblen identifies 'unfeminine' knowledge as that which expresses the unfolding of the learner's own life, 'the acquisition of which proceeds on the learner's own cognitive interest ... without reference back to a master whose comfort and good repute is to be enhanced by the employment or the exhibition of it' (Veblen [1899] 1998: 376).

This would, of course, explain why it is that the study of women in the history of economics often dies with women. Not only is women's work overlooked through what has been called the 'systematic misattribution', but it has been undervalued particularly when it is work that focuses on women (Dimand *et al.* 1995). As Robert Dimand points out,

> ... the "malestream" of the discipline did not care to read Abbott on *Women in Industry*, Breckinridge on *Women in the Twentieth Century*, Campbell on *Prisoners of Poverty*, Gilman on *Women and Economics* or McMahon on *Women and Economic Evolution* for the same reasons that male economists

wrote little on the economic experience of the female majority of the population.

(Dimand *et al.* 1995: 7)

Scholarly work was masculine business and rightly concerned itself with the unfolding of the learner's own life, the acquisition of which proceeds on *his* own cognitive interests.[8]

Veblen's description of 'unfeminine' (masculine) knowledge is particularly apt as it is a description that emphasizes independence not dependence – a distinction that, at its root, reflects a highly gendered notion of knowledge production and one that was long used as a foundation to argue against women's inclusion in the higher learning. From the philosopher Johann Erdmann in Germany to G. Stanley Hall in the US, the 'Woman Question' in higher education would often end in arguments about women's capacity for independent judgement and ability to master the subjects while male attributes and metaphors were invoked to describe the characteristics of academic citizenship (Mazón 2003).

As Patricia M. Mazón so carefully describes, the German system of higher education in the nineteenth century, which served as a model for the modern research university throughout much of the world, viewed the academic enterprise as a community of scholars perpetuated by an apprentice system aimed at cultivating independent judgement and resting upon 'masculine images of power and appropriation' (Mazón 2003: 37). As Erdmann saw it, the student's task was to mature by working his way up the ladder of knowledge first learning as a school boy, then studying as a university student, and finally pursuing knowledge as an academic scholar (Mazón 2003: 37). Comparing the relationship of a student to his discipline as a marriage of sorts, Erdmann envisioned that 'true devotion to the subject of intellectual love' consisted not of submission but 'mastering it and winning power over it' (Mazón 2003: 38). That women would hardly be viewed as scholars in such an enterprise is not surprising.

As the mechanism for training students to become faculty in the higher learning, graduate work was especially troublesome terrain for women. Just as undergraduate education was to be a bridge between childhood and adulthood for young boys, graduate work represented a bridge between learning as a student and generating knowledge as a scholar. As consumers in the academic enterprise, women were far less menacing than as potential colleagues and it is the political economy of this location that created an additional layer of difficulty for women.

In the end, it was the fear of women as colleagues and fellow professionals that sustained the controversy of the 'Woman Question'. The issue of women's role in the higher learning could not be settled without some discussion of what careers women would pursue at the conclusion of their education. Women as well were focused on the career question and pushed hardest to enter medical schools with this career in mind. It was the competition from women doctors that stiffened the resolve of medical faculty in denying access to medical education for women (Mazón 2003: 95). Pecuniary drift had its impact on women's access to the academy as men feared competition from women.

Gender and knowledge production today

The sweeping transformation in industrial society that accompanied the rise of the market system brought a fundamental transformation in the higher learning itself. Universities, particularly elite universities, became the gateway to professions in both politics and commerce while the pecuniary drift of industrial society changed the institution of the higher learning itself. Thus, universities played a central role in the formation of status in society. It is little wonder then, that the expansion of higher education brought increased competition within the higher learning along with new efforts to maintain status within the institution of the higher learning.

Veblen's observations on the relationship between the preservation of status and the representation of women as students at the turn of the century continues to resonate in higher education today in two distinct ways. On the level of faculty representation, there remains a close relationship between the status of the university and the representation of women. As a recent study of Carnegie I Research Doctoral Schools in the US confirms, representation of women as faculty is inversely correlated with status measures such as Barron's Profiles of American Colleges. While women in the most competitive category had an average of 27 per cent female faculty, the representation of women in the less competitive grouping was 75 per cent higher than the most competitive group. As status rises, women are increasingly absent in the halls of those Ivy League schools.[9]

Where students are concerned, institutional attempts at status preservation through gender discrimination have become increasingly public. In a widely read editorial appearing in *The New York Times*, Jennifer Delahunty Britz, Dean of Admissions at Kenyon College, went on to discuss the reality of the admissions process at elite institutions (Britz 2006). Britz describes how these institutions often accept less qualified male students over more qualified female students in an effort to maintain a more equal gender balance in undergraduate enrollment. While not justifying the practice, Britz argues that this particular form of 'affirmative action' for men reflects the impulse of colleges intending to preserve applications of both men and women which, it is believed, decline if the ratio of female to male students becomes too high. High status institutions feel compelled to preserve their status through gender balancing in enrollment.

The 'domestication of women' in higher education is reflected in continued segregation both as students and later as faculty. Today, women continue to be segregated by fields in higher education. They are over-represented in the fields of English, education, library science, and the health sciences and under-represented in the fields of science and engineering. In 2002, women received only 18 per cent of doctorates in engineering and 16 per cent of doctorates in physics and astronomy while receiving 66 per cent of doctorates in education. In the social sciences, women receive 55 per cent of total doctorates, yet they receive only 28 per cent of doctorates in economics while receiving 60 per cent of doctorates in anthropology and sociology (Hoffer *et al.* 2003).

The 'domestication of women' in higher education reflects itself not only in field choice but in the distribution of tasks within disciplines (Levit 2001; Park 1996; Moore and Sagaria 1991). As organizational theorists have argued, gendered divisions of labour emerge in organizations – divisions that 'carry characteristic images of the kinds of people that should occupy them' and replicating gender stereotypes that exist outside the organization (Kanter 1977). Within academe, a gendered division of labour exists such that not only is research valued more than teaching and service, but what constitutes good research, the science of discovery as Ernst Boyer would call it, is often identified with research that men do.

Moreover, as Shelly M. Park points out, the degree to which research is 'tainted' by its affiliation with teaching also serves as a measure of its status. Peer review journals are valued more than conference papers which is akin to lecturing and articles in scholarly journals to be read by other researchers are higher in status than publishing a textbook to be read by students (Park 1996: 48). Conversely, those teaching activities such as teaching graduate courses, that are more closely associated with research, are higher in status than other teaching such as the teaching of undergraduate courses (Park 1996: 49).

As Nancy Levit and others have shown, women are more often called upon to do the 'invisible work' of sustaining the academic community – activities such as student advising and committee work (Levit 2001: 784). As faculty, childcare, and housekeeping remain the purview of women in the academic household – and it is undervalued labour. A preponderance of undergraduate institutions, from Regents bylaws to state legislatures, still mouth the platitudes that 'teaching is our number one priority' at the same time that they sustain the practice of tenure and maintain a pecuniary reward structure almost exclusively on the basis of research.

While on one level Women's Studies as a field is surely feminized, in Veblen's description its marginalization along with the delayed and sometime outright failure of its insights to be incorporated into the body of knowledge in various disciplines may be explained by the delegitimation that comes with women doing 'unfeminine' work. Because Women's Studies deals with the unfolding of the learner's own cognitive interests – of women themselves, it is in this sense 'unfeminine' and hence unacceptable for enquiry for women. Women who study have proven themselves to be 'unexceptional' and hence unacceptable much like Pizan had done centuries ago.

Finally, the drift of pecuniary culture has permeated the culture of higher education in a way that would surely have been evident to Veblen. As Linda Hutcheon, former president of the Modern Language Association, has pointed out, the mode of professional discourse adopted by the adepts in the higher learning mimics most clearly the competitive model of the market (Hutcheon 2003). The adopted mode of discourse, she points out, is one of combat and conflict – a mode of discourse that is perhaps nowhere as evident as that of the discipline charged with rationalizing competition – economics. As anyone who has ever attended the American Economic Association meeting will observe, individuals present 'arguments' which are typically attacked by 'discussants', followed by questions which often are not really questions at all but statements intended to demonstrate the prowess and status of the questioner. Instead, we could envision an entirely different mode of discourse based upon thoughtful exchanges constructively intended to expand discussion, perhaps build consensus, or contribute to the full exposition of a topic or question (Keller 1985; Harding 1986).

Conclusion

Where allowed to function outside the constraints of ownership in its expression of marriage – that is, in the few professional jobs that women were legitimately allowed in the late nineteenth century, Veblen argues that women provide an example of learning that eschews honourific attachments. It is interesting that while Veblen finds most activity in the higher learning taken up by invidious activities of a ceremonial nature, he identifies the methods and ideals of kindergarten – the purview of women – as praiseworthy. According to Veblen, such instruction is primarily directed towards proficiency in the employment of impersonal facts by women who are 'ill at ease under the pecuniary code of reputable life' (Veblen [1899] 1998: 389). Neither driven by the ceremonial imperatives of the priestly class nor the pecuniary drive of consumer culture, Veblen sees women as teachers as a model of matter-of-fact learning.

In the end, Veblen argues that the introduction of women in the process of knowledge production might have wide-spread implications. Veblen concludes:

> In this way it appears that, by indirection, the institution of a leisure class here again favors the growth of a non-invidious attitude, which may, in the long run, provide a menace to the stability of the institution itself, and even to the institution of individual ownership on which it rests.
>
> (Veblen [1899] 1998: 390)

In this somewhat oblique reference, Veblen suggests that the leisure class itself may be threatened by the spread of non-invidious learning, such as that which women propound in primary education. Moreover, he suggests that this may also serve to undermine the 'institution of individual ownership' upon which it rests – ownership that, in its earliest form, Veblen describes as ownership of women by men (Veblen [1899] 1998: 22).

More recently, the growing number of women presidents at top universities introduces the possibility for further change as well. As the appointment of Drew Gilpin Faust as the first female President of Harvard University demonstrates, at least a few women have access to positions of influence. Whether those women are able to use their influence to pave the way for others to gain a full voice in the higher learning remains to be seen. While the true seat of power in the university system remains in the hands of the tenured full professors and the tenure system itself is under significant threat, the democratization of high administrative posts is underway.

Although the institution of the higher learning has in many ways successfully resisted change, the consequence of women gaining an authoritative voice in the higher learning could not be more revolutionary. The inclusion of women in the higher learning could alter existing values, threatening not only the patriarchy of knowledge, but patriarchy in other institutions that distribute power in society. It is little wonder, then, that there remains such strong resistance to women's inclusion as writers of the canon in the process of knowledge production.

Notes

1 See UNESCO, Institute for Statistics, 2005 Report and USAID reporting of UNESCO statistics at http://qesdb.usaid.gov/cgi-bin/broker.exe?_program=gedprogs. ged_theme_une_2.sas&_service=default&sscode=UNE530538+&cocode=ALL (accessed 22 February 2007). Statistics measure the number of females enrolled in tertiary education expressed as a percentage of total tertiary enrollment. Enrollment includes students of all ages in both public and private schools.
2 As Martha Nussbaum (2003) shows, despite advances in much of the industrialized world, education for women remains a challenge in many parts of the world.
3 For example, in 2000 the University of Oslo implemented a plan to improve gender diversity among faculty by reserving 12 full or associate professorships for female candidates. In January 2003, the European Free Trade Association Court ruled that it was illegal for the University of Oslo to reserve faculty positions for women. See *Chronicle of Higher Education*, World Beat, 'Court Bans Female-Professor Quota at U. of Oslo', February 298, 2003.
4 It is indeed telling that Lady Reason holds a mirror as a symbol of self-knowledge in an effort 'to demonstrate clearly and to show both in thought and deed to each man and woman his or her own special qualities and faults…' (Pizan [1431] 1982: 9).
5 Quoted in Pizan [1431] (1982: xxxvi).
6 Despite this, Pizan and others did not attack men directly, but male bias. As this quote from Mary Tattle-well and Joane Hit-him-Home argues, 'We do not menace the men, but their minds; not their persons, but their pens; the horridness of their humors, and the madness of their muses: which indeed towards us have been insupportable and intolerable …' (see Tattle-well and Hit-him-Home 1640: 109–110.)
7 See, for example, Thomas Kuhn *The Structure of Scientific Revolutions* (1962), Peter Berger and Thomas Luckmann *The Social Construction of Reality: a Treatise in the Sociology of Knowledge* (1966), Paul Feyerabend *Against Method: Outline of an Anarchistic Theory of Knowledge* (1975), Edward S. Herman and Noam Chomsky *Manufacturing Consent: The Political Economy of the Mass Media* (1988), and for a far different and more recent discussion see Steve Fuller *Philosophy, Rhetoric and the End of Knowledge: The Coming of Science and Technology Studies* (1993).
8 For a full discussion of the role of gender identities and their importance in economics see Pat Hudson, 'The historical construction of gender: reflections on gender and economic history', this volume.
9 Calculation by Elizabeth Moorhouse based upon AAUP data on Category I institutions and status as measured by Barron's Profiles of American Colleges. Regression run with dependent variable of percentage of women faculty at school 'i' and selectivity categories as independent variables.

References

Astell, M. (1730) *Some Reflections upon Marriage*, 4th edn, London: Printed for William Parker.

Bell, S. G. (1976) 'Christine de Pizan (1364–1430): Humanism and the Problem of a Studious Woman', *Feminist Studies* 3 (3/4): 173–184.

Berger, P. and Luckmann, T. (1966) *The Social Construction of Reality: a Treatise in the Sociology of Knowledge*. Garden City, NY: Doubleday.

Britz, J. D. (2006) 'To All the Girls I've Rejected', *The New York Times*, 23 March 2006.

Chronicle of Higher Education, World Beat, 'Court Bans Female-Professor Quota at U. of Oslo', 28 February 2003.

Dimand, M. A., Dimand, R. W. and Forget, E. L. (1995) *Women of Value: Feminist Essays on the History of Women in Economics*. Aldershot, UK: Edward Elgar.

Drake, J. (pseudonym) [1696] (1970) *An Essay in Defence of the Female Sex*. New York: Source Book Press.

Eliot, C. (1874) '*Remarks of President Eliot of Harvard College before the Trustees of the Johns Hopkins University*', in bind labeled 'Johns Hopkins University 1874', Special Collections Holdings, The Ferdinand Hamberger, Jr. Archives.

Feyerabend, P. (1988) *Against Method: Outline of an Anarchistic Theory of Knowledge*. Atlantic Highlands, NJ: Humanities Press.

Freeman, J. (1969) 'Women on the Social Science Faculties Since 1892' Paper delivered at the Political Science Association Conference, Winter 1969. Available: http://jofreeman. com/academicwomen/uc1892.htm (Accessed 22 February 2007).

Fuller, S. (1993) *Philosophy, Rhetoric and the End of Knowledge: The Coming of Science and Technology Studies*. Madison, Wisconsin: University of Wisconsin Press.

Harding, S. (1986) *The Science Question in Feminism*. Ithaca: Cornell University Press.

Harding, S. (1991) *Whose Science? Whose Knowledge?: Thinking from Women's Lives*. Ithaca: Cornell University Press.

Harding, S. (1993) 'Rethinking Standpoint Epistemology: What Is "Strong Objectivity?" ' in L. Alcoff and E. Potter (eds) *Feminist Epistemologies*. London: Routledge.

Herman, E. S. and Chomsky, N. (1988) *Manufacturing Consent: The Political Economy of the Mass Media*. New York: Pantheon Books.

Hoffer, T. B., Sederstrom, S., Selfa, L., Welch, V., Hess, M., Brown, S., Reyes, S., Webber, K. and Guzman-Barron, I. (2003) *Doctorate Recipients from United States Universities: Summary Report 2002*. Chicago: National Opinion Research Center.

Hutcheon, L. (2003) 'Rhetoric and Competition: Academic Agonistics', *Common Knowledge,* 9 (1): 42–49.

Jacobs, J. A. (1996) 'Gender Inequality and Higher Education', *Annual Review of Sociology,* 22: 153–185.

Jordansson, B. (1999) *The Politics of Gender Equality: The Encounter between Political Intentions and the Academy in the 'Tham Professorships'*, A Report from The Swedish Secretariat for Gender Research. Goteborg, Sweden. Available: http://www.genus.se/ digitalAssets/285_report.pdf (Accessed 22 February 2007).

Kanter, R.M. (1977) *Men and Women of the Corporation*, New York: Basic Books.

Kelly, J. (1982) 'Early Feminist Theory and the "Querelle des Femmes", 1400–1789', *Signs: Journal of Women in Culture and Society,* 8 (1): 4–28.

Keller, E. F. (1985) *Reflections on Gender and Science*. New Haven: Yale University Press.

Kuhn, T. (1962) *The Structure of Scientific Revolution*. Chicago: The University of Chicago Press.

Levit, N. (2001) 'Keeping Feminism in Its Place: Sex Segregation and the Domestication of Female Academics', *The University of Kansas Law Review*, 49 (4): 775–807.

Longino, H. E. (1990) *Science as Social Knowledge: Values and Objectivity in Scientific Inquiry*. Princeton: Princeton University Press.

Lopez-Claros, A. and Zahidi, S. (2005) 'Women's Empowerment: Measuring the Global Gender Gap', *World Economic Forum* 2005. Geneva, Switerland. Available: http://ncwo-online.org/data/images/WorldEconomicForum.pdf (Accessed 22 February 2007).

May, A. M. (1998) 'Women and the Higher Learning in America: Veblenian Insights on the Leisure of the Theory Class', in D. Brown (ed.) *Thorstein Veblen for the Twenty-First Century*. Northampton, MA: Edward Elgar.

May, A. M. (2006) '"Sweeping the Heavens for a Comet": Women, the Language of Political Economy, and Higher Education in the US', *Feminist Economics*, 12 (4): 625–640.

Mazón, P. M. (2003) *Gender and the Modern Research University: The Admission of Women to German Higher Education, 1865–1914*. Stanford, CA.: Stanford University Press.

Ministry of Children and Family Affairs (2000) '*Mainstreaming of Gender Equality in Norway*', Oslo, Norway.

Moore, K. M. and Sagaria, M. A. D. (1991) 'The Situation of Women in Research Universities in the United States: Within the Inner Circles of Academic Power', in G. P. Kelly and S. Slaughter (eds) *Women's Higher Education in Contemporary Perspective*. Netherlands: Kluwer Academic Publishers.

Nordic Research Board (NORBAL) (2005) 'Statistics on awarded doctoral degrees and doctoral students in the Baltic countries'. Available: http://english.nifustep.no/norbal__1/eng/startpage (Accessed 22 February 2007).

Nussbaum, M. (2000) *Women and Human Development: The Capabilities Approach*. Cambridge: Cambridge University Press.

Nussbaum, M. (2003) 'Women's Education: A Global Challenge', *Signs: Journal of Women in Culture and Society,* 29 (2): 325–355.

Park, S. M. (1996) 'Research, Teaching, and Service: Why Shouldn't Women's Work Count?' *The Journal of Higher Education,* 67 (1): 46–84.

Pizan, C. [1431] (1982) *The Book of the City of Ladies*. Translated by Earl Jeffrey Richards. New York: Persea Books.

Schibanoff, S. (1983) 'Comment on Kelly's "Early Feminist Theory and the Querelle des Femmes, 1400–1789"', *Signs: Journal of Women in Culture and Society,* 9 (2): 320–326.

Sen, A. (1999) *Development as Freedom.* New York: Alfred A. Knopf.

Smith College Archives. Available: http://www.smith.edu/collegerelations/traditions.php (Accessed 22 February 2007).

Tattle-well, M. and Hit-him-Home, J. (pseudonyms) (1640) *The Women's Sharpe Revenge: or an answer to Dir Seldome Sober that write those railing pamphelets called the the Iuniper and Crabtree lectures*, London. Available online from Early English books.

Tullberg, R. M. (1998) *Women at Cambridge*. Cambridge, England: Cambridge University Press.

UNESCO, Institute for Statistics, 2005 Report and USAID reporting of UNESCO statistics. Available: http://qesdb.usaid.gov/cgibin/broker.exe?_program=gedprogs.ged_theme_une_2.sas&_service=default&sscode=UNE530538+&cocode=ALL   (Accessed 22 February 2007).

Veblen, T. [1899] (1998) *The Theory of the Leisure Class*. Amherst, New York: Prometheus Books.

Veblen, T. (1917) *An Inquiry Into the Nature of Peace and the Terms of its Perpetuation*, New York: B.W. Huebsch.

Veblen, T. [1918] (1993) *The Higher Learning in America*. New Brunswick, New Jersey: Transaction Publishers.

Walsh, M. R. (1977) *"Doctors Wanted: No Women Need Apply:" Sexual Barriers in the Medical Profession, 1835–1975*. New Haven: Yale University Press.

Zimmer, A. (2003) Women in European Universities Final Report 2000–2003. Munster, Germany: Westfalische Wilhelms-Universitat. Available: http://www.goodfood-project. org/www/Gender/FinalReport_Zimmer_20.11.2003.pdf (accessed 22 February 2007).

Author index

page references followed by f indicate an illustrative figure; n indicates a note; t indicates a table

General index

page references followed by f indicate an illustrative figure; n indicates a note; t indicates a table